LUTHERAN QUARTERLY BOOKS

Editor

Paul Rorem, *Princeton Theological Seminary*

Associate Editors

Timothy J. Wengert, *The Lutheran Theological Seminary at Philadelphia*
Steven Paulson, *Luther Seminary, St. Paul*
Mark C. Mattes, *Grand View University, Des Moines, Iowa*

Lutheran Quarterly Books will advance the same aims as *Lutheran Quarterly* itself, aims repeated by Theodore G. Tappert when he was editor fifty years ago and renewed by Oliver K. Olson when he revived the publication in 1987. The original four aims continue to grace the front matter and to guide the contents of every issue, and can now also indicate the goals of *Lutheran Quarterly Books:* "to provide a forum (1) for the discussion of Christian faith and life on the basis of the Lutheran confession; (2) for the application of the principles of the Lutheran church to the changing problems of religion and society; (3) for the fostering of world Lutheranism; and (4) for the promotion of understanding between Lutherans and other Christians."

For further information, see www.lutheranquarterly.com.

The symbol and motto of *Lutheran Quarterly,* VDMA for *Verbum Domini Manet in Aeternum* (1 Peter 1:25), was adopted as a motto by Luther's sovereign, Frederick the Wise, and his successors. The original "Protestant" princes walking out of the imperial Diet of Speyer in 1529, unruly peasants following Thomas Müntzer, and from 1531 to 1547 the coins, medals, flags, and guns of the Smalcaldic League all bore the most famous Reformation slogan, the first Evangelical confession: The Word of the Lord remains forever.

Lutheran Quarterly Books

Living by Faith: Justification and Sanctification, by Oswald Bayer (2003).

Harvesting Martin Luther's Reflections on Theology, Ethics and the Church, essays from *Lutheran Quarterly*, edited by Timothy J. Wengert, with foreword by David C. Steinmetz (2004).

A More Radical Gospel: Essays on Eschatology, Authority, Atonement, and Ecumenism, by Gerhard O. Forde, edited by Mark Mattes and Steven Paulson (2004).

The Role of Justification in Contemporary Theology, by Mark C. Mattes (2004).

The Captivation of the Will: Luther vs. Erasmus on Freedom and Bondage, by Gerhard O. Forde (2005).

Bound Choice, Election, and Wittenberg Theological Method: From Martin Luther to the Formula of Concord, by Robert Kolb (2005).

A Formula for Parish Practice: Using the Formula of Concord in Congregations, by Timothy J. Wengert (2006).

Luther's Liturgical Music: Principles and Implications, by Robin A. Leaver (2006).

The Preached God: Proclamation in Word and Sacrament, by Gerhard O. Forde, edited by Mark C. Mattes and Steven D. Paulson (2007).

Theology the Lutheran Way, by Oswald Bayer (2007).

A Time for Confessing, by Robert W. Bertram (2008).

The Pastoral Luther: Essays on Martin Luther's Practical Theology, edited by Timothy J. Wengert (2009).

Preaching from Home: The Stories of Seven Lutheran Women Hymn Writers, by Gracia Grindal (2011).

The Early Luther: Stages in a Reformation Reorientation, by Berndt Hamm (2013).

The Life, Works, and Witness of Tsehay Tolessa and Gudina Tumsa, the Ethiopian Bonhoeffer, edited by Samuel Yonas Deressa and Sarah Hinlicky (2017).

The Early Luther

Stages in a Reformation Reorientation

Berndt Hamm

Translated by
Martin J. Lohrmann

Fortress Press
Minneapolis

THE EARLY LUTHER
Stages in a Reformation Reorientation

Copyright © 2017 Fortress Press. All rights reserved. Except for brief quotations in critical articles or reviews, no part of this book may be reproduced in any manner without prior written permission from the publisher. Email copyright@fortresspress.com or write to Permissions, Fortress Press, PO Box 1209, Minneapolis, MN 55440-1209.

Originally published 2010 in German as
Der frühe Luther. Etappen reformatorischer Neuorientierung

Interior contents have not been changed from prior English editions.

Paperback ISBN: 978-1-5064-2721-8
eBook ISBN: 978-1-5064-2722-5

In memory of Dr. Christel Hamm
November 5, 1941 – June 19, 2009

Contents

Foreword, by Timothy J. Wengert — ix

Translator's Preface — xiii

Preface to the English Edition — xvi

Preface — xvii

Abbreviations — xix

1. From the Medieval "Love of God" to Luther's "Faith": A Contribution to the History of Repentance — 1

2. Impending Doom and Imminent Grace: Luther's Early Years in the Cloister as the Beginning of His Reformation Reorientation — 26

3. Why Did Luther Turn Faith into the Central Concept of the Christian Life? — 59

4. The Ninety-five Theses: A Reformation Text in the Context of Luther's Early Theology of Repentance — 85

5. Luther's Instructions for a Blessed Death, Viewed against the Background of the Late Medieval *Ars Moriendi* — 110

6. Luther's Discovery of Evangelical Freedom — 154

Contents

7. Freedom from the Pope and Pastoral Care to the Pope: The Compositional Unity of *The Freedom of a Christian* and Its Dedication Letter to Pope Leo X — 172

8. How Mystical Was Luther's Faith? — 190

9. Justification by Faith Alone: A Profile of the Reformation Doctrine of Justification — 233

Bibliography — 258

Name Index — 279

Topic Index — 281

Foreword

When Matthias Pollicarius compiled and published the first set of biographical reflections on Martin Luther's life in 1547, already the early Luther played an important role, highlighted by material that recalled Luther's birth, his reception of the master of arts degree at the University of Erfurt, his struggle with Tetzel, and his appearance before the emperor in Worms.[1] In Johann Mathesius's more well-known *Historien von des ehrwirdigen Martini Luthers anfang, lehr, leben vnd sterben*, a set of sermons first published in 1566, the first three sermons dealt with Luther's life up through 1521.[2] This concentration on the younger Luther continued into the twentieth century, where Roland Bainton's classic English biography, *Here I Stand*, devoted fully half of its pages to Luther's life through 1521.[3] At the same time, other historians, notably Heinrich Boehmer and

---

1. Johannes Pollicarius, ed., *Historia de vita et actis reverendiss. Viri D. Mart. Lutheri, uerae Theologiae Doctoris, bona fide conscripta a Philippo Melanthone*... (Erfurt: Gervasius Sturmer, 1548). See VD 16: M 3416. This version included a distich on Luther's life, Melanchthon's preface to the second volume of Luther's Latin works, and the *Acta* of Luther's appearance in Worms. Later versions included Luther's preface to the first volume of his Latin works and a more detailed, prose version describing Luther's life.

2. Johann Mathesius, *Historien von des Ehrwirdigen in Gott Seligen thewren Manns Gottes/ Doctoris Martini Luthers/ anfang/ lehr/ leben vnd sterben: Alles ordendlich der Jarzal nach/ wie sich alle sachen zu jeder zeyt haben zugetragen* (Nuremberg: Ulrich Neuber, 1566).

3. Roland Bainton, *Here I Stand: A Life of Martin Luther* (New York and Nashville: Abingdon, 1950).

Gordon Rupp, even produced studies that concentrated exclusively on the "young Luther."[4]

The development of Luther's thought, with the twists and turns of his early biography, has commanded attention from scholars precisely because of the Reformation and its remarkable effects upon the history of Christianity in the West. Older scholarship, far from exhausting all avenues of research into the young Luther, has often become so enthralled by certain later debates that it has ignored many important sources of Luther's thought and has distorted the context in and against which that thought developed. In the present study, however, Berndt Hamm, armed with expertise in both late medieval intellectual life and Luther, develops new perspectives that leave old debates behind and shape a fresh look at some well-known sources. In so doing he builds creatively on the work of his teacher, Heiko Oberman, while providing new impulses for future research.

Perhaps the most important contribution of the essays in this book comes from Hamm's ability to provide new insights into the development of Luther's theology from his entry into the monastery through his early lectures on the Bible to his writing of the Ninety-five Theses in 1517 and *The Freedom of a Christian* in 1520. Instead of looking for a single breakthrough, Hamm carefully outlines a series of important shifts in Luther's late medieval theological worldview that unfold over the length of his early career. In so doing, he gives credence both to early scholarship of the twentieth century, which insisted on an early date for Luther's breakthrough (before or in the midst of his first lectures on the Psalms in 1513-15), and to scholarship of the last half of the twentieth century, which often preferred a much later date (usually 1518) for the proper beginning of Luther's evangelical theology.

How Hamm argues is as important as what he concludes. Here his lifelong analysis of late medieval texts unlocks the finer nuances of Luther's comments. By fiercely insisting on placing Luther within his late medieval milieu, Hamm discovers how, slowly but surely, Luther leaves behind the medieval theology of love for the certainty of faith. Having set up this argument in the first chapter, in chapter 2 Hamm goes after one of the

---

4. See Heinrich Boehmer, *Road to Reformation: Martin Luther to the Year 1521*, trans. John W. Doberstein and Theodore G. Tappert (Philadelphia: Muhlenberg, 1946), and Gordon Rupp, *Luther's Progress to the Diet of Worms* (London: SCM, 1951). See also the notorious psychiatric study by Erik Erikson, *Young Man Luther: A Study in Psychoanalysis and History* (New York: Norton, 1962).

most beloved legends of Luther research: that Luther's early life in the monastery was only darkness and despair. Instead, Hamm insists that radical *Anfechtungen* (assaults, struggles, etc.) were a hallmark of Luther's developing evangelical theology, not a medieval remnant to be overcome. This result leads inexorably to Hamm's third chapter, where he asks why faith became for Luther the central concept of the Christian life. Once again, the early biblical lectures loom large as an important source, showing just how the Reformation was, as Hamm puts it, an event embracing theology and piety. This combination begins to show up in Luther's insistence upon the hearing of faith, not the doing of works. As such, Hamm shows how the division between medieval continuity and Reformation breakthrough is a false distinction, where Luther is both medieval and evangelical at the same time.

In chapters 4 through 7 Hamm embarks on analysis of several crucial early texts of Luther: the Ninety-five Theses (chapter 4), the sermon on preparation for dying (chapter 5), and *The Freedom of a Christian* (chapters 6 and 7). Here, too, rather than abandoning his insights into the medieval roots of Luther's theology, Hamm actually underscores their importance and the subtle shifts in Luther's theology between the Romans lectures of 1515-16 and the Ninety-five Theses of 1517: where new insights about justification and faith are slowly being separated from the medieval contours of contrition and humility. Similarly, Luther grappled with the medieval *ars moriendi* (art of dying) and began to separate the Christian's approach to death from anxieties over mortal sin and proper preparation and to concentrate instead on what he saw as the only thing necessary for the dying: faith in God's promise *extra nos* (outside of us). With *The Freedom of a Christian* (1520), Luther's theology has fully matured and the authority of Scripture as a proclaimed Word of God that frees the Christian from the condemnation of the law comes to complete expression (chapter 6). Moreover (chapter 7), the dual life of a Christian as "lord of all" and "servant of all" finds a fascinating application in Luther's preface to Leo X, where the reformer demonstrates a remarkable freedom in the gospel while continuing to proclaim his service to the pope.

Chapter 8 introduces a further neuralgic theme in study of the early Luther: his relation to medieval mysticism. Here again, Hamm's far-reaching knowledge of the late medieval theological scene sheds new light on Luther's unique place in early modern intellectual history. What Hamm makes clear is that Luther knew this tradition intimately, that it structured his theology in terms of law and gospel, and that it helped him view justification experientially. Only under these conditions — and certainly not when mysticism is reduced to Meister Eckhart or Pseudo-Dionysius — can Luther's theology rightly be called mystical. Chapter 9 serves as a kind of homiletical conclusion to the entire work. With its origins in a lecture to pastors, this chapter summarizes Hamm's understanding of Luther's teaching on justification: With Luther the Reformation freed the entire understanding of salvation from the traditional religious logic of gift and gift in response (see p. 257). Instead, Hamm concludes, Luther replaced cooperation with the unconditional work of God's mercy and goodness.

    I want to extend special appreciation to Mohr Siebeck publishers for providing easy access to the original texts, to Paul Rorem for his willingness to accept this into the Lutheran Quarterly Books series, and most especially to the book's translator, Martin Lohrmann. I am pleased to have had a part in making this important contribution to Luther research available to the broader English-speaking audience.

TIMOTHY J. WENGERT
Commemoration of Bernard of Clairvaux, 2012
Philadelphia, Pennsylvania

Translator's Preface

With thorough research and elegant writing, Berndt Hamm's *Der Frühe Luther* has made a profound contribution to our understanding of Martin Luther's personal, professional, and pastoral formation. Dr. Hamm studies both Luther's personal piety and his theological acumen, examining how Luther's doctrinal views developed alongside practical and pastoral concerns. Throughout the book, he pays close attention to Luther's continuities with and breaks from the late medieval traditions he inherited. As a result, this work sheds new light on the great question of how Luther became Luther. It has been a delight for me to have learned from this book, one sentence at a time.

As a translator, my goal has been to express Dr. Hamm's writing and insights as clearly as possible for the English-reading public. This task includes the challenge of finding consistent and accurate translations for complex words and phrases. For instance, the concept of repentance *(poenitentia)* is full of nuance: it can refer to an internal feeling of sorrow for sin, an external change in one's way of life, a sacrament of the church (in whole or in part), or some combination of the above. Rather than trying to force a single word like "penance," "repentance," or "confession" to bear all the meaning in English, I have preferred to clarify the theological concepts being discussed, such that the German word *Reue* might be translated as remorse or repentance, while *Buße* might mean confession or penance, depending on context. Another choice facing a translator is what to do with the German word *Anfechtung* (plural: *Anfechtungen*), a term that has major significance for Luther's theology and for Dr. Hamm's study. *Anfechtung* can mean doubt, distress, assault, affliction, trials, or temptations. Since it has no clear single equivalent in English and is such an important term for understanding Luther, I have left it untranslated so that it can mean all those complicated things at once. A final example of a translation decision arises in the fact that the word "satisfaction" is often a technical term in theology, especially with respect to atonement or confession. Lost in this theological language is the fact that satisfaction is derived from the Latin for "doing enough" *(satis + facere)*. To get to the plain meaning behind the word, I translated the similarly literal German *Genugtuung* as "doing enough" wherever appropriate. Even though the German word has the same technical theological sense as the English, Dr. Hamm calls similar attention to the word's roots early in chapter 1 and in other places as he advances his argument. Satisfaction means "doing enough" to right a wrong, a definition that helps us get underneath several of the key concepts being debated during the early years of Luther's career.

Dr. Hamm's work makes it clear that he views "the Reformation" as a complex phenomenon rather than as this or that single heroic moment. In that sense, he often uses the word "reformation" as a general adjective that describes the new insights that followed Luther's adaptation of or break with existing traditions; that sense of gradual change should not be lost. Following common English usage and Dr. Hamm's own intentional juxtapositions, however, I have chosen to capitalize "Reformation" throughout, trusting the reader to remember the paradox that "the Reformation" is both a watershed moment in world history and something that happened so subtly that it can be almost impossible to define. The word "evangelical" is similarly used with some self-consciousness. At its most basic, the word comes from the Greek, meaning "of the good news" or "of the gospel." Early in the Reformation, the word came to describe the general message of gospel freedom that was preached and taught in common by many different reformers. In this public proclamation of a shared message, "evangelical" can therefore be used as a near synonym for Protestantism in general (chapter 9, in particular, deals with this issue of finding what is common among Protestants). More specifically in German, however, "Evangelical" also refers to the institutional Lutheran church, especially in contrast to the "Reformed" churches that followed the lead of reformers like Zwingli and Calvin more than Luther. By letting words like "Reformation" and "Evangelical" retain their ambiguity, we are following Dr. Hamm in taking time to discover what we really mean by concepts like these in light of the historical record.

As seen in these examples, my goal has been to let Dr. Hamm's thought-provoking work speak as clearly as possible in the English language. I also hope that this book finds value not only among experts in the field but also among students, interested nonspecialists, and all who are looking for a good introduction to the life and thought of Martin Luther.

To this end, I retranslated essays that have already appeared in English. Chapters 1 and 3 of this book can be found in *The Reformation of Faith in the Context of Late Medieval Theology and Piety: Essays by Berndt Hamm*, edited by Robert J. Bast and published by Brill (2004). Ms. Helen Heron of Erlangen translated those chapters for that volume. For the sake of clarity and consistency in this book, however, it was important that they be translated anew. I am extremely grateful for Ms. Heron's work, as well as for the access I had to her unpublished translations of several other chapters. I also retranslated the English version of chapter 7, which was published in *Lutheran Quarterly* 21, no. 3 (2007), as translated by Ms. Heron and me. It appears here in a new version.

I am very grateful to my family for their support and patience as this work has been under way. My congregation in Philadelphia has also provided me with a great community of faith in which to see how Luther's teaching remains so fruitful and vibrant today. Thanks also to Eerdmans Publishing for printing this book and to Mark Dixon for his assistance with the bibliography and some footnotes and also preparation of the indexes. Finally, I thank Dr. Paul Rorem of Princeton Theological Seminary, Dr. Timothy Wengert of the Lutheran Theological Seminary at Philadelphia, and Dr. Hamm himself for inviting me to help add *The Early Luther* to the list of works published in the Lutheran Quarterly Books series. *Verbum domini manet in aeternum.*

MARTIN J. LOHRMANN
Philadelphia, Pennsylvania
Advent 2012

Preface to the English Edition

I would like to preface the English edition of my Luther book by saying thank you. My thanks go first of all to Timothy J. Wengert, who had the idea and took the initiative of having this book translated into English, thereby making it available to a wider international audience. In Martin J. Lohrmann, he found a theologically and linguistically perceptive translator, who has recast my fairly elaborate German prose into good, readable English. His patient and effective striving for the right phrase has earned my great thanks. Finally, I also thank Paul E. Rorem for supporting this translation project and being willing to publish this book in the Lutheran Quarterly Books series.

Most of all, it fills me with joy and thanks that these three American colleagues in Philadelphia and Princeton have given readers access to my book's central thesis: to set Luther free from the usual historical shorthand of "medieval" or "modern" — or even "late medieval" and "early modern" — and, in both his traditional aspects and his remarkable innovations, to see Luther amid a field of continuities, ruptures, and efforts toward normalization.

BERNDT HAMM
Erlangen/Ulm
Advent 2012

Preface

The following book presents nine chapters about the early Luther, from his entrance into the cloister in the summer of 1505 until his writing of *The Freedom of a Christian* in the autumn of 1520. The last two chapters span that entire period, while also referring to some of Luther's later writings. Chapters 4 and 9 were written specifically for this book; all the other chapters were written and published earlier as essays.

The chapters share a common disinterest in diagnosing Luther's "Reformation turn" or "Reformation breakthrough" either biographically or theologically. This stands in contrast to the efforts of many researchers of the twentieth century, especially systematic theologians. As readers will see, I am quite inclined to bid farewell to this "breakthrough" construct and to revisit the history of Luther's journey. This is the path of a person who was a member of a religious order, a scholastic and mystical theologian, interpreter of the Bible, writer of devotional literature, and controversialist in conflict with the church hierarchy. For this reason, I approach the young Luther from the perspective of the Middle Ages onward and place him in the dynamic context of various late medieval innovations and changes. This helps show how much of what Luther changed and pushed should be understood as the intensification of strong, previously tested abilities. At the same time, I would also like to explain how and why there were not only gradual continuous steps in Luther's religiosity but also frequent qualitative leaps. These made it possible for him to break with essential patterns of previous religious thought. In this way, Luther not only advanced a late medieval church agenda but caused a "Reformation." In other places, I have described the complex interrelationship between individual points of continuity and "system failure" as an overall "emergence" that changed the entire nature of the religiosity of the time. Near the end of his life, in his well-known preface to the first volume of his Latin works (March 5, 1545), Luther himself described this process as "emerging from errors." He wrote, "Here, in my case, you may also see how hard it is to struggle out of and emerge from errors which have been confirmed by the example of the whole world and have by long habit become a part of nature, as it were" (WA 54:183.21-33; *LW* 34:334).

I received much valuable help in the final editing of this book. My heartfelt thanks go especially to my student assistants Anna-Lena Geyer, Franziska Gruber, and Paula Svoboda, as well as Siglinde Scholz, Kerstin Kristen, Heidrun Munzert, Dr. Henning Jürgens, and Dr. Gudrun Litz.

I am very grateful for the rigorous yet pleasant collaboration with the book's original publisher, Mohr Siebeck, especially with Dr. Henning Ziebritzki and Mr. Matthias Spitzner.

This book is dedicated to my late wife. She accompanied me and supported me in my theological and historical work for forty-two years, with loving, sharp-witted corrections and wings of inspiration.

Berndt Hamm
Erlangen-Uttenreuth
June 19, 2010

Abbreviations

BC   *The Book of Concord.* Edited by Robert Kolb and Timothy J. Wengert. Minneapolis: Augsburg Fortress, 2000.

BSLK   *Die Bekenntnisschriften der evangelisch-lutherischen Kirche.* 5th ed. Göttingen, 1963.

CCSL   Corpus Christianorum. Series Latina. Turnhout: Brepols, 1953-.

CR   *Corpus Reformatorum. Opera quae supersunt omnia,* by Philip Melanchthon. Edited by C. G. Bretschneider and H. E. Bindseil. Halle and Brunswick: Schwetschke, 1834-60.

LW   *Luther's Works* [American edition]. 55 vols. Philadelphia: Fortress; St. Louis: Concordia, 1955-86.

PL   Patrologia Cursus Completus: Series Latina. Edited by J.-P. Migne. Paris, 1844-64.

StA   *Martin Luther Studienausgabe.* Edited by Hans-Ulrich Delius. Vols. 1ff. Berlin: Evangelische Verlangsanstalt, 1979ff.

WA   *Luthers Werke: Kritische Gesamtausgabe.* 65+ vols. Weimar: H. Böhlau, 1883-.

WA Br   *Luthers Werke: Kritische Gesamtausgabe: Briefwechsel.* 18 vols. Weimar: H. Böhlau, 1930-85.

WA TR   *Luthers Werke: Kritische Gesamtausgabe: Tischreden.* 6 vols. Weimar: H. Böhlau, 1912-21.

CHAPTER 1

From the Medieval "Love of God" to Luther's "Faith": A Contribution to the History of Repentance

The rule that one can understand the Reformation only through the Middle Ages belongs among the key principles of a properly grounded working history of the Reformation. This does not mean looking merely at that era's later decades; it means looking also at the theologies, piety, and worldviews that had developed over centuries. Above all, we should notice the diversity of the Middle Ages, its own new beginnings and continuities. This will show us to what extent the Reformation was embedded in the Middle Ages and in what sense it can be considered a departure. To explain the symbiotic biblical words "love" and "grace," which are so central to the religiosity of the Christian West, I will draw a long line from the twelfth century to the early writings of Martin Luther in the first quarter of the sixteenth century.

Anyone who wants to speak of love in the Middle Ages, whether erotic love between people or the love of Christ experienced by mystics, runs into the twelfth century as a time of discontinuity.[1] Before this, the sources show that love — by which I mostly mean love as an emotional part of life and a central desire and motivation in one's existence — was not a remarkable theme. This may seem surprising, since both pagan and Christian antiquity had already developed a highly refined emotional culture around love, either sensuous love in the style of Catullus or Ovid, or love as a purely spiritual and transcendental sensibility, as in Augustine's

---

1. Peter Dinzelbacher, "Liebe II. Mentalitäts- und literaturgeschichtlich," in *Lexikon des Mittelalters* (Munich and Zürich, 1991), 5:1965-68, and Dinzelbacher, "Über die Entdeckung der Liebe im Hochmittelalter," *Saeculum* 32 (1981): 185-208.

concept of the love of God. All imaginable shades of physical and spiritual inclination ran between these loves, including parental love, brotherly love, friendship, and altruism.²

Nevertheless, the early Middle Ages, as seen preeminently in the Franks after the time of Clovis (that is, around the year 500), created entirely different terms, upending the basis of a refined emotional culture. In place of an urban culture with high educational achievements came a primarily uncivilized agrarian world with very primal and "archaic" (rather than simply crude) patterns for behaving and thinking.³ This change in worldview shows itself, for instance, in how the main factor in both law and religion shifted entirely to external actions. In considering both a legal case and a sin, the deciding point was what actually happened, that is, whether someone killed or did not kill. By contrast, the question of inner feelings and personal intentions went totally to the background, rendering moot the question of whether one killed with intent or killed unintentionally through an unfortunate chain of events.

Wrongdoing and sin were thus defined entirely on the basis of physical deeds. In that period, the church's penitential system made a similarly strong move to prioritize the external works of repentance (as seen in "doing enough" and making satisfaction in the flesh) rather than the inner pain of contrition for sin. The Irish penitential books, which exerted their great influence over the Western penitential system beginning in the seventh century, made fasting the most important penitential practice: the worse the sin, the longer the corresponding fast. Only after a sinner had performed an obligatory fast or another penalty (that is, after the sinner had "done enough") could the penitent be reintegrated into holy Christian community.⁴

Looking at the penitential system of the early Middle Ages is there-

---

2. Leo Pollmann, *Die Liebe in der hochmittelalterlichen Literatur Frankreichs. Versuch einer historischen Phänomenologie,* Analecta Romanica 18 (Frankfurt am Main: Klostermann, 1966), 11-32. On the relationship of the religious love of God, self, and neighbor (in this order) in Augustine, see John Kevin Coyle, *Augustine's "De Moribus Ecclesiae Catholicae": A Study of the Work, Its Composition, and Its Sources* (Fribourg: University Press, 1978), 267-302; see also Augustine, *De doctrina Christiana* 1.26f., CCSL 32:21f.

3. Arnold Angenendt, *Das Frühmittelalter: Die abendländische Christenheit von 400 bis 900,* 2 vols., 2nd ed. (Stuttgart: W. Kohlhammer, 1995).

4. Angenendt, *Das Frühmittelalter,* 210-12 and 334f. See also Cyril Vogel, "'Buße (liturgisch-theologisch),' D: Westkirche I: Bußdisziplin und Bußriten," in *Lexikon des Mittelalters* (Munich: Artemis Verlag, 1999), vol. 2, cols. 1132-35 (with bibliography).

fore incredibly revealing for our theme, because through this one central religious point we see the dominant fixation upon restoration and attendant rituals; conversely, there was apparently no need to spend time uncovering the inner themes of spiritual pain or love of God. During the twelfth century, however, this relationship between external and internal, doing and feeling, was reversed in an almost breathtaking way. Along with an ethically refined culture of chivalry, dramatic reforms of monastic life, and rapidly expanding cities and their blossoming urban cultures, there arose the entirely new phenomena of internalization and individualization.[5] This means that love was discovered as a central emotion in life. To be more precise: love was rediscovered.[6]

This new appreciation of sensual and spiritual love was closely tied to the intense twelfth-century renaissance of Ovid and Augustine.[7] It was the same twelfth century that on one hand saw the worldly ideal of chivalrous courtly love,[8] for instance, in the transformation of a story like that of

---

5. Colin Morris, *The Discovery of the Individual, 1050-1200*, Church History Outlines 5 (London: SPCK for the Church Historical Society, 1972); Peter Dinzelbacher, *Vision und Visionsliteratur im Mittelalter*, Monographien zur Geschichte des Mittelalters 23 (Stuttgart: Hiersemann, 1981), 243-50 (with bibliography); John F. Benton, "Consciousness of Self and Perceptions of Individuality," in *Renaissance and Renewal in the Twelfth Century*, ed. Robert L. Benson and Giles Constable (Cambridge: Harvard University Press, 1982), 263-95.

6. See the programmatic title of Dinzelbacher's article in n. 1 above.

7. On the Ovid renaissance, see Franco Munari, *Ovid im Mittelalter* (Zurich: Artemis, 1960); on the continuing effect of Augustine, see Grete Lüers, "Die Auffassung der Liebe bei mittelalterlichen Mystikern," *Eine heilige Kirche* 22 (1940): 110-18, with the beautiful but inaccurate sentence at the beginning: "Since Augustine, to whom Christian art assigned as emblem a burning heart in true recognition of his being, the question of the essence of love never let go of the mediaeval philosophers and the pious." It did, in fact, let go of thinking and pious Christians in the early Middle Ages for centuries, so that in the twelfth century there really was a *Re-naissance* of the Augustinian *caritas*. On the concept of the "Renaissance of the twelfth century," see the standard text by Charles Horner Haskins, *The Renaissance of the Twelfth Century* (Cambridge, Mass., 1927), and the bibliography in Hermann Jakobs, *Kirchenreform und Hochmittelalter: 1046-1215*, 2nd ed., Oldenbourg Grundriß der Geschichte 7 (Munich: R. Oldenbourg, 1988), 123f.

8. See Leslie T. Topsfield, *Troubadours and Love* (Cambridge: Cambridge University Press, 1975); Francis X. Newman, ed., *The Meaning of Courtly Love* (Albany: State University of New York Press, 1968); Herbert Kolb, *Der Begriff der Minne und das Entstehen der höfischen Lyrik* (Tübingen: M. Niemeyer, 1958); Joachim Bumke, *Höfische Kultur: Literatur und Gesellschaft im hohen Mittelalter*, vol. 2, 3rd ed. (Munich: Deutscher Taschenbuch Verlag, 1986), 503-82.

Tristan and Isolde into a romantic novel.⁹ On the other hand, that century first experienced and described the mystical journey of sharing intimate love with Jesus.¹⁰

The biblical Song of Solomon, which had previously been interpreted in continuity with the exegetical tradition of the early Middle Ages as an allegory of the relationship between the bridegroom Christ and his bride the church, went through a dramatic reinterpretation.¹¹ The Cistercian abbot Bernard of Clairvaux wrote his famous sermons on the Song between 1135 and 1153, setting an influential precedent for the later Middle Ages. Delivered in the monasteries, Bernard's Latin sermons substituted the individual soul for the church.¹² The soul is the bride who embraces her divine bridegroom with a rousing, burning passion, which would rather suffer than be reasonable.¹³ This love of God pays no heed to honor and privilege, profit and reward, but is its own fulfillment. "Its pleasure," wrote Bernard, "is its own reward. I love *because* I love; I love *in order to love*."¹⁴ The way of salvation is the ascent of the loving soul, beginning with the meditative remembrance of the suffering Christ, leading to mystical union with the divine Spirit. Bernard and so many mystics after him sensuously pictured this *unio* as embrace and kiss.¹⁵ With this typically

---

9. See Francoise Barteau, *Les Romans de Tristan et Iseut* (Paris: Larousse, 1972); Gerhard Schindele, *Tristan: Metamorphose und Tradition* (Stuttgart: Kohlhammer, 1971); and Denis de Rougemont, *Die Liebe und das Abendland*, trans. Friedrich Scholz (Cologne: Kiepenheuer u. Witsch, 1966).

10. Dinzelbacher, *Vision und Visionsliteratur im Mittelalter*, 150-55.

11. For information on the medieval interpretation of the Song of Solomon, see Friedrich Ohly, *Hohelied-Studien: Grundzüge einer Geschichte der Hoheliedauslegung des Abendlandes bis um 1200* (Wiesbaden: F. Steiner, 1958); Helmut Riedlinger, *Die Makellosigkeit der Kirche in den lateinischen Hoheliedkommentaren des Mittelalters*, Beiträge zur Geschichte der Philosophie und Theologie des Mittelalters 38/3 (Münster: Aschendorff, 1958).

12. According to Ohly (*Hohelied-Studien*, 147), this signifies "a transfer of the Church's *Heilsgeschichte* to the sphere of spiritual experience."

13. The relevant passages from Bernard's interpretation of the Song of Solomon are cited in Kurt Ruh, *Geschichte der abendländischen Mystik*, vol. 1, *Die Grundlegung durch die Kirchenväter und die Mönchstheologie des 12. Jahrhunderts* (Munich: Beck, 1990), 258f.

14. "Fructus eius usus eius. Amo quia amo; amo, ut amem." *Sermo* 83.4, in *Sermones super Cantica canticorum*, in *Sancti Bernardi opera*, vols. 1-2, ed. Jean Leclercq (Rome: Editiones Cistercienses, 1957-58), vol. 2, 300.25f.

15. Ruh, *Geschichte der abendländischen Mystik*, 258, 265. The Benedictine Rupert von Deutz (1070-1129) was one of the first — before the time of Bernard — to describe the em-

monastic theology of spiritual experience,[16] Bernard became the great pioneer who made love *(amor Dei, dilectio, caritas)* the heart of theology and piety for centuries to come. That line extended from his foundational treatise *De diligendo Deo (On the Loving God)*[17] to Johannes von Staupitz's 1517 tract *Von der Lieb Gottes (On the Love of God)*.[18]

If Bernard was a kind of modern man in his own century, a pioneer with his emotionally oriented theology of love, he nevertheless stood adamantly opposed to the cathedral and monastery schools in France, which also had their intellectual beginnings in that era. In theology, the twelfth century shows these two faces: the model of a pious, humble, contemplative theology represented by Bernard,[19] and the countermodel of a budding scholastic theology and its sharp dialectical methods. This movement was embodied by Peter Abelard from Brittany (1079-1142), whom Bernard bitterly hounded.[20] Abelard stood for the new type of theological intellec-

---

brace and kiss of Christ as an experience; cf. Dinzelbacher, "Über die Entdeckung der Liebe," 197: "Again and again as he contemplates the Cross the crucified Christ turns his eyes upon him and benevolently accepts his salutation: 'But that was not enough for me: I wanted to touch him, embrace and kiss him . . . I sensed that he desired it . . . I held him, embraced him, kissed him for a long time. I sensed how hesitantly he permitted these caresses — then he himself opened his mouth so that I might kiss more deeply.' Naturally Rupert then interprets his experience allegorically on the basis of the Song of Solomon; but what he described was what he experienced: French kisses with God. And in the event he is driven by a loving yearning such as no one had evinced in *this* way to the best of our knowledge for the Son of God who in the early Middle Ages was far more the *Rex tremendae maiestatis*, the awful avenger who lives on a plane far above humanity." On the mystical kissing, cf. also below, n. 37.

16. Ulrich Köpf, *Religiöse Erfahrung in der Theologie Bernhards von Clairvaux*, Beiträge zur historischen Theologie 61 (Tübingen: Mohr, 1980).

17. The treatise is typical of the new program of independent thematic examinations of Christian love; edited in the edition by Leclercq et al., vol. 3 (Rome, 1963), 109-54, bilingual in the edition edited by Gerhard B. Winkler, *Bernhard von Clairvaux: Sämtliche Werke lateinisch/deutsch*, vol. 1 (Innsbruck, 1990), 57-151. From the same period, cf., e.g., Hugo von St. Viktor (d. 1141): *De laude caritatis*, Migne, PL 176:969-76.

18. *Johann von Staupitzens sämmtliche Werke*, vol. 1, *Deutsche Schriften*, ed. Joachim Karl Friedrich Knaake (Potsdam: Krausnick, 1867), 88-119. Staupitz dedicated the tract for the new year 1518, which grew out of his Advent sermons of 1517, to Kunigunde, widow of the duke of Bavaria. It then also appeared in printed form in 1518.

19. Jean Leclercq, *Wissenschaft und Gottverlangen: Zur Mönchstheologie des Mittelalters*, trans. Johannes Stöber and Nicole Stöber (Düsseldorf: Patmos, 1963).

20. See the colloquium papers of Abelard: *Petrus Abaelardus (1079-1142): Person, Werk und Wirkung*, ed. Rudolf Thomas, Trierer theologische Studien 38 (Trier: Paulus-Verlag, 1980).

tual and for a new rational search for knowledge and understanding.²¹ Of course, the intellectual development of reason should not be understood as simply the polar opposite of the emotionally oriented development of love, but also as participating in the new expression of internalization and individualization during the twelfth century. Like the urgent desires of love, reason's urgent search for causes brings an inner unrest, which is not content with the devout reception of the contents of faith and wants to go beyond the superficial world of facts and move to the dimension of motives and causes. This explains why such a rational, philosophical, and systematic thinker like Abelard not only was a renowned lover (Heloise and Abelard are likely the most famous couple in the history of the church) but also established love as the deciding factor for salvation in early scholastic theology.

Unlike Anselm of Canterbury a few decades earlier, Abelard and Bernard no longer saw the essential reason for the incarnation and for Christ's passion as being God's offended honor, which demands that people "do enough" *(satisfactio)*,²² but found that reason in the love of God that gives itself freely to humankind. The experience of this divine love fires the human heart with love for others.²³ In this way, sinners reach true repentance for sin, inner sorrow, and a sighing and a crying of the heart that do not come from fear of punishment but from thankful love of God and the loving compassion of the loving Christ.²⁴ Unlike the early Middle Ages,

---

21. Jacques Le Goff, *Die Intellektuellen im Mittelalter* (Stuttgart, 1986); on Abelard as "the first great modern intellectual," see 40-54.

22. Anselm of Canterbury (d. 1109) in his *Cur deus homo*, completed in 1098; in the Latin/German, edited by Franciscus Salesius Schmitt (Darmstadt, 1965).

23. On Abelard's teaching on reconciliation, see especially his commentary on the epistle to the Romans: PL 178:833D-836D; also Reinhold Seeberg, *Lehrbuch der Dogmengeschichte*, vol. 3, *Die Dogmengeschichte des Mittelalters*, 6th ed. (Darmstadt: Wissenschaftliche Buchgesellschaft, 1959), 239-43. On the doctrine of reconciliation in Bernard of Clairvaux, see particularly *Sermo* 43.1-3, in his *Sermones super Cantica Canticorum*, ed. Leclercq et al., vol. 2, pp. 41-43; and Dinzelbacher, "Über die Entdeckung der Liebe," 193f., 195.

24. On Abelard's teaching on repentance and remorse, see in particular *Ethico* ("*Scito te ipsum*"), chaps. 17-25, PL 178:660-73; *Peter Abelard's "Ethics,"* ed. David E. Luscombe (Oxford: Oxford University Press, 1971), 76-111; and Martin Ohst, *Pflichtbeichte: Untersuchungen zum Bußwesen im Hohen und Späten Mittelalter*, Beiträge zur historischen Theologie 89 (Tübingen: Mohr, 1995), 56-59. On the relationship to Christ's passion of human love of God, see Abelard's commentary on Romans: PL 178:836B. Admittedly, in the understanding of repentance in the first half of the twelfth century, we

Abelard no longer understood sin as a matter of external deeds but wholly instead as coming from the inner participation of the will and the soul. The decisive point, therefore, is not whether I have actually killed but whether I intended to kill and could have avoided the murder. The question of blame *(culpa)*, now posed in a new way, came to depend solely on the doer's intention and awareness of the actions.[25]

Quite analogously, the whole weight of understanding repentance fell upon changing the inner direction of the will — the intention to love and the pangs of regret — and no longer the actual acts of repentance. Just as with the incarnation and Christ's passion, the aspect of "doing enough" *(satisfactio)* in the theological analysis of the penitential system took a backseat to the motive of love. This example shows how closely Bernard's mystical, affective theology related to Abelard's intellectual, scholastic theology and how strongly the central love motif in the one theology also dominated the doctrinal system of the other. Where Bernard the monastic theologian meditated on the experience of love, Abelard the theological dialectician reflected on the logic of love.

We should keep in mind that with his internalized understanding of repentance, Abelard stood entirely within the early scholastic trend of his era. Before him, in the first decades of the twelfth century, the school of Anselm of Laon had so fully moved the emphasis to the inner penitential feeling of regret that succeeding generations and schools of scholastic theology had to engage the complex problem of what should remain of external repentance *(poenitentia exterior)*, that is, confession to a priest, the priestly absolution of sins, and then "doing enough" by completing the works of repentance imposed by the priest.[26] The idea shared by many

---

can only see initial approaches to the whole imaginative field of the pangs of remorse motivated by Christ's passion and, in imitation thereof, entering into it (according to Bernard's saying in *Sermones super Cantica Canticorum* 20.8: "qui Christo passo compatitur, compungitur"). This theme was increasingly explored up to the end of the fifteenth century; Ruh, *Geschichte der abendländischen Mystik*, 242-44.

25. Benton, "Consciousness of Self," 271-74 ("Guilt, shame and intention") with bibliography; Arnold Angenendt, "*Deus, qui nullum peccatum impunitum dimittit*: Ein 'Grundsatz' der mittelalterlichen Bußgeschichte," in *Und dennoch ist von Gott zu Reden: Festschrift für Herbert Vorgrimler*, ed. Matthias Lutz-Bachmann (Freiburg im Breisgau: Herder, 1994), 142-56; and Seeberg, *Lehrbuch der Dogmengeschichte*, 238f.

26. On the doctrine of repentance in the school of Anselm of Laon (d. 1117), see Ludwig Hödl, *Die Geschichte der scholastischen Literatur und der Theologie der Schlüsselgewalt*, part I, *Die scholastische Literatur und die Theologie der Schlüsselgewalt von ihren*

around the year 1200 seemed natural: all guilt and punishment were wiped out by love's contrition, so that neither the earthly acts of satisfaction nor the otherworldly purifying punishments of purgatory were necessary anymore.[27]

In the twelfth and thirteenth centuries, a consensus arose among the majority of early scholastic theologians. The deciding factor in repentance comes primarily in a truly loving contrition, which the Holy Spirit effects in the heart of the sinner. As soon as sinners feel this bitter pain of love (as Peter did after his threefold betrayal [John 21:17]), God gives them direct forgiveness of sins, forgiving both the guilt and the eternal punishment of hell.[28] In the love motif, repentance gives the conclusive justification of the sinner. Whoever feels such pangs of regret, such *vera contritio* (true contrition), should always then humbly desire to receive the priestly sacrament of confession and absolution, committing themselves to the church's discipline of penance. In that way, every true repentance is based on the church's power of the keys. Should sinners die in this spiritual state of *contritio* before contact with the priest takes place, they are nevertheless saved on the basis of the inner reconciliation with God. Thus, beginning in the twelfth century, the decisive weight of repentance no longer lay on the doing of *satisfactio* but on the emotional plane of wounded, mourning love. Here salvation or damnation is decided. Himself explaining penitential love, Jesus said of the sinful woman in Luke 7:47, "Her sins, which were many, have been forgiven, for she has shown great love."[29]

Anfängen an bis zur Summa Aurea des Wilhelm von Auxerre, Beiträge zur Geschichte der Philosophie und Theologie des Mittelalters, vol. 38 H.4 (Münster: Aschendorff, 1960), 6-45 (especially 26, 28f., 38f., 44f., and the summary in 376-80).

27. Hödl, *Die Geschichte der scholastischen Literatur und der Theologie der Schlüsselgewalt*, 281 and 293f.

28. The "as soon as" is based on an earlier aphorism derived from a combination of Ezek. 33:12 and 18:21: "In quacumque hora peccator ingemuit, non recordabor iniquitatum eius" (God says: "But if the wicked turn away from all their sins that they have committed and keep all my statutes and do what is lawful and right, they shall surely live"). See *Decretum Gratiani, De poenitentia*, d. 1, c. 32, ed. Aemilius Ludovicus Richter and Aemilius Friedberg, vol. 1 (Leipzig, 1879), 1165; Hödl, *Die Geschichte der scholastischen Literatur und der Theologie der Schlüsselgewalt*, 81, 87, and 96; Ohst, *Pflichtbeichte*, 56 with n. 32. Even in the late Middle Ages, this aphorism remained a classical proof text for the direct connection between repentance and the forgiveness of sins.

29. This translation follows the medieval tradition. On the use of this passage in early scholasticism, see, e.g., Hödl, *Die Geschichte der scholastischen Literatur und der Theologie der Schlüsselgewalt*, 226, and Ludwig Hödl, "'Busse (liturgisch-theologisch),'

This change of emphasis from satisfaction to penitential love also helped justify a common, long-developing change in the church's penitential practice: the priestly absolution of sin was moved forward. Unlike the early Middle Ages, this meant that the normal situation was no longer an entire penitential process, including the sinner's "doing enough" through works of repentance, but simply became the statement of remorse and confession. The works of satisfaction imposed by the priest then related only to a certain residual amount of temporal punishment for sin. Whoever did not complete this punishment in this life had to wipe it out in the hereafter under the harsher conditions of purgatory before reaching paradise.[30] Even then, the decisive condition for a sinner to be able to inherit eternal salvation was not any act of repentance or merit but the state of the heart at the moment of death. What mattered was whether it was in a state of loving God and therefore contrite for sin (already being in a kind of emotional orbit around God, so to speak) or whether the love of self had caused it to remain trapped in orbit around itself.

In principle, this decisive center point of the love of God did not change during the rest of the Middle Ages. People in the late Middle Ages were told in memorable ways that God the Father would judge each individual soul personally at the moment of death, according to the rule "I will show mercy to all those who depart this life with true repentance."[31] That has remained the decisive point for salvation in the Roman Catholic understanding since the twelfth century. Good works "only" have the effect of decreasing temporal punishments and increasing the blessings of paradise.

What changed in the high and late scholasticism of the thirteenth to fifteenth centuries and in the pastoral theology of piety of the late Middle Ages will become clear to us if we now make a great leap from the twelfth century to the four decades leading up to the Reformation, the years between

---

D. Westkirche, II, Scholastische Bußtheologie," in *Lexikon des Mittelalters,* vol. 2 (Munich: Artemis-Verlag, 1983), cols. 1137-41.

30. On the early and high scholastic theory of purgatory as it developed from the second half of the twelfth century, see Jacques Le Goff, *La naissance du purgatoire* (1981).

31. Thus the text of a banner on a picture of the divine judgment of the individual painted by Hans Holbein the Elder in 1508; see Berndt Hamm, "Von der spätmittelalterlichen *reformatio* zur Reformation: Der Prozess normativer Zentrierung von Religion und Gesellschaft in Deutschland," *Archiv für Reformationsgeschichte* 84 (1993): 36f. The same text could also be seen on a gravestone in the choir of the church in the Franciscan monastery in Nuremberg; see Ulrich Schmidt, *Das ehemalige Franziskanerkloster in Nürnberg* (Nuremberg: Nurnberger Volksseitung, 1913), 18.

1480 and 1520. The following points seem to me particularly important if we want to locate and characterize the salvific role of penitential love during that later period and compare it to the theology of the twelfth century.

1. The love of God *(caritas)* was no longer identified with the coming of the Holy Spirit to human souls, as people like Peter Lombard, the influential teacher of the early scholastic period (ca. 1100-1160), had put it.[32] No longer was this kind of immediate experience of God simply the awakening of the soul through the power of the divine spirit. Instead, as a gift of the Holy Spirit, the love of God became its own particular quality of the soul, providing the foundational habit of virtue and giving all other virtues their loving orientation to God.[33] With this, though, the love of God was absorbed so much into the human psyche that it could be disconnected from the gracious working of the Holy Spirit, as seen in the work of William of Ockham (ca. 1285-1347) and his students. Ockhamists like Gabriel Biel (d. 1495) could say that a person could produce acts of pure love of God and true repentance by natural powers.[34] Most theologians around the year 1500 contested this possibility, seeing the love of God being poured instead into a person's soul, constituting an unformed but justifying mercy of God. They also stressed the rule, however, that sinners had to prepare to receive this grace, this true love of God, and this true repentance through the exertions of their own souls.

---

32. Petrus Lombardus, *Sententiae,* Lib. I, dist. 17, cap. 1 (Quod spiritus sanctus est caritas, qua diligimus deum et proximum), in *Sententiae in IV libris distinctae,* ed. Collegium S. Bonaventurae, Tome I, Pars II, Liber I et II, 3rd ed., Spicilegium Bonaventurianum 4 (Rome: Grottaferrata, 1971), 141.25–143.20; on this kind of Augustinian doctrine of grace, which was unable to assert itself in the early scholasticism of the twelfth century but reveals that it was only in the first half of the thirteenth century that the idea of the habitual character of justifying grace and love was developed, see Artur Michael Landgraf, *Dogmengeschichte der Frühscholastik,* vol. I/1 (Regensburg: Pustet, 1952), 220-37.

33. Landgraf, *Dogmengeschichte der Frühscholastik,* 141-219; Johann Auer, *Die Entwicklung der Gnadenlehre in der Hochscholastik mit besonderer Berücksichtigung des Kardinals Matteo d'Acquasparta,* part 1, *Das Wesen der Gnade* (Freiburg im Breisgau: Herder, 1942); and the article "Grâce," in *Dictionnaire de Spiritualité ascétique et mystique,* vol. 6 (1967).

34. Leif Grane, *Contra Gabrielem: Luthers Auseinandersetzung mit Gabriel Biel in der Disputatio contra Scholasticam Theologiam 1517,* trans. Elfriede Pump, Acta Theologica Danica 4 (Copenhagen: Gyldendal, 1962), 223-61; Heiko A. Oberman, *Der Herbst der mittelalterlichen Theologie,* trans. Martin Rumscheidt and Henning Kampen (Zurich: EVZ-Verlag, 1965), 139-46; originally published in English as *The Harvest of Mediaeval Theology* (1963).

2. Near the end of the Middle Ages, the image of the suffering Christ, the pitiable Man of Sorrows, moved to the center of theology and piety.[35] In the same way, God's love for people became more intensely and almost exclusively related to the earthly figure of the Christ of the passion. The love that responds to Christ's suffering love awakens the soul's greatest depths of penitential sorrow. This true repentance, along with all the sinner's work of "doing enough," then becomes nothing other than suffering with the suffering Christ, following his way of the cross, and being conformed to his passion.[36]

3. This unbreakable connection between the love of God, penitential sorrow, and inner reenactment of Christ's suffering signaled an essential change with respect to the role of the love of God as seen in the mysticism of the twelfth to fourteenth centuries. For mystical theologians like Bernard of Clairvaux, the love for Jesus, the suffering Son of God who had become human, was only the first stage in a mystical ascent that — transcending all that is earthly and profane — unites the soul directly with the otherworldly spirituality of the eternal word of God.[37] Love climbs upward over the purifying, purgatorial, confessional stages of inward sighing. Near the end of the Middle Ages, if I see it correctly, this brand of spiritual "alpinist" had left the scene. People still recognized, as always, that there

---

35. Hamm, "Von der spätmittelalterlichen *reformatio* zur Reformation," 24-41.

36. Martin Elze, "Das Verständnis der Passion Jesu im ausgehenden Mittelalter und bei Luther," in *Geist und Geschichte der Reformation: Festschrift für Hanns Rückert*, ed. Heinz Liebing and Klaus Scholder, Arbeiten zur Kirchengeschichte 38 (Berlin: De Gruyter, 1966), 127-51; Petra Seegets, "'Das alles menschlich heyl an dem leiden Christi steet': Stephan Fridolin — ein spätmittelalterlicher Frömmigkeitstheologe zwischen Kloster und Stadt" (Ph.D. diss., Erlangen, 1994).

37. See Ruh, *Geschichte der abendländischen Mystik*, 234-75, esp. 242: "For Bernard the recalling of Christ's sufferings is always only a starting-point and has scarcely any intrinsic value." On the stages of love according to Bernard, cf. 229-34 and 258 (the ascent of the bride/soul from kissing the feet and the hands, and then the union with the heavenly Bridegroom in the kiss on the mouth [cf. above, n. 15]). Kissing the feet corresponds to the humble attitude of contrition: "First we fall before the feet of him who created us and weep for all (the evil) that we have done" *(Sermo 3.5*, in *Sermones super Cantica Canticorum)*. See also the gradual path of the "impetuous" love of God in the tract *De quattuor gradibus violentae caritatis* by the mystical theologian Richard of St. Victor (d. 1173) in Ruh, 387-95; on the first step, 389f.: "The first step — that of wounding love — reveals most clearly the Ovidian model. It pierces the heart, love's fiery arrow penetrates the spirit to the marrow. This then 'burns with desire, glows with ardor, it blazes, it pants, it groans from the bottom of its heart and long-drawn sighs burst from it.'"

were stages in the love of God, levels of intensity,[38] but all those stages of love now had to do with the inner relationship of the painful, contrite heart to the suffering Christ and a lifelong existence of identifying with the martyred Son of Man. This reduction and concentration of the mystical love of God to the *via purgativa*, in which one claimed the passion for oneself, were particularly characteristic of the instructions for piety before and after 1500. The artwork of these decades, for instance, clearly aimed to raise emotions and provide instructive images concerning this passion-driven way of salvation.

4. Despite the importance for the later Middle Ages of the decisive point of penitential love, in comparison with the twelfth century the weight nevertheless shifted back to the external dimensions of repentance: the priestly sacrament of confession and absolution, along with works of satisfaction. There were several reasons for this. Because of the doctrine of purgatory that had been developing since the end of the twelfth century, it became more important to know whether one had truly made satisfaction and repaid all one's temporal punishments for sin.[39] The fearful punishments of purgatory were painted in ever more excessive, detailed, and terrifying ways during the late Middle Ages.[40] As a result, the faithful made increasingly frantic efforts to save themselves from purgatory and enter into paradise immediately after death, either by "doing enough" through fasting, prayer, almsgiving, and making endowments or by buying indulgences. The more that priests and laity imagined purgatory as a place of frightening punishment rather than an experience of purification, the more the importance of "doing enough" increased. The religiosity of the later Middle Ages was marked by the popular understanding that attaining salvation depended on works done out of love for God and neighbor. That is, good works of repentance paid the penalties of sin and earned rewards.

---

38. On the "gradualism" characteristic of medieval theology, piety, and devotion — a thinking in terms of ascending and descending steps and stages further intensified in comparison with the early old church and its Neoplatonic impulses, see Günther Müller, "Gradualismus," *Deutsche Vierteljahrsschrift für Literaturwissenschaft und Geistesgeschichte* 2 (1924): 681-720; see also my contribution in Berndt Hamm, Bernd Moeller, and Dorothea Wendebourg, *Reformationstheorien: Ein kirchenhistorischer Disput über Einheit und Vielfalt der Reformation* (Göttingen, 1995), 69-71.

39. See n. 30 above.

40. See the articles and illustrations in Peter Jezler, ed., *Himmel, Hölle, Fegefeuer: Das Jenseits im Mittelalter*, exhibition catalogue (Zurich: Verlag Neue Zürcher Zeitung, 1994).

The mercantile mentality of the time revolved less around the God-loving soul's receiving a heavenly treasure and more around accessing the "treasury of good works."

5. Along with this, the priestly power of the keys with respect to absolution gained new significance from a separate source, namely, the various doctrinal streams of scholasticism.[41] In particular, the following theory of absolution gained great weight in the school of Duns Scotus (ca. 1265-1308). In short, this theory said that most people, due to emotional weakness, are not in a position to achieve a true penitential love (*contritio*, "contrition") without help from the sacrament of confession itself. When such people come to the priest and confess their sins to him, they have only an imperfect sorrow for sin (the so-called *attritio*, "attrition"). But through the sacramental absolution, specifically through the words *Ego te absolvo a peccatis tuis* ("I absolve you of your sins"), the imperfect is changed to a perfect and true repentance. Justifying grace enters the sinful hearts through the power of the words of absolution, turning *attritio* into *contritio*. Thus the sinner is given the gift of the forgiveness of sins *(remissio peccatorum)*, which means being freed from guilt and eternal damnation.[42] Further, a person's weak internal repentance can be balanced out externally by the priest's authority and the sacrament's efficacy, thereby in-

---

41. Herbert Vorgrimler, *Buße und Krankensalbung,* Handbuch der Dogmengeschichte, vol. 4, sec. 3 (Freiburg im Breisgau: Herder, 1978), 131-38; Vorgrimler, considering the heightened evaluation of priestly absolution, speaks of a "change of direction in the Scholastic theology of repentance" in the thirteenth century (e.g., in Bonaventure, Thomas Aquinas, and Duns Scotus). What is new, for example, is that the efficacy of the grace of *contritio* is attributed to the performance of the sacrament.

42. On the medieval Scotist teaching on repentance, see the works of Valens Heynck, e.g., his essay "Zur Lehre von der unvollkommenen Reue in der Skotistenschule des ausgehenden 15. Jahrhunderts," *Franziskanische Studien* 24 (1937): 18-58. Cf. also Ohst, *Pflichtbeichte,* 117-38; he shows how this theory of the sinner's imperfect striving for repentance was transformed and ennobled by the sacramental absolution evidently beginning with William of Auvergne (d. 1249). Ohst connects the fact that repentance became a problem in the thirteenth century directly to a sophisticated legal set of standards that were increasingly obscure for laypeople: "How can a person ever find spontaneous, genuine repentance for a deed which objectively, measured by the prevailing standards, is sinful but which he himself does not recognize as such because he does not understand the standards?" (p. 118). Whether there really is, as Ohst assumes in his richly faceted study, a direct connection between this problem of an understanding of sin that was becoming more complicated legally and the sacramental reinterpretation of absolution along with the corresponding theory of *attritio/contritio* needs to be explored further in the sources.

stantly raising a saving and true penitential love through the magic of the church's ritual, so to speak. Beginning in the thirteenth century, this massive new sacramentalism became increasingly prevalent as people trusted less in their own inner spirituality.[43] Theologians and priests had an obvious, but also ambiguous, interest in seeing the effective authority of their ecclesiastical roles grow in prestige, which compounded consciousness about sin, anxieties, and the need for assurance among the faithful. Therefore, external repentance — the sacrament of penance, penitential works, and indulgences — gained in importance at the same time that repentance was being internalized by continuous developments that stretched from the twelfth century to the end of the Middle Ages. This tendency grew even stronger among the mystics of the fourteenth century.

6. A typical question of theologians near the end of the Middle Ages was the following: As religious subjects after the Fall, what remains of human understanding, emotion, will, and action when people push themselves to the limit of their innate spiritual powers?[44] What kind of love and repentance are people capable of without the pull of the Holy Spirit and without the power of God's grace flowing into their hearts? The formulation of this question clearly shows how much theologians had learned to observe the natural, earthly realm of human existence as its own conceptual sphere, focusing on this-worldly subjects. Theologians around the year 1500, however, diverged widely in how they answered questions about the religious capacities of the natural sinful person.

7. Which gaps reveal these divergent opinions? The Ockhamist approach was discussed earlier. Theologians holding this view trusted people's natural ability to have the moral freedom to love God above all things and thereby reach true repentance.[45] This was a moral optimism, which could not really say with any clarity why people need the gracious work of

---

43. This exaggeration of the effect of the sacraments and indulgences in contrast to man's minimal ability to repent attains its most extreme form in the Augustinian monk Johannes von Paltz (d. 1511), who was a member of the Erfurt community at the very time Luther joined it (in July 1505). Cf. Berndt Hamm, *Frömmigkeitstheologie am Anfang des 16. Jahrhunderts: Studien zu Johannes von Paltz und seinem Umkreis,* Beiträge zur historischen Theologie 65 (Tübingen: Mohr, 1982), 266-91.

44. This is the question so typical for late medieval theology of the *facere quod in se est* (What can the sinner before God achieve when he does all that he can?); cf. Heiko A. Oberman, "Facientibus quod in se est deus non denegat gratiam: Robert Holcot, O.P., and the Beginnings of Luther's Theology," *Harvard Theological Review* 55 (1962): 317-42.

45. See n. 34 above.

God within them.[46] The theologians of the Augustinian Order (the order whose Erfurt cloister the young Luther entered in 1505) represented the sharpest contrast to this Ockhamist view of confession. Luther could learn from the scholastic theologians and spiritual instructors of his order that the natural powers within sinful people were capable only of rousing the heart in selfish directions.[47] Sinful people cannot feel the love of God or make a true repentance in loving accord with Christ's passion but can only go as far as the sorrow for sin that comes from the egotistical motive of fearing punishment. These sinners are like the criminal who is led to the gallows and regrets his crimes not because he understands them as such or inwardly abhors them but because he is afraid of the gallows. Therefore, every sinner who does not have God's justifying and reforming grace is only capable of a shabby kind of "gallows remorse." The merciful love of God entering the soul is the only thing that brings sinners back into God's orbit. Only its gracious spiritual power can transform sinners into truly loving and repentant people who follow in Christ's footsteps.

In the years immediately before the Reformation, the Augustinian monk Johannes von Staupitz (ca. 1468-1524) preeminently stressed that the sinner's repentance depended entirely on grace from beginning to end.[48] Staupitz was not only Luther's teacher and superior in the order but also his pastoral counselor and fatherly friend.[49] In later years, Luther repeat-

---

46. Consequently the Ockhamist school based the need to be filled with grace not on the sinful deficiency of human nature but on God's voluntary bond with humankind: in total divine freedom, God has decided to accept as worthy of merit and satisfactory only such acts of love for God and one's neighbor as have been created by the divine quality of grace and love instilled in them. No qualitative or ethical change is brought about in the essence of one's ability to love through this infusion. Cf. Berndt Hamm, *Promissio, Pactum, Ordinatio: Freiheit und Selbstbindung Gottes in der scholastischen Gnadenlehre*, Beiträge zur historischen Theologie 54 (Tübingen: Mohr, 1977), 361-65.

47. Adolar Zumkeller, *Erbsünde, Gnade, Rechtfertigung und Verdienst nach der Lehre der Erfurter Augustinertheologen des Spätmittelalters*, Cassiciacum 35 (Würzburg: Augustinus-Verlag, 1984), and "Das Ungenügen der menschlichen Werke bei den deutschen Predigern des Spätmittelalters," *Zeitschrift für katholische Theologie* 81 (1959): 265-305.

48. Lothar Graf zu Dohna and Richard Wetzel, "Die Reue Christi: Zum theologischen Ort der Buße bei Johann von Staupitz," *Studien und Mitteilungen zur Geschichte des Benediktinerordens und seiner Zweige* 94 (1983): 457-82.

49. For orientation (with bibliographical details) on Staupitz and the topic "Staupitz and Luther," see Wolfgang Günter, "Johann von Staupitz (ca. 1468-1524)," in *Katholische Theologen der Reformationszeit*, ed. Erwin Iserloh, Katholisches Leben und

edly emphasized both in letters to Staupitz and in reminiscences about Staupitz that he owed his groundbreaking insights to his elder, even though Staupitz did not agree with Luther's break from the papal church.[50] When we take a closer look at the theological proximity of the two, Luther's step beyond Staupitz will show us the decisive transition from the soteriological centrality of the "love of God" in the Middle Ages to the centrality of justification by faith alone in the Reformation. This piece of theological microhistory changed the course of world history.

When Luther published the detailed explanation of his crisp Ninety-five Theses on indulgences in the early summer of 1518, he prefaced the edition with an accompanying letter to Staupitz, in which he described how the esteemed father had helped him come to a new understanding of repentance some years earlier.[51] Through his guidance, the bitter word "repent" *(poenitentia)* became sweet. Earlier — no doubt under Ockhamist influences[52] — Luther had understood repentance as something forcibly

---

Kirchenformen im Zeitalter der Glaubenspaltung 48 (Münster: Aschendorff, 1988), 5:11-31; Lothar Graf zu Dohna, "Staupitz und Luther: Kontinuität und Umbruch in den Anfängen der Reformation," *Pastoraltheologie* 74 (1985): 452-65; Richard Wetzel, "Staupitz und Luther," in *Martin Luther: Probleme seiner Zeit,* ed. Volker Press and Dieter Stievermann, Spätmittelalter und Frühe Neuzeit 16 (Stuttgart: Klett-Cotta, 1986), 75-87; a revised version of Wetzel's essay appears in Ebernburg-Hefte 25 (1991): 369(41)-395(47).

50. Cf. Luther's last letter to Staupitz, dated September 17, 1523, WA Br 3:155f.6-8, no. 659 (*LW* 49:48f.), and Otto Scheel, ed., *Dokumente zu Luthers Entwicklung (bis 1519),* 2nd ed. (Tübingen: J. C. B. Mohr, 1929), 30, no. 74: Staupitz is the one "per quem primum cepit evangelii lux de tenebris splendescere in cordibus nostris" (2 Cor. 4:6); letter to Count Albrecht of Mansfeld, dated February 23, 1542, WA Br 9:627.23-25, no. 3716, and Scheel, p. 167, no. 461: "Jnn disen gedancken oder anfechtungen . . . ich etwa [= einst] auch drinnen gestecket. Vndt wo mihr D. Staupitz, oder viel mehr Gott durch Doctor Staupitz, nicht heraus gehofffen hette, so were ich darin ersoffen vndt langst in der helle" ("I was once bogged down in such thoughts and *Anfechtungen.* And if Dr. Staupitz — or rather God through Dr. Staupitz — had not helped me, I would have drowned in them and long been in hell").

51. Letter from Luther to Staupitz dated May 30, 1518, WA 1:525-27 (*LW* 48:64ff.); Scheel, *Dokumente zu Luthers Entwicklung (bis 1519),* 9-11, no. 18; Wetzel, "Staupitz und Luther" (as n. 49, version in the Ebernburg-Hefte), 374-85.

52. Since it is well known that Luther's theological development was strongly influenced by the Ockhamist theologian Gabriel Biel, the following reminiscence (from his *Enarratio Psalmi LI,* 1538) clearly relates to the contritionism of the Biel school (see n. 34 above): "Hac doctrina [scil. de contritionibus et attritionibus] sane ita sum ego in scholis corruptus, ut vix magno labore, Dei gratia, me ad solum 'auditum gaudii' (Ps 51.10) potuerim convertere. Nam si expectandum eo usque est, donec sufficienter conteraris,

coerced, a strained attainment whose goal was true penitential love, confession, and works of satisfaction. Staupitz, however, opened Luther's eyes to what true repentance really is. First, the love of God and God's righteousness is not an end point but a starting point, a love that is not strained but owes its existence to the encounter with the suffering of the "sweetest redeemer." Second, the biblical sense of repentance should not be understood in terms of human doing but as a fundamental reversal in attitude and emotion *(transmutatio mentis et affectus)*. Third, this existential change of direction is not a human achievement but is the grace of God; put precisely: it is not changing oneself but being changed.

Much of what Luther described here as a joyful discovery of true biblical repentance bequeathed to him by Staupitz may remind us of certain characteristics of the reorientation of the understanding of repentance in the twelfth century. At that time, the accent shifted from the external level of "doing enough" to the inner penitential emotion of regret. That regret was understood to come from the impulse of God's love, was reciprocated by human love, and was anchored in the fact of Christ's incarnation and passion. The changes of the twelfth century were tied to an Augustine renaissance, just as we should understand the theological insights of Staupitz and Luther through the Augustine renaissance of their day.[53] In their time, they too had to contend with the forms of an archaic piety based on deeds and payments. Just as after the year 1100, so also in 1500 the "true" biblical meaning of *poenitentia* needed to be rediscovered. But that meant something different in the later Middle Ages than it did in Abelard and Bernard's time. By revisiting Staupitz's sermons and tracts from the years before the Reformation, we see that the great gap between the beginning of the twelfth century and 1500 is unmistakable.

For the theologians of the high Middle Ages, there was absolutely no doubt that the love awakened in the heart of the sinner by God's Spirit supplied the power in life for spiritual conversion and advancement. Consequently, a direct inner causal relationship existed between penitential

---

nunquam pervenies ad auditum gaudii. Id quod in monasterio magno cum dolore saepissime expertus sum, sequebar enim hanc doctrinam de contritionibus" (in contrast to the Scotist *doctrina de attritionibus*); WA 40/II:411.36–412.17; Scheel, *Dokumente zu Luthers Entwicklung (bis 1519)*, 95, 11-16, no. 241.

53. See Heiko A. Oberman, *Werden und Wertung der Reformation: Vom Wegestreit zum Glaubenskampf* (Tübingen: Mohr, 1977), 82-140 (regarding the Augustinian renaissance in the late Middle Ages); on the Augustinian renaissance of the twelfth century, see n. 7 above.

love, forgiveness of sin, and justification. As an attentive pastoral counselor, however, Staupitz quite intensely acquired the spiritual disillusionment of the later Middle Ages and worked within his own radically Augustinian theology of grace. He placed the pitiful lowliness and spiritual poverty of humanity in contrast to the abundant mercy of God in Jesus Christ.[54] He certainly shared the opinion that the sinner's soul is led to a true penitential love through the gift of transforming grace. Indeed, all people who are pulled in by the gravity of Christ's passion experience the spiritual rebirth that makes them capable of true love of God and genuine sorrow for sin. But this human sorrow, as Staupitz would emphasize in the same breath, is always so pitifully small that it definitely cannot attain the forgiveness of sins on the basis of its own emotional quality.[55] Only Christ's infinitely priceless sorrow for human sin in the Garden of Gethsemane and the spiritual suffering of his passion (which far exceeded his physical pain on the cross) compensated for all the inadequacy of our human repentance. Only in that is there any causal connection between the sinner's penitential love and the forgiveness of sins. Human love of God is elevated through Christ's passion alone. Only in this way can one speak of a justifying and saving love.[56] In Staupitz's eyes, it was absurd that a sorrow

---

54. See Staupitz's tract printed at the beginning of 1517 (arising from his Advent sermons in Nuremberg in 1516): *Libellus de exsecutione aeternae praedestinationis*, in Johann von Staupitz, *Sämtliche Schriften*, vol. 2, *Spätmittelalter und Reformation*, ed. Lothar Graf zu Dohna and Richard Wetzel, Texte und Untersuchungen 14 (Berlin: De Gruyter, 1979), §64 (p. 150): "Ego admiror coniunctionem summae misericordiae cum summa miseria."

55. Cf. Staupitz, Salzburger Predigten 1520, Codex St. Peter 6 V 8, Pr. 6.fol. 96v-97r; quoted in Dohna and Wetzel, "Die Reue Christi," 466: "O mein got, wie ain klaine reu ist es umb mich [= bei mir], das ich ain missfallen umb mein sündt hab und traur darüber" ("Oh, my God, what a tiny remorse that is in me, that I have displeasure and sorrow for my sin").

56. The Staupitz text in n. 55 continues: Christ answers the sinner — who surely feels a true contrition from his love to God but is aware of the lifelong worthlessness and inadequacy of his own pangs of remorse — by pointing to his own remorse in the Garden of Gethsemane. The sinner can make this perfect, eternally precious vicarious remorse his own if he only relates his own suffering to this suffering of Christ: "Nain, nain, fleuch nuer zu meinem herzenlaid und zeuchs in dich, so ist die sündt schon volkömen pereut" ("No, no, fly only to my heart's suffering and draw it to yourself and so your sin is fully repented of"). Quotation from Dohna and Wetzel, "Die Reue Christi," 466. See also the theologically even more dynamic text of a sermon on repentance that Staupitz preached in Nuremberg in Lent 1517 and was recorded by the Nuremberg council clerk, Lazarus

for sin as egocentric and anxious as "gallows remorse" could be transformed into true penitential love through the power of the sacrament of confession, a view held by many of his contemporaries.[57] A disposition that truly deserved the name "confession" should only have heartfelt love of God as its central point of departure. But according to Staupitz, only the power of Christ's vicarious suffering turns this true penitential love by humans into a repentance that has "done enough," that is, a repentance that is satisfactory and "is enough" to receive divine forgiveness for the guilt and punishment of all sins.[58] To use an illustration: only because we humans with our tiny feelings of love can climb onto the shoulders of Christ's great love and great suffering, can our repentance — which by itself is so insufficient — become a repentance that nevertheless wipes out our sins. Diminutive human repentance can reach heaven on the shoulders of the giant Christ.[59]

Spengler (ed. Knaake), 15-19, especially 16: that people must "ground" their contrition on that of Christ, that is, find in this the ground for the forgiveness of sins. On the relationship between human contrition and that of Christ in Staupitz — like that of the analogous relationship of human merit and that of Christ — see Dohna and Wetzel, passim, and Hamm, *Frömmigkeitstheologie am Anfang des 16. Jahrhunderts*, 238-43.

57. Staupitz, Nuremberg sermon on repentance (see n. 56), ed. Knaake, p. 16: gallows repentance, the characteristic of which is that it only relates to "human gain and loss," is "totally useless and sterile."

58. Staupitz, Nuremberg sermon on repentance, p. 16: through the "schmerzen, rew und traurigkeit unsers seligmachers" ("suffering, remorse, and sadness of our Savior"), one's true loving contrition is "allererst angezundet und lebendig gemacht und dan zu abtilgung unnser sondere mer dann genugsam" ("first kindled and brought to life and then increasing more than enough to wipe out our sins"). Here, as is clear from the context and his other writings, Staupitz has in mind a twofold effect of Christ's suffering: on the one hand, as an inner working of grace, it enflames the answering contrition of the sinner; on the other, through its immeasurable merit it complements externally all the imperfection of this human contrition so that it becomes "more than enough" to achieve forgiveness of sin. Consequently the valency of contrition to wipe out sin is an external valency bestowed by God for Christ's sake. Cf. Hamm, *Frömmigkeitstheologie am Anfang des 16. Jahrhunderts*, 240-43 and n. 59 following.

59. The "sufficiency" of repentance is thereby the assumption of Christ's contrition, of which Staupitz says (Nuremberg sermon on repentance [see n. 56], p. 16): "Dieser schmerz und berewung Christi, wo wir unser rew darein ergrunden, ist zu abwaschung aller unser missethat genugsam und so vellig [voll ausreichend], wo es moglich were, das tausent welt weren, das sie durch diese engstliche plutschwaissung Christi [Luke 22:44] irer sonden entledigt wurden" ("This pain and remorse of Christ upon which we base our repentance is sufficient to wash away all our transgressions, and is so plenteous

Precisely here lies the decisive point at which Luther goes beyond the typical late medieval horizon of a person like Johannes von Staupitz.

The question of sufficient repentance is typically late medieval. What kind and what amount of repentance, confession, works of satisfaction, and purchase of indulgences are necessary and "enough" for eradicating the guilt and punishment of sin, both temporally and in the hereafter? What kind of help does the sinner need to stoke at least a spark of that true love of God, that painful love of true repentance, without which no one reaches salvation in the end? Finally, how does this true repentance become a saving repentance? When Luther wrote his letter to Staupitz on true repentance at the end of May 1518, having "enough" sufficient confession and repentance was no longer a question for him.[60] He, too, had once started with this question,[61] but the radicality of his own experience as a sinner and his encounter with the sovereignty of free divine mercy led him to realize that it can never be the quality of people's inner love of God and feelings of remorse that allows them to be blessed with the forgiveness of sins and saved from damnation. In whatever form and upon whatever shoulders it rests (including the penitential love that rests on Christ's vicarious repentance), repentance can never be a sufficient, saving repentance, when viewed in light of the forgiveness of sins and heavenly salvation. Therefore, people should not base the peace of a troubled conscience on it, either.[62]

---

that if there were a thousand worlds their sins would be discharged through Christ's fearful sweating of blood"). The comparison with the giant's shoulders is not taken from the sources.

60. See Luther's polemic against the question of *satis contritum esse* — of "sufficient" contrition — in his commentary on the thirty-eighth thesis on indulgences, written quite some time before the letter to Staupitz. In the justification of the sinner, it is not a question of the *fervor contritionis* but of the *fides absolutionis*. Whatever the state of your contrition *(quicquid sit de contritione tua)*, however inadequate it is, the only important thing is the faith in Christ's word of forgiveness (given by the priest): WA 1:594.37–595.5.21-34 (*LW* 31:191ff.), and *Luthers Werke in Auswahl*, ed. Otto Clemen, vols. 1-4, 6th ed. (Berlin: De Gruyter, 1966-68), vol. 1, pp. 105.5-16 and 105.37–106.14.

61. See Luther's retrospective glance in 1538, already cited in n. 52, which began with the question that once tormented him: *Utrum fuerit contritio sufficiens:* WA 40/II:411.10f., and in Scheel, *Dokumente zu Luthers Entwicklung (bis 1519)*, 94.27.

62. See Luther's theses (which were probably developed in the early summer of 1518) *Pro veritate inquirenda et timoratis conscientiis consolandis*, WA 1:629-33, e.g., thesis 18 (631.23f.): "Super contritionem edificantes remissionem super arenam, id est super opus hominis, fidem dei edificant," and theses 8 and 9 (631.5-8): "Remissio culpe non

From the Medieval "Love of God" to Luther's "Faith"

It is precisely because Luther was so aware of the lifelong human perversion through sin that he could not imagine a Christian life without the sorrow of true repentance. By this, he meant that when people reach the end of their own possibility, security, and certainty, they become acutely aware that before God they are beggars with empty hands[63] and that they should heartily regret their sin. The letter to Staupitz shows how important such a confession of the heart was for Luther, just as he was similarly concerned in the famous Ninety-five Theses with the same true confession and true repentance.[64] The difference in comparison with the Middle Ages, however, is that in Luther's eyes this pain of true repentance that comes from love of God is not a justifying or saving repentance. That is, the confession is not "good enough."[65] On the contrary, such a repentance is simply the self-understanding that a person can contribute absolutely nothing to salvation, not even the smallest little spark of a loving, penitential feeling. For Luther, this was not simply a subjective humble attitude of piety coming from a sighing self; it was an objective, doctrinal reality. Hu-

---

innititur contritioni peccatoris, nec officio aut potestati sacerdotis, innititur potius fidei, quae est in verbum Christi dicentis: 'Quodcunque solveris etc.'" On this, see the interpretation by Oswald Bayer, *Promissio: Geschichte der reformatorischen Wende in Luthers Theologie,* Forschungen zur Kirchen- und Dogmengeschichte 24 (Göttingen: Vandenhoeck & Ruprecht, 1971), 164-202, especially 182-202.

63. Note the famous words of the onetime mendicant Luther in his last note and in Heiko A. Oberman's commentary: "Wir sein pettler: *Hoc est verum:* Bund und Gnade in der Theologie des Mittelalters und der Reformation," *Zeitschrift für Kirchengeschichte* 78 (1967): 232-52.

64. See from the Ninety-five Theses (October 31, 1517), thesis 4: "The penalty of sin remains as long as the hatred of self, that is, true inner repentance, until our entrance into the kingdom of heaven," and thesis 40: "A Christian who is truly contrite seeks and loves to pay penalties for his sins; the bounty of indulgences, however, relaxes penalties and causes men to hate them — at least it furnishes occasion for hating them." WA 1:233.16f. and 235.16f. (*LW* 31:25 and 28) and in *Luthers Werke in Auswahl,* vol. 1, 3.26-28 and 5.37f. In interpreting the Ninety-five Theses we must consider the fact that they do not discuss justification (and consequently also not faith) but indulgences (and consequently also repentance and remorse). This means that Luther did not try to explain in a comforting way how sinners enter into Christ's grace and righteousness but wished to make it clear, in a sharp and provocative way, how sinners — on the basis of the grace bestowed upon them and in imitation of Christ — leave themselves open to the gravity of the penitential life with its destruction of human possibilities and certainties, thereby denying themselves the escape of a deceptive assurance of grace and salvation.

65. See the quotation from the theses *Pro veritate . . .* in n. 62 above and n. 69 below.

man beings, no matter how great their love of God and sorrow for sin, cannot really contribute anything to their salvation, whether through pious emotions or moral actions. *Hoc est verum!*[66]

From 1513 to 1518, Luther gradually distanced himself theologically from the medieval spirituality of love of God and penitential love to such a degree that he replaced the medieval centerpiece of love with the centerpiece of faith.[67] Because of this, faith and repentance went their separate ways after 1516.[68] Faith remained tied up with repentance (for there is no faith in Christ without the pain of repentance),[69] but faith itself lost its characteristic note of sorrow and took on for Luther the character of the comforting, joyous confidence that clings to the words of promise in the gospel: that biblical promise that personally pledges itself to me, saying, "your sins are forgiven." Luther thus replaced the medieval alliance between penitential love and the forgiveness of sins by linking faith with the words of forgiveness. But what does that mean? Is not faith as Luther sees it a kind of radical love of God, even if it is a joyful, comforting love of God instead of a painful, penitential love? As Luther constantly reiterated, faith is a sure confidence in God's saving goodness, in God's unconditional mercy on account of Jesus Christ. Can this faith then be understood as anything other than a warming of the conscience through the power of the Holy Spirit and, consequently, as a true and trustworthy love since it expects and receives all things from God?[70]

---

66. See n. 63 above. Already in Luther's first lectures on the Psalms, the statements about the subjective-existential prayerful attitude before God *(humilitas)* and the didactic objectified truth coincide in one and the same *modus loquendi;* see also chap. 3.

67. Already in this form in the *Dictata super Psalterum* (1513-15); see also chap. 3.

68. This development can first be seen in the second half of Luther's lectures on Romans; cf. Matthias Kroeger, *Rechtfertigung und Gesetz: Studien zur Entwicklung der Rechtfertigungslehre beim jungen Luther,* Forschungen zur Kirchen- und Dogmengeschichte 20 (Göttingen: Vandenhoeck & Ruprecht, 1968), 152-63. This development reached its conclusion in the theses *Pro veritate . . .* (as in n. 62). To detect this in no way signifies that, like Oswald Bayer, we should see in this set of theses Luther's first reforming texts.

69. See the theses *Pro veritate . . .* Thesis 40: "Finge casum (per impossibile) sit absolvendus non contritus, credens tamen sese absolvi, hic est vere absolutus." Here Luther could not imagine a justifying faith without a simultaneous loving repentance inextricably bound to this faith ("impossible!"); yet what he wanted to say in the thesis is that it is not the repentance but the faith that receives the justifying forgiveness of sins. No faith without contrition, but no *contritio justificans!*

70. On the metaphor of "being warmed," see Luther's sermon from June 9, 1532, on

Although it effectively functioned this way, Luther displayed the greatest restraint, even a kind of timidity, about describing faith as love of God.[71] He talked effusively about God's self-giving, saving love,[72] and of the highest love of Christ the bridegroom for his bride (believers),[73] just as he characterized the living, active essence of faith as love of neighbor.[74]

God's love to humanity: "Denn es nicht moglich ist, were solch fewr seiner liebe fulet, das er nicht auch solt ein wenig davon erwermet und entzundet werden" ("For it is impossible for one who feels the fire of his love not to be a little warmed and inflamed by it"). WA 36:429.28-30 (though without mention of the concept of faith). See also occasional phrases used by Luther that characterize the essence of faith and its "joy" as love of God, e.g., in the tract *Von der Freiheit eines Christenmenschen*, § 21: "die seel durch den glauben reyn ist und gott liebet"; §27: "also fleusset auß dem glauben die lieb und lust zu got"; §20: "und stett all seyn [des Glaubens] lußt darynn, das er widderumb mocht gott auch umsonst dienen ynn freyer lieb," in Martin Luther, *Studienausgabe*, ed. Hans-Ulrich Delius, vol. 2 (East Berlin, 1982), 287.24f.; 299.14f.; 287.9f. (*LW* 31:357). On the character of faith as love of God, see also Luther's sermon postille: WA 10/I/1:73.8f.; 102.11; 260.15f.; 10/I/2:187.25. See also n. 73 below (Elert) and Peter Manns, "Fides absoluta — Fides incarnata: zur Rechtfertigungslehre Luthers im Großen Galater-Kommentar," in *Reformata Reformanda, Festgabe für Hubert Jedin*, vol. 1, ed. Erwin Iserloh and Konrad Repgen (Münster: Aschendorff, 1965), 288-312. I must thank my colleague Reinhard Schwarz for allowing me to read his typescript "Die Umformung des religiösen Prinzips der Gottesliebe in der frühen Reformation: Ein Beitrag zum Verständnis von Luthers Schrift 'Von der Freiheit eines Christenmenschen,'" which appears in the papers of the *Verein für Reformationsgeschichte*. There Schwarz comments on Luther succinctly and relevantly: "Provided with a strongly affective component, faith contains within itself the emotion of love of God."

71. See, for instance, Luther's exegesis of the first commandment in the Large Catechism, *BSLK*, 560-72; *BC*, 386-92. The faith that carries out the first commandment is here described by Luther as trust and sincere confidence but is not called love — in contrast to the famous exegesis of the first commandment in the Small Catechism: "We are to fear, love and trust God above all things" (*BSLK*, 507.42f.; *BC*, 351.2).

72. The divine Being as "feur offen und brunst solcher liebe, die himel und erden fullet" ("the fiery oven and heat of such love as fills heaven and earth"), WA 36:424.18f. (sermon from June 9, 1532); see also WA 36:429.1-5, 13-24.

73. Werner Elert, *Morphologie des Luthertums*, vol. 1, *Theologie und Weltanschauung des Luthertums hauptsächlich im 16. und 17. Jahrhundert* (Munich: Beck, 1931), 147-54. Elert shows how, in Luther's understanding, the "moment of reciprocity" is contained in this "relationship of love," i.e., "that God's love engenders our love for him" (with reference to WA 10/III:157.9ff.); hence for Luther faith is "the relationship of a mutual love between the I and Thou in the most personal sense," 151.

74. Rudolf Mau, "Liebe als gelebte Freiheit der Christen: Luthers Auslegung von G 5,13-24 im Kommentar von 1519," *Lutherjahrbuch* 59 (1992): 11-37.

Love flows from God to believers and from believers to neighbors.[75] But concerning the reciprocating and trustworthy relationship of people to God, Luther significantly stopped using the traditionally favored concept of love as his foundation. Instead, he worked out a concept of faith, which had in scholastic theology stood as the emotionally weakest and least pious dimension of Christian existence.[76] By turning this concept of faith into the central concept for the justification of the ungodly, Luther wanted to say that people are not justified and saved through their spiritual feelings or through pious emotions like love of God and penitential love. They are justified and saved instead through the passive reception of that which is outside them. For Luther, faith is the path of pure reception, of being gifted with the righteousness of Jesus Christ.[77] Faith is given to believers when they trust in the gospel; they themselves are nothing, but they can trust all things to the saving activity of God.

In contrast, the concept of the love of God was quite problematic in Luther's eyes. All across the theological tradition, it was easily bound up with the notion of a spiritual quality that might improve a person's affective and effective abilities. Luther, however, wanted to keep the sinner's relationship with God and salvation absolutely free of exactly those kinds of ideas about religious quality and activity. This also corresponded to his original and foundational experience that as a sinful human being he was unable to truly love God through his emotions[78] and would be lost if the gate of salvation were somehow based on his own ability to love, even if that ability to love were given to him first through God's mercy and Holy Spirit. Therefore, the concept of faith was supposed to dispel any connotation of quality, virtue, being good, or doing good works, presenting instead a relationship of "only" receiving a gift. Faith then means being liberated from all the conditions of salvation that have to do with feelings and actions. Yes, faith is a kind of loving feeling, even the most radical form of

---

75. Cf. Luther, *Von der Freiheit eines Christenmenschen*, §29: *Studienausgabe*, 305.1-11.

76. Piety (*pietas, devotio*), here in the sense of a manner and structuring of one's life in relationship to God. On the medieval concept of faith, see chap. 3.

77. "Ingressus in Christum est fides, quae nos colligit in divitias iustitiae dei," *Operationes in Psalmos*: WA 5:408.4f.

78. Luther traced the experience of the *semper peccator* in his first lectures on the Psalms and the *simul iustus et peccator* in his lectures on Romans back to that attitude of faith with which he could perceive himself as a hopelessly lost sinner who is incapable of love while at the same time able to see himself in the light of Christ's righteousness.

love, because it leaves everything to God alone. However, faith does not justify and save through feelings or through any affective ardor or fervor; it justifies only because it receives. Faith is love of God, but it is always a broken love because of the original sin of not loving. It is a radical love in the suffering *(Anfechtung)* of radical sins. Thus faith justifies and saves not through its loving but through its receiving; the sinful person rather than the loving person is declared to be free. This is what Luther wanted to say when he named faith, rather than love, as the saving bond between humans and God.[79] Distancing the justifying nature of faith from love and penitential love was a reason why, with increasing clarity and beginning in 1516, Luther separated faith from penitential remorse and a groaning humility. This is the receiving, justifying, and saving faith that alone is in relationship with the liberating word of God.

Allow me to summarize the main points of this chapter. For the theology of the twelfth century, it was a pioneering discovery to overcome the fixation on outwardly effective religious acts by turning to the inner emotion of love of God. Almost 400 years later, however, Luther did not only turn against a religiosity of good works. For him it was liberating to overcome the fixation on both outward pious actions and inward true love of God. He did this by listening to the absolving word of the gospel and, consequently, by receiving the saving righteousness that comes from outside us *(extra nos)*.[80] That was his discovery of faith. In doing this, Luther took a position beyond the late medieval tendencies to both externalize and internalize repentance.

---

79. In contrast to Luther, Zwingli had no qualms about identifying faith and love within the existential movement of trust in God; Berndt Hamm, *Zwinglis Reformation der Freiheit* (Neukirchen-Vluyn: Neukirchener Verlag, 1988), 76-78.

80. Cf. Karl-Heinz Zur Mühlen, *Nos extra nos: Luthers theologie zwischen Mystik und Scholastik*, Beiträge zur historischen Theologie 46 (Tübingen: J. C. B. Mohr, 1972), and Wilfried Joest, *Ontologie der Person bei Luther* (Göttingen: Vandenhoeck & Ruprecht, 1967).

CHAPTER 2

Impending Doom and Imminent Grace: Luther's Early Years in the Cloister as the Beginning of His Reformation Reorientation

1. The Usual View of Luther's Years in the Erfurt Cloister: A Dark Time before the Reformation Change

The 500th anniversary of Martin Luther's entry into the Augustinian monastery in Erfurt on July 17, 1505, provided an occasion for renewed thinking about how much weight to give those early years when considering both his biography and the Reformation as a whole. According to traditional Protestant views, there was really nothing to celebrate in 2005; at least, no real Reformation jubilee. Conventional wisdom supposes that the time between Luther's entry into the monastery and his permanent transfer to Wittenberg in autumn 1511 was not the source of the Reformation metamorphosis in his theology and piety. The dominant consensus today still seems to be that important characteristics of a changed Reformation theology do not appear before his first lectures on the Psalms (1513-15). In recent decades, even more Luther scholars have concluded that the lectures on Romans (1515-16) do not reveal the so-called Reformation turn, either; instead, one must look to the indulgence controversy and then the unfolding process with Rome during 1518.[1] Even though early-twentieth-century researchers

1. For reviews of the literature on this subject, see Otto Pesch, "Zur Frage nach Luthers reformatorischer Wende: Ergebnisse und Probleme der Diskussion um Ernst Bizer, 'Fides ex auditu,'" in *Der Durchbruch der reformatorischen Erkenntnis bei Luther*, ed. Bernhard Lohse (Darmstadt: Wissenschaftliche Buchgesellschaft, 1968), 445-505, and Pesch, "Neuere Beiträge zur Frage nach Luthers 'Reformatorischer Wende,'" *Catholica* 37

like Karl Holl and Otto Scheel recognized a strong and dynamic "change before the change"² in Luther's time in Erfurt, more recent research insists that Erfurt does not belong to Luther's *initia reformationis* but to a dark prehistory before the change. They view the years at the Erfurt monastery under the dominant auspices of terrible *Anfechtungen* (doubts and afflictions), the experience of which was definitely a part of the later shape of Luther's new theology but nevertheless clearly belongs on the mundane side of the watershed moment. It was the personal intensification of a late medieval religious crisis that struck the young monk ever deeper and failed to provide him with an exit. Erfurt thus functions as a negative medieval foil from which a bright, liberating Reformation change arises.

2. Departing from the Scholarly Construction of Luther's "Reformation Turn"

The trusty and ingrained way of speaking about Luther's "Reformation turn"³ or his "breakthrough to Reformation awareness"⁴ is admittedly less plausible than it appears to be at first blush. It fulfills all too well the deep need of historians to find clear, nameable epochs. Even more, it satisfies the desires of systematic theologians to find a central theological truth that can serve as the epitome of a decisive Reformation change and can stand as the liminal experience that defines before and after moments in Luther's life. Above all, an intensive fusion of historical and systematic theology in the twentieth century forced this rhetoric of "change" that continues to dominate the discussion about the young Luther.

(1983): 259-87. See also Volker Leppin, "Luther-Literatur seit 1983, Teil II," *Theologische Rundschau* 65 (2000): 431-54.

    2. For another instructive review of the literature, see Wilhelm Link, *Das Ringen Luthers um die Freiheit der Theologie von der Philosophie* (Munich: Kaiser, 1940).

    3. Pesch, "Zur Frage nach Luthers reformatorischer Wende," 500. See also Oswald Bayer, "Die reformatorische Wende in Luthers Theologie," *Zeitschrift für Theologie und Kirche* 66 (1969): 115-50, and Bayer, *Promissio: Geschichte der reformatorischen Wende in Luthers Theologie*, Forschungen zur Kirchen- und Dogmengeschichte 24 (Göttingen: Vandenhoeck & Ruprecht, 1971).

    4. Lohse, *Der Durchbruch der reformatorischen Erkenntnis bei Luther*, and Lohse, ed., *Der Durchbruch der reformatorischen Erkenntnis bei Luther: Neuere Untersuchungen* (Stuttgart: Franz Steiner Verlag, 1988). See also Thomas Kaufmann, *Martin Luther* (Munich: Beck, 2006).

For me, revisiting Luther's time in Erfurt means nothing other than attempting to displace this whole "change" construction through a kind of rehistoricizing. It is well known that in his later recollections Luther stressed how laboriously, slowly, and gradually he found a way out of the errors of that early time and how his incremental progress was bound up with the intense experience of *Anfechtungen*.[5] I will simply refer to that famous passage in a table talk of 1532 where Luther said, "I did not learn my theology all at once but had to constantly dig deeper and deeper; my *Anfechtungen* brought me to this because one cannot learn anything without practice."[6] On the other hand, it is also known that Luther — according to his own testimony — often gained sudden insights of monumental importance that moved him deeply; above all, his insights about the biblical meaning of repentance, the forgiveness of sins, the righteousness of God, the difference between law and gospel, and the nature of the papacy and the devil.[7] Insofar as Luther mentioned cognitive and affective discov-

---

5. WA 54:186.25-29; *LW* 34:338: "I relate these things, good reader, so that, if you are a reader of my puny works, you may keep in mind, that, as I said above, I was all alone and one of those who, as Augustine says of himself, have become proficient by writing and teaching. I was not one of those who from nothing suddenly become the topmost, though they are nothing, neither have labored, nor been tempted, nor become experienced, but have with one look at the Scriptures exhausted their entire spirit."

6. WA TR 1:146.12-14, no. 352; *LW* 54:50: "I didn't learn my theology all at once. I had to ponder over it ever more deeply, and my spiritual trials [*tentationes, Anfechtungen*] were of help to me in this, for one does not learn anything without practice."

7. On repentance, see Luther's letter to Staupitz, May 30, 1518, WA 1:525-27; *LW* 48:64-70. On the forgiveness of sins, see Luther's lectures on Romans, WA 56:273.3–274.11; *LW* 25:260, especially the autobiographical words, "on the basis of this in my foolishness I could not understand in which way I should regard myself a sinner like other men and thus prefer myself to no one, even though I was contrite and made confession.... Thus I was at war with myself, not knowing that it was a true forgiveness indeed." On the righteousness of God, see n. 5 above. See also WA 5:144.1-23 (*Operationes in Psalmos*, 1519-21) and WA 56:171.26–172.15 (Lectures on Romans [1:17]); *LW* 25:151. On the difference between law and gospel, see WA TR 5:210.6-16, no. 5518, "Aber do ich das discrimen fande, quod aliud esset lex, aliud euangelium, da riß ich her durch"; *LW* 54:442: "But when I discovered the proper distinction — namely, that the law is one thing and the gospel is another — I made myself free." On the nature of the papacy, see n. 5 above, especially Luther's description of how he came to the recognition that the pope was not head of the church by "divine right" *(iure divino)* and how he conceded the pope's human right to rule *(ius humanum)* until he realized that if the papacy were not from God then it must necessarily be from the devil. On Luther's conviction (gained in 1520) that the pope was the Antichrist, see the October 11, 1520, letter written to Spalatin after the arrival of the pa-

eries and breakthroughs, he gave details about essential steps in a very complex and ongoing journey of theological awareness, which led him to a new overall understanding of Christian faith. How much he stylized or condensed these recollections is anyone's guess. But what seems essential to me is that he did not cast his theological biography in light of one all-defining central change or conversion. He spoke of important clarifications, which took place within a contextually specific and defined theological scope. That also applies to his oft-mentioned new understanding of the righteousness of God, *iustitia Dei* (Rom. 1:17),[8] which provided the basis for Luther's so-called tower experience.[9] That was nothing more or less than an electrical interpretive discovery of great (albeit also bounded) significance, which rearranged a string of new and important Reformation concepts. We need to very carefully differentiate between Luther's accounts of surprising discoveries and the varied attempts of modern scholarship to nail down a central biographical Reformation insight or a decisive moment of discovery. Otherwise those modern efforts will be used to determine a defining qualitative breakthrough or to build an essential theological vocabulary of what is or is not "the Reformation" within a narrower or wider period of time.

By lifting this up, I can address various research directions that have already relativized the construct of the "Reformation turn." I recall, for instance, recent publications by Volker Leppin and Martin Ohst.[10] Above all,

---

pal bull, in WA Br 2:195.22f., no. 341: "Iam multo liberior sum, certus tandem factus papem esse Antichristum et satane sedem manifeste inventum." On the devil, see Luther's 1539 tract *Against the Antinomians*, WA 50:473.34-57; *LW* 47:113: "For the devil is lord of the world. I myself could never believe this, that the devil should be the lord and god of the world. But I experienced often enough that this too is an article of faith: He is 'prince of the world, god of this age.'" See also Heiko Oberman, *Werden und Wertung der Reformation: Vom Wegestreit zum Glaubenskampf* (Tübingen: Mohr, 1977), 200-202.

8. See n. 7 above and WA 5:144.1-23 (*Operationes in Psalmos*, 1519-21) and WA 56:171.26–172.15 (Lectures on Romans [1:17]); *LW* 25:151. Luther most aptly described his new understanding of *iustitia Dei* in a late table talk (no. 5518; see n. 7 above) as revolving around a set of distinctions in his life. Unlike other places where he recalled his struggles with Rom. 1:17, here the entire weight falls on the distinction between law and gospel.

9. The textual basis for the label "tower experience" comes from WA TR 3:228.6-32, no. 3232; *LW* 54:193. On the location of the tower, see Heinrich Bornkamm, "Iustitia Dei in der Scholastik und bei Luther," *Archiv für Reformationsgeschichte* 39 (1942): 1-46. On the theological meaning of the tower experience and "bathroom experience" *(cloaca-Erlebnis)*, see Oberman, *Werden und Wertung*, 94-101.

10. Leppin, "Luther-Literatur seit 1983, Teil II," 449f.; Leppin, "Von Sturmgewittern,

decades ago Heiko Oberman had already pointed out how wrong the supposed need to choose between an early or later dating of Luther's "theological breakthrough" was.[11] At the same time, he opened up new questions about the positive coherency between the spectrum of insights and discoveries gained during the Erfurt years and his mature Reformation theology. Oberman insisted especially upon the lasting effects of Erfurt's *via moderna*, which made Luther a nominalist as long as he lived.[12] But quite regardless of the precise scholastic settings of the universities, researchers such as Reinhard Schwarz and Ulrich Köpf have perceived an intense and causal connection between the early years at the cloister and Luther's later theological profile. His entire life was characterized by certain elements of a monastic experience-oriented theology.[13] Amid such reflections, one can also suppose that Luther had already by 1511 come under the strong influence of specific theologies and spiritualities of his order and of his monastic superior, confessor, and teacher, Johannes von Staupitz; this influence may have especially affected how he worked out his understandings of sin and grace.[14]

A new question arises at this point. Is it possible that at the beginning of the sixteenth century a Reformation break with a previously all-encompassing church, theology, and piety (which simultaneously retained key dynamics of medieval religiosity) might have only been possible

---

Turmstuben und der Nuss der Theologie: Martin Luther (1483-1546) zwischen Legende und Wirklichkeit," in *Wittenberger Lebensläufe im Umbruch der Reformation*, ed. Evangelischen Predigerseminar (Wittenberg: Drei-Kastanien-Verlag, 2005), 11-27; and Leppin, *Martin Luther* (Darmstadt: Wissenschaftliche Buchgesellschaft, 2006), 107-17. Martin Ohst, "Die Lutherdeutungen Karl Holls und seiner Schüler Emanuel Hirsch und Erich Vogelsang vor dem Hintergrund der Lutherdeutung Albrecht Ritschls," in *Lutherforschung im 20. Jahrhundert: Rückblick — Bilanz — Ausblick*, ed. Rainer Vinke (Mainz: P. von Zabern, 2004), 19-50.

11. Oberman, *Werden und Wertung*, 93f. Oberman identified a "tower experience" tradition in which Luther stood and which would have represented a kind of theological topography.

12. Heiko Oberman, *Luther: Mensch zwischen Gott und Teufel* (Berlin: Severin und Siedler, 1982), 126-30.

13. Reinhard Schwarz, "Luthers unveräußerte Erbschaft an der monastischen Theologie," in *Kloster Amelungsborn 1135-1985*, ed. Gerhard Ruhbach and Kurt Schmidt-Clausen (Hanover: Kloster Amelungsborn, 1985), 209-31; Ulrich Köpf, "Monastische Traditionen bei Martin Luther," in *Luther — Zwischen den Zeiten*, ed. Christoph Markschies and Michael Trowitzsch (Tübingen: Mohr Siebeck, 1999), 50-57.

14. See section 7 of this chapter below.

within the constellation of an observant order, maybe even only within an observant Augustinian cloister?

Questions like this — whether something could only have happened in this way and not in quite a different manner — are naturally unanswerable. There are nevertheless many reasons to suppose the answer to this one is yes. In fact, Luther's Reformation beginnings present a far-reaching story of experience and knowledge, which began during his time in the Erfurt cloister and was stamped by the early impressions of life in the order. Therefore, my thesis is that there are not only important religious continuities between Erfurt and Luther's later biography, but that also the Reformation's new and pioneering directions were set in motion already in the years from 1505 to 1511. This period includes the time at Erfurt from July 1505 until autumn 1508, the first days in Wittenberg (autumn 1508 to autumn 1509), and finally the second time in Erfurt from autumn 1509 until the late summer of 1511, which was interrupted by Luther's journey to Rome in the winter of 1510-11.

If, in view of Luther's development during these years, I use the term "Reformation," it is only with great reservation. Yes, it is evident how strongly his own use of the term is influenced by his earlier views about what was doctrinally normative. For that reason, one can rightly doubt whether "Reformation" is a methodologically suitable term for historical writing. On the other hand, the concept should also not be avoided if we want to ask what was new, epoch changing, and church dividing about Luther's work. I would therefore still like to use the term "Reformation," with three conditions. First, it helps me describe those factors that led to a fundamental "system-crashing" departure from medieval religiosity. Second, the concept should be handled so loosely that it cannot be fixed to one central discovery or change; instead, it should span a wide arc of changes and an entire ensemble of discoveries.[15] Third, the concept signifies the material and historically observable connection between Luther's early theology (hidden from the general public of his time) and his later published works of theology, which became the foundation for the evangelical church and its confessional identity.

---

15. For a summary of that which can generally be called "Reformation writings" of the 1520s, see Berndt Hamm, "Einheit und Vielfalt der Reformation — oder: was die Reformation zur Reformation machte," in *Reformationstheorien: Ein kirchenhistorischer Disput über Einheit und Vielfalt der Reformation*, ed. Berndt Hamm, Bernd Moeller, and Dorothea Wendebourg (Göttingen: Vandenhoeck & Ruprecht, 1995), 85-97.

3. The Roots of *Anfechtung* in Luther's Theology

By wanting to situate the development of Luther's "Reformation turn" within the span of 1505 to 1511, I am basically lifting up what Luther himself held to be the central theological element of his and any salvific life-changing experience. His oft-repeated statements that one can only become a Christian and a theologian through experience (that is, only by going through *Anfechtung*) are famous.[16] Self-awareness comes to sinners through God's word, in which people are afflicted by their own sins, God's judgment, and Satan's demonic power. Without this awareness, the gospel cannot give its liberating message about God. The older Luther emphasized precisely this point in the conflicts with the antinomians.[17]

In the center of Luther's doctrine of justification belongs the familiar idea that God's actions drive people into such a tight corner that in the end all their possibilities and efforts toward salvation come up short.[18] This is God's alien work *(opus alienum)*. Thus the comfort given by the gospel always happens when despair gets consoled.[19] While Luther theologically pegged *Anfechtung* and consoling faith closely together (including in the early Erfurt years), he placed his personal history of *Anfechtung* in the context of his Reformation theology. Thus he wrote in *The Bondage of the Will* about his former despair about predestination: "I myself was offended more than once, and brought to the very depth and abyss of despair, so that I wished I had never been created a man, before I realized how salutary that despair was, and how near to grace *(gratiae propinqua).*"[20]

A few months after his first period in Erfurt, in a March 17, 1509, letter to his friend Johannes Braun, Luther expressed his aversion to the university's philosophical and scholastic teaching models and his desire for a theology that "explores the kernel of the nut, the innermost part of the

---

16. Oswald Bayer, *Martin Luthers Theologie: Eine Vergegenwärtigung* (Tübingen: Mohr Siebeck, 2003), 20.

17. Joachim Rogge, "Innerlutherische Streitigkeiten um Gesetz und Evangelium, Rechtfertigung und Heiligung," in *Leben und Werk Martin Luthers von 1526 bis 1546: Festgabe zu seinem 500. Geburtstag*, vol. 1, ed. Helmar Junghans (Berlin: Evang. Verl.-Anst., 1983), 187-204.

18. Paul Althaus, *Die Theologie Martin Luthers*, 5th ed. (Gütersloh: Gütersloher Verlagshaus Gerd Mohn, 1980), 111.

19. WA Br 1:35.34 (April 8, 1516, no. 11); LW 48:11-14: note the words *fiducialis desperatio*. Note also *salutaris desperatio* in the following footnote.

20. WA 18:719.9-12; LW 33:190.

wheat, the marrow of the bone."²¹ Here he quite clearly had a vision of a theology that does not lose itself in idle speculations but devotes itself to the central existential problem of the afflicted conscience and its consolation. In this sense, he would say in a later table talk, "Gerson was the first to tackle the matter which concerns theology; he also experienced many *Anfechtungen*."²² On the basis of his own experience, the *tentatio* (the Latin equivalent of *Anfechtung*) that leads people to the abyss of doubt, taking them in endless circles around the gracious God, became the foundation of every true theology. Only those who have been broken on the illusion of their *iustitia activa* (active righteousness) will recognize salvation in the *iustitia passiva* (passive righteousness) received from Jesus Christ. That is why Luther included the story of his early *Anfechtung* and doubts in the birth narrative of his new liberating theology, saying, "My *Anfechtungen* have brought me to my theology."²³

At this latest point in my argument, the problematic use of the concept of *Anfechtung* becomes clear when applied to Luther's early years in the cloister. For it is not a term from Luther's history but is rather a theological concept from the perspective of faith within Luther's recollections about his life. Nevertheless, he was referring to the real history of the despair, disillusionment, and doubt that he experienced. In this sense, one can use such an interpretation of *Anfechtung* as a shorthand expression for the larger idea itself being interpreted and for all that Luther experienced during his life as religiously frightening, terrifying, and soul crushing.

4. Luther's *Anfechtungen* in the Cloister as the Intensification of a Systemic Crisis within Late Medieval Religiosity

4.1 Posing the Question

As I view this existential and theological connection between fundamental experiences of *Anfechtung* and Luther's career as a reformer, I come first to

---

21. WA Br 1:17.41-46, no. 5.
22. WA TR 2:114.1-3, no. 1492. On Luther's interpretation of the French theologian Jean Gerson as a theologian of *Anfechtung* and comfort, see Sven Grosse, *Heilsungewißheit und Scrupulositas im späten Mittelalter: Studien zu Johannes Gerson und Gattungen der Frömmigkeitstheologie seiner Zeit* (Tübingen: J. C. B. Mohr, 1994), 1f. and 140-58.
23. Compare with text cited in n. 6 above.

essential questions amid my reflections: Does this distress caused by the problem of conscience in Luther's early years in the cloister really belong to what is new in Luther's Reformation theology? Were there not countless other members of religious orders near the end of the Middle Ages who endured uncertainty over their state of grace and salvation? Is not *tentatio* a typical late medieval monastic problem, heightened by Luther's overly scrupulous and sensitive conscience? If so, might we say that while it was certainly closely interwoven with his Reformation theology, it ought not belong itself to his new breakthrough? If this should be the case, then we have simply returned to the conventional scholarly wisdom that I described in the beginning of the chapter.

4.2 Contradictions within Late Medieval Spirituality

One can certainly see the emotional distress of the young Luther as the escalation of a basic problem of the late Middle Ages. We might say that the systemic crisis within the period's religiosity came to its head in the personal crisis of Luther's agonizing *Anfechtungen* about sin and judgment. If one views the spirituality of the observant orders around 1500, the concept of a "crisis in piety" can appear in a perhaps surprising light. And yet, this crisis did not come from elements that are normally perceived to be the signs of crisis within the late medieval church, namely, certain "abuses" in pastoral care or in an "externalization" of piety.[24] Instead, the fundamental problem lay basically reversed. In a spiritual golden age, the internalization and intensification of the spiritual life were forced, as communities of lay-

---

24. Volker Leppin, "Von der Polarität zur Vereindeutigung: Zu den Wandlungen in Kirche und Frömmigkeit zwischen spätem Mittelalter und Reformation," in *Frömmigkeit — Theologie — Frömmigkeitstheologie: Contributions to European Church History, Festschrift für Berndt Hamm*, ed. Gudrun Litz, Heidrun Munzert, and Roland Liebenberg (Leiden and Boston: Brill, 2005), 299. Despite Bernd Moeller's well-known counterthesis that the fifteenth century was quite possibly the most pious century of Christian history (cited in Leppin above), the typical Protestant view remains much more pessimistic about the era as one that prepared the way for the Reformation due to its medieval church life and religiosity. For another view of late medieval theological polarities (e.g., external and internal, fearful and comforting, individual and communal relationships), see Berndt Hamm, "Theologie und Frömmigkeit im ausgehenden Mittelalter," in *Handbuch der Geschichte der evangelischen Kirche in Bayern*, ed. Gerhard Müller, Horst Weigelt, and Wolfgang Zorn (St. Ottilien: EOS, 2002), 1:188-190.

men and clerics of the *devotio moderna* (which were close to the monastic orders) also show.[25] This development led to intense contradictions, which threatened to overtax a traditionally proven monastic spirituality and pastoral care, and — in Luther's case — caused it to collapse. For one thing, there was the tension between a heightened awareness of sin and the recently intensified emphasis on striving for obedience and perfection. The increasing focus on internalization introduced the new need to track down sin in the soul's most secret hiding places and to observe one's own spiritual powerlessness both humbly and anxiously.[26] In weekly confession, the observant monk was supposed to reveal to his father confessor the results of his most scrupulous self-analysis.[27] The increasingly subtle understanding of sin made the entire confession a terrible hurdle.[28] But at the same time and often in the same sources, a lofty ideal about the perfection of *homo spiritualis* was also preached. In this, people should not be content to observe good works but should strive for the perfection of a pure conscience, selfless love of God, and the entirely self-denying imitation of the cross, doing even the hardest things out of the innermost willingness and delight.[29]

A distinction between two late medieval religious ways of speaking joined this tension, so that there was a kind of division of labor within the

---

25. Nikolaus Staubach, ed., *Kirchenreform von unten: Gerhard Zerbolt von Zutphen und die Brüder vom gemeinsamen Leben* (Frankfurt am Main: P. Lang, 2004); Anne Bollmann, "'Apostolinne van Gode gegeven': Die Schwestern vom gemeinsamen Leben als geistliche Reformerinnen in der Devotio moderna," in *Frömmigkeit — Theologie — Frömmigkeitstheologie*, 131-44. On the connection between music and meditation in the *devotio moderna*, see Ulrike Hascher-Burger, *Gesungene Innigkeit: Studien zu einer Musikhandschrift der Devotio moderna* (Leiden and Boston: Brill, 2002), especially 95-146.

26. Berndt Hamm, "Wollen und Nicht-Können in der spätmittelalterlichen Bußseelsorge," in *Spätmittelalterliche Frömmigkeit*, ed. Berndt Hamm and Thomas Lentes (Tübingen: Mohr Siebeck, 2001), 111-146.

27. See the 1504 reform-minded constitution for the observant Augustinians that Staupitz had overseen, in Johann von Staupitz, *Gutachten und Satzungen*, ed. Wolfgang Günter and Lothar Graf zu Dohna (Berlin: De Gruyter, 2001), 173.37-39.

28. Ronald K. Rittgers, *The Reformation of the Keys: Confession, Conscience, and Authority in Sixteenth-Century Germany* (Cambridge: Harvard University Press, 2004), 23-46; Martin Brecht, *Martin Luther: Sein Weg zur Reformation, 1483-1521* (Stuttgart: Calwer, 1981), 74-77. See also WA TR 5:439.32–440.8, no. 6017.

29. The coexistence of a sin's subtle but ever-present nature and the highly idealistic drive for perfection can be seen in Thomas à Kempis, *De imitatione Christi*, especially in book 3, chap. 3.

pious person.[30] On the one side, a subjective and humble prayer was put in people's mouths: they ought to acknowledge and confess before the vastness of God's severity and kindness that they are entirely unworthy sinners, miserable nobodies, who only deserve punishment and are totally dependent on God's mercy.[31] On the other side, however, stood the objectifying doctrine of the church, which said that people, especially conscientious members of religious orders, are perfectly qualified and required to be worthy of eternal life before God through love and repentance, to bear all the temporal punishments for sin here on earth by practicing a perfectly penitential life and thereby earning a rich heavenly reward. The nun and the monk should therefore ever more deeply search and express their sinful unworthiness before God, even as they simultaneously strive for the highest peak of well-deserved merit on the path of salvation through inner and outer active righteousness *(iustitia activa)*. It is easy to see that crises of conscience were bound to occur within a devotional system with such contradictory tendencies. In fact, the logic of this internalized and individualistic quest for piety included the potential that the spiritual conflict might escalate into something unbearable.

For this reason, the problem of certainty gained new significance near the end of the Middle Ages. On the one hand, it is striking how emphatically life in an observant monastery was extolled as a *via securior* (a safer path) and as an exclusive way of life with the maximum certainty for gaining grace and salvation.[32] On the other hand, this same religious system refused to grant the individual any final personal certainty of grace and salvation,[33] even though the rule of personal, mystically oriented meditation and the forced concern with one's own conscience encouraged an exact and individualized longing for certainty. Around 1500 the full religious drive for perfection required perfect certainty. But this was unattainable through the existing mechanisms, despite many collective offers through even the most ascetic lifestyles or through sacraments, indulgences, endowments, and prayers.

30. For more on this distinction, see chap. 3 below, especially point 9.
31. See n. 29 above.
32. See Ralph Weinbrenner, *Klosterreform im 15. Jahrhundert zwischen Ideal und Praxis: Der Augustinereremit Andreas Proles (1429-1503) und die priviliegierte Observanz* (Tübingen: Mohr, 1996); and Berndt Hamm, *Frömmigkeitstheologie am Anfang des 16. Jahrhunderts: Studien zu Johannes von Paltz und seinem Umkreis*, Beiträge zur historischen Theologie 65 (Tübingen: Mohr, 1982), 291-99.
33. On the "certainty of hope," see Grosse, *Heilsungewißheit*, 106-11 and 230-36.

This desire for protection and certainty reached its dramatic peak in a boiling eschatological religiosity, which brought up new and panicky fears about the nearness of divine wrath. The *ars moriendi* (art of dying) literature of the fifteenth century placed an extremely final and eschatological focus of one's entire life on the hour of death.[34] At the same time, this also meant that the divine judgment as *iudicium particulare* — the judgment of individuals immediately after death, with the prospect of terrible punishments in the hereafter — came excruciatingly near.[35] Of course, the impending and terrifying hour of death, judgment of sin, hell, and purgatory "in the midst of life" corresponded to an equally intense emphasis on the imminence of the mercy of God, Christ, Mary, and the entire "communion of saints" *(communio sanctorum)*. The impending *disfavor* was juxtaposed with the imminence of protecting mercy, especially in the form of the suffering Christ.[36] In any case, this *extra nos* (outside us) dimension of nearby grace was placed in direct relationship to the Holy Spirit's inner working of grace, filling sinners with regenerating righteousness and the ability to be virtuous. Sinners are thus given the spontaneous ability to love, repent, and suffer, which then allows them to pass individual judgment at the hour of death and be made worthy of eternal life.

But the anxious pious person still asks, "Do I — either now or at the hour of my death — really have this quality, without which I have no merciful judge? Have I really made reparation for all my sin by activating this quality?" This uncertainty remained, driving people to great lengths to reach the hereafter.

4.3 The Intensification of the Late Medieval Piety Crisis and Luther's Personality Crisis

When we return to the Luther who was between twenty-one and twenty-seven years old during his time in Erfurt, we clearly see how the intensifications and contradictions of piety in his day (described above) coalesced around him. In the storm of July 2, 1505, near Stotternheim, the terrifying nearness of an angry divine judgment, combined with the frightful nearness of impending death, entered the realm of Luther's personal experi-

---

34. On *ars moriendi* literature, see chap. 5 below.

35. Peter Dinzelbacher, *Die letzten Dinge: Himmel, Hölle, Fegefeuer im Mittelalter* (Freiburg im Breisgau: Herder, 1999), 47-57.

36. See chap. 5 below.

ence. I leave it open as to how much other frightening realizations of the nearness of death and impending judgment had already taught Luther to interpret such a distressing experience by deciding to enter the cloister.[37] As he described it to his father in 1521, he felt himself called to a life in the cloister "through terrors from heaven." He wrote, "I was walled in by the terror and the agony of sudden death and forced by necessity to take the vow."[38] The contrast between the terrifying nearness of God's holiness and his own sins, unholiness, and unworthiness also remained acute in the following years in the cloister.[39] Thus, as we see in his later recollections, the celebration of the Mass and the awareness of Christ's holy presence in the communion elements could cast Luther into a panicked horror about being near God's majesty.[40] Martin Brecht put this aptly: "The configuration of the experience of Stotternheim clearly arose ever and again in a new form for the monk Luther: He thought that he was compelled to encounter the divine judgment in life-threatening proximity."[41]

Above all, Luther experienced God's holy imminence at that time as a distressing demand of the imperious, judging God.[42] Karl Holl rightly directed our attention to how the uncompromising strictness of this image of God became the basis for all of Luther's later development.[43] This was an ethical strictness that required not only outer correctness and purity but also the full devotion of love to God and neighbor: "the fervor, entirety, joyfulness of the will."[44] In this, Holl viewed the "breakthrough" of Luther's "new moral awareness" as happening in the Erfurt years "between 1509 and 1511,"[45] combined with what was at that time an unusual intensity in studying the Bible.[46] This reference to Luther's extraordinary familiarity

---

37. Brecht, *Martin Luther*, 54-58.
38. WA 8:573.30–574.1; *LW* 48:332.
39. WA Br 1:10.9–11.14-28, no. 3; *LW* 48:3-4.
40. Brecht, *Martin Luther*, 79-81.
41. Brecht, *Martin Luther*, 82.
42. See again the letter to Hans Luther (WA Br 8:573.12-15; *LW* 48:331): "I wish you to know that your son has reached the point where he is altogether persuaded that there is nothing holier, nothing more important, nothing more scrupulously to be observed than God's commandment."
43. Karl Holl, "Der Neubau der Sittlichkeit (1919)," in *Gesammelte Aufsätze zur Kirchengeschichte I: Luther*, 7th ed. (Tübingen: J. C. B. Mohr, 1948), 197-217.
44. Holl, "Neubau," 206.
45. Holl, "Neubau," 197
46. Holl, "Neubau," 197f.

with the Bible at a very early stage is very important and has been positively corroborated by recent research on Luther, for instance, by Martin Brecht and Helmar Junghans.[47] Nevertheless, one must stress just as clearly against Holl that Luther's experience of a confrontation with God — which claimed his innermost heart in all its dimensions — does not indicate a breakthrough, but rather has grown out of late medieval religiosity and remains closely attached to that period's rigorism. Holl himself pointed out how Luther picked up the observant orders' dynamic views of piety, which included the ideals of unconditional obedience to God and perfect emulation of Christ.[48] These inward-looking monastic schools had pushed the spirituality of renunciation so far that they expected people to abandon their own self-worth under the guise of yearning for reward and salvation.[49] The goal was total submission to God's will, even up to the highest degree of perfection. This was the *resignatio ad infernum*, the willingness of the God-loving soul to let itself be led, in imitation of Christ, into the hell of deepest God-forsakenness.[50]

Luther's later reminiscences agree in how he zealously adopted this observant monastic ideal during his Erfurt years. He increasingly wanted to perfectly fulfill the strict discipline of the observant rules by means of excessive confession, vigils, fasting, prayer, and hard labor; even more, he wanted to present his innermost being to God in perfect purity and sinlessness. The Ockhamist teaching of Gabriel Biel, which he acquired during his theological studies in Erfurt, could only strengthen his religious drive for perfection. In this teaching, he learned that people can reach a state of pure love of God and true repentance by their own natural powers, *ex puris naturalibus*.[51] Behind Luther's quest for spiritual perfection clearly

---

47. Brecht, *Martin Luther*, 88-96; and Helmar Junghans, "Bibelhumanistische Anstöße in Luthers Entwicklung zum Reformator," *Revue d'histoire et de philosophie religieuses* 85 (2005): 17-42.

48. Holl, "Neubau," 198-203.

49. See Reinhard Schwarz, "Die Umformung des religiösen Prinzips der Gottesliebe in der frühen Reformation: Ein Beitrag zum Verständnis von Luthers Schrift 'Von der Freiheit eines Christenmenschen,'" in *Die Reformation in Deutschland als Umbruch*, ed. Bernd Moeller and Stephen E. Buckwalter (Gütersloh: Gütersloher Verlagshaus, 1998), 130-32.

50. On the pious ideal of an absolutely selfless *resignatio ad infernum*, see Thomas à Kempis, *De imitatione Christi*, book 2, chap. 11, especially nos. 10, 19-21.

51. Heiko A. Oberman, *Der Herbst der mittelalterlichen Theologie*, trans. Martin Rumscheidt and Henning Kampen (Zurich: EVZ-Verlag, 1965), 139-52; Leif Grane, *Contra*

stood that obsessive image of God as oppressively holy, even as God's ominous vengeful judgment grew ever closer. In 1531 Luther said, "I am not speaking now about the ungodly monks, who worshiped their belly as god (Phil. 3:19) and committed horrible sins that I would just as soon not mention, but about the best of them, to whom I and many others belonged, who lived holy lives and tried with might and main to appease the wrath of God and to merit the forgiveness of sins and eternal life by the observances of their religious order."[52] As Luther repeatedly testified, his image of Christ at the time (including the Man of Sorrows of the passion) was entirely characterized by the image of the relentless judge who required atonement for every sin and who granted no remission without the holiness of repentance through true remorse, confession, and works of satisfaction.[53] In Luther's eyes, the revelation that God's Son became flesh and was therefore even closer to us made the frightening imminence of the Judge even more agonizing and tormenting.[54] The sight of the Crucified One thus drove him even deeper into the dilemma of an achievement-based piety of judgment.

As we know, in this confrontation with the accusing and angry God, Luther's inner need and desperate straits came from the direct interaction between his all-consuming drive for purity and holiness (to which he felt bound as an observant, come what may) and an ever-deepening awareness of the general sinfulness behind each particular sinful act. And it was precisely the theologians of his own order who so strongly emphasized the human fall into sin and the insufficiency of human nature.[55] Nevertheless, what they thought provided a delicate balance became a violent collision within Luther. Therefore, for him the traditional monastic guides about

---

Gabrielem: Luthers Auseinandersetzung mit Gabriel Biel in der Disputatio contra Scholasticam Theologiam 1517, trans. Elfriede Pump, Acta Theologica Danica 4 (Copenhagen: Gyldendal, 1962), 223-61, especially 242-50.

52. WA 40/1:485.20-24; *LW* 26:458.

53. WA 38:148.11f.; Brecht, *Martin Luther*, 83; and Berndt Hamm, "Normative Zentrierung im 15. und 16. Jahrhundert: Beobachtungen zu Religiosität, Theologie und Ikonologie," *Zeitschrift für historische Forschung* 26 (1999): 196 n. 104.

54. On Luther's view of the terror of the crucified Christ, see Luther's "Meditation [Sermon] on Christ's Passion" (1519), WA 2:137.10-139.31; *LW* 42:3-14, especially paragraphs 4-11. See also n. 104 below.

55. Adolar Zumkeller, *Erbsünde, Gnade, Rechtfertigung und Verdienst nach der Lehre der Erfurter Augustinertheologen des Spätmittelalters*, Cassiciacum 35 (Würzburg: Augustinus-Verlag, 1984), especially xxxiiif.

intently striving for perfection and conscientious self-observation unraveled into an unstoppable dynamic of uncertainty, self-doubt, and desperate anxiety. The more he related God's imperious desire for holiness to the entirety of his existence and strove toward perfect purity, the stronger he grew aware of his total unworthiness. The more vigilantly he recognized his unworthiness, sin, and guilt, the more urgent grew his desire for perfection and certainty, so that the complete failure of his striving for holiness and the total imminence of a damning judgment advanced ever closer in front of him. Finally, he no longer saw a point at which he might connect God's desire for holiness, his forgiveness, and the heavenly reward of eternal salvation to some quality in his own heart or to a genuine piety that came from his life in the cloister. To put it another way: his conscience could no longer be sure of any *iustitia activa* of its own but could only recognize its radical failure, with the result that he reached a disturbing level of self-doubt about his eternal election. Thus did Luther's *Anfechtungen* bring him "to the very depth and abyss of despair"[56] and into a subtle hatred of the God who predestines and judges, who demands from him what seemed to be unattainable: the purity of mind that loves God above all, for God's own sake.[57]

5. The Turning Point for Luther's *Anfechtung*: A Change Worthy of the Word "Reformation"

I have briefly sketched the agonizing and escalating distress within Luther's conscience, which he experienced during his theological studies in Erfurt and Wittenberg and which he later experienced in other forms. To a certain degree, Luther had dealt with this problem by means of the best available pastoral tools of the later Middle Ages. It was a process of humbling self-awareness and *Anfechtung* that brought all vain self-righteousness to nothing, thereby leading the terrified but hopeful sinner to trust in a reconciliation with the heavenly Father through Christ. As Luther knew, this same God gives grace to a sanctified and worthy penitent who "does enough." This quality of holiness never could or should be fully certain, for

---

56. WA 18:719.9-12; *LW* 33:190.

57. WA 54:185.24-25; *LW* 34:336: "I did not love, yes, I hated the righteous God who punishes sinners, and secretly, if not blasphemously, certainly murmuring greatly, I was angry with God."

which reason spiritual *Anfechtung* would remain an essential feature of Christian life. Nevertheless, this humble attitude should not turn into despair but instead be borne by the comforting hope in God's mercy and merited faithfulness.[58]

Comparing Luther's experience of *tentatio* in the cloister with this late medieval view of despair and comfort, we can recognize how a new and intensified quality of *Anfechtung* came to him. The critical tensions of late medieval piety, especially within the spirituality of the observant orders, led the young brother and theologian into an inconsolable hopelessness that he described in 1518, only a few years later, in this way: "At such a time God seems terribly angry, and with him the whole creation. . . . All that remains is the [soul's] stark-naked desire for help and a terrible groaning, but it does not know where to turn for help."[59]

In my view, this sense of hopelessness is the basic situation in which Luther began to give up trying to coordinate the established forms of theology, piety, and pastoral care, including the advice of spiritual teachers such as Bernard of Clairvaux and Jean Gerson. This is also the point at which even the sympathetic pastoral counselors of his order could no longer help him. Staupitz himself, who knew how to comfort Luther better than any other spiritual adviser, had to confess the limit of his own understanding and counsel here.[60] Luther had surpassed even the familiar category of "scrupulosity," of having too active a conscience.[61] Amid this *Anfechtung*, a turning point becomes apparent that can be understood as the beginning of a Reformation reorientation. What is new is that Luther reached the end of his monastic drive for perfection by realizing the total emptiness of his efforts toward holiness before God and by seeing that there was no longer any possibility of ascending to God by his own spiritual powers. He believed that he could no longer escape his crisis of conscience through an intensification of spiritual virtuosity or works of holiness. Luther then confessed that, with respect to God's judgment, people have nothing to offer but sins and absolute unworthiness all their lives.[62]

---

58. Grosse, *Heilsungewißheit*, 35-44.

59. WA 1:557.37–558.5; *LW* 31:129.

60. WA TR 1:62.1f., no. 141; 1:240.12-15, no. 518 (*LW* 54:93-95); 2:26.4-6, no. 1288 (*LW* 54:132-33); 4:403.19-22; 6:106.32–107.3, no. 6669.

61. WA TR 1:240.15-17, no. 518; *LW* 54:94: "In short, no confessor wanted to have anything to do with me. Then I thought, 'Nobody has this temptation except you,' and I became as dead as a corpse."

62. In his first lectures on the Psalms, Luther repeatedly developed the fundamen-

This now became for him a subjective, prayerful confession and an objective statement of truth and doctrine.[63] This overturned the medieval vocabulary, a key move for the entire Reformation.[64] The humble message of the choral prayer: "Lord, I stand before you as an unworthy sinner who deserves only wrath and punishment!" no longer competed against the message of the podium from which the professor of theology expressed the catholic truth of faith, which had said that the one who is justified has no mortal sin and can earn eternal life through deeds of merit *(merita de condigno)*. For Luther, the doctrine of faith and the prayerful posture of humility started to come together as one. This meant, though, that humility was no longer a virtue of self-humiliation but rather a radical and disillusioning awareness of real personal lowliness. In the humility of confessing sins, people do not make themselves lower than they are[65] but rather apply the truth of God's judgment to themselves, realizing that as creatures and sinners they are truly nothing and can contribute absolutely nothing to their own salvation.[66] With this, Luther set aside the scholastic idea of forming a habit *(habitus)* of grace and virtue, in which justified people might actively move into eternal life. The fires of *Anfechtung* had proven all the ideas and ambitions of finding a way of salvation by means of the *iustitia activa* to be lies and illusions.

In summary, we can say that in Luther's early years at the cloister, a crisis in the structure of medieval religiosity became an acute personal crisis as he strove for perfection. At the same time, the escalation of this dilemma revealed the shift to a fundamentally new way of viewing how people stand before God. Sins started to be perceived anew as the personally

---

tal thought that people are always captive to radical original sin. Thus he wrote in his exegesis of the Vulgate's Ps. 50:5-7 (Ps. 51): "Therefore it is true that before Him we are always in sins, so that in His covenant and testament which He has established with us He Himself might be the justifier" (WA 3:289.5-7; *LW* 10:237).

63. To see this arc across Luther's career, compare "it is true" of n. 62 above to Luther's last handwritten note (February 16, 1546): "We are beggars. That is true" (WA TR 5:318.2f., no. 5677; *LW* 54:476).

64. See section 9 of chap. 3 below.

65. In late medieval piety, it was a sign of humility to confess sins where there was no guilt, as in this sentence from Gregory the Great: "Bonarum mentium est ibi culpam agnoscere, ubi culpa non est" (PL 77:1195B).

66. See chap. 3 below. For a critical evaluation of the Finnish school of Luther research, see Volker Leppin, "Luther-Literatur seit 1983, Teil III," *Theologische Rundschau* 68 (2003): 330-32.

and profoundly all-encompassing loss of the image of God in the creature intended to be loved and to do works of love. This existential and theological consequence of Luther's early experiences of *Anfechtung* in the cloister was the first turning point of Reformation significance. It was therefore also a long process of change over time and not a precise moment; it was a gradual experience of learning to see things differently and not a breakthrough experience in the all-too-tempting typology of Paul's Damascus road experience: "And immediately something like scales fell from his eyes" (Acts 9:18).

By keeping the gradual nature of this change in mind, we can differentiate three essential and closely connected elements: first, the element of inconsolable hopelessness, in which Luther experienced his own spiritual failure; second, the element of understanding this deep *Anfechtung* not as an unfortunate irritation to be overcome but as an important step in which sinners can recognize their real wretchedness before God now and in perpetuity; third, the element of interpreting this desperate situation no longer as simply an attack by God or the devil but much more as the saving work of the Holy Spirit, who precisely in this way reveals an exit from such a hell. In this way, the experiential concept of *Anfechtung* opened up a new theological and christological meaning: *Anfechtung* (or *tentatio*) as cross and as grace. It was clearly and especially Staupitz who pointed the way to this interpretation of Luther's spiritual anguish. In 1530, for instance, Luther comforted his sorrowful friend and pupil in Wittenberg, Hieronymus Weller, by saying that he had once experienced something similar after he entered the cloister. When Luther sought advice from his father confessor and opened up to him about the terrible thoughts he suffered, Staupitz said, "You do not know, Martin, how useful and necessary for you this *Anfechtung* is; for God does not test you in this way without a reason: You will see that he will use you as his servant to do great things."[67] Even though Staupitz could not really understand the spiritual anguish of Luther's spiritual *Anfechtungen*, he helped him see them as necessary afflictions rooted in God's merciful direction.

The three aforementioned elements describe a slow emotional and theological progression, which had already begun during Luther's years in Erfurt. They also allow us to guess why it was Luther who followed this path instead of someone else. The high demands of observant life collided with

---

67. Recorded in a 1530 letter from Luther to his friend Jerome Weller, WA Br 5:519.24-32, no. 1670.

his unique personal sensitivity and conscientiousness. This then awakened in him an extreme need for certainty, plunging him with equally unusual intensity into reading the Bible and into an attempt to penetrate the truth of God's word theologically and existentially. The historical contingency of Luther's early reorientation process came from the interaction of many factors, especially from his independent efforts to study the Bible (even if that was mediated by humanistic and monastically specific impulses), from his having been stamped by the particular spiritual and theological traditions of the Augustinian Order (in which — as will be made yet clearer — his superior and mentor Staupitz played a prominent role), and from his ability to experience things very personally.[68] The new thing that emerged from all this can certainly be described academically. However, like everything that is historically contingent and personal, it is never without some loose ends. It is thus, strictly speaking, never entirely explainable.

6. Luther's First Lectures on the Psalms (1513-15) as the Theological Harvest of His Prior Reorientation

Luther's first lectures on the Psalms document in detail the result of this emerging Reformation reorientation; they are, so to speak, the theological harvest of his *Anfechtung* in the cloister.[69] From their very beginning, we find the radical destruction of any human quality of holiness or virtue that was just described above. Luther's reorientation had clearly already taken place before the summer of 1513 when he started to prepare his interpretation of the Psalms. An elaborate, scripturally adept, experientially tested, and theologically innovative set of first lectures like these required a long preparation in *experientia*, along with reflection on how to apply it. In all likelihood, Luther resolved to take on the Psalms precisely because he wanted to test his new balance of existential subjectivity and doctrinal objectivity *coram Deo* (before God) by means of these central texts of monastic prayer life.

> 68. Karl Holl noted the relationship between an experiential theology and Luther's Bible studies, in Sebastian Degkwitz, *Wort Gottes und Erfahrung: Luthers Erfahrungsbegriff und seine Rezeption im 20. Jahrhundert* (Frankfurt am Main: Lang, 1998), 21-29.
>
> 69. For more on Luther's *Dictata super Psalterium*, see Karl-Heinz Zur Mühlen, "Luther II," in *Theologische Realenzyklöpadie* (Berlin: De Gruyter, 1991), 21:562; Reinhard Schwarz, *Luther* (Göttingen: Vandenhoeck & Ruprecht, 1986), 61; and Jared Wicks, *Man Yearning for Grace: Luther's Early Spiritual Teaching* (Wiesbaden: F. Steiner, 1969), 41-94.

Luther's consequence-laden process of reorientation — that long arc of Reformation change — must have already begun in the years before the first lectures on the Psalms. Significant indications of this already appeared in his marginal notations *(Randbemerkungen)* on Peter Lombard, which he made in Erfurt in 1509-10 and in which he made his first attack on the concept of *habitus* with respect to the scholastic doctrine of grace.[70] His early letters also reveal the same change of direction, particularly his aforementioned letter to his friend Johannes Braun from March 17, 1509. After expressing his desire for a theology that gets to the kernel or marrow of the matter, he himself pushed forward to the "kernel" and "marrow" of things, before abruptly writing, "But God is God; human judgment is frequently — or rather, always — mistaken. He is our God, he will lead us in kindness (*suavitas* or 'sweetness') and that forever."[71]

With this, Luther found his life's theme: the sharp contrast between human errors and evils and God's merciful loving-kindness.[72] His *Anfechtungen* had led him to the point where he could recognize the error of his main monastic question, "O, when will you ever become pious and do enough to grab hold of a merciful God?"[73] His accused conscience no longer sought an escape through his own purity, holiness, and righteousness. To apply the vocabulary of Luther's first lectures on the Psalms, he took God's accusing and damning verdict to be his own rightful self-judgment.[74] By doing this, he had traveled the path of failure in his monastic quest for perfection to the recognition that God saves sinners out of pure mercy.

Already in the marginal notes on Peter Lombard mentioned above, Luther pointedly emphasized that Paul's statement "it depends not on human will or exertion, but on God who shows mercy" (Rom. 9:16) was incompatible with any notion of cooperation in grace. One must much more understand this to be an absolute: "everything should be attributed to

---

70. See especially WA 9:42.35–43.8.

71. WA Br 1:17.41-46, no. 5.

72. WA Br 1:10.9–11.2, no. 3; *LW* 48:3: "God, who is glorious and holy in all his works, has deigned to exalt me magnificently — a miserable and totally unworthy sinner — by calling me into his supreme ministry, solely on the basis of his bounteous mercy. Therefore I have to fulfill completely the office entrusted to me so that I may be acceptable (as much as dust can be acceptable to God) to such great splendor of divine goodness."

73. "Predigt über die Taufe," WA 37:661.23f.

74. See especially the notes on Ps. 51, WA 3:287.20–293.21; *LW* 10:235-43.

God"; it depends entirely *(tantum)* on God's mercy.⁷⁵ Behind the judging wrath of God that appears in the humiliation of *Anfechtung*, Luther recognized the merciful God who makes his promise true. On account of Christ, God forgives sinners who have nothing good to offer and leads them to eternal life out of pure mercy.⁷⁶

The concept of faith, which Luther turned into the central concept of the Christian life in his Psalms lectures, thereby contains two elementary and relational truths about God's word: it is first the humbling realization of the divine word of judgment in the unsparing recognition of one's own affliction; after this, it is the trustworthy hope in the realization of the divine word of salvation, with an equally radical awareness of having been given God's sure promises.⁷⁷ Both encounters contain a fundamentally christological character. Afflicted and humbled sinners experience the existential afflictions of Christ's cross in their own lives.⁷⁸ As Luther could put it in 1518 when reflecting on his own attacks of *Anfechtung*, one's soul is then "stretched out with Christ so that all the person's bones may be counted, and every corner of the soul is filled with the greatest bitterness, dread, trembling, and sorrow in such a manner that all these last forever."⁷⁹ But under the form of opposites *(sub contrario)*, the cross conceals the saving presence of God. When afflicted people recognize themselves in Christ's suffering, then they can also base their certainty of salvation on the Crucified One.⁸⁰

7. The Realization of God's Mercy in Luther's Early Years in the Cloister (1507-13)

From all this, it is clear that a new view of God's generous overtures to humanity came directly out of Luther's experiences of *Anfechtung*. During

---

75. Luther's *Randbemerkungen* on Lombard's *Sentences* II, dist. 26, c. 2, in WA 9:70.32–71.3.

76. See chap. 3 below.

77. See chap. 3 below.

78. See Erich Vogelsang, *Der angefochtene Christus bei Luther* (Berlin: De Gruyter, 1932). For a more recent interpretation of Luther's Christology, see Jens Wolff, *Metapher und Kreuz: Studien zu Luthers Christusbild* (Tübingen: Mohr Siebeck, 2005).

79. WA 1:558.5-8; *LW* 31:129.

80. Many researchers persist in the error that Luther had not yet recognized the "certainty of faith" in the theology of his early Psalms and Romans lectures. See chap. 3, especially nn. 44 and 45.

his cloistered years in Erfurt and Wittenberg before the beginning of the first lectures on the Psalms, *iustitia activa* disappeared entirely as a way of procuring salvation. At the same time, Luther learned to understand *iustitia Dei* (the righteousness of God) as a righteousness that both destroys and gives a gift. He was already on the Reformation path to the *iustitia passiva* (passive righteousness) of salvation freely bestowed.[81] The terrifying and bitter nearness of the God who damns all sin and impurity turns into the sweet and comforting imminence of the God who gives blessing.[82] Based on his experiential theology and biblical reflection, Luther encountered God's generous and grace-driven action, which descends into a sinner's deepest misery. Still, this early theology was fully located within the dominant notion of judgment. Judgments by God and by the self prove to be gracious judgments; liberating mercy finds its reality by unmasking judgment.

On this path of gradual Reformation reorientation, Luther's superior, father confessor, and teacher, Johannes von Staupitz, clearly gave the downcast brother such essential help that Luther could later say, "If Doctor Staupitz — or rather, God through Doctor Staupitz — had not helped me [out of my *Anfechtungen*], I would have drowned in them and long ago been in hell."[83] In another place, Luther said, "I have everything from Doctor Staupitz; he gave me *occasionem*."[84] It is true that during his study of theology Luther had not yet adopted the Augustinian teachings of his order, which came from Gregory of Rimini. However, in Staupitz he encountered the man who — appealing to the later anti-Pelagian Augustine — transformed this radical theology of grace from its late scholastic form into a pastoral theology of piety that could be used in the confessional and in the pulpit.[85] That was something extraordinary for the beginning of the sixteenth century. It belongs to the unique constellation of Luther's life that, of all people, this distinctive theologian of mercy could stand by him and provide pastoral care during his heaviest attacks of *Anfechtung* in the cloister. The two men shared their first extended time together in 1508-9, when Luther interrupted his studies in Erfurt to take up residence in Wittenberg for several

---

81. Karlmann Beyschlag, *Grundriß der Dogmengeschichte*, vol. II/2 (Darmstadt: Wissenschaftliche Buchgesellschaft, 2000), 345.

82. See n. 79 above.

83. WA Br 9:627.23-25, no. 3716.

84. WA TR 1:80.6f., no. 173.

85. Oberman, *Werden und Wertung*, 82-140.

months.[86] That could have already been the time of that important conversation about repentance that Luther recalled in the May 30, 1518, letter to Staupitz that accompanied his explanation of the Ninety-five Theses.[87] More likely, this discussion first took place after the summer of 1511 when Luther had been permanently transferred to the cloister in Wittenberg. In any case, it must have happened before he began his lectures on the Psalms, because it reflects exactly the understanding of repentance that is to be found from the beginning to the end of the *Dictata super Psalmarium*. If some Luther researchers have come to date it later, it is mainly because they take too little account of the fact that in this letter of 1518 Luther differentiated four chronological steps in the development of his understanding of true repentance.[88] The discussion with Staupitz, which I shall now describe in more detail, can only be assigned to the first step.

In the beginning was the impulse that Staupitz gave him, the word that pierced him "like the sharp arrow of the Mighty" (Ps. 120:4), doing its work in him for a long time.[89] Luther wrote, "Therefore I accepted you as a messenger from heaven when you said that *poenitentia* is genuine only if it begins with love for justice and for God and that what they consider to be the final stage and completion is in reality rather the very beginning of *poenitentia*."[90] If we read this sentence against the background of Staupitz's theology[91] and at the same time in the context of Luther's early handling of *Anfechtung* as documented in his Psalms commentary, then the following meaning arises: a true repentance worthy of that name does not flee from the righteousness of God that judges and punishes that which is sinful in a person, but willingly makes it its own; indeed, repentant sinners love this righteousness because they recognize in it the same

---

86. Brecht, *Martin Luther*, 98.

87. I find it problematic to describe this letter to Staupitz as a "dedication" letter in the same way that the letter to Pope Leo X is a dedication letter to *The Freedom of a Christian*. Because it serves as an explanation to his superior in the order about the ongoing indulgence controversy, I rather prefer to call this a "companion" letter (Brecht calls it a *Beibrief* [*Martin Luther*, 281]).

88. Note the four transitional markers: *aliquando, deinceps, post haec,* and *denique*; WA 1:525.6; 525.16; 525.24; 526.1; *LW* 48:65-66.

89. WA 1:525.10-14; *LW* 48:65-66.

90. WA 1:525.10-14; *LW* 48:65-66.

91. For Staupitz's view of confession and his emphasis on true repentance, see Richard Wetzel, "Staupitz und Luther: Annäherung an eine Vorläufer-Figur," *Blätter für pfälzische Kirchengeschichte und Religiöse Volkskunde* 58 (1991): 78-81.

righteousness of God that comes to them in the loving and saving way of Christ's suffering for sin.

In this sense the word "repentance," as Luther went on to describe it, gained a sweet and lovable ring in his ears because he began to understand it through the "wounds of the sweetest Savior."[92] The mystic concept of "sweetness" implies the immediate "good-tasting" experience of being near the merciful favor of God, which meets the afflicted sinner in Christ, the Man of Sorrows. Staupitz helped Luther free himself from all doctrines of repentance, especially the Ockhamist and Scotist teachings, which viewed love as the goal and consummation of active striving and self-effort by sinners going through the penitential process. Instead, true repentance is love of divine righteousness from beginning to end, a penitential love that justifying grace has always and already made active in the heart of the penitent. God's love, mercy, and righteousness always precede human abilities to love, repent, and be righteous. Staupitz's connection of love and righteousness became the motivation for Luther to see his agonized existence in light of Christ's passion and so to perceive the sweetness of divine mercy amid the bitterness of *Anfechtung*. Against this background came Luther's statement in the lectures on the Psalms that having no *Anfechtung* is the greatest *Anfechtung*, and that God rages most when God is not raging.[93]

As Luther himself stressed, we only do justice to his memory of discussing repentance with Staupitz by setting it within an entire series of conversations in which Staupitz comforted him in a fatherly way over a long period of time.[94] The center of these talks was the personal application of the passion, which highlighted Staupitz's canny ability to update Bernard of Clairvaux's passion mysticism in the language of his own or-

---

92. WA 1:525.18-23; *LW* 48:66: "I began to compare your statements with the passages of Scripture which speak of *poenitentia*. And behold — what a most pleasant scene! Biblical words came leaping toward me from all sides, clearly smiling and nodding assent to your statement. They so supported your opinion that while formerly almost no word in the whole Scripture was more bitter to me than *poenitentia* (although I zealously made a pretense before God and tried to express a feigned and constrained love for him), now no word sounds sweeter or more pleasant to me than *poenitentia*. The commandments of God become sweet when they are read not only in books but also in the wounds of the sweetest Savior."

93. See n. 67 above.

94. WA 1:525.4-6; *LW* 48:65: "Reverend Father: I remember . . . your most delightful and helpful talks, through which the Lord Jesus wonderfully consoled me."

der.[95] He advised Luther to look on the wounds of the Crucified One[96] and to imprint this image in his mind so that his desperate brooding and personal anguish over predestination would give way to a comforting assurance of hope.[97] Through Staupitz, Luther learned that in light of the suffering and afflicted Christ who bitterly repented on our behalf, we should interpret the humbling experience of being far from God as a time of particular closeness to the God who saves; precisely because of our afflictions we can know a close and intimate connection with Christ.

In addition to Staupitz, Luther had other pastors and father confessors who showed him *Christus pro me* (Christ for me) and who held before his eyes the grace of salvation and forgiveness of sin that was valid for him personally and could help him out of his agonizing doubts by revealing a merciful judge. From his first years in Erfurt, the young brother was obviously given similar references to the nearby, effortless, accessible, and profligate generosity of God's mercy.[98] To think otherwise of the theological and spiritual climate of cloistered life in Erfurt and Wittenberg is unimaginable. Around 1500 the observant Augustinians, like no other religious order, accentuated the sharp contrast between the sin-filled distress of humans and the infinite mercy of God, in whom people should confidently take refuge.[99] In Staupitz's voice, this comforting language of mercy attained an extraordinary power of theological and popular persuasion. When Luther became aware that his monastic attempt for perfection had collapsed, it was a result of his great rigor within the context of the pastoral care provided by his order. The total destruction of his own active holiness was precisely the point at which he perceived a similarly total reception of grace through God's holiness. The Christology of the cross became his hermeneutical key to comprehending both the impending doom of divine judgment and the imminence of divine mercy as two sides of the same

---

95. Eric L. Saak, *High Way to Heaven: The Augustinian Platform between Reform and Reformation, 1292-1524* (Leiden: Brill, 2002), 467-583.

96. See the source material in Berndt Hamm, "Johann von Staupitz (ca. 1468-1524) — spätmittelalterlicher Reformer und 'Vater' der Reformation," *Archiv für Reformationsgeschichte* 92 (2001): 32f.

97. Hamm, "Johann von Staupitz (ca. 1468-1524)"; Brecht, *Martin Luther*, 87; and Luther's table talk of February 18, 1542 (WA TR 5:293.5ff., no. 5658a). For an interpretation of this table talk, see Wetzel, "Staupitz und Luther," 78-81.

98. Brecht, *Martin Luther*, 68, 75, and 87. For more on Christ *pro me*, see also the preface written by Philip Melanchthon in CR 6:159.

99. See n. 55 above.

event. Because he had experienced judgment, wrath, and destruction in a way that remained foreign to Staupitz,[100] he also came to a new radicality in his theological thinking about the freely given righteousness of God.[101]

8. The Nearness of Heaven and the New Experience of Sweetness: The Mystical Element in Luther's Reformation Reorientation

In the terrifying experience of God's wrath, as well as in the comforting encounter with God's grace, an intense closeness to God developed for the young brother. This pushed the late medieval intensification further, strengthening it and allowing it to turn into a new quality of relationship with God. Luther's experience and his stylized biographical reminiscences show this experience of closeness to come directly from contact with the terrifying, threatening, and ultimately blessed opening of heaven. Here reality and symbolism are joined together. Thus, during the thunderstorm at Stotternheim, Luther saw himself "called by heaven through terror."[102] Later (in 1539) he also referred to the flash of lightning that shook him so much that he vowed to Saint Anne that he would enter a monastery.[103] This heavenly terror spread into his *Anfechtung* in the cloister. As he testified in a sermon of the later 1530s, the sight of the Crucified One struck him like a flash of lightning.[104] In a 1532 table talk, he said, "The words 'righteous' and 'righteousness of God' struck my conscience like lightning. When I heard them I was exceedingly terrified. If God is righteous [I thought], he must punish"; in 1538, he spoke in the same sense of a "thunderbolt" in his heart.[105]

Similarly, Luther heard Staupitz as a voice from heaven, *velut e caelo sonantem*.[106] Just as the heaven of love and mercy opened up for him in this way, he could then likewise in his famous autobiographical reflection of 1545 describe his breakthrough to a new understanding of *iustitia Dei* as

---

100. See n. 60 above.
101. The difference between Staupitz and Luther lay in their views of the human ability to love and of their ability to truly confess and repent. See chap. 1 above.
102. WA 8:573.30–574.1; *LW* 48:332.
103. WA TR 4:440.5-11, no. 4707.
104. "Predigt über Mt. 24:25f." (December 7, 1539), WA 47:590.1-6.
105. WA TR 3:228.24-26, no. 3232c; *LW* 54:193, and WA TR 4:72.27-31, no. 4007; *LW* 54:308: "That expression 'righteousness of God' was like a thunderbolt in my heart."
106. See n. 90 above.

an entry into paradise: "Thus that place in Paul [Rom. 1:17] was for me truly the gate to paradise,"[107] and "Here I felt that I was altogether born again and had entered paradise itself through open gates."[108] As in the letters to Braun[109] and to Staupitz,[110] the mystical concept of "sweetness" arose here again. As much as he had hated the phrase "the righteousness of God" before, it now became pleasant and sweet to him. The direct contact between heaven and earth in God's movement toward humanity always includes both elements together. It is a revelation of wrath and mercy, of sin and righteousness.[111] Only when contrasted to the impending doom of heaven overtaking us does the opened heaven of blessedness become the liberating presence of God.

We have started with these semantics about heaven being near and being open and about the new experience of sweetness and love. From this point, we can begin to understand Luther's Reformation reorientation as a process with a thoroughly mystical dimension. Of course, this is only possible if we free ourselves from too fixed a concept of mysticism and keep the element of close personal experience foremost in our minds. By this, I mean that we ought to understand mysticism as a personal, direct, and holistic experience of the blessed nearness of God, which leads all the way to a profound union with God.[112] If one wants to characterize Luther's early development as a way to a new kind of mystical theology,[113] that should not in any case mean the same thing as medieval understandings of a change in the essential quality of a person or in a gradual ascent to God on the ladder of love's inspiration. Luther's theology of the comforting and blessed nearness of God includes the close experience of judgment, wrath, and terror. It

---

107. WA 54:186.8f.; *LW* 34:337.

108. WA 54:186.14-16; *LW* 34:337.

109. See n. 71 above.

110. See n. 92 above.

111. Note Luther's treatment of Rom. 1:17-18 in his first lectures on the Psalms, WA 3:174.15-20; *LW* 10:145, "For [Paul] says (Rom. 1:18, 17): 'The wrath of God is revealed from heaven;' again: 'The righteousness of God is revealed, etc.' The meaning is this: No human being knew that the wrath of God is upon all men and that all are in sin before God, but through His Gospel He has revealed from heaven both how we may be saved from that wrath and by what righteousness we may be set free, namely, through Christ."

112. On my use of the mystical concept of "nearness," see Bernard McGinn, *The Presence of God: A History of Western Christian Mysticism*, vols. 1 and 3 (New York: Crossroad, 1991 and 1998).

113. This will be developed more fully in chap. 8.

moves on the basic level of *Anfechtung* within the conscience and it remains a theology of "condescension." God's mercy — that is, God's good news of Jesus Christ — comes down to an eternally sinful, pitiful, and afflicted humanity.[114] Luther therefore emphasized the from-heaven-to-earth nature of justifying righteousness as an *externa et aliena iustitia* (an external and alien righteousness). "God does not want to redeem us through our own, but through external, righteousness and wisdom; not through one that comes from us and grows in us, but through one that comes to us from the outside; not through one that originates here on earth, but through one that comes from heaven. Therefore, we must be taught a righteousness that comes completely from the outside and is foreign."[115]

With this intense connection between what is external *(extra nos)* and what is internal,[116] Luther represents a new mysticism of faith and word. In the early theology of his first lectures on the Psalms (and the subsequent lectures on Romans), this means two different things. Faith is a bitter sighing *(gemitus)* that comes from the close experience of unrelenting divine law and judgment, which shatters any appeal by the conscience to its own quality and merit. Simultaneously, faith is the sweet and joyful consolation of being lifted up on high *(raptus, exstasis)*, because in the midst of judgment, faith hears the gospel of Christ's saving righteousness and trusts in this.[117] This does not thus become an internal righteousness that is infused into the soul. Instead, for believers it remains *iustitia extra nos:* the external, sheltering, perfect, and eternal righteousness of the Son of God for us. Still, through faith in the gospel people are profoundly united with this righteousness of Christ in a kind of *unio mystica* (mystical union).[118] For believers, this faith becomes a "sweet" and intimate experience of being given a perfect gift against all the experiences of *Anfechtung* that come through the law, sin, death, judgment, and condemnation.

114. Beyschlag, *Grundriß*, 322-88.

115. WA 56:158.10-14; *LW* 25:136.

116. Karl-Heinz Zur Mühlen, *Nos extra nos: Luthers theologie zwischen Mystik und Scholastik*, Beiträge zur historischen Theologie 46 (Tübingen: J. C. B. Mohr, 1972).

117. Heiko A. Oberman, "Simul gemitus et raptus: Luther und die Mystik," in his *Die Reformation: Von Wittenberg nach Genf* (Göttingen: Vandenhoeck & Ruprecht, 1986), 45-89.

118. On union and communion in Luther's thought, see Schwarz, *Luther*, 192-200; Erwin Iserloh, "Luther und die Mystik," in *Kirche, Mystik, Heiligung und das Natürliche bei Luther*, ed. Ivar Asheim (Göttingen: Vandenhoeck & Ruprecht, 1967), 62-87; and chap. 8 below.

Faith's experience of such union always remains a broken experience, because — when confronted with the experiential evidence of the devilish powers of corruption — it can "only" be based on Christ's nearness in the gospel and the sacraments and not on a direct experience of sanctification in one's own life. In the years after the Psalms lectures when Luther went back to some of the authors and themes of medieval mysticism,[119] he did so always and only with a sense of this characteristic brokenness.[120] In that way he could stress the intimacy that comes with the merciful nearness of God and the sinful soul, that the self-giving mercy of God has come down to human suffering. The soul does not achieve this. Instead, the soul suffers it in the total passivity of its connection to Christ through faith.

9. Conclusion: *Anfechtung* as an Ingredient in Luther's Reformation Reorientation

The two-sided nature of Luther's early theology integrated impending doom with the scandalous imminence of mercy in its understanding of faith. This theology appeared already in his first lectures on the Psalms, clear evidence of his Reformation reorientation. The fundamental change with respect to late medieval views about the nearness of God's judgment and grace is obvious. It is also clear that this theological reorientation went through further important steps in the years leading up to 1520,[121] and that this Reformation view generally developed around the significant and essential interaction between personal experiences of *Anfechtung* and intense engagement with the interpretation of biblical texts. The extent to which the theology of the Psalms lectures had already been established during the preceding years in Erfurt and Wittenberg must remain an open question. Nevertheless, we can say with a high degree of certainty that between 1507 and 1513 the young brother and theologian experienced that

---

119. Brecht, *Martin Luther*, 137-44, and Henrik Otto, *Vor- und frühreformatorische Tauler-Rezeption: Annotationen in Drucken des späten 15. und frühen 16. Jahrhunderts* (Gütersloh: Gütersloher Verlagshaus, 2003).

120. On Luther's sense of how he fit into the mystical tradition before him, see the excellent essay by Susanne Köbele, "*Heiligkeit durchbrechen:* Grenzfälle von Heiligkeit in der mittelalterlichen Mystik," in *Sakralität zwischen Antike und Neuzeit*, ed. Berndt Hamm et al. (Stuttgart: Steiner, 2007), 147-69.

121. See n. 7 above.

radical *Anfechtung* that opened him up to a new insight about how human sin can never be totally eliminated. This was an insight into the basic personal sinfulness that lies beneath the surface of individual and visible sinful acts. In a movement that is both existential/affective and theological/cognitive, this final despair over one's own possibilities of winning salvation signifies a departure from the medieval model, which balanced *Anfechtung* and assurance, fear and trust, humility and hope. With this, Luther's process of Reformation reorientation had already begun. It was a break with all late medieval programs — great or small — that taught human cooperation in salvation. To put it in terms of the theology of repentance, it was a break with the "contritionism" of thinkers like Gabriel Biel and with the "attritionism" of people like Johannes von Paltz.[122] The only thing left for people to do was to confess that they could not do anything and to make that the earnest prayer of supplication to God.[123]

Without this result coming from his early *Anfechtungen* and without this total despair of one's own quality, holiness, and worth before God, Luther's new view of God's unilateral generous encounter with humanity is unimaginable. His holding on to both the judging and the saving righteousness of God required the total failure of his monastic drive for godliness; he could later describe the indissoluble connection of these two elements as a "confident doubt."[124] This intense connection allows us to suppose that he had not only experienced his failure before 1513 but also had arrived at the first stages of his new understanding of grace and Christ. The idea about the christological symbiosis of judgment and grace probably first opened his eyes to how deep were his sins (and consequently his complete dependence on God) and, consequently, how bottomless was God's gift of mercy. It is just as probable that the intense theology of grace and christocentric direction of his order played an essential role in Luther's twofold reorientation, especially as he encountered it in the pastoral care and theology of Johannes von Staupitz. The first impulse in this direction can almost certainly be found already in the first years in the cloister in Erfurt.

---

122. On the breadth of this theology of piety, see Hamm, *Frömmigkeitstheologie*, 275-84.

123. Berndt Hamm, *Promissio, Pactum, Ordinatio: Freiheit und Selbstbindung Gottes in der scholastischen Gnadenlehre*, Beiträge zur historischen Theologie 54 (Tübingen: Mohr, 1977), 377-83.

124. See n. 19 above.

Nevertheless, speculation or questions about when to date moments such as Luther's conversations with Staupitz are not essential for my reflections. As soon as we no longer fixate on isolating the great decisive "Reformation turn" doctrinally or chronologically but can discern a wide arc of Reformation development with various moves and clarifications, the issue of dates becomes relative anyway. The wider view of gradual change displaces the need to define breakthroughs.[125] For Luther research, however, the decision of whether or not to exclude Luther's experiences of *Anfechtung* during the early years in the cloister from his trajectory toward a Reformation reorientation is intrinsically important. The essential question is whether we want to recognize the substance of "Reformation" first in the clear, bright, and liberating features of his later theology or already in the desperate hopelessness of his striving for holiness.[126]

When it is viewed historically, I believe, everything points to seeing the beginning of Luther's Reformation reorientation already in this experience of *Anfechtung* and failure. The unique nature of *Anfechtung* itself already presents a fundamental change in the direction of the divine encounter that first led Luther into the cloister. For inasmuch as he did not see himself in the free spontaneity of pure love to God and neighbor but rather in the poison of egoism and repugnance to the God whose demanding, judging, and retributive righteousness drove him into a corner, there ripened within him the existential admission and the theological recognition that God's salvation had nothing to do with the quality and worthiness of his soul. Here already lay the break with a medieval religiosity that invariably taught a causal relationship between a person's virtuous quality and actions and the attainment of eternal life.

Theologically — especially with respect to the theology of the cross — it is also hard to justify why we should really view the turn toward a "Reformation" relationship with God solely in terms of the comforting and liberating joy of certain salvation but not in a new dimension of darkness and bitterness, pain and sighing, and in an angst-ridden doubt about God and oneself. In any case, for Luther the two sides of the path of salvation belong inseparably together, in his autobiographical recollections as well as in the architecture of his theology: the law terrifies and the gospel

---

125. I have adapted the concept of the "wider view" from the field of aesthetics. I am grateful to the following work: Wilhelm Genazino, *Der gedehnte Blick* (Munich: C. Hanser, 2004).

126. On the delicate use of the word "Reformation," see section 2 of this chapter.

blesses. He understood the destruction of *Anfechtung* to be a necessary condition for the faith that trusts in God's promises alone.[127] Under God's good guidance, he saw both elements as being fastened together: the nearness of impending doom and the imminence of saving grace.[128]

---

127. Brecht, *Martin Luther*, 59.

128. On Luther's memory of the storm near Stotternheim and his invocation of Saint Anne, see WA TR 4:440.9-11, no. 4707: "'Hilff du, S. Anna, ich will ein monch werden!' Sed Deus tum Hebraice meum votum intellexit: 'Anna,' id est sub gratia, non legaliter." See also WA TR 1:134.32-35, no. 326: "Singulari Dei consilio factus sum monachus, ne me caperent. Alioqui essem facillime captus. Sic autem non poterant, quia es nham [*sic*] sich der gantz orden mein an."

CHAPTER 3

Why Did Luther Turn Faith into the Central Concept of the Christian Life?

Faith's central role as a key concept that unites different streams of the Reformation is well known.[1] From every side in the pamphlets and tracts, we meet the programmatic slogan "We are justified by faith alone and not by works!" Here faith means direct access to God's word and thereby the sure reception of salvation.[2] The question of how *sola fide* (faith alone) could become such a stereotypical reformation slogan leads us to the roots of the Reformation and confronts us with the elementary fact that the Reformation began as an event of theology and piety, rooted in the doctrines of medieval theology and the experiences of observant monasteries. In short, the question leads us to the starting point of a new theology in the young Augustinian brother in Erfurt and Wittenberg, Martin Luther. Luther addressed the question in his own hand in the marginal notes *(Randbemerkungen)* on Peter Lombard in 1509-10,[3] and especially in the notes for his first lectures on the Psalms (1513-15)[4] and on Romans (1515-16).[5]

1. I owe many suggestions for the following lecture to the students who took part in my Erlangen seminar "Luther's Discovery of Faith" in the summer semester of 1996 and to my assistant Dr. Petra Seegets.
2. For a recent example, see Thomas Hohenberger, *Lutherische Rechtfertigungslehre in den reformatorischen Flugschriften der Jahre 1521-22* (Tübingen: Mohr, 1996).
3. WA 9:28-94. For the same period, see Luther's marginal notes on Augustine, WA 9:2-27.
4. The first edition of the *Dictata super Psalterium* can be found in WA 3 and 4 (*LW* 10 and 11); the new edition is found in WA 55/I (glosses) and WA 55/II 1:1, *Lieferung* (scholia on Pss. 1–15).
5. WA 56; *LW* 25.

Still, I would like to ask this question from the medieval perspective. How did such an astonishing shift to the side of faith take place, since love — not faith — had defined Christian salvation during the Middle Ages, at least since the twelfth century? I emphasize the perspective of the Middle Ages not only because I am looking at the Reformation's disruptions, although that is certainly customary in Luther research. No, I emphasize this point because I want to go beyond the scholarly consensus in order to lift up the continuities that Reformation faith shares with important medieval understandings. My thesis can be formulated like this: without Luther's positive use of familiar late medieval scholastic doctrine and piety, the new centrality of *sola fide* in his theology would be incomprehensible. Particular elements of the medieval concept of faith were important for Luther when — for the first time in his 1513 lectures on the Psalms — he turned the terms *fides, fidelis,* and *credere* ("faith," "faithful," and "believe," respectively) into key concepts for Christian existence and church life.[6] At the same time he was building this connection, Luther also gave faith that new defining content that allowed it to supersede the medieval centrality of love *(caritas)* and its works *(opera).*

But how did he accomplish this process of displacement that was so basic to the Reformation? To describe this, I need to sketch out common features in the high and late medieval concept of faith; I shall naturally start with those authors who would have been especially dear to a certain inquisitive Augustinian brother. The understanding of faith that would have been mediated to him by, shall we say, Gabriel Biel[7] and Johannes

---

6. On the centrality of the concept of faith in Luther's *Dictata super Psalterium,* see the seminal study by Reinhard Schwarz, *Fides, spes und caritas beim jungen Luther, unter besonderer Berücksichtigung der mittelalterlichen Tradition* (Berlin: De Gruyter, 1962). See p. 212 for thoughts on *caritas* and p. 227 for *spes*. On occasion, though not yet as a formula, the young Luther also already used the verbal combination *sola fides,* for example, WA 4:380.19f.; *LW* 4:518. On the significant comparison with the exegetical tradition of medieval interpretation of the Psalms, see n. 36 below.

7. Gabriel Biel, *Canonis misse expositio,* ed. Heiko A. Oberman and William J. Courtenay, 4 vols. (Wiesbaden: Franz Steiner, 1963-67); Biel, *Collectorium circa quattuor libros Sententiarum,* ed. Wilfrid Werbeck and Udo Hofmann, 5 vols. (Tübingen: Mohr Siebeck, 1973-84), with indexes by Werbeck. Biel not only shows himself in his commentary on the Mass (first printed 1489) and commentary on the *Sentences* (first printed 1501) to be a decided adherent of the Ockhamist line of teaching, but also presents in his quotations a certain breadth and "harvest" of the medieval scholastic tradition. In this respect he serves as a source for finding common traits on the understanding of faith in the vari-

Why Did Luther Turn Faith into the Central Concept?

von Staupitz[8] provides the following characteristics:

1. Together with baptism, faith was the fundamental principle for Christian life in the Middle Ages. It was the basic attitude that separated Christians from non-Christians. It was the fundamental principle, and yet it was also the smallest part of being a Christian, as yet completely insufficient for the attainment of salvation.

2. Faith always has an essential relationship with the revealed truth of God. In this sense, it understands truth by hearing that which people cannot say or discover on their own; instead, it understands what has been communicated to it through the authority of Holy Scripture and the church.

3. From this arises faith's basic orientation to the word: its own hearing and obeying come from the authoritative word of divine truth.[9]

4. With respect to the binding doctrine about the reality of God, faith

---

ous streams of the high and late Middle Ages. For instance, Thomas Aquinas is the most frequently cited theological authority in Biel's commentary on the *Sentences;* see the indices in the *Collectorium,* 140-44. On Biel's concept of faith, see Heiko A. Oberman, *Der Herbst der mittelalterlichen Theologie,* trans. Martin Rumscheidt and Henning Kampen (Zurich: EVZ-Verlag, 1965), 68-87.

8. Johann von Staupitz, *Lateinische Schriften 1: Tübinger Predigten,* in *Sämtliche Schriften: Abhandlungen, Predigten, Zeugnisse,* ed. Richard Wetzel (Berlin: De Gruyter, 1987), 552f. and 564f. (hereafter cited as Staupitz, *Tübinger Predigten*). Luther, of course, did not know these sermons on Job, extant only in Staupitz's handwritten copy, which probably date from between 1495 and 1500. Yet they show what kind of theology of piety was represented by the man who enjoyed such intense contact with the young monk Luther as the superior of his order, as his teacher and confessor. Certainly Staupitz showed himself in this cycle of sermons to be a great pupil of Augustine, but at the same time he represents a broad spectrum of theologically reflected spirituality, and in the situating of faith, for example, he closely follows formulations of Jean Gerson, so that he too, like Biel in his different way, can be read as representative of a certain theological consensus in the field of high and late medieval understanding of faith.

9. It appears to me that medieval theology was never able to make clear what the so-called infusion and formation of faith by grace (*fides infusa* and *formata*) actually meant for the character of faith itself — as a virtue of the Christian in its own right distinguished from hope and love — beyond the elementary stage of faith acquired by hearing. This formation of faith was always qualitatively determined by the formative *caritas* but not described as a feature of the virtue of faith itself. Consequently *fides ex auditu* (Rom. 10:17) in its elementary meaning was decisive for the description of the specific nature of the *virtus fidei,* while the intensified forms of infused and formed faith as *fides* remained remarkably pale and acquired their whole coloring from love.

is always recognition, knowledge, and consent by the intellect *(intellectus)*. Therefore, in the Middle Ages, faith was essentially cognitive.[10]

5. As Biel put it with respect to the Christian tradition,[11] faith is the firm adherence to the truth. Thus its recognition of truth possesses an infallible certainty, *certitudo* and *securitas*, about the contents of faith.

6. Faith is invariably receptive. It receives and accepts the truth as taught and preached. It does not create, act, or work, standing in contrast to the medieval view of *caritas*, which was always described as having an active and operative dimension.

7. Faith was therefore in the first instance a concept about the relationship to something beyond *(ad extra)*, describing the receptive relationship of a person to the church's truth. Love, meanwhile, was the dominant qualitative concept for a person's inner heart. Where faith is the way that a person comes to a sure knowledge of God, love is the way in which God comes to dwell in the heart.

8. Taken together, this means that among all the medieval theological terms for describing people's spiritual change and internal attitudes,

---

10. It can be said without qualification that faith has its place in that human capacity to know and understand *(intellectus)* that is directed toward spiritual truths. Certainly the will is also always involved in faith — in ways variously defined according to the different schools — insofar as believers willingly assent to what they recognize, that is, they allow it to stand as true. Yet these willed acts of *assensus* are directly coupled with the rational character of the *intellectus*; there is no shifting of faith to the level of the powers of emotion (affects) in the "heart." The reference to *voluntas* underscores the free nature of faith, whose subject remains solely the *intellectus* and its *ratio*. Faith is thus the freely willed movement from apprehension of the content of faith through its cognition and recognition to rational comprehension of what is believed. See Karl Lehmann and Wolfhart Pannenberg, eds., *Lehrverurteilungen — kirchentrennend?* vol. 1, *Rechtfertigung, Sakramente und Amt im Zeitalter der Reformation und heute* (Freiburg im Breisgau: Herder, 1986), 56: "Die Trienter Konzilsväter denken mit der mittelalterlichen Tradition bei dem *Wort* 'Glaube' (in der semantischen Spannung von *fides* und *credere*!) zunächst an die Zustimmung des Verstandes zum geoffenbarten Wort Gottes einerseits und an den 'objektiven' Glauben andererseits, wie er in Bekenntnis und Lehrverkündigung der Kirche niedergelegt ist."

11. Biel, *Collectorium*, vol. 3, dist. 23, q. 2, art. 1, not. 1 (p. 407.3-5): "Fides est notitia adhaesiva certa et firma veritatis ad religionem pertinentis per revelationem accepta." See also pp. 408.18f. *(intellectus adhaesio)*, 410.3 *(firmitas adhaesionis)*, 411.9 *(apprehensio credibilis, id est veritatis credendae)*, and 424.23f. (the *fides acquisita* as "intellectualis virtus seu habitus derelictus ac causatus ab actibus intellectus apprehensivis vel adhaesivis, inclinans intellectum ad obiecti cognitionem aut ad veri adhaesionem").

"faith" had the least qualitative definition. Faith was only a moral virtue in a limited sense,[12] because it was primarily receptive and not active. While *caritas* (love) reshaped sinners' lives for intimate relationship with God's goodness, freed them from their egoism, and qualitatively changed the direction of lives, faith was not constituted by the existential relationship with God's goodness but by the cognitive relationship to God's truth. Faith led people out of error rather than made them good. Therefore, being faithful did not necessarily lead to being good or doing good. Faith in itself — as unformed, naked faith — was totally compatible with lovelessness and a state of damnation. Even Judas Iscariot had believed.

9. Thus, as Christians made their climb to paradise, faith was the lowest rung on the ladder. To be sure, *fides* had a part to play in the ascent, providing different styles and steps of faith, ways to go from inherited faith to infused faith or from unformed faith to formed faith. Nevertheless, the principle of perfection did not lie in faith itself but in the form of the justifying grace and love that flowed into sinners. The formative principle of grace-filled love would first lift faith to the next step of spiritual quality and morality, which made gaining salvation possible. The end point of the Christian life in medieval theology and piety was therefore not *fides* but *caritas*, which motivated meritorious and satisfactory works of justification.[13]

Thus far we have located where faith stood in comparison to the central concept of love. To understand Luther's new approach, however, we need to go beyond the nine points above, because the medieval view of faith differentiated not only between faith and love but also between faith and hope. Above all, I am reminded of the theology of piety of the fifteenth century, which — as one can see in the example of Johannes von Staupitz[14] — was shaped especially by Jean Gerson.[15] Gerson's pastoral theology gave hope

---

12. Biel, *Collectorium*, vol. 3, art. 3, dub. 4, pp. 424.1–425.38; see also Schwarz, *Fides, spes und caritas*, 44f.

13. A characteristic example is the following formulation of Johann von Staupitz on the human faith in salvation — closely bound up with hope and love — worked by the Spirit: "Vitam autem gloriae non vidimus, sed speramus et cognovimus per fidem, movemur autem ad eam per caritatem; ipsa namque caritas pondus est quo coelum attingimus. Caritas autem non consentit malo, ideo simul cum peccato mortali non stat." See Staupitz, *Tübinger Predigten*, 368, ll. 191-95.

14. On Staupitz's reception of Gerson, see Staupitz, *Tübinger Predigten*, 517f. For the definition of the relation of *fides* to *spes* and *caritas*, see Sermo 24, ll. 287-315 (pp. 371-73); most of this section consists of direct citations of Gerson.

15. Certainly every theology must somehow deal with piety, but in the late Middle

(spes) a new value. In contrast to faith, hope was ranked next to love. For in the general medieval understanding, *spes* — like *caritas* — was rooted not in a cognitive ability but in being a matter of human will and emotional life; it was not a cognitive but an affective realm for the higher spiritual soul.[16] Faith accepted doctrinal content and specific ways of thinking, therefore using the intellect and reason to grasp the truth about God. Hope, however, was a way of life like love, directing the soul to God's goodness and the riches of paradise. But at this point there arose a very significant distinction in the theology, piety, and even devotional art[17] of the later Middle Ages. This was a visible split, which I would like to characterize as follows.

Faith and hope were assigned to different modes of speech, which means that they offered different kinds of certainty and assurance. In the professing and confessing of the Christian faith, faith belonged to an objective and general realm of discourse; that is, it belonged to the church's realm of truth and certainty and transcended individual opinions. Believers who stood on this plane knew that their relationship to God was defined by the divine saving revelation and its universal rules, as expressed in the rule that the only people who reach salvation are those who die without mortal sins and who are in a state of justifying grace. In practice, that meant loving God with one's whole heart and feeling true penitential sorrow for sin. Knowing this rule was part of having certainty of faith. What faithful people could not concretely know was the answer to the decisive

---

Ages only that type of theology I call *theology of piety* was totally orientated toward piety in the sense of the pious (authentic) shaping of life — and indeed, so exclusively that all theological themes and modes of reflection not directly relevant for piety fall out of the program of the theology of piety or are reshaped to fit it. See Berndt Hamm, "Von der spätmittelalterlichen *reformatio* zur Reformation: Der Prozess normativer Zentrierung von Religion und Gesellschaft in Deutschland," *Archiv für Reformationsgeschichte* 84 (1993): 7-82. For the relation of the theology of piety to scholastic and monastic theology of the fifteenth century, see 18-41, and especially 19f. n. 26.

16. See, for example, Jean Gerson, *De consolatione theologiae*, in *Oeuvres complètes* (hereafter cited as JGOC), vol. 9, ed. Palémon Glorieux (Paris: Desclée, 1973). See also Thomas Aquinas, *Summa theologiae* II/II, q. 18, art. 1 *(voluntas* as *subiectum* of *spes)* and q. 24, art. 1 *(voluntas* as *subiectum* of *caritas)* in comparison with q. 4, art. 2 *(intellectus* as *subiectum* of *fides)*. On the doctrine of hope (and its certainty) in Thomas and other scholastic theologians, see the work of Basse cited below in n. 23.

17. Think particularly of sayings, particularly those ribbons of text that appear on the pious pictures of the century before the Reformation. Such illustrated texts, often doctrinal formulations or short prayers, can be precisely assigned to the various levels of expression that I distinguish below.

personal question of whether they were in a state of grace and love and were thereby worthy of salvation. While one could know the truth with the certainty given by faith, there was no personal, individual certainty of having grace or salvation; at best, there could only be conjecture about being in a state of grace.[18]

The realm of discourse surrounding hope was quite different, for it was always also the level of humility *(humilitas)*. For Gerson and for other spiritual teachers before and after him, *spes* and *humilitas* were two sides of the same emotional Christian posture.[19] In contrast to faith, humility and hope expressed themselves on the subjective and existential level; they were prayer rather than doctrine. They formed the personal posture of prayer in which people confessed their sins before the righteous, judging God and confidently cast their hopes on the merciful, saving God. Here faith's fixed knowledge of truth and its objective uncertainties vanished. For in the posture of humility, the consciousness of the normal need to follow the rules for salvation and the ensuing need to "do enough" and earn merit were at once wiped out. That is when sinners could see only their own emptiness before God, accuse themselves, and despair (as Gerson demanded of them) of their own ability to reach salvation by their own merits.[20] In humility, people made themselves even more insignificant than they actually were; they confessed guilt where there was no guilt, in a manner of speaking.[21] This meant that humility's self-condemnation

---

18. On this *coniecturaliter,* see Thomas Aquinas, *Summa theologiae* I/II, q. 112, art. 5.

19. Gerson, *De consolatione theologiae;* see also Staupitz, *Tübinger Predigten,* ll. 21-27 (p. 186).

20. Jean Gerson, *De vita spirituali animae,* in JGOC, vol. 3 (Paris: Desclée, 1962), 126: "Denique perspicuum est, quanta necessitate desperare debeamus de viribus nostris . . . nec confidere in homine, sed projicere totam spem nostram in Deum, ne confundamur, sed liberemur et nutriamur et glorificemur." Gerson, *De praeparatione ad missam,* in JGOC, vol. 9 (Paris: Desclée, 1973), 50: "Deum time, de te desperans, in se fidens, et mandata eius observa, quod in te est non omittens; hoc est omnis homo." With this pregnant summing up, Gerson's text closes.

21. This corresponds to a much quoted sentiment of Gregory the Great: "Bonarum mentium est ibi culpam agnoscere, ubi culpa non est." (See *Epist.* 11.64, in PL 77:1195B.) It is typical that this dictum is received and applied by Gerson (in the version of the text quoted) in the sense that the sinner should exaggerate his sense of guilt *(exaggerans quantum potest)* as his own prosecutor, witness, and judge (Gerson, *De consolatione theologiae,* pp. 232f.). See also Sven Grosse, *Heilsungewißheit und Scrupulositas im späten Mittelalter: Studien zu Johannes Gerson und Gattungen der Frömmigkeitstheologie seiner Zeit* (Tübingen: J. C. B. Mohr, 1994), 54 and 122.

blocked out the truth and reality of one's actual standing before God, so that precisely such humility became the de facto highest spiritual quality and merit.[22] In quite the same way, hope (humility's sister) would then leap over the characteristic uncertainty of faith. In a posture of pure trust, hope released itself from the problem of uncertainty, bound itself to God's loving promises alone, and gained a personal certainty of salvation that was impossible for the intellect to know.[23]

In medieval theology and piety there was therefore a very telling difference between the uncertainty of faith's knowledge and the hopeful certainty of abject humility. Here we see the division between a theoretical, objective, and highly rational teaching of doctrine and the existential way of life with its personal standing before God. It is a polarity between the rationalized religion of the lecture hall[24] and the affective religion of monastic prayer. As the later Middle Ages wore on, the latter form of an internalized, mystical piety of prayer outgrew its originally monastic borders to become a spirituality not only for members of the various orders but also for pious secular clergy and laypeople. Institutional histories reveal how these conversations about "certainty" took place back in the twelfth and thirteenth centuries when cathedral schools and nascent universities were making room for the new pervasive spirit of rational and philosophical theology,

---

22. Grosse, *Heilsungewißheit*, 113-18.

23. Gerson, *De consolatione theologiae*, 195f.; see also Grosse, *Heilsungewißheit*, 106-11. On this whole theme, see Michael Basse, *Certitudo Spei: Thomas von Aquins Begründung der Hoffnungsgewißheit und ihre Rezeption bis zum Konzil von Trient als ein Beitrag zur Verhältnisbestimmung von Eschatologie und Rechtfertigungslehre* (Göttingen: Vandenhoeck & Ruprecht, 1993). Note: this study doesn't take account of Gerson and medieval theology of piety and pays only minimal attention to late scholasticism; it is, in a word, one of the systematic-theological Thomas-Luther studies typical of an older style. On personal certainty of hope according to Staupitz, see the texts cited below in n. 27.

24. The concept "lecture hall" is quite pointed and refers as *pars pro toto* to the entire field of the church's academic and catechetical mediation of knowledge in teaching and instruction. Equally selective is the following description, "religion of monastic prayer," with which I refer to the whole expressive dimension of the stance of prayer before God. The reading in the lecture hall and the prayer in the choir or in the monastic cell represent in particularly typical fashion the difference between the objectified form of doctrinal teaching and the existential living out of faith in humility and hope. On the corresponding existential type of expression in Gerson's theology of consolation, which aims to accentuate humility and the certainty of hope, see Sven Grosse, "Existentielle Theologie in der vorreformatorischen Epoche am Beispiel Johannes Gersons: Historische Überlegungen zum ökumenischen Disput," *Kerygma und Dogma* 41 (1995): 80-111.

thereby mixing it with the formation that came through the prayer life of spiritual communities.[25] The late medieval concept of faith took its expression from the earlier academic disruption of scholasticism, which had focused on a didactic, cognitive understanding of ecclesiastical truth that might impart a universally valid *certitudo*. In contrast to this, the theme of intimate emotional community with God, which lifted sinners out of nothingness up to the assurances of salvation, focused on humility and hope. This was the same twelfth century in which the theologians of western Europe discovered both a new rational basis for faith and a new emotional inwardness of love, including its penitential emotions of humility and hope.[26] For this reason, the theological and devotional course of history was set for a new polarization of knowledge and emotion in Western Christianity.

The opposition of faith and humility/hope once again exemplifies how faith could not be the central concept for Christian life in the Middle Ages, because the level of truth for "faith alone" had not yet reached the humility and hope of a truly spiritual life. In the medieval view, only love could open up the inner relationship of the heart both to truth and to God's goodness, thus making possible the humble confidence of hope.

25. It is characteristic when Petrus Comestor (d. 1179) concludes: "Sunt qui orationi magis operam dantes lectioni minus insistunt, et hi sunt claustrales. Sunt alii qui lectioni invigilant, rarius orantes, et hi sunt scholares" (*Sermo* 9, in PL 198:1747A). Arnold Angenendt quotes this in his forthcoming book on medieval religiosity, which he generously allowed me to see in manuscript form; see in that work the section on the high Middle Ages, which briefly and appropriately characterizes the shift in the history of science in the twelfth and thirteenth centuries, and also provides a helpful bibliography.

26. Peter Dinzelbacher, "Über die Entdeckung der Liebe im Hochmittelalter," *Saeculum* 32 (1981): 185-208. Theologically important in the framework of this reorientation "inward" is above all the shifting of the center of gravity from the external penitential works of satisfaction to the inner penitential sense of contrition (of humble pain at one's sins) and of hope (which takes flight to God's forgiveness). This new view of repentance, which comes to the fore above all in the school of Anselm of Laon (d. 1117) and with Abelard (d. 1142), understands the genuine contrition and attrition of the heart as an awakening of love to God. From the twelfth century on the *vera contritio* arising from the motive of love to God comes to constitute the decisive condition at the moment of death for admission to purgatory and/or paradise. See the article "Buße," in *Lexikon des Mittelalters*, vol. 2 (1983), cols. 1123-41, especially 1137-39; Ludwig Hödl, *Die Geschichte der scholastischen Literatur und der Theologie der Schlüsselgewalt*, part I, *Die scholastische Literatur und die Theologie der Schlüsselgewalt von ihren Anfängen an bis zur Summa Aurea des Wilhelm von Auxerre*, Beiträge zur Geschichte der Philosophie und Theologie des Mittelalters, vol. 38 H.4 (Münster: Aschendorff, 1960), passim.

As soon as faith could be understood as "faith formed by love" and thereby seen in a closer connection with humility and hope, the concept of faith could unreservedly articulate the saving relationship of the sanctified person to God. For this reason, we repeatedly encounter pre-Reformation sermons that use this concept of a more fulfilling faith in order to express the intense relationship of trust in God's mercy and Christ's saving righteousness.[27] Especially in the language of the theology of piety and its focus on the spiritual life *(vita spiritualis)*, the tension between *intellectus* and *affectus* could be bridged, but the divergence between these two discursive realms within Christian existence could not be undone.

Amid the typically late medieval questions of *Anfechtung* (especially among the more scrupulously religious people), the difficulty and even the impossibility arose about how to keep these divergent intellectual and pastoral issues under control.[28] How could people reach the pure, humble,

---

27. Note the way in which the Franciscan Stephan Fridolin in his sermons on Compline toward the end of the fifteenth century related "by faith alone" to the righteousness in the passion of Jesus Christ, quoted by Hamm, "Von der spätmittelalterlichen *reformatio* zur Reformation," 39 n. 98. See also Petra Seegets, "'Das alles menschlich heyl an dem leiden Cristi steet': Stephan Fridolin — ein spätmittelalterlicher Frömmigkeitstheologe zwischen Kloster und Stadt" (Diss. theol., Erlangen, 1994), especially 70 and 228-31. Staupitz too, in his Tübingen sermons on Job (see n. 8 above), frequently employed the concept of faith in the full soteriological sense of *fides caritate formata*, without specially mentioning the (naturally assumed) "infused" quality of love, an abbreviated form of speech that elsewhere too seems to be quite common in texts of the theology of piety; see also Staupitz, *Tübinger Predigten*, Sermo 22, ll. 108-11 (p. 341): "Tertium fundamentum in bonitate collocatur. Et secundum hoc sic imbuendi pueri sunt, quod deus optimus dedit nobis sua bonitate fidem rectam, in qua sperantes salvi erimus. Cuius fidei fundamentum positum in Christo." A comparison with other passages shows how carefully Staupitz distinguished in the traditional style between *fides, spes,* and *caritas,* in particular between general certainty and personal uncertainty of faith on the one hand and the personal certainty of salvation given in hope on the other as well as particularly in regard to the decisive key position of love, which alone can save and build the form of life for faith and love; see *Tübinger Predigten*, Sermo 4, ll. 194-203 (p. 83); Sermo 24, ll. 203-12 and 300-315 (pp. 368f., 372f.); Sermo 27, ll. 219f. (p. 403); and Sermo 28, ll. 113-18 (p. 408f.), as well as Staupitz's tract published at the beginning of 1517: *Libellus De exsecutione aeternae praedestinationis*, ed. Lothar Graf zu Dohna et al. (Berlin: De Gruyter, 1979), §51 (p. 138), §171 (p. 236), §228 (p. 278), §237 (p. 284), and §§238-40 (pp. 286-88). In the Staupitz literature, as far as I can tell, the relation between *fides, spes,* and *caritas* is not presented with the clarity that might be wished.

28. See Wilfrid Werbeck, "Voraussetzungen und Wesen der scrupulositas im Spätmittelalter," *Zeitschrift für Theologie und Kirche* 68 (1971): 327-50; Grosse, *Heilsungewißheit und Scrupulositas im späten Mittelalter*.

Why Did Luther Turn Faith into the Central Concept?

and sure assurance of hope when they were well aware of the church's binding teaching that no one would be saved without the sanctifying quality of justifying love and its possibilities to earn merit? What to do with the fact that church teaching also denied that they could have any certain knowledge of their own state of grace and love? How could people find the consolation of hope alone in the *pro nobis* sufferings of Christ when they also had to wonder whether Christ even lived in their hearts *(in nobis)* through the power of love? To have the primary consolation without the secondary doubt, Staupitz described as "too immodest a trust in God's mercy," because Christ's suffering *pro nobis* only leads to salvation insofar as it is *in nobis*.[29] In saying this, he expressed the whole dilemma facing late medieval pastoral care as being the tension between strenuously examining one's conscience and having a comforting trust in God's mercy.

When we again turn to the early Luther, it is immediately remarkable — but not totally surprising — how vigorously he appropriated the medieval concept of faith that I sketched above in his *Randbemerkungen* (marginal notations) on Lombard's *Sentences* of 1509-10 and in his first lectures on Psalms and Romans beginning in 1513. Following the theological tradition, he deemed it particularly important that faith was defined not as an operative virtue or as a moral activity but as the receptive event of comprehending and assenting to the truth about God, which God's authoritative word of revelation loudly proclaimed.[30] This relationship between truth and the word remained essential for Luther's view of faith,[31] as he held fast

---

29. Johannes von Staupitz, "Von der Nachfolgung des willigen Sterbens Christi," in *Johann von Staupitzens sämmtliche Werke*, vol. 1, *Deutsche Schriften*, ed. Joachim Karl Friedrich Knaake (Potsdam: Krausnick, 1867), p. 66; see also Heiko A. Oberman, *Werden und Wertung der Reformation: Vom Wegestreit zum Glaubenskampf* (Tübingen: Mohr, 1977), 106-8.

30. See Luther's marginal notes on the *Sentences* of Peter Lombard (Petrus Lombardus) in WA 9:91.4-6: "Videt quisque intellectualiter fidem suam certissima scientia, hoc est non actu secundo, sed actu primo, id est intellectus habet eam praesentem sibi certissime, sed non per opera etc." See also WA 9:92.13-36, especially the closer definition of *fides ex auditu* (Rom. 10:17) as "sensus seu intellectus, id est qui recipit sensum illorum *(verborum sonantium,* that is, the word of Christ), ille habet fidem; assensus enim ad istum sensum est fides, licet non videat, quomodo sensus ille verus sit" (ll. 23-27) — "fides, id est assensus, fit ex auditu, id est apprehensione [*perceptione*] significationis seu sensus verborum" (ll. 28-30). A shift away from the tradition reveals itself at the point where Luther pointedly summarized the content of faith in the concept of the "verbum Christi"; see Schwarz, *Fides, spes und caritas,* 51-54.

31. For Luther the concepts *veritas, intellectus,* and *fides* belong together, whereby

to the emphasis on the cognitive and doctrinal basis of faith. For him, faith is fundamentally a hearing and understanding of verbal truth, a perceptive recognizing and knowing *(cognoscere* and *intelligere).*[32]

---

he stressed with the tradition that the relational truth of believing apprehension of truth is not a *seeing* of the truth (see n. 30 above: *non videat*), but rather a *firmiter credere* in what the Holy Spirit has revealed (WA 9:92.13-17). See also WA 9:38.12-15: "Veritas est intellectio activa/passiva rei, sicut se habet. Bonitas est amatio activa/passiva amabilis sive rei." The orientation of faith to *veritas* and *intellectio* is directly connected with the fact that faith is related to preaching and teaching, leading to the sequence *fides, spes,* and *actio:* "Spes enim servat, quae fides praedicat et docet" — "sine qua [fide] nemo potest sperare et per consequens bene agere" (WA 9:91.12-33). These thoroughly traditional differentiations between *veritas* and *bonitas* or *fides* and *spes* respectively reflect Luther's theological thinking at the time of the marginal comments on Peter Lombard. At the same time, these marginalia are evidence for what was so important to him in the medieval understanding of faith that he reproduced it in his own formulations and in later years did not give it up but integrated it into his significantly altered understanding of faith.

32. This line of cognitive/intellectual understanding of faith is continued by Luther beyond his comments on the *Sentences* in the lectures on the Psalms (see n. 47 below: "solum intellectu et fide," and WA 3:507.35; *LW* 10:452: "solo intellectu et fide"), whereby admittedly it must be observed (as we shall see) that it is by no means rationally and intellectually confined. It is rather that the *cognoscere* and *intelligere* of faith spread out into the entire emotional life of the human "heart." How strongly the cognitive recognition of truth remained the basis of Luther's concept of faith — in the connection between apprehension, knowledge, recognition, and confession — can be seen more than clearly, for example, in his exegesis of the Vulgate Ps. 95:6 (the words *confessio et pulchritudo*), where in Gerson's style he linked faith as the light of the soul to *intelligentia* and its *intellectus, ratio,* and *speculativa virtus,* while assigning spiritual *amor* as the beautifying color of the soul to *voluntas* and its *affectus, practica virtus,* and *vis appetitiva* (WA 4:109.12-31; *LW* 11:260-61). See also Bernhard Lohse, *Ratio und fides: Eine Untersuchung über die ratio in der Theologie Luthers* (Göttingen: Vandenhoeck & Ruprecht, 1958), 38-41; Albert Brandenburg, *Gericht und Evangelium: Zur Worttheologie in Luthers Erster Psalmenvorlesung* (Paderborn: Verlag Bonifacius-Druckerei, 1960), 73-76; for the *intellectus fidei* see Schwarz, *Fides, spes und caritas,* 134-53. The specific recognition and understanding of faith is not a natural human capacity but a gift of the biblical revelation of Christ and therefore stands sharply opposed to all natural cognitive human ability. The latter proves itself to be blind to divine truth, that is, to the recognition of Christ (see WA 4:356.23f.; *LW* 11:485: "Sic enim fides non intellectum illuminat, immo excecat"). In his *Dictata super Psalterium,* Luther differs from medieval theologians like Gerson and Biel by interpreting the *intellectus fidei* emphatically not in philosophical style as a faculty of the soul of the *homo intelligens,* but exclusively in terms of the truth of Christ that opens the way to its own recognition (see WA 3:176.3f.; *LW* 10:147f.: "In the Holy Scriptures *understanding*

Why Did Luther Turn Faith into the Central Concept?

It was therefore essential for Luther that this faithful reception of the truth should not be ethically qualified according to the medieval view. That is, even without the quality and activity of love, it is possible to have faith, even for the person who is conscious of internal lovelessness and mortal sin. In contrast to love, faith is not a pious quality; it is an externally oriented relationship, characterized by its receptive, grasping relationship to the absolutely certain and reassuring word of the truth of revelation.[33] This is the late medieval dowry, so to speak, that came with Luther's concept of faith in his early theology. From the perspective of late medieval theology and piety, no other concept could appear to him so well suited to express what was most important in the relationship between God and humanity than this ready-made view of faith. But how could faith suddenly attain its new soteriological centrality in Luther's first lectures on the Psalms when for centuries — during a great era of rediscovered and further-developed Augustinian religiosity — it had occupied a place subordinate to the decidedly more important concept of love?

This turning point was only possible because faith, love, and the other ingredients of the spiritual life got mixed up in a kind of whirlpool of a radically new experience of truth and untruth, which fundamentally altered their positions. By the phrase "experience of untruth," I mean that crisis of *Anfechtung* that the young theologian and brother was processing theologically in the Psalms lectures.[34] In a very unsettling way, Luther had experienced the deep divide between divine and human realities. He had personally reached the end of his human possibilities before God in every

---

takes its name from the object rather than from any capacity, the opposite of what it is in philosophy." See also Gerhard Ebeling, *Lutherstudien*, vol. 1 (Tübingen: Mohr, 1971), 39f. This exclusive conditioning of the *intellectus fidei* by grace did not prevent Luther from relating the theological *cognoscere/intelligere* and the theological *velle* to the anthropological base of the *intellectus* with its *ratio* and *voluntas* respectively (see above), yet only to the extent that he was concerned with the existential movement of the human soul and its real cognition and will, not because he had a psychological interest in its various areas.

33. See n. 30 above: *apprehensione, perceptione;* see also n. 11 above (*fides* as *apprehensio* in Biel).

34. The most important literature on Luther's *Dictata super Psalterium* is collected in Karl-Heinz Zur Mühlen, "Luther II," in *Theologische Realenzyklöpadie* (Berlin: De Gruyter, 1991), 21:562; Reinhard Schwarz, *Luther* (Göttingen: Vandenhoeck & Ruprecht, 1986), 24f.; Bernhard Lohse, *Luthers Theologie in ihrer historischen Entwicklung und in ihrem systematischen Zusammenhang* (Göttingen: Vandenhoeck & Ruprecht, 1995), 61. See also Jared Wicks, *Man Yearning for Grace: Luther's Early Spiritual Teaching* (Wiesbaden: Franz Steiner, 1969), 41-94.

respect: both as a thinking subject and as an ethical agent. In his eyes, all human speculation, speech, and judgment about God became untrue, just as he denied human nature any ability to truly love God and neighbor. He saw humanity caught up for life *(semper!)* in the radical original sins of blindness and egoism.[35]

Here we hit the nerve of a fundamentally new theological approach. For this means that while he was delivering his *Dictata super Psalterium*, Luther was no longer thinking in the categories of a qualitative, habitual, and operative human nature. If he ever did, then it was only to show that human quality could only be an "unquality" in the face of God's judgment and mercy. Salvation or damnation does not depend on quality, because the human quality of being and acting can only be seen theologically as sin. For Luther, therefore, a love that is understood in qualitative and active terms can no longer be the central concept of a Christian life journeying toward salvation. The decisive point was no longer the question of quality but of one's perspective on the judgment that happens between God and people: how God has judged me and how I have judged myself before God. With this, Luther shifted the problem of truth from being a matter of quality to being a matter of relationship and judgment. In this move — as we will soon see — he found the initial escape from the agonizing question of how healing truth can come into a deeply untruthful and perverse human existence. He changed the question of salvation into a question about faith, because — entirely within the sense of the traditional terminology — he

---

35. In addition to n. 37 below on the Lutheran *semper*, see also WA 3:289.5-7; *LW* 10:237: "Therefore it is true that before Him we are always in sins, so that in His covenant and testament which He has established with us He Himself might be the justifier." The concepts *pactum* and *testamentum* point to Luther's view — explored in more detail below — that the justifying reorientation of sinful human existence does not consist in a natural, qualitative change, but in a new definition from without through the address of the divine word of covenant; see Berndt Hamm, *Promissio, Pactum, Ordinatio: Freiheit und Selbstbindung Gottes in der scholastischen Gnadenlehre*, Beiträge zur historischen Theologie 54 (Tübingen: Mohr, 1977), 377-89. On the problem of sin and truth as developed in the following, see especially WA 3:287.20–293.21, *LW* 10:235-43; WA 4:266.1-4 and 266.22–273.23; *LW* 11:400-409 (with the intensive combination of *veritas* and *fides* to the point of their identification in WA 4:266.25-27; *LW* 11:401, or in the new version WA 55/I:756: "When I was afflicted because of the Word of God, then I learned that I must trust neither in myself not in any other man, because every man is a liar, while God is truthful and I must trust in Him and faithfully proclaim Him against the fury of all persecutors"). See also, Hamm, "Martin Luthers Entdeckung der evangelischen Freiheit," *Zeitschrift für Theologie und Kirche* 80 (1983): 54-56.

turned the human relationship to God's truth into the divine truth of a relationship based on faith. Since everything now peaked at the question of relationship, the concept of faith could assume its new dominance.[36]

How this actually happened first grows clear when we look more closely at the relationship between faith and truth in Luther's first lectures on the Psalms. Amid radical personal crisis, Luther found truth only where people stopped speaking and God began. He thereby reduced the sinner's real encounter with God exclusively to the relationship that comes from believing God's word *in the Bible,* namely, the word about Christ; the earliest tendencies in this direction can be seen in 1509.[37] With this critical reduction (which also deeply criticized the church) came an essential broadening of what is meant by truth and faith. For Luther did not relegate the truth of God's word simply to the human cognitive sphere of *intellectus* or *ratio* (reason). As a word of direct address, God's word moves the whole of human existence, and its truth surrounds the affective emotional life of the soul.[38]

---

36. See n. 6 above. The centrality of faith is repeatedly emphasized by Luther, as in WA 3:648.23–651.22; *LW* 11:144-49, where he characterized the *fides Christi* as fountain and source of the whole Christian life and the foundation of the church, e.g., in the formulation: "Indeed, faith, which is given by God's grace to the ungodly and by which they are justified, is the substance, foundation, fountain, source, chief, and the firstborn of all spiritual graces, gifts, virtues, merits, and works," in WA 3:649.17-20, *LW* 11:146. The new dominance of the concept of faith in Luther's theology can be impressively underlined if one compares his exegesis of the Psalms at the many places where he spoke of *fides, fidelis,* or *credere,* although the Psalms text itself does not provide these terms with the previous tradition of exegesis of the Psalms. One will then observe that in the majority of these cases Luther's employment of the concept of faith ran counter to the tradition. See the commentary apparatus to Luther's glosses interpreting Pss. 1–30 in WA 55/I:1-288; further Ebeling, *Lutherstudien,* 1:143-45, 167-75, 181.

37. See the way Luther centered his understanding of faith on the Bible and the word as early as his marginal notes on the *Sentences* of Peter Lombard in WA 9:45.2-7 ("veritas scripturae et fidei"); 46.16-20; 62.19-24 ("quicquid supra fidem [i.e., to the biblical Word of God] additur, certissimum est figmentum esse humanum"); 65.11-22; 66.9f.; 84.6-8 ("credere oportet et verbis scripturae fidem profiteri et linguam illis aptare et non econtra"). Essentially this already implies the believing relation to the *verbum Christi* in WA 9:92.24 and 30-33. See also Luther's letter to Johannes Braun on March 17, 1509, and the sentence "Sed deus est deus; homo saepe, imo semper fallitur in suo iudicio." WA Br 1:17.44f., n. 5. On this topic, see Heiko A. Oberman, *Luther: Mensch zwischen Gott und Teufel* (Berlin: Severin und Siedler, 1981), 170f.

38. WA 3:649.1-5; *LW* 11:145. The word of Christ and faith in it are fixed in the heart: "in corde, id est in affectu sunt." See also WA 4:313.29; *LW* 11:425-26 ("Vivifica," i.e., *veritate*

As Luther continued to express it, this happens in a twofold way. God's speech — the biblical word about Christ — encounters sinners as a word of judgment and promise, *iudicium* and *promissio*.³⁹ People respond to both sides of the divine speech in faith. The judgmental word exposes and condemns them in their profound evil. At that point, faith means admitting the truth of this judgment, recognizing the desperate condition before God, and prayerfully confessing sins to God by personally applying that divine judgment that accuses, judges, and condemns.⁴⁰ Luther bun-

---

fidei) along with 314.7 ("Revela," i.e., "a cecitate primi peccati in intellectu, sicut 'vivifica' in affectu"). On Luther's understanding of the affects in his *Dictata super Psalterium*, see Günther Metzger, *Gelebter Glaube: Die Formierung reformatorischen Denkens in Luthers erster Psalmenvorlesung, dargestellt am Begriff des Affekts* (Göttingen: Vandenhoeck & Ruprecht, 1964); Schwarz, *Fides, spes und caritas*, 172-91; see also n. 48 below.

39. *Iudicium* and *promissio*, judgment and promise, are contrasting ways in which God encounters us in the biblical word. Since, however, as Luther continually emphasized in the *Dictata super Psalterium*, the salvific presence of God is always hidden for those on earth under the opposing form of the cross of Christ, the saving word of the gospel and its promise of future glory always meet the sinner as the message of the cross and therefore at the same time as the humbling judgment upon all the glory of the world and humankind, just as conversely the assurance of salvation is also hidden within the word of judgment for those who allow themselves to be humbled. *Iudicium* und *promissio* are thus to be clearly distinguished in their character yet at the same time intimately bound together in the spiritual understanding of the word of Christ — in the same way in which, as we shall see, *humilitas* and *spes* are bound together in the *fides Christi*. Thus Luther could let the afflicted request in prayer: "That is to say, 'Do not let the word of faith be silenced by me because of the opposition of the adversaries, but help me to speak and preach it all the more, because in Your judgments, etc., that is, in the very words of Your promise of things to come I have set my hope.' Or, secondly and better: 'When I am in Your judgments, that is, in Your sufferings and crosses, then I do not only hope, but hope exceedingly, that is, I hope more abundantly than otherwise, when I am outside.' Rom. 5:4 says: 'Patience works hope, etc.'; Ps. 60:8: 'Moab is the pot of my hope.' Indeed, that we too, acknowledging the grace of God, might indicate that we are making progress in writing and reading, it seems to me that 'judgments' and 'judgments of the mouth' are altogether different. 'Judgments' are the sufferings of Christ themselves, which abound in us, and the cup of the Lord which must be drunk" (WA 4:330.21-32; *LW* 11:449f.). On the two sides of Luther's understanding of the cross (judgment and peace), see WA 3:652.24-27; *LW* 11:150: "For according to its spiritual understanding, Holy Scripture is a nest. There Christ is concealed, to be sought and to be found. And the altar means the same, for it is the cross to which the flesh with its desires is nailed, as Christ was to His cross. When the flesh has been crucified, the rest and peace of the soul follows." On this topic, see also Brandenburg, *Gericht und Evangelium*, especially 33-42 and 86-88.

40. WA 3:287.20–293.21; *LW* 10:235-243.

dled this recognition, acceptance, confession, and self-condemnation together under the concept of humility *(humilitas)*. Faith now works in concert with humility.[41] Luther made this possible by setting humility in direct relationship to truth.[42] In humility, people do not make themselves less significant than they really are; instead, they apply the truth of the judgmental word of God to themselves, realizing that, as sinful creatures, they truly are nothing before God.[43] For Luther, the church's objective and doctrinal view of truth now begins with the personal existential prayer life of individual sinners.

At the same time this is happening, those who have come to the end of their possibilities for winning salvation are raised up and comforted by

41. WA 3:452.27-30; *LW* 10:404: God judges "First, tropologically, for He condemns the works of the flesh and the world. He shows that all that is in us and in the world is abominable and damnable in God's sight. Thus whoever clings to Him by faith necessarily becomes vile and nothing, abominable and damnable, to himself. And that is true humility." See also n. 53 below. The understanding of faith as *humilitas* continues unbroken into Luther's lectures on Romans (for example, with such formulations as *humilis fidei gemitus* or *humilitas fidei* in WA 56:276.34 and 282.12; *LW* 25:264 and 269); see also Matthias Kroeger, *Rechtfertigung und Gesetz: Studien zur Entwicklung der Rechtfertigungslehre beim jungen Luther,* Forschungen zur Kirchen- und Dogmengeschichte 20 (Göttingen: Vandenhoeck & Ruprecht, 1968), 41-85. It seems to me important, however, that while Luther integrated *humilitas* completely into *fides*, faith is not reduced without remainder to the dimension of *humilitas*, as became clear in the following discussion of the *spes* dimension of faith.

42. On the fundamental moment of truth in *fides* as *humilitas*, Kroeger rightly remarks that Luther's main concern in his lectures on the Psalms and Romans is "Gott selber nur überhaupt als Wirklichkeit zu gewinnen, und sei es in Zorn und Unheil, d.h. im Bekenntnis der Sünde und in der Rechtfertigung Gottes allein"; "Dieses Wiedergewinnen von Gottes Wirklichkeit, das nur im Bekennen der Wahrheit und im Glauben geschieht, ist der erschütternde und leidenschaftliche Sinn dieser frühen Theologie. Darum ist fides iustificans durchweg als confessio und humilitas verstanden." Kroeger, *Rechtfertigung,* 45.

43. WA 4:267.29-33; *LW* 11:401: "Therefore, in this consternation, that is, in this confusion, I said and experienced that man alone will not stand but become a liar, unless by help from above he remains truthful in the confession of faith. Or, because he said, 'I have been humbled exceedingly,' he learned in this affliction that every man is a liar and nothing, because he does not stand in temptation but falls from the truth and agrees to what is false, unless the Lord helped him." See also WA 4:272.32-38; *LW* 11:408. See also the central thought extended by Luther from the mendicant sphere to the universally Christian sphere that the faithful (the *pauperes Christi*) *are* poor and *confess* themselves as poor, in WA 3:87.12–88.14, and in the new series WA 55/I:80.7–84.5.

the divine word of promise. The truth of the promise lies in the truthfulness of God, that is, in God's trustworthiness to do what God has promised: on account of Christ, God forgives sin and brings people to eternal life out of pure mercy.[44] This firmly established word of promise awakens people to the bright and joyful side of faith. Faith is now identical with a confident hope, with *spes* and *fiducia* (faithfulness).[45] Humility and hope are tightly connected to each other (just as in the traditional views), but now within the bonds of faith.[46] Not only humility's deep doubt, which makes people unsure of themselves, but also hope's personal assurance of

---

44. WA 4:360.5-13; *LW* 11:490f.: "This, however, is a happy inheritance because it is eternal, for he says, 'I have purchased [it] for a heritage forever.' The promises of God gladden the heart of those who believe and hope in them. Therefore in the meanwhile we rejoice in faith and hope of things to come which God has promised us. We rejoice, however, because we are certain that He does not lie but will do what He promised and will remove from us every evil of body and soul and will grant us every good thing, and this without end. Who will not rejoice if he is certain that his body will be clothed with glory and immortality, brightness, strength, etc.? But he is certain if he believes. So great is it that he waits for it, because what he waits for will undoubtedly come to be." See also WA 3:287.1-9 and, in the new series, WA 55/I:776 ("Haec me consolata est spes, quia certa est, deus enim verax est in promissis, in humilitate mea") and WA 4:17.4–18.4; *LW* 11:170-71. On Luther's understanding of promise in the early lectures, see James Samuel Preus, *From Shadow to Promise: Old Testament Interpretation from Augustine to the Young Luther* (Cambridge: Harvard University Press, Belknap Press, 1969); Oswald Bayer, *Promissio: Geschichte der reformatorischen Wende in Luthers Theologie,* Forschungen zur Kirchen- und Dogmengeschichte 24 (Göttingen: Vandenhoeck & Ruprecht, 1971); Hamm, *Promissio,* 377-89.

45. WA 3:640.11–641.10, in the new series WA 55/I:584 ("Beati fideles omnes, qui habitant per fixam spem . . . in domo tua"); WA 4:332.26-33; *LW* 11:453 (the connection of *fides, spes, certificari, consolari,* and *gaudium* with the *verbum evangelii tui*); WA 4:264.14-16, 31-35, and in new series WA 55/I:754 (the *certe credere* establishes the *certa spes*); WA 4:314.10; *LW* 11:426 ("fac me confidere et certificari"); WA 4:380.33–382.24; *LW* 11:517-21 (on the joy of the one who believes/hopes in God's word of promise), as well as n. 44 above. What applies to *humilitas* (see n. 41 above) also applies to *spes*: Luther integrated them in the fulfillment of faith without reducing faith to hope; the hope that trusts and is assured of salvation is one of the significant dimensions of faith. To put it another way: faith is the basis of hope (as Luther emphasized particularly with reference to Heb. 11:1). See Schwarz, *Fides, spes und caritas,* 112f., 163-69, and 227-40. On Christ as ground of the trust and assurance of hope, see WA 3:56.31-42; *LW* 10:68.

46. WA 3:566.36-39; *LW* 11:47 (combination of *fides* with "de se et mundo desperare" and "nudus in domino sperare") and WA 4:207.7-12, in the new series WA 55/I:718 ("humiliati . . . desperantes de se et in deum sperantes").

salvation find their place through the right relationship to faith.[47] To medieval theologians, this kind of certainty of faith remained understandably foreign. As we saw earlier, such theologians had pushed the certainty of faith to an abstract level of truth, so that faith had to remain uncertain about how its inner qualities of virtue were being worked out on the personal level. By freeing the question of salvation from this question of qualitative and moral character, Luther was able to turn the certainty of hope into the certainty of faith. Here again, the general nature of the truth about faith fit together with the existential prayerful posture of the sinner before God.

From these observations, I offer the following conclusions and their significance:

1. For Luther, as in the preceding theological tradition, faith was related to the verbalized truth of revelation. For him, however, this should be understood exclusively as the biblical word of God. In this sense, word and faith create an essential unity within faith, so that what belongs to true faith has come through the new pathos of divine speech.

2. Because Luther described biblical truth as both the judging and the saving word of God that is addressed to the totality of human cognitive

---

47. See the evidence of the texts quoted in nn. 44 and 45 above. In regard to Luther's view of the firm assurance of faith and hope in his first two lecture series, it must admittedly be kept in mind that the character of assurance of salvation is also conditioned by the opposed forms of the divine revelation *sub contrario* (see n. 39 above). That explains the peculiarly fractured nature of his understanding of faith's assurance of salvation, which has misled some scholars into thinking that in his lectures on the Psalms and Romans Luther did not yet know the personal certainty of faith. He set great value on this firm *certitudo*, but combined it immediately with the complete despair of the sinner over all he possesses and can dispose of. Just as the saving message of the gospel is experienced as judgment on all "flesh" and its self-glorying, so too the believers' assurance in hope, holding fast to God's promise, is closely tied to that existential unsettling and *Anfechtung* that the humbling word of God works by confronting them with the reality of their desolate state and with the ire of the *deus iudex*. The situation of the believing sinner is thus characterized by an oscillation between assurance and uncertainty, between *spes* and *timor*. To this corresponds the formula, taken over from Augustine and repeatedly used in the Psalm lectures, that the believer has grace and salvation "only" in hope, not yet however in present reality: "tota vita fidelium est tantummodo in spe et nondum in re" (WA 4:259.2f., and in the new series WA 55/I:752); "omnis nostra letitia est in spe futurorum et non in re presentium" (WA 4:380.35f.; *LW* 11:518); "opera enim dei sunt intelligibilia, id est solum intellectu et fide perceptibilia in spe, non in re" (WA 3:367.34-36; *LW* 10:310); on this topic, see Lohse, *Luthers Theologie*, 74.

and affective existence, the concept of faith gained a new holistic breadth and depth.[48]

3. In a way that is also typical of the Middle Ages, faith is fundamentally a cognitive perception of revelation, a firm grasp of and adherence to the truth. In a manner very unlike the Middle Ages, however, faith then becomes conceptually identical with *humilitas* and *spes*, with both their distressing self-accusation and certainty of personal salvation.

4. To put it more precisely, the concept of faith incorporated humility and hope into itself, while *humilitas* and *spes* conversely aligned themselves with the concept of *fides*. They should no longer be understood as an inwardly formed quality of love but are now purely relational concepts, expressing a passive stirring of the heart through the speech of divine truth and goodness.[49]

5. In Luther's first lectures on the Psalms, the same thing happened to the concept of love. He assimilated it into faith — into faith's perceiving and judging — inasmuch as he understood the synonyms *caritas, dilectio,* and *amor* to describe the external relationship of the sinner to God's goodness and mercy, a warming of the heart through the power of the Holy Spirit. In this external sense, love is faith, together with humility and hope.[50] On the other hand, however, the active and operative side of love is quite different, with Luther distinguishing it as something that follows the justifying faith that leads to salvation.[51] He completely abandoned the

---

48. On the relation between *intellectus* and *affectus* in Luther's understanding of faith, see WA 4:107.31-34; see also Karl-Heinz Zur Mühlen, "Affekt II," in *Theologische Realenzyklöpadie* (Berlin: De Gruyter, 1977), 1:607, and "Luther II," 21:546; see also n. 38 above.

49. See Schwarz, *Fides, spes und caritas*, 169-72 (on *humilitas*, in critical response to Ernst Bizer), and 231-33 (on *spes*, especially on Luther's formulation of the *nuda spes*, which ought to cling to the *nuda verba* of God).

50. On the unity of faith, hope, and love, see WA 4:380.35-37; *LW* 11:518: "For this reason we rejoice, because we believe the divine promises, and we hope for and love the things which He promises." WA 4:8.10f.; *LW* 11:158: God "is united spiritually with our spirit through faith and love." On the understanding of faith as love in the power of the Holy Spirit, see Schwarz, *Fides, spes und caritas*, 112f., 187, 191, and 253f.

51. The believer, loving God and hoping in God, performs the works of love, as Luther puts it, "on the backside" (*posteriora dorsi*, Ps. 67:14 from the Vulgate) of his life: WA 3:396.14–397.2; *LW* 10:332. The fact that for Luther good works no longer constituted the contact between humankind and salvation did not prevent him at the same time from still describing works as *merita*, as in WA 3:396.39; *LW* 10:332; and WA 4:389.39; *LW* 11:531; see also Hamm, *Promissio*, 382 n. 177.

qualitative or habitual understanding of *caritas* that had been imparted so readily in tradition.⁵²

6. The entire trajectory of human salvation thus rested on faith. This is the faith that justifies.⁵³ As many research papers on the Psalms lectures have shown, for Luther this meant that faith puts sinners in their most basic relationship with Christ. It is a cognitive and affective relationship to Christ's righteousness that is brought existentially near through the word of judgment and salvation.⁵⁴ In its connection with the biblical word, faith thus became *the* christocentric relational basis for participation in Christ.⁵⁵

7. With this, faith took the central soteriological and eschatological place that love had held in the Middle Ages, a central place that had long been bound up in love's formative and operative qualities. After Luther, however, the formula went like this: love no longer forms faith; faith itself has become the form of a life guided by love.⁵⁶

8. The new central role of faith depended on Luther's rejection of the medieval difference — indeed separation — between the objective teaching about the limits of human self-awareness and the subjectivity pursued in an affective spiritual way of life. Through his concept of faith, he combined the abstract language about the church's doctrinal truth with the subjective and existential language of prayer.

Because it is so striking, I want to make absolutely clear that Luther

---

52. Schwarz, *Fides, spes und caritas*, 210-13.

53. See, for example, the evidence of the texts quoted above in n. 36 and below in n. 55; on the specific *humilitas* character of the *fides iustificans* of those who are "born" out of the word of God, see WA 3:345.26-30; *LW* 10:290.

54. Justification as an event of communication between the *iustitia Christi* and the *fides Christi* through the medium of *iudicium* and *evangelium/promissio* consists in the humbling of the believer together with the humiliated Christ and in being placed upright again with the exalted Christ; WA 3:431.40–432.25; *LW* 10:372; and WA 3:458.1-7; *LW* 10:401f. See also Schwarz, *Fides, spes und caritas*, 188-90.

55. WA 3:369.4; 3:458.8-11; 3:466.26f.; *LW* 10:312, 402, and 407f. ("Iustitia dei . . . tropologice est fides Christi"); WA 4:19.37-39; *LW* 11:174 ("Christus non dicitur iustitia . . . in persona sua nisi effective; sed fides Christi, qua iustificamur, pacificamur, per quam in nobis regnat"). See also Erich Vogelsang, *Die Anfänge von Luthers Christologie nach der ersten Psalmenvorlesung, insbesondere in ihren exegetischen und systematischen Zusammenhängen mit Augustin und der Scholastik dargestellt* (Berlin: De Gruyter, 1929), as well as nn. 57 and 58 below.

56. Luther's relational understanding of faith leaves no room for faith as a "form" in the sense of the Aristotelian *forma*.

first developed this new understanding of faith in a course on the Psalter. He, the professor of Holy Scripture and observant Augustinian monk, chose the prayer book of the canonical hours to be his teaching text. He understood the Psalms to be very much both christological and existential, as words of Christ and words about Christ,[57] which (in their tropological or moral sense) should relate to faith's perceiving, comprehending, and believing way of life.[58] We might indeed say that Luther's focus on the connection between the christological and tropological meaning of the Psalms — that is, the move toward the personal appropriation of Christ — shows what he meant by letting the truth of God's word communicate with believers' minds and emotions.[59] Far better than any other biblical text when interpreted and applied this way, the Psalter allowed him to express the kind of theology that was most important to him in that period around 1513. It was a kind of integrative biblical theology whose *modus loquendi* (way of speaking) connected the lecture hall with monastic prayer life. It was a theology that connected *lectio* and *oratio* (Scripture and prayer), *intellectus* and *affectus*, thinking and feeling, truth and experience.[60] This

---

57. See especially Luther's preface to the first Psalm lectures, which presents the hermeneutical foundations of his christocentric understanding of the Psalms in WA 3:12.11-13, 32; *LW* 10:4f., and in the new series WA 55/I:6-11; see also Ebeling, *Lutherstudien*, 1:109-31. See also Luther's view that all the works of creation and the old covenant are signs pointing to Christ as their fulfillment: "ideo Christus finis omnium et centrum, in quem omnia respiciunt et monstrant" in WA 3:368.18-24; *LW* 10:311.

58. Luther described the method of his tropological exegesis of the Psalms in this way: "Immo pro tropologia hec regula est. [Canon:] Quod ubicunque Christus in Psalmis conqueritur et orat in afflictione corporali ad literam, sub eisdem verbis queritur et orat omnis fidelis anima in Christo genita et erudita et in peccatum se tentatam vel lapsam agnoscens. Quia Christus usque hodie conspuitur, occiditur, flagellatur, crucifigitur in nobis ipsis. Item insidiatur ei usque modo sine intermissione caro sum sensibus, mundus cum voluptatibus suis et diabolus cum suggestionibus suis et tentationibus, sicut Christo Iudei secundum carnem." WA 3:167.20-28; 3:458.8-11; *LW* 11:402; on this topic, see also Ebeling, *Lutherstudien*, 1:1-68. See also n. 55 above.

59. On this christological sense of God's *iudicium* and *promissio*, see n. 39 above.

60. See also Luther's early letter of March 17, 1509, to Johannes Braun (n. 37 above); the sentence quoted above in n. 37 is preceded by the following characterization of a genuine theology that he wishes to emulate: ". . . ea inquam theologia, quae nucleum nucis et medullam tritici et medullam ossium scrutatur" (l. 43f.). So on the basis of its integrative character Luther's theology moves both on the "existential" and on the "objective" or "sapiential" level of expression; for an opposing view, see Otto Hermann Pesch, *Theologie der Rechtfertigung bei Martin Luther und Thomas von Aquin: Versuch eines systematisch-*

Why Did Luther Turn Faith into the Central Concept?

integrative theological program encapsulated Luther's new understanding of faith, that faith is not only awareness and mind but also integrates the darkness of grief and the brightness of joy.[61]

Luther did not stop at this concept of faith. In the years following he developed it so much further[62] that modern research cannot agree about whether the understanding of faith in the lectures on the Psalms and on Romans even belongs to the Reformation.[63] I content myself with the con-

---

theologischen Dialogs (Mainz: Matthias-Grünewald-Verlag, 1967), 937-41. Pesch interprets the difference between Luther and Thomas Aquinas essentially as the "Unterschied zwischen existentieller und sapientialer Theologie."

61. See Heiko A. Oberman, "Simul gemitus et raptus: Luther und die Mystik," in *Die Reformation: Von Wittenberg nach Genf* (Göttingen: Vandenhoeck & Ruprecht, 1986; original 1967), 45-89. Remarkable as it is that mystical terminology found its way into Luther's understanding of faith, especially after 1515, it is equally apparent on the other side that he did not come to his specific concept of faith via medieval mysticism, but found access to particular mystical traditions and concepts on the basis of his new concept of faith (the first lectures on the Psalms). This can be observed with the mystical concepts of *raptus* and *exstasis*, which he emphatically did not regard in the traditional mystical sense of being transported above the sphere of mere belief (see Oberman, 74-79), but as the illuminated recognition of faith, as in the gloss on Ps. 115:11 (Vulgate): "Exstasis illa ... est raptus mentis in claram cognitionem fidei, et ista est proprie exstatis," in WA 4:265.32f., in new series WA 55/I:756. On this topic, see Wolfgang Böhme, ed., *Von Eckhart bis Luther: Über mystischen Glauben* (Karlsruhe: Evan. Akad. Baden, 1981), especially the contributions of Heiko A. Oberman, Reinhard Schwarz, and Karl-Heinz Zur Mühlen on Luther's understanding of ecstasy. See also chap. 8 below.

62. This further development had already begun in the second half of the lectures on Romans; see Kroeger, *Rechtfertigung*, 152-63. See also Jared Wicks, *Luther's Reform: Studies on Conversion and the Church* (Mainz: Verlag P. von Zabern, 1992), 15-42.

63. It is striking that those scholars who dispute the Reformation character of this understanding of faith generally do not argue immanent-historically from a comparison with late medieval texts, but take their bearings from a predetermination within systematic theology and from a systematic theological interpretation of Luther. The historiographical value of such an obviously dogmatic interpretation of history is correspondingly limited. See, for example, the early attempt at such interpretation by Lennart Pinomaa, *Der existentielle Charakter der Theologie Luthers: Das Hervorbrechen der Theologie der Anfechtung und ihre Bedeutung für das Lutherverständnis* (Helsinki: Finnische Literaturgesellschaft, 1940); Pinomaa sees the "hervorbrechende Neue" in Luther (p. 143) first in the texts between spring 1515 and spring 1518, without drawing in any medieval texts at all for comparison. The same problem manifests itself in Ernst Bizer, *Fides ex auditu* (Neukirchen-Vluyn: Verlag der Buchhandlung des Erziehungsvereins, 1958). It is also discernible in those influenced by him to advocate a late dating of the Reformation breakthrough.

clusion that we can already observe a significant break (and maybe even the most important change) from the medieval view of faith in Luther's first series of lectures on the Psalms. For here already, the concept of faith displaced the medieval primacy of love as the central element for attaining salvation in the Christian life. And yet, his continuity with the medieval concept of faith could still be clearly seen. From his early theological training onward, the concept of faith presented itself to Luther as precisely the right way to express what was most important for him in 1513-15 and beyond: faith became the new fundamental relationship of the inner person to divine truth, which consisted not in working but in receiving.

In conclusion, we need to give a short reply to a fair question: Why appeal to the Middle Ages at all? Are not the biblical text and its clear language enough to explain why faith became the central concept for the Christian life in Luther's first lectures on the Psalms? There are many reasons for speaking against such a simple explanation, primarily the fact that the concept of faith occurs quite infrequently in the Vulgate translation[64] and that, as a consequence, Luther's view of faith in those lectures was neither purely biblical nor simply Pauline.[65] The biblical text itself does not explain the manner of its interpretation.[66] In this case, the decisive point is

---

64. The Vulgate formulation of Ps. 115:10, "Credidi, propter quod locutus sum," is at any rate significant; WA 4:266.23–268.28; *LW* 11:400. Generally, it is striking that at the numerous places where Luther's exegesis of the Psalms uses the terms *fides*, *fidelis*, and *credere*, the Psalm text itself hardly ever supplies them. One can indeed speak of a specific Paulinism in Luther even at the time of the lectures on the Psalms, yet he quotes relevant passages from Paul relatively seldom when emphasizing the concept of faith in the *Dictata*. It would therefore be an extreme short circuit to try to explain the new centrality of faith in the first lectures on the Psalms simply by reference to his intensified reference to the biblical text. It is remarkable, for example, that in seven of ten cases where the Vulgate Psalm text speaks of *intellectus*, Luther's glosses and/or scholia introduce the concept of faith without explicit reference to Paul, as in WA 4:342.4f.; *LW* 11:465: "'Da mihi intellectum,' id est spiritualem intelligentiam veritatis et fidei in litera latentis." The combination of *intellectus*, *veritas*, and *fides* indicates the wide horizon of Luther's theological training.

65. The weight placed in Luther's early concept of faith as humble self-recognition, self-judgment, self-damnation, and confession of sin is alien to the Pauline understanding, as are the style and fashion in which Luther contrasts faith and love.

66. For late medieval theologians heavily engaged in the study and interpretation of Paul (such as Johann von Staupitz), it would have been quite natural around 1513, when Luther began his work on the Psalms, to understand the Pauline *fides* in the sense of the *fides caritate formata* of standard teaching, just as Augustine's biblical exegesis was re-

the lens through which an interpreter reads the Bible to connect with various interpretive horizons within the text. Therefore, the key to understanding Luther's new role for faith can be found in how the personal horizon of his theological education and his existential *Anfechtung* engaged with the challenges of the biblical text.

In view of the frequently discussed question whether the Reformation should be understood as an event of radical change when compared to the world of the late Middle Ages or as a continuing process, I think that — within the paradigm of the theological *initia reformationis* (beginnings of the Reformation) — this chapter can show to what extent the Reformation is both. With its break from tradition and rapid change in values, it is a clear turning point. In its continuities, however, it carried on and developed traditional forms.

The impression of either sudden or gradual change depends mostly on which historical perspective one uses when viewing the fifteenth and sixteenth centuries and on which interests and questions one brings to the sources. This holds true for all epochal breaks that take place within a generation, for instance, for momentous years in twentieth-century Germany and Europe such as 1918, 1945, and 1989. Because the generation that experienced a period of radical change has nevertheless grown up in the rational and emotional categories of better or worse times, sudden new things are always seen as combinations or adaptations of the old. This is exactly what we can observe with Luther. He had, for instance, absorbed the teachings of late scholasticism and the practices of piety that were typical around the year 1500 with every fiber of his being. Thus, all his new theological discoveries stayed in a continuous stream with the so-called late Middle Ages. Naturally, we should always remember that this late medieval period of the fifteenth and early sixteenth century can also be seen as the early modern period, in which characteristic developments of the sixteenth and seventeenth century were already being announced. My own methodology about the "normative centralization" of religion and society is also meant to address the two-sidedness of the age.[67] In this case, the

---

ceived in this sense. Neither the concentration of Luther's work on the biblical text nor the influence of an intensified Paulinism can alone offer an adequate explanation for his new way of bringing the concept of faith into play.

67. See Berndt Hamm, "Reformation als normative Zentrierung von Religion und Gesellschaft," *Jahrbuch für biblische Theologie* 7 (1992): 241-79; Hamm, "Von der spätmittelalterlichen *reformatio* zur Reformation."

new central position of faith (first visible in Luther around 1513-15) had an essential role to play in that age's process of centralization. What I have described here is the process of clarification that led Luther to this new elevation of faith as the radiant center of the Christian life. The track record of Luther's public impact and his concept of faith after 1518-19 then stand on another level.[68] The successes of Luther the Bible professor who worked in the cloister and the lecture hall and of Luther the popular writer are naturally and inextricably bound together.[69]

---

68. See Bernd Moeller, "Das Berühmtwerden Luthers," *Zeitschrift für historische Forschung* 15 (1988): 65-92.

69. See Berndt Hamm, "Die Reformation als Medienereignis," *Jahrbuch für biblische Theologie* 11 (1996): 137-66.

CHAPTER 4

The Ninety-five Theses: A Reformation Text in the Context of Luther's Early Theology of Repentance

1. The Question of the "Reformation" Nature of the Ninety-five Theses

Quite apart from the famous question of whether or not Luther actually nailed the Ninety-five Theses onto the door of the Castle Church in Wittenberg (he did send them to his archbishop, Elector Albrecht von Brandenburg, on October 31, 1517), there arises a curious contradiction between the theses as a famous and monumental break in history and the judgments concerning them in recent research. Their publication is rightly considered to be the beginning of Luther's becoming well known, indeed famous, and thereby to mark the beginning of the Reformation as a public event. Luther quite publicly and intentionally overstepped the recognized limits when, with the criticism of the church presented in the theses, he addressed not only an internal university audience but also the church's hierarchy, those people responsible for the circulation of indulgences.

Therefore, he too remembered the day of October 31, 1517, as representing a fundamental break and the beginning of his public activity against the papacy.[1] To this very day, the Ninety-five Theses stand as most prominent of all the Reformation texts in Lutheran memory. It is thus all the more curious that a significant amount of Luther research has good reason for denying the "Reformation" or "evangelical" character of pre-

---

1. See Luther's letter to Nicholas von Amsdorf on November 1, 1527, WA Br 4:275.25-27 (no. 1164), and a table talk, WA TR 2:467.27-32 (no. 2455a/b).

cisely this text. In his unsurpassed 1981 biography of Luther, Martin Brecht offered the pregnant formulation: "When Luther was caught up in the dispute over indulgences he was not yet Evangelical."[2] He explained: "The attack on indulgences was therefore made strictly on the basis of a late medieval theology and piety."[3]

2. The Fundamental Attack on the Relevance of the Papacy and the Church Hierarchy for Salvation in the Hereafter

Even those who do not share this general assessment of the theses must nevertheless agree that, at least on first inspection, wide swaths of the theses move entirely in the reforming realm of the late Middle Ages. They stand in the tradition of a strongly internalized and mystically influenced theology of repentance;[4] they also continue sharp critiques of the hierarchy's use of indulgences, especially the papal jubilee indulgence campaign of the previous thirty years.[5] Regardless, what is immediately apparent is that Luther not only criticized indulgences as being scandalous, superficial, and harmful but also dared to make a fundamental attack on the church's reigning structures of authority. He made the connection between the church's penitential requirements and God's punishment of sin to be the overarching principle of his disputation, in the course of which he denied the pope's authority to bind and loose sins in the hereafter.[6] Luther leveled the authority and efficacy of the papacy, along with all the hi-

---

2. Martin Brecht, *Martin Luther: Sein Weg zur Reformation, 1483-1521* (Stuttgart: Calwer, 1981), 215.

3. Brecht, *Martin Luther*, 215f.

4. Volker Leppin, "'Omnem vitam fidelium penitentiam esse voluit' — Zur Aufnahme mystischer Traditionen in Luthers erster Ablassthese," *Archiv für Reformationsgeschichte* 93 (2002): 7-25.

5. On this topic see Wilhelm Ernst Winterhager, "Ablaßkritik als Indikator historischen Wandels vor 1517: Ein Beitrag zu Voraussetzungen und Einordnung der Reformation," *Archiv für Reformationsgeschichte* 90 (1999): 6-71, and David Bagchi, "Luther's Ninety-five Theses and the Contemporary Criticism of Indulgences," in *Promissory Notes on the Treasury of Merits: Indulgences in Late Medieval Europe*, ed. Robert N. Swanson (Boston: Brill, 2006), 331-55.

6. See Luther's theses on indulgences 5, 6, 8-13, 20-22, 25, 26, 28, 34, 61; *LW* 31:17-34. Since there are a multiplicity of German collections of the Ninety-five Theses, this chapter will use the American Edition of Luther's Works *(LW)* in reference to them. This chapter's preferred source is the *Studien Ausgabe*.

erarchical channels underneath it. According to Luther, papal and ecclesiastical sanctions should only apply to this world of the living and not extend somehow beyond death into an ominous purgatory. They have no valid relationship to the transcendent. The pope can therefore release people only from the earthly punishments he himself imposes, not from the punishments that God imposes. God's judgment is thereby removed in principle from papal authority.[7] Luther sharpened his attack on papal authority when he forcefully challenged the traditional doctrine of the church's treasury of merit, which was administered by the pope and through which the pope could grant the grace of indulgences that had been made available through the vast reservoir of the merits of Christ and the saints.[8] Again, he revoked papal claims on the hereafter. By the presumptuous authority of plenary indulgences, the pope magnanimously promised to release Christians from all earthly punishments for sin, in return for a payment of money. But to Luther, a repentant person receives all of that for free at the end of his or her life, even without the pope, bishops, and priests.[9] When viewed in the light of the human hopes for salvation and blessedness in the hereafter (the ubiquitous and definitive end goals of religiosity at that time), the church hierarchy represented by the pope became totally superfluous.[10] At the very least, those theses that relate to the punishment of sins in this life and beyond — papal and divine punishments — already reveal in retrospect a Reformation quality, the beginning of the break with traditional authority structures within Western Christendom.

---

7. This holds good not only for the remission of divine punishment but also for the forgiveness of sin, which, in Luther's view, lies solely in God's power, while the pope (as also the priests when giving absolution in confession) can only declare and confirm that God has released from sin: "Papa not potest remittere ullam culpam nisi declarando et approbando remissam a deo." Theses 6 and 38.

8. Theses 56-66, especially 58.

9. Theses 13 and 36.

10. Luther stressed, however, that one should not despise priests and the pope but should humbly subordinate oneself to the declarative function of their office (see n. 7 above and theses 7 and 38). So, too, the pope's authority to reserve for himself the remission of particular canonical church punishments *(casus reservati)* should not be scorned on pain of incurring new sin before God's judgment (thesis 6).

3. Luther's New Understanding of the Justifying Righteousness of God in the Years before the Ninety-five Theses

Still, the question remains whether this point concerning ecclesial authority gives enough reason to understand the Ninety-five Theses as a Reformation text that parted ways with the medieval views of grace and salvation. This does not appear to be the case. In any event, it is clear that the Ninety-five Theses do not give voice to the groundbreaking theology of justification that Luther had inaugurated in the previous years as a biblical interpreter and that he was at that same exact time articulating and pushing even further precisely through his lectures on Hebrews during the autumn, winter, and spring of 1517-18.[11] In short, our question becomes one of how Luther's new understanding of justification — especially his view of the righteousness of God *(iustitia Dei)* that justifies and accepts a person into eternal life — fundamentally differed from medieval theology. For him, justification was not a compartmentalized trait within God, which diagnosed and then rewarded or punished people on the basis of their qualities and their moral behavior. Instead, it was identical with the generous loving-kindness and mercy of God toward the sinner, for the just and merciful God had reckoned *(anrechnet* or *reputat)* the totally unworthy person as having the righteousness of the Son, Jesus Christ. Forgiveness of all sins and acceptance into eternal blessedness will be given to all who accept the promise *(promissio)* of this grace through firm faith in Christ, without needing to peer sideways at their own worthiness.

We know that in his famous autobiographical reflections of 1545 Luther described this relationship between the generous righteousness of God and its passive reception through faith as a door to a liberating under-

---

11. On the wealth of literature on the early Luther's theology of justification, the following works remain unsurpassed: Matthias Kroeger, *Rechtfertigung und Gesetz: Studien zur Entwicklung der Rechtfertigungslehre beim jungen Luther,* Forschungen zur Kirchen- und Dogmengeschichte 20 (Göttingen: Vandenhoeck & Ruprecht, 1968), especially 164-203 and 235-38, and Oswald Bayer, *Promissio: Geschichte der reformatorischen Wende in Luthers Theologie,* Forschungen zur Kirchen- und Dogmengeschichte 24 (Göttingen: Vandenhoeck & Ruprecht, 1971), 203-25. Researchers differ as to whether one should date the course on Hebrews (with Kroeger) in the summer semester of 1517 and the winter semester of 1517-18 or (with Bayer) in the winter semester of 1517-18 and the summer semester of 1518. I prefer Bayer's dating, but leave this lecture course out of consideration in my argumentation because of the problem of its dating and so that I can work exclusively with texts that can be dated with certainty.

standing of the apostle Paul's letter to the Romans.[12] And, in fact, we do find the basic structure of the theology of justification outlined above from the very beginning of Luther's 1515-16 lectures on Romans, including the new interpretation of *iustitia Dei*. Even the interpretation of the key passage, Romans 1:17, contains all the precision one could hope for.[13] Luther first made this new understanding of salvation, which could no longer be fitted into existing theological categories, available to the wider public in his first printed pamphlet of all: an interpretation of the seven penitential psalms that appeared in the spring of 1517. In that work, Luther reaped the harvest of his learned exegesis of Paul by transforming the theology of justification into a theology of piety for poorly educated "rough Saxons," as he described them in a letter.[14] This transformation can be seen in the interpretation of the first words of the seventh penitential psalm (Ps. 143:1), which in Luther's translation reads, "Hear my prayer, O Lord; give ear to my supplications because of Thy faith! Answer me in Thy righteousness!"[15] He commented,

> Here it should be noted that the little words "Thy faith" and "Thy righteousness" do not refer to the faith and the righteousness with which God believes and is righteous, as some have thought, but to the grace whereby God works faith in us and makes us righteous. Thus the apostle Paul in Rom. 1, 2, and 3 speaks of the righteousness and the faith of God given to us by the grace of Christ. A token or a painted gulden is not the real thing; it is only a representation. In fact, it is worthless and a fraud if it is given or considered as a real gulden, while a genuine gul-

---

12. Luther's preface to the first volume of his *Opera Latina* (March 5, 1545), WA 54:185.12–186.24; *LW* 34:336-37. On the interpretation of these texts within the framework of the question of Luther's "reforming change of direction," see the two volumes edited by Lohse: *Der Durchbruch der reformatorischen Erkenntnis bei Luther* (Darmstadt: Wissenschaftliche Buchgesellschaft, 1968) and *Der Durchbruch der reformatorischen Erkenntnis bei Luther: Neuere Untersuchungen* (Stuttgart: Franz Steiner Verlag, 1988), and Volker Lepping, "Luther-Literatur seit 1983, Teil II," *Theologische Rundschau* 65 (2000): 448-54.

13. WA 56:171.26–172.15; *LW* 25:151-53.

14. See Luther's letter to Christoph Scheurl on May 6, 1517, WA Br 1:93.6-8, on his exegesis of the penitential psalms: "Non enim Nurenbergensibus, id est delicatissimis et emunctissimis animabus, sed rudibus, ut nosti, Saxonibus, quibus nulla verbositate satis mandi et praemandi potest eruditio christiana, editae sunt."

15. "Ach Gott, erhore mein gebeet! Nym tzu deyn oren mein flehen yn deiner warheit, erhore mich yn deiner gerechtickeit!" WA 1:211.15f.; *LW* 14:195.

den is such in truth and without deception. So the life, work, and righteousness of the conceited saints is, in comparison with the righteousness and work of the grace of God, only a semblance and a deadly, harmful fraud if it is held to be the real thing. This is not truth; but the real truth is that of God, who gives the genuine and fundamental righteousness, namely, faith in Christ.[16]

4. The Absence of the Theme and Vocabulary of Justification in the Ninety-five Theses.

Luther had laid the foundations for his new Reformation views of justification, grace, and salvation well before the conflict over indulgences. In his first lectures on the Psalms (1513-15), he had also already shifted the central concept of a truly Christian life from love (so typical of the Middle Ages) to faith.[17] Despite all this, there is no trace of this language in the theses against indulgences. This is also seemingly absent in Luther's "Sermon on Indulgences and Grace,"[18] which appeared in March 1518. In that first published sermon in German, he intended to teach the people his pastoral objections to indulgences better than in the Ninety-five Theses.[19] Neither in the sermon nor in the theses did Luther speak of the themes and concepts of justification. The entire vocabulary of faith, trust, and certainty; of the peace and quiet of the comforted conscience; of the gospel as the assuring word of promise and forgiveness; and of the blessed righteousness of Christ as a *iustitia extra nos*, which gives saving protection to sinful humanity, was already well rehearsed. And yet, in his protest against the deceptive and seductive grace of the indulgences, Luther did not mention these ways of talking about the grace and goodness of God at all. In the Ninety-five Theses, he mentioned the grace of God and the gospel only briefly and generally.[20] Thesis 62 did oppose the teaching about the "treasure of the church" as a storehouse for the surplus merits of Christ, Mary, and the saints: "The true treasure of the church is the most holy gospel of the glory and grace of

---

16. WA 1:212.33–213.2.5-9; *LW* 14:196.
17. See chap. 3 above.
18. WA 1:239-46.
19. See the introduction by Clemen to the edition of the sermons in *Luthers Werke in Auswahl*, WA 1:10.
20. There is mention of *gratia* in theses 58 and 68. The "gospel" is discussed in theses 55, 62f., and 65.

God."²¹ But he did not say more. The main topic of the Ninety-five Theses is not the *gloria et gratia Dei* (the glory and grace of God) as the gift of righteousness and salvation, but rather, the lifelong repentance of the faithful, as seen in thesis 1. That is, the point was not faith itself but the life of the faithful *(vita fidelium)* as a life of continuous repentance.²²

5. The Saint Peter's Indulgence as an Offer of Relief and Security

It was quite natural that Luther addressed the problem of indulgences with theses from the practical perspective of confession rather than justification. Indulgences pertained to the ongoing task of people "doing enough" to pay off the temporal punishments of their sins until the hour of their deaths, taking care to see that their souls would be helped even amid the threats of purgatory; they were not related to the theological themes of guilt for sin, absolution, or justification. This process of "doing enough" *(satisfactio, Genugtuung)* was characterized by great insecurity, as no one could know how much temporal punishment God had assigned him or her. In the same manner as the jubilee indulgences of the previous decades, the Saint Peter's indulgence bundled together many offers of relief and security for the living and the dead who were making their way to salvation, so that — as the indulgence commissioners and preachers promised — even great sinners could attain the highest possible amounts of divine grace quickly and easily.²³ The plenary indulgence, which gave complete liberation from all temporal punishments and works of satisfaction, was only one of the three main elements within the papal package of grace.²⁴

---

21. *LW* 31:31. Thesis 62: "Verus thesaurus ecclesiae est sacrosanctum euangelium gloriae et gratiae dei."

22. *LW* 31:25, thesis 1: "When our Lord and Master Jesus Christ said, 'Repent' [Matt. 4:17], he willed the entire life of believers to be one of repentance."

23. Berndt Hamm, *Frömmigkeitstheologie am Anfang des 16. Jahrhunderts: Studien zu Johannes von Paltz und seinem Umkreis*, Beiträge zur historischen Theologie 65 (Tübingen: Mohr, 1982), 284-91.

24. Hamm, *Frömmigkeitstheologie*, 289: The jubilee package of grace also contained, along with the plenary indulgence for the living and the dead, special reductions for the admittance to the sacrament of confession, that is, to a complete forgiveness of all guilt for sin through the absolution in the sacrament. Moreover, a third main grace of the jubilee was the *fraternitas papalis oder generalis*, that is, the participation *(participatio)* granted by the pope in works of satisfaction, intercessions, and other spiritual goods of

6. Luther's Counterpoint in the Ninety-five Theses: A Lifetime of True Christian Repentance

Luther answered the church hierarchy's campaign for relief and certainty by making a counterpoint about true Christian repentance in the theses and in their accompanying letter to Archbishop Albrecht.[25] He characterized this as a lifelong process of radically giving up all the relief and assurances of confession. Instead, Christian repentance finds its truth and authenticity in the innermost soul as true inner repentance *(poenitentia vera intus)*[26] because the person is filled with true sorrow for sin *(veritas contritionis)* under the influence of God's grace.[27] True repentance fills the soul with *odium sui*,[28] the hatred of one's own sinful self. As Luther stressed, this repentant conversion of the inner person *(homo interior)* changes one's fundamental attitude to the suffering and activities of the outer person *(homo exterior)*.[29] While the offer of indulgence tempts one to scorn God's punishments and to take flight from them, the true attitude of repentance proves to be an internal agreement with the punishments, a "piety of the cross" *(crucis pietas)*.[30] For Luther, this meant that the motivation of love spans one's entire life. *Contritio* itself is an effect of grace that comes from the love of God. It is therefore also a love of God's righteousness[31] and the opposite of *odium sui*.

---

the *ecclesia universalis* and her members. Everyone could acquire this brotherhood for himself or in favor of other living people or even for the dead. On these three principal graces, see also the instruction on the jubilee indulgence by Cardinal Albrecht, the *instructio summaria* for the archbishopric of Magdeburg and the diocese of Halberstadt in 1517 in Peter Fabisch and Erwin Iserloh, eds., *Dokumente zur Causa Lutheri, I* (Münster, 1988), 246-93. The total indulgence for the souls in purgatory is cited here specifically as a fourth principal grace of the jubilee.

25. Luther's letter to Cardinal Albrecht of Brandenburg, October 31, 1517, WA Br 1:108-13 (no. 48); LW 48:43-48.

26. LW 31:25, thesis 4: "The penalty of sin remains as long as the hatred of self, that is, true inner repentance, until our entrance into the kingdom of heaven."

27. Luther speaks of the *contritionis veritas* in theses 39 and 40.

28. See n. 26 above.

29. Luther differentiates between *homo interior* and *homo exterior* in this sense expressly in thesis 58.

30. LW 31:31, thesis 68: "They are nevertheless in truth the most insignificant graces when compared with the grace of God and the piety of the cross."

31. On *amor iustitiae*, see n. 77 below and Luther's companion letter to the explanation of the Ninety-five Theses to Johann von Staupitz on May 30, 1518, WA 1:525.12; LW 48:64-69.

For these reasons, *contritio* faces the punishments that plague the outer person all through life with love and eagerness instead of an attempt to avoid them. Thesis 40 thus states, "A Christian who is truly contrite seeks and loves to pay penalties for his sins."[32]

Growing from the innermost pain of contrition, this agreement with the punishment and cross of the *homo exterior* means that Christians have a way to keep their bodies in check. That is, their entire lives can practice the repentance demanded by Christ as "various outward mortifications of the flesh" *(varias carnis mortificationes),* as Luther put it in thesis 3.[33] He later took up this idea in his 1520 tract on freedom *(The Freedom of a Christian),* in which he drew out the conclusions about how the faithful orientation of the inner person addresses the command given to the outer person about the "mortification of the desires" *(mortificatio concupiscentiarum),*[34] defining the *mortificatio* in terms of the triad of "fasting, watching, working," whose tasks are to subdue the "mischief" of the body.[35] Without a doubt, Luther was taking up the monastic understanding of repentance that described the lifelong task of *satisfactio* above all as self-castigation, as mortification of the desires of the flesh.

Along with traditional requirements about "doing enough" also belonged the large but often misunderstood concept of almsgiving *(eleemosyna),* namely, the merciful care of one's neighbors. Because of this, it was natural that Luther identified the outward effect of true, internal, God-loving repentance as a central theme in the Ninety-five Theses. Calling these effects "good works of love" *(bona opera charitatis)*[36] or "works of mercy" *(opera misericordiae),*[37] he spent two theses addressing the old saying, "Repentance is better than indulgence."[38] He wrote in theses 43 and

---

32. *LW* 31:29.
33. *LW* 31:25.
34. *StA* 2:286.35; *LW* 31:357-58.
35. *StA* 2:287.84f.; *LW* 31:358: "here he must indeed take care to discipline his body by fastings, watchings, labors, and other reasonable discipline and to subject it to the Spirit so that it will obey and conform to the inner man and faith and not revolt against faith and hinder the inner man, as it is the nature of the body to do if it is not held in check."
36. Thesis 41.
37. Thesis 42.
38. On the meaning of this phrase in the late Middle Ages, see Jean Gerson, *De indulgentiis* 13, in *Oeuvres complètes,* ed. Glorieux, 10 vols. (Paris: Desclée, 1960-73), 9:656; Johannes von Paltz, *Supplementum Coelifodinae,* ed. Berndt Hamm (Berlin: De Gruyter, 1983), 71.26–72.8; Johann von Staupitz, *De exsecutione aeternae praedestinationis,* §195

44: "Christians are to be taught that he who gives to the poor or lends to the needy does a better deed than he who buys indulgences. Because love grows by works of love, man thereby becomes better. Man does not, however, become better by means of indulgences but is merely freed from penalties."[39] In the Ninety-five Theses, this second outward dimension of true lifelong repentance (caring for neighbors) clearly outweighed the first outward dimension (the mortification of the flesh). This care for neighbors quite naturally also raised the highly controversial financial aspect of the indulgences.[40] The inward and outward sides of repentance each raised alternatives to buying indulgences. Instead of the easy escape from punishment, they offered the willing, arduous, and lifelong way of repentance: a way of self-punishment and self-giving.[41]

In addition to this, Luther's theses raised a third dimension of perpetual arduous repentance, which Luther likewise attached to the outer person. It belongs to the first two dimensions but goes beyond them by asserting that a person's entire life is an experience of the cross and punishment, death and hell, and a destruction of all earthly and religious certain-

---

(p. 254 with n. 79). See also Willigis Eckermann, "Buße ist besser als Ablaß: Ein Brief Gottschalk Hollens an Lubertus Langen," *Analecta Augustiniana* 32 (1969): 323-66; Hamm, *Frömmigkeitstheologie*, 285f.; and Lothar Graf zu Dohna and Richard Wetzel, "Die Reue Christi: Zum theologischen Ort der Buße bei Johann von Staupitz," *Studien und Mitteilungen zur Geschichte des Benediktinerordens und seiner Zweige* 94 (1983): 475 and 481.

39. *LW* 31:29. See also Luther's letter to Albrecht von Brandenburg, *LW* 48:47.

40. The financial aspects of the Saint Peter's indulgence in continuity with the combination of indulgences and the financial system that was already a century old and Luther's criticism of this are depicted clearly and concisely in Ulrich Barth, "Die Geburt religiöser Autonomie: Luthers Ablaßthesen von 1517," in *Aufgeklärter Protestantismus* (Tübingen: Mohr Siebeck, 2004), 62-69. The research on this topic generally overlooks that, at the end of the Middle Ages, most indulgences could be attained without a payment of money — e.g., by offering particular prayers before a print or a pictorial epitaph with an inscription; see also Berndt Hamm, "Die Nähe des Heiligen im ausgehenden Mittelalter: Ars moriendi, Totenmemoria, Gregorsmesse," in *Sakralität zwischen Antike und Neuzeit*, ed. Berndt Hamm, Klaus Herbers, and Heidrun Stein-Kecks (Stuttgart: Steiner, 2007), 197-219.

41. Luther stressed the difficulty of this way to salvation particularly in his letter to Albrecht of Brandenburg in October 1517; WA Br 1:111.27-32; *LW* 48:46. On the late medieval tradition in which Luther stands here, see Berndt Hamm, "Die 'nahe Gnade' — innovative Züge der spätmittelalterlichen Theologie und Frömmigkeit," in *"Herbst des Mittelalters"? Fragen zur Bewertung des 14. und 15. Jahrhunderts*, ed. Jan A. Aertsen and Martin Pickavé (Berlin: De Gruyter, 2004), 543, 546, 556.

ties. This is not simply an active repentance but even more the passive experience of hardships and afflictions that Luther called *tribulationes*.[42] These existential tremors wrest away from the penitent person everything that the indulgence preachers valued: ease, certainty, and peace. They block the indulgences' escape route into a false confidence of salvation. By contrast, with the basic attitude of *contritio*, Christians can take up their cross[43] in love and thereby take on the form of Christian discipleship. Passivity and activity, the outer and the inner person, are therefore no longer to be separated. This is precisely the sense in which Luther reinterpreted the first thesis about the lifelong repentance of the faithful[44] in his last two theses: "Christians should be exhorted to be diligent in following Christ, their head, through penalties, death, and hell; And thus be confident of entering into heaven through many tribulations rather than through the false security of peace [Acts 14:22]."[45]

In conclusion, therefore, we can say that the trajectory of true repentance that Luther contrasted to the relief and security offered by the sale of indulgences is an arc that defines all aspects of human existence: internal and external, passive suffering and active formation. It is a trajectory of difficulty and uncertainty, of the cross and love. It is a life on the edge of despair, a *desperatio sui*,[46] in which penitent people cannot even be sure of the authenticity of their *contritio*.[47] Luther understood this lifelong repentance as a purgatory on earth: a healing purgatory in which the fear of punishment departs to the extent that love enters.[48] Where punishment is recognized and loved as a divine instrument of healing, it loses its terror.

---

42. See n. 45 below; thesis 95.

43. On the life of the cross ("Crux, crux!"), see thesis 93 and (in n. 30 above) thesis 68: *crucis pietatem*.

44. See n. 22 above.

45. *LW* 31:33.

46. See nn. 60 and 79 below.

47. *LW* 31:28, thesis 30: "No one is sure of the integrity of his own contrition, much less of having received plenary remission." See also Luther's letter to Albrecht of Brandenburg, in which he wrote that people could be certain of salvation through the grace poured into them; WA Br 1:111.27f.; *LW* 48:46-47.

48. See theses 14-17. On Luther's existentialization of purgatory, see Notger Slenczka, "'Allein durch den Glauben': Antwort auf die Fragen eines mittelalterlichen Mönchs oder Angebot zum Umgang mit einem Problem jades Menschen?" in *Luther und das monastische Erbe*, ed. Christoph Bultmann, Volker Leppin, and Andreas Lindner (Tübingen: Mohr Siebeck, 2007), 301-9.

7. The Ninety-five Theses in the Context of the Late Medieval Internalization of Repentance

From this aspect of the Ninety-five Theses, the question of their Reformation character arises anew and with more intensity. Where do these theses depart from the typical medieval understanding of repentance? Many reform-minded authors from the fourteenth to the beginning of the sixteenth century, especially mystical theologians and theologians of piety influenced by mysticism, appear to have anticipated the potential theological content of the theses in all essential points. Time and again, their writings highlighted the centrality of repentance as a comprehensive way of life, which grows on the foundation of true penitential love and reverence for Christ's passion. The lifelong process of "doing enough" comes less in external works but much more in the internal conformity to the Crucified as an ongoing process of humility and equanimity. People should surrender their self-will and entrust themselves in patient, prayerful devotion to all that the righteous and gracious God asks of them through cleansing punishments, including sufferings, afflictions, and even the bitter experience of being forsaken by God. In this internal understanding of repentance, a central role comes in the idea that true repentance with abhorrence of sin is always connected to love of God's righteousness, an *amor iustitiae*, which perceives the "sweetness" of God's desire to be merciful amid the "bitterness" of God's justice.[49] Volker Leppin has interpreted Luther's first thesis on indulgences — and thereby the concept of repentance across the Ninety-five Theses — as an "assimilation of mystical traditions" influenced by Luther's mentor Staupitz and Staupitz's 1515 lectures on Tauler.[50] In doing so, he has placed the theses in this wider context of the late medieval internalization of repentance, which I have briefly described here. In fact, the succession of authors and texts who appear to have anticipated the penitential theology of the Ninety-five Theses stretches from Johannes Tauler to Johannes von Staupitz.[51]

---

49. A typical representative of such a spiritual understanding of penitence in the years before the Reformation was Luther's superior in the order, his teacher and father confessor Johann von Staupitz. See Dohna and Wetzel, "Die Reue Christi," and chap. 2 above. On Staupitz's key phrase *amor iustitiae*, see n. 31 above.

50. Leppin, "'Omnem vitam fidelium penitentiam esse voluit' — Zur Aufnahme mystischer Traditionen in Luthers erster Ablassthese."

51. While Leppin (see n. 50) interprets the Ninety-five Theses from the late medieval internalization and making immediate of ideal penitence, there is also in the current

The question, however, is whether this interpretation does justice to the intention of the Ninety-five Theses in the context of late 1517, when Luther had already gained new insights into the theology of justification and repentance in the preceding years. The classification of the Ninety-five Theses hangs decisively on this point. Therefore, I will now remind us of important aspects of Luther's theological biography before October 1517, paying close attention to the significance of the concept of faith and the relationship between justification and repentance.

8. The Years of Luther's First Two Lectures (1513-16): An Integrative Concept of Faith and a Unity in the Theology of Justification and Repentance

When inquiring into the beginning of Luther's Reformation reorientation, we arrive at the period just before his first lectures on the Psalms, which he started preparing in the summer of 1513. From its very beginning, the interpretation of Psalms reveals that Luther had reached the end of his monastic drive for perfection and had realized the total worthlessness of his attempts to achieve sanctification before God. Confronted with the damning judgment of God, as Luther then asserted, a person has nothing to offer but sins and total unworthiness.[52] From that perspective, the Psalms lectures document a radical theology of repentance and the complete demolition of any human quality of holiness and virtue. It is a work that articulated the same inner attitude of repentance that Luther later described in thesis 4 as self-hatred and the abhorrence of one's own self *(odium sui)*.[53] Most remarkable

---

interpretation of Luther a tendency to perceive "the new religious ideal" of the Reformation in Luther's inward turn such as can be seen in his high regard for lifelong "true repentance"; thus Barth, "Die Geburt religiöser Autonomie," 78 and 80. Similarly, for Karl Holl the theses are interpreted as proof of Luther's epochal discovery of the "religion of the conscience" and — beyond Holl — "as the birth of religious autonomy." In Luther's "liberating act" can be heard the free voice "of the religious awareness itself which has achieved certain knowledge of its true being and consequently sues for the recovery of its free, unhindered fulfillment" (94). In what follows I shall show that this interpretation of the Ninety-five Theses that focuses on the inwardness and subjectivity of the conscience is too narrow and leaves out of consideration their important progression beyond the late medieval variants of the spiritualization of repentance.

52. On this interpretation of Luther's first lectures on the Psalms, see chap. 2 above.
53. See n. 26 above.

of all is how this interpretation of the Psalms integrated a theology of justification into this penitential attitude, such that the penitential attitude grounds its humility *(humilitas)* within the larger concept of faith.[54] Given a new central role in God's justification of sinners by Luther (contrary to the received tradition), faith presents two basic relationships to God's word. First, faith as humility accepts the divine word of judgment by shamelessly recognizing one's own wretchedness, despairing of oneself, confessing sins, and personally condemning oneself. Second, faith as a confident hope allows for the appropriation of the divine word of salvation in the equally radical recognition of God's gift of faithfulness to the divine promise. In this way, amid the destruction of all that they are and can do, believers are restored and comforted. Both the relationship of humility to the *iudicium Dei* and the relationship of hope to the *promissio Dei* have fundamentally christological roots, in which afflicted and humbled sinners experience the afflictions of Christ's cross themselves. Under the "form of opposites," however, the cross masks the saving presence of God. When afflicted people see themselves in Christ's suffering, they can also base their own salvation on the certainty offered by that same Crucified One.

In Luther's lectures on the Psalms, faith is an integrative concept, whose two-sided theology of justification assimilates the poles of condemnation and acquittal, despair and confidence, humility and hope, uncertainty and certainty. Faith also integrates the lifelong journey of repentance with the justification of sinners. The basic principles of true repentance and the love of God's righteousness and goodness similarly belong to the essence of faith. In the medieval tradition, all these concepts like humility, hope, and love were described as habits of virtue and as qualities. Now, through their alignment with faith, they became purely relational concepts for expressing the heart's being moved passively by God's call, while offering no spiritual basis for a way of salvation through the *iustitia activa*.

In his lectures on Romans (1515-16), Luther further extended his integrative, two-sided understanding of faith.[55] The new understanding of *iustitia Dei* came to have such a value that Luther could turn this righteousness of God into the comprehensive saving reality that God gives to sinners, which also puts a limit on righteous condemnation. Similarly, the negative attitude of humility and self-condemnation on the part of the

---

54. On what follows, see chap. 3 above.
55. On the following, see Kroeger, *Rechtfertigung*, 41-163.

sinner is surrounded by the positive attitude of faithful and hopeful trust. Luther clearly showed the relational (rather than the qualitative, substantial, or ontological) character of *iustificatio*[56] by describing justification as a decisive instance of imputation *(reputatio* or *imputatio)*,[57] when the imputed righteousness of Jesus Christ becomes *iustitia externa* and *aliena*.[58] The righteousness that protects and saves sinners is therefore an external, alien righteousness because it never becomes personal property but always remains — as the righteousness of Jesus Christ — a righteousness that is imputed. It only becomes liberating divine gift of salvation for sinners through the trusting and humble relationship of faith.

In a well-known letter of April 8, 1516, written to Georg Spenlein, a former fellow brother in Wittenberg's Augustinian cloister, Luther quite succinctly expressed that integrative view of faith from his first lectures, with its combinations of dark and light, bitterest despair and "sweetest consolation" *(dulcissima consolatio)*.[59] He extended this two-sided structure to the phrase "trusting despair" *(fiducialis desperatio)* when he wrote, "you will find peace only in him and only when you despair of yourself and your own works. Besides, you will learn from him that just as he has received you, so he has made your sins his own and has made his righteousness yours."[60] The despair of self and of all one's own quality and morality can therefore become a comforting resignation, because believing

---

56. Luther spoke expressly of *relatio* in the early Romans lectures; WA 56:269.8 and 13; *LW* 25:257. The Aristotelian category of relation here stands in antithesis to the categories of *qualitas* and *habitus*. See also the later text from the doctoral disputation of Joachim Mörlin (1540): "Christianus est dupliciter considerandus, in praedicamento relationis et qualitatis. Si consideratur in relatione, tam sanctus est quam angelus, id est imputatione per christum, quia Deus dicit se non videre peccatum propter filium suum unigenitum, qui est velamen Mosi, id est legis. Sed christianus consideratus in qualitate est plenus peccato." WA 39/II:141.1-6. The *velamen Mosi* is a reference to 2 Cor. 3:12-16.

57. WA 56:268.26–273.2, particularly 269.2 ("ex sola dei reputatione"); *LW* 25:257-60.

58. WA 56:158.10–159.24; *LW* 25:136f.

59. WA Br 1:33-36, no. 11; *LW* 48:11-14. To the "de te ipso desperans" ("despairing of yourself") there stand in contrast the words "Istam charitatem eius [Christi] rumina, et videbis dulcissimam consolationem eius" ("Meditate on this love of his and you will see his sweet consolation").

60. *LW* 48:13; WA Br 1:35.33-36: "Igitur non nisi in illo, per fiducialem desperationem tui et operum tuorum, pacem venies; disces insuper ex ipso, ut, sicut ipse suscepit te et peccata tua fecit sua, et suam iustitiam fecit tuam."

sinners know that they are received into the reciprocal event of the "happy exchange" in which their sins will be reckoned to Christ and Christ's righteousness reckoned to them.[61] Like the contemporaneous lectures on Romans, the letter to Spenlein is a clear witness to the complete unity of the theology of justification and repentance within Luther's early theology, a unity in which the experience of penitential change and remorse is so extensively pervaded and altered by the theology of justification that the classical penitential term *contritio*, which one might actually expect at every turn, is almost totally missing, replaced or eclipsed by concepts such as humility, self-condemnation, and despair.

9. The Fascination with Tauler's Mysticism and Luther's "Journey Outward"

When he was working on Romans and writing the letter to Spenlein (1515-16), Luther came across the mystical sermons of the south German writer and Dominican friar Johannes Tauler, to which he added marginal notes (*Randbemerkungen*).[62] The experience reading Tauler was electrifying for Luther. A few months later he had a similar experience when reading the lectures of a late medieval author, the so-called Frankfurter, who had also been strongly influenced by Tauler. At first, Luther even thought that this was a tract genuinely written by Tauler.[63]

However one weighs the importance of Tauler's mysticism, in terms of Luther's theological development it seems clear to me that these strong

---

61. Luther had already used this motif of exchange to talk about justification when he was composing his lectures on Romans and the letter to Spenlein. This motif appears most prominently then in *The Freedom of a Christian* (1520) (*LW* 31:351f.; §12: WA 7:25.26–26.12 [German] and 54.31–55.36 [Latin]). Luther articulated what is surprising in this exchange, which, from the perspective of all earthly exchanges with their proportion of offer and gift in return, must appear absurd, at the end of this passage in the text with the exclamation: "Quae proportio! Sic, sic, etiam sic!" Thus, at the time the theses were written, this motif had already entered Luther's view.

62. Henrik Otto, *Vor- und frühreformatorische Tauler-Rezeption: Annotationen in Drucken des späten 15. und frühen 16. Jahrhunderts* (Gütersloh: Gütersloher Verlagshaus, 2003), 183-214.

63. Andreas Zecherle, "Die 'Theologia deutsch': Ein spätmittelalterlicher mystischer Traktat," in *Gottes Nähe unmittelbar erfahren: Mystik im Mittelalter und bei Luther*, ed. Berndt Hamm and Volker Leppin (Tübingen: Mohr Siebeck, 2007), 1-95.

impressions enriched and deepened Luther's new theology of faith in the realm of experience without changing its framework.[64] What fascinated Luther about Tauler's mysticism and what first resonated with his own work was the dominant leitmotif of passivity: people do not move actively and determinedly toward God; instead, all their own supports are taken away by God, leaving only the tranquility of being totally overwhelmed by God's healing work. Next, then, Tauler became Luther's teacher of doubt-filled *Anfechtung* and confident despair. Tauler showed him a mysticism that included the bitterest experiences of God's absence, his own triviality, and the twin poles of hellish distance from God and blessed nearness to God. Luther understood this polarity in terms of his two-sided and integrative view of faith. In doing so, however, he took an entirely different direction than medieval mysticism.[65] Where Tauler's radical internalization of repentance climaxed in the innermost soul's experience of a blessed birth in God, Luther countered by setting the desperate and total internal emptiness of personal unworthiness next to the external dimension of the alien righteousness of Christ *extra nos*.[66] Through faith, sinners are not driven ever deeper into themselves but are raised out of themselves from the innermost depths of their existence into the generous riches of divine righteousness and assurance of salvation.

10. Separating Luther's Theology of Justification and Repentance, of *Fides* and *Contritio*, in 1517

In the following months and years, Luther consistently pursued this outward journey in such a way that his overall Reformation reorientation exists as a wide arc that contains several main points and elaborations within it. In the first months of 1517 at the latest, the increasing turn from inward to outward led to a revision of his concept of faith, through which Luther released himself from an integrative understanding of faith that encompassed the two poles of humility and hope, of self-despair and comforting trust in Christ's promised righteousness, in order to combine the concept of *fides* only with the bright side of the relationship to God: assurance, trust, hope, joy, cer-

---

64. See chap. 8 below, especially sections 20 and 21.
65. See chap. 8 below, especially section 22.
66. Karl-Heinz Zur Mühlen, *Nos extra nos: Luthers theologie zwischen Mystik und Scholastik*, Beiträge zur historischen Theologie 46 (Tübingen: J. C. B. Mohr, 1972).

tainty, and security.⁶⁷ But this meant a change in the whole structure of his theology. Up to this point, he had followed the theological traditions of the late Middle Ages, especially in the functional unity of the theology of piety, justification, and repentance.⁶⁸ Now, however, justification and repentance separated from each other. True repentance lost its relevance in the theology of justification. Concepts like *poenitentia, humilitas, desperatio sui, odium sui, gemitus* (lamentation), and the now prominent concept of true sorrow for sin *(contritio)* describe a basic attitude in which people who love God willingly accept God's just punishments as a life under the cross without thereby being taken away from their mental anguish and their being justified. By contrast, with its relationship to concepts like *fiducia* and *spes*, the concept of faith denotes the inner focus on God's justifying righteousness, which gives peace, rest, certainty, and security to troubled consciences. This separation of terms later found its final expression when Luther described the new understanding of repentance he received from Staupitz without mentioning its theological origins in justification.⁶⁹ Conversely, he related his discovery of the Pauline sense of "the righteousness of God" without getting into its earlier implications for the theology of repentance.⁷⁰

This separation of concepts can be seen very clearly in the interpretation of the seven penitential psalms mentioned earlier, which in the spring of 1517 was Luther's first published pamphlet. As I showed in an example from the text, he related the concept of faith exclusively to the righteousness of God given in Christ, without entering into the vocabulary of repentance⁷¹ and without mentioning themes like confession, humility,

---

67. A certain tendency in this direction can already be seen in the later parts of the lectures on Romans; see Kroeger, *Rechtfertigung*, 152-63. In my opinion, the change becomes obvious already at the end of 1516 when, in his sermon of December 7, Luther names the real intention of the gospel — in contrast to despair, which arises from the effect of the law understood spiritually — as help, healing, and joy and links particularly this joyful gospel with faith; WA 1:105.19-31. See also Kroeger, 229f. and 233f.

68. A typical representative of the theology of piety in the years before the Reformation was the Augustinian hermit from Erfurt, Johannes von Paltz (d. 1511). Paltz is also typical in that in his handbook for pastors, *Supplementum Coelifodinae*, he treats the topic of justification *(iustificatio impii)* in the large section on repentance and here under the wider topic of remorse (223-32).

69. Luther's letter to Staupitz, WA 1:525-27; LW 48:64-69; see also Leppin, "Omnem vitam," 8-14, and chap. 2 above, especially section 7.

70. See n. 12 above.

71. See n. 16 above. All the other places in the interpretation of the penitential psalms that mention faith likewise do not include humility, regret, despair of oneself, and

and penitence.[72] For example, he began his interpretation of Psalm 51:1 ("Have mercy on me, O God, according to your steadfast love") with the words: "A true and penitent heart sees nothing but its sin and misery of conscience."[73]

Luther had separated the concept of faith from the vocabulary of repentance. When he did that, he began to differentiate more clearly between the theology of justification and the theology of repentance, prying faith and justification away from the otherwise continuously oscillating poles of despair and comfort, judgment and grace, law and gospel, the inner state of mind and the external gift of salvation. As one who has faith and is justified, the sinner now clearly stands on the bright side of a conscience that has found rest, peace, and certainty. It is clear that salvation is not dependent on some disposition or quality of repentance.

This separation of the perspectives of repentance and justification in the period before the Ninety-five Theses explains how, in 1517, Luther published a sermon on repentance and another on indulgences and a tract on indulgences without mentioning a word about faith and its comforting relationship of trust in God.[74] This is particularly true of the sermon on in-

---

condemnation as part of faith: WA 1:165.20-24; 175.15f.; 187.32f.; 188.20f.; 199.7; 206.8; 209.18-23; 210.9-13, 15-23; 212.21; 216.9 (the penitential psalms appear in *LW* 14:137-205). It is typical that Luther equated faith with firm trust, confidence, and hope (WA 1:175.15f.), or waiting, hoping, trusting, and depending on God (WA 1:209.19 and 21f.), and so set faith absolutely on its positive foundation of God's promise: "und dasselb wort und vorheyßen gottis ist der gantze enthalt des newen menschen" (WA 1:209.22f.).

72. WA 1:165.11-17; 175.17-22; 178.2-4; 185.26–186.8; 186.11-15; 197.1f.; 198.8-11, 16-19; 199.34–200.2; 201.10-21; 202.3-5, 16-25; 206.29-32; 213.25f.; 216.28-32.

73. *LW* 14:166; WA 1:185.35-38: "'Erbarme dich meyner, ach got, nach deyner großen barmhertzickeit!' Eynen warhafftigem rewigen hertzen ligt nichtz vor augen dan seyne sund und elend ym gewissen."

74. I am referring here to the sermon on Saint Matthew's Day from February 24, 1517 (WA 1:138-41; *LW* 51:26-33), the *Sermo de indulgentiis pridie dedicationis* from the spring of 1517 (WA 1:94-99; on its dating, see n. 76), and the *Tractatus de indulgentiis* (WA 1:65-69), which must have been written very much contemporaneously with the Ninety-five Theses; on its dating, see Jared Wicks, "Martin Luther's Treatise on Indulgences," *Theological Studies* 28 (1967): 481-518, and Brecht, *Martin Luther*, 165f. The *Sermo in die purificationis Mariae* (February 2; WA 1:130-32), which likewise dealt with indulgences, should not be dated with Loscher (cf. WA 1:130 n. 1) in 1517 but, according to an earlier tradition and Bayer (*Promissio*, 118 n. 496a), in 1518. Luther treated indulgences only briefly in a sermon on January 4, 1517 (WA 1:505-14; especially 509.36–510.8). He complained that the pastors delight in the fantastic stories of the legends and neglect the

dulgences *(Sermo de indulgentiis)*,⁷⁵ which Luther most likely delivered near the beginning of Lent 1517⁷⁶ and which anticipates and elucidates the Ninety-five Theses on many points. There he said that true confession and repentance "hates sin because of its love of righteousness and love of the righteous punishment of sin, and because it wants the injured righteousness to be avenged. Therefore it does not ask for indulgences but for the cross."⁷⁷ The sermon closes with the thought that a sermon on true repentance is incompatible with the proclamation of easy and gratuitous indulgences, because the latter teach laxity and escape from punishment while true repentance seeks a *rigida exactio*, a rigid fulfillment of the divine law and its commandments.⁷⁸

11. The Ninety-five Theses as a Reformation Text

Against this background of Luther's theological development from 1513 to 1517, the Ninety-five Theses now appear in a new light. As I have shown, what is typical of the Reformation in them is not the individual elements of their theology of confession or contrition; it is also not the way they present true repentance as a lifelong process of the inward and outward

---

preaching of the gospel, and demanded a *maxima reformatio ecclesiae;* this alternative — high regard for indulgences or for the gospel — was then taken up again in the Ninety-five Theses, but neither in the sermon nor in the theses was the content of the gospel defined as the message of forgiveness of sin and righteousness through faith. This was also true of the three places in Luther's preaching on the Lord's Prayer in 1517 in which he spoke of indulgences (WA 9:144.5-8; 152.30-32; 159.2-7). These sermons, however, are not authentic but are only handed down in Johann Agricola's revision; cf. Brecht, 185.

75. WA 1:94-99, especially 98.12–99.28.

76. For the dating in the spring of 1517 and not October 31, 1516 (thus Knaake, WA 1:94 n. 1), or October 31, 1517 (thus Löscher, WA 1:94 n. 1, and Bayer, *Promissio*, 166 n. 2), see Brecht, *Martin Luther,* 183 with n. 12, and Norbert Flörken, "Ein Beitrag zur Datierung von Luthers Sermo de indulgentiis pridie Dedicationis," *Zeitschrift für Kirchengeschichte* 82 (1971): 344-50. Flörken dates the sermon somewhat later than Brecht, to May 30, 1517. These variations in date within the spring of 1517 do not affect my argument.

77. WA 1:99.15-17. "Alia est vera [scil. contritio seu poenitentia interior], de qua dixi, quod amore iustitiae et poenarum odit peccatum, quia cupit ulcisci iustitiam laesam. Ideo non petit indulgentias, sed cruces."

78. WA 1:99.22-24. "Qua enim facilitate simul et semel possunt praedicari contritio vera et tam facilis largaque indulgentia, cum vera contritio rigidam exactionem cupiat et illa nimis laxet?"

person who follows Christ and the cross. We find only traces of the Ninety-five Theses' Reformation character when we read them as a witness to Luther's reorientation, in which he had abandoned the traditional combination of repentance and justification. He redefined "true repentance" so that it was no longer (as in the medieval tradition) a quality in the human soul necessary for salvation and no longer a part of faith; instead, repentance became the ever-present dark flip side of faith[79] and an aftereffect of it. It radiated both the *odium sui* and the *amor iustitiae* to the whole life of the Christian, even though by itself it could not impart salvation. Repentance had lost its soteriological function. Viewed in this way, the Ninety-five Theses are not about justification, characterized by the "vertical" dimension of the salvation bestowed freely and received in faith; instead, in a typically "reforming" way, they stand as a text that only ad-

---

79. The consoled and joyful confidence of faith always coexists with the painful insight into one's own nothingness before God and the despair of all attempts to be able to withstand God's judgment with a quality and morality of a holiness of one's own. In Luther, this radical humiliation and destruction of the person is so closely connected with the justifying faith in salvation that in his treatise *The Freedom of a Christian* (1520) it can be described as an effect of grace through Christ's gospel: "Should you ask how it happens that faith alone justifies and offers us such a treasure of great benefits without works in view of the fact that so many works, ceremonies, and laws are prescribed in the Scriptures, I answer: First of all, remember what has been said, namely, that faith alone, without works, justifies, frees, and saves; we shall make this clearer later on. Here we must point out that the entire Scripture of God is divided into two parts: commandments and promises. Although the commandments teach things that are good, the things taught are not done as soon as they are taught, for the commandments show us what we ought to do but do not give us the power to do it. They are intended to teach man to know himself, that through them he may recognize his inability to do good and may despair of his own ability. That is why they are called the Old Testament and constitute the Old Testament. For example, the commandment, 'You shall not covet' [Exod. 20:17], is a command which proves us all to be sinners, for no one can avoid coveting no matter how much he may struggle against it. Therefore, in order not to covet and to fulfil the commandment, a man is compelled to despair of himself, to seek the help which he does not find in himself elsewhere and from someone else, as stated in Hosea [13:9]: 'Destruction is your own, O Israel: your help is only in me'" (*LW* 31:348; cf. *StA* 2:269.9-18 [§6]). As closely, then, as faith and repentance (separated from all *iustitia activa*) belong together in Luther, so clearly can we recognize the total theological direction of his writings after 1517: Luther did not see the justifying character of faith in the human self-condemnation and the regret connected to this but solely in the receptive alignment to the gift of the forgiveness of sin and the righteousness of Christ. Consequently, he also in principle detached faith terminologically from the vocabulary of repentance.

dresses the "horizontal" level of the sanctification of life, which neither "does enough" nor earns merit. This is the painful shattering of every imagined security: the good works of brotherly love, the emulation of Christ's cross, suffering, and bitter hardships. Late medieval indulgences had combined these two dimensions, displacing the "satisfactory" function of good works and thereby supposedly easing and securing the attainment of salvation by helping people avoid purgatory. Luther, however, denied any relevance of indulgences for the hereafter and, as I have shown, consequently subjected them and papal authority to the "horizontal" level alone: their authority only extends to the earthly plane of existence.[80] With this "horizontalization" in the Ninety-five Theses, Luther thus completely invalidated and desacralized indulgences, contrasting them with the priceless treasure of a holy life of repentance, which takes the form of the disillusioning cross and loving action. On this level there is nothing of the ease promised by indulgences but only the rigor of a way of life that exposes itself uncompromisingly to the divine claim on total and undivided human obedience.[81] The theological basis of the Ninety-five Theses exists in how this view of the divine law stands face-to-face with the divine gift of the gospel. The paradox briefly flares up,[82] but — in light of the problem of indulgences — it was not the main theme of the theses.

---

80. See n. 7 above.

81. See n. 78 above, regarding *rigida exactio*. Because of this, many interpreters (e.g., Barth, "Die Geburt religiöser Autonomie," 80) believe that in the Ninety-five Theses and other texts written around the same time Luther was following the late medieval position of contritionism rather than the model of alleviation in attritionism. In truth, however, long before the formation of the theses he had turned away not only from attritionism but also from contritionism because he no longer saw salvation to be dependent on a particular quality of repentance. Unlike Staupitz in 1517, he was no longer moved by the problem of sufficient "satisfactory" repentance and remorse. In a biographical reminiscence of 1538 (quoted in chap. 1, n. 52 above), he said that he earlier (which to me means the time before his first lectures) followed the *doctrina de contritionibus*, i.e., the contritionism of the school of Biel (in contrast to the *doctrina de attritionibus* of Scotus). He gave a clear "no" to the ideal of perfection in this doctrine of contrition in the first lectures on the Psalms (1513-15). But what Luther vigorously reinforced in comparison to Biel's Ockhamism was the important word of sanctification and repentance, through which he saw how the sinful person was confronted by the oppressive holiness and the wrath of God.

82. See nn. 20 and 21 above.

12. Beyond the Theses: The New Connection between the Theologies of Justification and Repentance, between *Fides* and *Absolutio*

The Ninety-five Theses stand as a Reformation text precisely in how they do *not* talk about faith and justification, comforting trust, and the certainty of salvation. Even so, looking at the broader form of Luther's theology of repentance, we might say that he would not have written a similar tract on true Christian repentance even a few months later. The Ninety-five Theses, the *Tractatus de indulgentiis*[83] (written about the same time), and the sermon on indulgences and grace[84] represent only an interim stage on the way to an essentially different view and evaluation of the church's sacrament of confession. This change could already be seen clearly in Luther's explanation of the Ninety-five Theses and in other texts written during the spring and early summer of 1518.[85] By 1519, he was reaping the fruits of these new views in his sermon on the sacrament of confession.[86] What was most remarkable about Luther's continuing progression was how he once again closely connected the theologies of justification and repentance, even letting them mix together, although in quite a different sense than in his first lectures. In the future, too, Luther would keep a firm hold on the separation of faith and repentance that began in 1517. This is because he did not make the inner penitential attitude of radical humility the main ingredient or the basis of faith's relationship to God; he gave that role instead to the *verbum externum*, the external spoken word of priestly absolution that he connected to faith in the forgiveness of sins and the reception of salvation for Christ's sake. Receiving this certain word of assurance

---

83. See n. 74 above.

84. See nn. 18 and 19 above.

85. See the careful documentation and interpretation of this development in Bayer, *Promissio*, 164-225. The key text in which Bayer finds Luther's new theology of repentance clearly formulated for the first time is found in the series of theses *Pro veritate* (WA 1:629-33), especially in 182-202. The fact that I cannot share Bayer's opinion that Luther's "Reformation turn" lay in this new understanding of the sacrament of confession in 1518 is clear from what I have already said. What we can see here in Luther is no more and no less than an important further stage on his way to the Reformation reorientation, which had already begun before he started his first lectures on the Psalms. On this "extended view" of the development of Luther's Reformation theology and criticism of the church, see chap. 2 above.

86. WA 2:709-23.

thus became the pivotal and central point of his understanding of confession and the gospel. In this, the *absolutio* (the priest's word of absolution) depends not on priestly status but solely on the promise of one Christian to another of the forgiveness of his sins by the authority of Christ,[87] a word that can be firmly and joyfully believed as the promise of God. In this way, Luther reached the end of his journey outward: he allowed the saving external dimension of the divine *iustitia externa* to correspond to the ability of the *verbum externum* to be received, in contrast to the frailty of everything internal. Faith therefore means that people allow themselves to be freed through this liberating word from all obsessions about their own sins or their own holiness.

As in the Ninety-five Theses, Luther later considered true loving repentance, sorrow for one's own sins, and humble self-despair ongoing tasks within a Christian life, directly connected to the drive for a sanctified life and good works.[88] And yet, beginning in the spring of 1518, he contrasted faith and repentance with a new kind of sharpness in order to emphasize that Christians can never build their own salvation on their own repentance but must build it solely on Christ's liberating word of forgiveness.[89] "Although repentance and works should not be dismissed, one can in no way build on them but solely on the sure words of Christ, who tells you that when the priest absolves you, you will be absolved.... If you build

87. WA 2:722.36f.: "aber ym Newenn Testament hat sie [Die 'gewalt, die sund zu vorgeben und alßo eyn urteil an gottis statt zu fellenn'] eyn yglicher christenmensch, wo eyn priester nit da ist, durch die zusagung Christi...."
88. WA 2:719.34–720.3: "Das nit abermall yemandt myr schuld gebe, ich vorbiete gute werck, szo sage ich, mann soll mit allem ernst rew unnd leyd haben, beichte un gutt werck thun. Das were [verteidige, schütze] ich aber, wie ich kann, das man den glaubenn des sacraments laß das heubt gutt seyn und das erbe, da durch man gotis gnade erlange, unnd darnach vill gutt thue, alleyn gott zu eehr und dem nehsten zu nutz, unnd nicht darumb, das man sich drauff vorlassen soll als gnugsam, vor die sund zu bezalen; dann got gibt umb sunst, frey seyn gnade, szo sollen wir auch umb sunst, frey widderumb yhm dienen."
89. This sharp contrasting of faith and repentance is first to be found explicitly in Luther's explanation of thesis 38 of the theses on indulgences (WA 1:594.37–596.23; *LW* 31:191-96) and — probably shortly afterward — in the *Sermo de poenitentia* (WA 1:323–324.19), which, according to Knaake, was composed "before Easter in 1518." Already in the explanation of the seventh thesis on indulgences, Luther contrasted the peace of the conscience bestowed by faith in God's word of promise with the false outlook which seeks peace by the way of inner experience *(experientia intus)* (WA 1:541.5-7; *LW* 31:98-107).

on this with a sure faith, you are standing on the rock against which the gates and all the power of hell cannot win."[90]

Thus convinced of the total reliability of the words of absolution, Luther brought to completion his remodeled theology of repentance. Nevertheless, the beginnings of this Reformation reorientation — the path away from a salvation based on personal quality or morality and the journey toward a salvation based on the external truth of God's word — were already present in the time before Luther began his first lectures on the Psalms.

In contrast to much of the previous research, this chapter paints a relatively unique picture of how Luther's view of repentance and justification changed over time. We especially notice an important phase between the close of the lectures on Romans and the theology of the external word of salvation, which first came to the fore after the Ninety-five Theses. In this phase, the relationship between justification and faith arose out of the matrix of a particular theology of repentance defined by remorse, humility, and despair. On one hand, this simultaneously theological and existential clarification in Luther's writings reveals a gradual transition, for which reason I have deliberately avoided the teleological side of concepts like "development" and "process." But to say that the change was "gradual" is misleading if we simply mean a gradual shift of emphasis.[91] For, on the other hand, the changes described here have the character of sudden leaps,[92] which cannot be derived either from the previous state of Luther's religiosity or as continuous modifications. Instead, they appear each time as something qualitatively and surprisingly new.

---

90. WA 2:716.5-12: "Wie woll die rew und gute werck nit nachzulassen seyn, ist doch auff sie keynerweyß zu bawenn, ßibderbb alleinn auff die gewisse wort Christi, der dir zusagt, wan dich der priester loeßet, soltu loß seyn. Dein rew und werck mugenn dich triegenn, und der teufell wirt sie gar bald umbstossen ym todt und yn der anfechtung. Aber christus, deyn gott, wirt dir nit liegen noch wancken, und der teuffell wirt ym seyne wort nit umbstossen; und bawst du darauff mit eynem festen glauben, ßo stehst du auff dem Felß, da widder die pforten und alle gewalt der hellen nit mugen besteen [MT 16.18]."

91. Kroeger rightly stresses this in *Rechtfertigung*, 218f.

92. See Berndt Hamm, "Die Emergenz der Reformation," in *Die Reformation: Potentiale der Freiheit*, ed. Berndt Hamm and Michael Welker (Tübingen: Mohr Siebeck, 2008), 1-27.

CHAPTER 5

Luther's Instructions for a Blessed Death, Viewed against the Background of the Late Medieval *Ars Moriendi*

1. Luther's "Sermon on Preparing to Die" in Its Time

The Reformation's deep roots in late medieval religiosity and, at the same time, the serious break with traditional piety are both exemplified in the pastoral instructions for a Christian death. The first Reformation writing on the subject of the well-prepared death is especially telling on this point, also deserving of attention because it was one of the most widely spread and influential writings about death from the period. This was Martin Luther's "Sermon on Preparing to Die," which was probably written in the first half of October 1519 and published before the end of that month.[1] Only two short 1529 tracts on dying by the Augsburg theologians Caspar Huberinus and Urbanus Rhegius (often printed together) enjoyed a similar, if not greater, circulation.[2]

Luther's sermon belongs to a whole chain of sermons that he wrote in early modern High German in 1519 and 1520.[3] By putting these works in

---

1. *LW* 42:99-115. The first edition, printed by Johann Grunenberg in Wittenberg, serves as the critical edition of the work, WA 2:680-97; *StA* 1:230-43. The remainder of the chapter will cite *StA* and *LW*, also citing the sectional numbers that organize the sermon. For the history of the publication and reception of the sermon, see WA 2:680-84.

2. Gunter Franz, *Huberinus — Rhegius — Holbein: Bibliographische und druckgeschichtliche Untersuchung der verbreitetsten Trost- und Erbauungsschriften des 16. Jahrhunderts* (Nieuwkoop: De Graaf, 1973).

3. See Ursula Stock, *Die Bedeutung der Sakramente in Luthers Sermonen von 1519* (Leiden: Brill, 1982); Thomas Hohenberger, *Lutherische Rechtfertigungslehre in den*

the genre of "sermon," Luther emphasized that they were not learned tracts that rationally discussed problems and provided detailed authoritative references; instead, they were simple documents in everyday language that were close to the pastoral situations of the pulpit, the confessional, and the deathbed. They were intended to communicate the essential elements of his theology in a basic, elementary, and catechetical way to a theologically untrained public.[4] In this, Luther was continuing the popularizing impulse of the late medieval theology of piety, which sought to help Christians live out and deepen their spirituality, overlooking those complicated questions and disputes that were typical of the academic and systematic theologies of the "schools."[5]

2. The *Ars Moriendi* Literature between Suso and Luther

Catechetical efforts to simplify theology into the language of the people appeared in the many themes of *praxis pietatis* (the practice of piety), above all in the literature concerning *ars moriendi* (the art of dying).[6] Although this was really an innovation of the fifteenth century, we must not forget that the mystic Henry Suso (Heinrich Seuse) wrote the first *ars moriendi* tract in German lands — and in the German language — sometime between 1328 and 1330. This was not a separate book but was instead chapter 21 of his *Little Book of Eternal Wisdom,* entitled "How One Should Learn to Die and How

---

reformatorischen Flugschriften der Jahre 1521-22 (Tübingen: J. C. B. Mohr, 1996), 46-105; Matthieu Arnold, "Les sermons de 1518-1519," in *Luther et la réforme: Du Commentaire de l'Épître aux Romains à la Messe allemande,* ed. Jean-Marie Valentin (Paris: Ed. Desjonquères, 2001), 149-67; and Martin Brecht, "Luthers reformatorische Sermone," in *Fides et pietas, Festschrift für Martin Brecht,* ed. Christian Peters and Jürgen Kampmann (Münster: Lit, 2003), 15-32.

4. For this concept's reception among the laity, see n. 20 below. On the genre of sermon, see Beverly Mayne Kienzle, ed., *The Sermon* (Turnhout: Brepols, 2000), 159-64.

5. Berndt Hamm, "Was ist Frömmigkeitstheologie? Überlegungen zum 14. bis 16. Jahrhundert," in *Praxis Pietatis: Beiträge zu Theologie und Frömmigkeit in der Frühen Neuzeit, Festschrift für Wolfgang Sommer,* ed. Hans-Jörg Nieden and Marcel Nieden (Stuttgart: Kohlhammer, 1999), 9-45.

6. See the foundational work by Franz Falk, *Die deutschen Sterbebüchlein von der ältesten Zeit des Buchdruckes bis zum Jahre 1520* (Cologne: Bachem, 1890; Amsterdam: Rodopi, 1969). See also Helmut Appel, *Anfechtung und Trost im Spätmittelalter und bei Luther* (Leipzig: M. Heinsius nachfolger, 1938), and Rainer Rudolf, *Ars moriendi: Von der Kunst des heilsamen Lebens und Sterbens* (Cologne and Graz: Böhlau, 1957).

an Unprepared Death Happens."⁷ No other German text of the Middle Ages had as wide a circulation as the handwritten form of this work.

By synthesizing mystical inwardness and practical everyday piety, Suso gained a prominent and quintessential place in how theology was applied to spiritual instruction, edification, admonition, and consolation. The removal of chapter 21 of Suso's book and its transmission either as a separate manuscript or publication show how the teaching about dying grew apart from its wider original context and became an independent theme.⁸ But the real beginning of *ars moriendi* as its own genre came with Jean Gerson, whose small tract *De arte moriendi* (written around 1400-1401) created the definitive prototype for the next century.⁹ The work was originally written in French as *Médicine de l'âme* or *La science de bien mourir*, but was soon thereafter translated into Latin, and after that into other vernacular languages.¹⁰ Above all, the tract set the mold through its concentration on the deathbed scene, its pragmatic brevity and clear structure, its simple way of speaking, its elementary pastoral and catechetical

---

7. Henry Suso [Heinrich Seuse], *Deutsche Schriften*, ed. Karl Bihlmeyer (Stuttgart: Kohlhammer, 1907; Frankfurt am Main: Minerva, 1961), 278-87; Suso, *Deutsche mystische Schriften*, ed. Georg Hofmann (Zurich: Benziger, 1999), 289-97; the later (ca. 1331-34) Latin edition of the "Büchleins der ewigen Weisheit" in Suso's *Horologium Sapientiae*, ed. Pius Künzle (Fribourg: Universitätsverlag, 1977), chap. 21, pp. 526-40. On the interpretation of Suso, see Alois M. Haas, "Didaktik des Sterbens: Zur Botschaft der spätmittelalterlichen Sterbebüchlein," in *Gewißheit angesichts des Sterbens*, ed. Joachim Heubach (Erlangen: Martin-Luther-Verlag, 1998), 16-20.

8. On the separate transmission of chap. 21 of the "Büchleins der ewigen Weisheit," see Alois M. Haas and Kurt Ruh, "Seuse, Heinrich OP," in *Die deutsche Literatur des Mittelalters: Verfasserlexikon* (Berlin: De Gruyter, 1992), vol. 8, col. 1115.

9. Jean Gerson, "De arte moriendi, lateinisch ediert, kommentiert und deutsch übersetzt von Fidel Rädle," in *Literatur — Geschichte — Literaturgeschichte*, ed. Nine Miedema and Rudolf Suntrup (Frankfurt am Main: Lang, 2003). On the prototypical nature of this work, see Bernd Moeller, "Sterbekunst in der Reformation: Der 'köstliche, gute, notwendige Sermon vom Sterben' des Augustiner-Eremiten Stefan Kastenbauer," in *Vita Religiosa im Mittelalter, Festschrift für Kaspar Elm*, ed. Franz J. Felten and Nikolas Jaspert (Berlin: Duncker und Humblot, 1999), 757.

10. Gerson, "De arte moriendi," 722f. It is important that Gerson's work belongs to a lifelong and catechetical doctrine of piety. It was originally a French tract, which Gerson later turned into a Latin trilogy. The *ars moriendi* stood as the last part of the "opus tripartitum," the previous two parts of which covered the Ten Commandments and confession. See Sven Grosse, *Heilsungewißheit und Scrupulositas im späten Mittelalter: Studien zu Johannes Gerson und Gattungen der Frömmigkeitstheologie seiner Zeit* (Tübingen: J. C. B. Mohr, 1994), 227.

theology, and — last but not least — its successful use of the vernacular. These traits also mark Luther's sermon.

For the period between Gerson and Luther, we should especially mention those writings about death that were seen as important and typical representatives of *ars moriendi* within German-speaking lands. The widely circulated *Speculum artis bene moriendi* was written in Latin by an unknown author in the second quarter of the fifteenth century; it then appeared in several German translations, as well as in other languages.[11] Somewhat later (probably around 1450) was published the *Illustrated Ars Moriendi* (hereafter, the *Illustrated Ars*) with its five *Anfechtungen*. Related to the *Speculum* and combining series of wood engravings with its texts, it was available in Latin and in vernaculars and beloved everywhere.[12] Other works included "Die Künst von dem heilsamen sterben," written by the court priest in Vienna, Thomas Peuntner (d. 1434),[13] and a booklet by the preacher in the cathedral at Strasbourg, Johannes Geiler von Kayserberg, entitled "Wie man sich halten sol by eym sterbenden menschen" (1482),[14] along with Kayserberg's brief instruction "Ein ABC. Wie man sich schicken sol zü einem kostlichen seligen tod" (1497).[15] Finally, we should mention the writings of two Augustinian monks from Luther's immediate vicinity: the booklet "Die himlische funtgrub" by the professor of theology in Erfurt, Johannes von Paltz, with its third sermon, "Von der wollgebrau-

---

11. On the composition and transmission of the *Speculum* (whose author it is thought belonged to the University of Vienna), see Rudolf, *Ars moriendi*, 75; Karin Schneider, "Speculum artis bene moriendi," in *Die deutsche Literatur des Mittelalters: Verfasserlexikon* (Berlin: De Gruyter, 1993), vol. 9, cols. 40-49; and Nigel F. Palmer, "Ars moriendi und Totentanz: Zur Verbildlichung des Todes im Spätmittelalter, mit einer Bibliographie zur 'Ars moriendi,'" in *Tod im Mittelalter,* ed. Arno Borst et al. (Constance: Universitätsverlag Konstanz, 1993), 318f.

12. On the composition and transmission of the *Bilder-Ars-moriendi*, see Palmer, "Ars moriendi," 321-25, and Dick Akerboom, "'. . . Only the Image of Christ in Us': Continuity and Discontinuity between the Late Medieval *Ars Moriendi* and Luther's *Sermon von der Bereitung zum Sterben*," in *Spirituality Renewed: Studies on Significant Representatives of the Modern Devotion*, ed. Hein Blommestijn, Charles Caspers, and Rijcklof Hofman (Leuven: Peeters, 2003), 209-72.

13. See the edition and commentary in Rainer Rudolf, *Thomas Peuntners "Kunst des heilsamen Sterbens" nach den Handschriften der Österr. Nationalbibliothek* (Berlin: E. Schmidt, 1956).

14. Johannes Geiler von Kaysersberg, *Sämtliche Werke*, part I, section I, vol. 1, ed. Gerhard Bauer (Berlin and New York: De Gruyter, 1989), 1-13.

15. Geiler von Kaysersberg, *Werke*, 97-110.

chung des todes"[16] (which appeared in twenty-one editions between 1490 to 1521), and the booklet "Von der nachfolgung des willigen sterbens Christi" (1515) by Johannes von Staupitz, Luther's superior in the order and his predecessor in the chair at Wittenberg.[17]

3. Addressing the Reading Public: The Great Importance of the Lay Element

Asking about the audience for the late medieval *ars moriendi* literature reveals insightful information about how Luther's sermon came to work.[18] Markus Schart (d. 1529), one of the court counselors of Elector Frederick the Wise, had asked Luther in the spring of 1519 for instruction on how to prepare for dying. Because he was overworked, Luther initially declined to write this. He first recommended that Schart read the booklet on dying by his fatherly friend Staupitz[19] before he himself took up the pen. Here is the typically strong connection between *ars moriendi* literature and the pastoral care of the laity. Texts in Latin were primarily meant to be practical handbooks for pastoral care. Works in the vernacular, however, were directed not only to priests or members of a monastic order with less linguistic proficiency but even more to the bourgeois and noble laypeople who could read or who were at least interested in increasing their piety. These were the ones who pressed for written and illustrated works of pas-

---

16. Johannes von Paltz, *Opuscula*, ed. Christoph Burger et al. (Berlin: De Gruyter, 1989). "Himmlische Fundgrube" appears at pp. 155-284; "Sermon 3" appears in early modern High German on 239-48 and in Low German on 276-82.

17. Staupitz, *Johann von Staupitzens sämmtliche Werke*, vol. 1, *Deutsche Schriften*, ed. Joachim Karl Friedrich Knaake (Potsdam: Krausnick, 1867), 50-88. A good (but incomplete) overview of Christian literature about dying from Saint Cyprian until the end of the Middle Ages is available in Haas, "Didaktik des Sterbens," 21f.

18. See n. 1 above. It would be interesting to compare Luther's sermon on dying with another related work he had written just prior (in August or September 1519), namely, the letter of comfort for Elector Frederick the Wise entitled *Tessaradecas consolatoria pro laborantibus et oneratis* (WA 6:99-134), which George Spalatin translated into German in the winter of 1519-20. On this topic, see Reinhard Schwarz, "Das Bild des Todes im Bild des Lebens überwinden: Eine Interpretation von Luthers Sermon von der Bereitung zum Sterben," in *Gewißheit angesichts des Sterbens*, ed. Joachim Heubach (Erlangen: Martin-Luther-Verlag, 1998), 33 and 38; and Ute Mennecke-Haustein, *Luthers Trostbriefe* (Gütersloh: G. Mohn, 1989), 71-82.

19. WA Br 1:381.17-20; LW 42:95.

toral care and catechesis for dying.[20] They desired not only better instruction from the clergy but also the pious self-help that they could receive through their own reading, recitation, and visual contemplation. In this way, in the immense circulation of literature about dying from the time of Gerson until the Reformation, two innovative tendencies met and reinforced one another. On the one hand, there was the popular impetus of a practical reforming theology, which sought to reach into the daily lives of as many people as possible. On the other hand, there was the need of more discriminating educated and religious citizens, their wives, nobility, nuns, and other readers who did not have formal theological training.[21]

It is therefore telling that Staupitz dedicated his comforting work about dying to a secular noblewoman, Countess Agnes von Mansfeld: "To the blessed instruction of Your Grace and anyone else who may well come to it."[22] Johannes von Paltz also wrote and published his very successful "Heavenly Treasury" at the request of Elector Frederick the Wise (to whom he dedicated the work) and Frederick's brother Duke John.[23] This connection to the laity was characteristic of the *ars moriendi* literature as a whole, ever since its very beginning in France around 1270[24] and in Germany with Suso's instructions for dying, written in the vernacular. It is therefore misleading to assert that the *ars moriendi* was originally intended for instructing priests in their care of the dying and that only later — when there were not enough priests during outbreaks of the plague — laypeople were also

---

20. Palmer, "Ars moriendi," 315, and Hamm, "Was ist Frömmigkeitstheologie?" 29-31 and 20 n. 28. See also Dieter Harmening, "Katechismusliteratur: Grundlagen religiöser Laienbildung im Spätmittelalter," in *Wissensorganisierende und wissensvermittelnde Literatur im Mittelalter: Perspektiven ihrer Erforschung*, ed. Norbert Richard Wolf (Wiesbaden: L. Reichert, 1987), 91-102, and Annette Maria Bollmann, "Frauenleben und Frauenliteratur in der Devotio moderna: Volkssprachige Schwesternbücher in literarhistorischer Perspektive" (Ph.D. diss., Groningen, 2004), 35f.

21. Werner Williams-Krapp, "The Erosion of a Monopoly: German Religious Literature in the Fifteenth Century," in *The Vernacular Spirit: Essays on Medieval Religious Literature*, ed. Renate Blumenfeld-Kosinski, Duncan Robertson, and Nancy Bradley Warren (New York: Palgrave, 2002), 239-59.

22. Staupitz, *Werke*, 52.

23. Berndt Hamm, *Frömmigkeitstheologie am Anfang des 16. Jahrhunderts: Studien zu Johannes von Paltz und seinem Umkreis*, Beiträge zur historischen Theologie 65 (Tübingen: Mohr, 1982), 111f.

24. This teaching about dying — like those before it — also belongs to an entire Christian catechesis. See Palmer, "Ars moriendi," 315, and Dieter Briesemeister, "Ars moriendi," in *Lexikon des Mittelalters* (Munich: Artemis Verlag, 1999), vol. 1, cols. 1041f.

instructed as to how they "could effectively accompany their neighbors in the last affliction."[25] In the period that followed, Gerson led the way by writing his instructions about dying for a wide readership of less educated people who needed it. He wrote as much for priests *(sacerdotes)* and ministers *(curati)* who were engaged in pastoral care as for laypeople *(personae saeculares)* and members of religious orders *(personae religiosae)*.[26] He could also hope "to teach the ordinary people *(simplices)* who never or rarely heard a sermon, or if they did, then only a bad one."[27]

4. The Goal of *Ars Moriendi* Literature: To Visualize Death and Prepare to Die

Right in the introduction of the Latin version of his work, Gerson formulated the broad and popular goal of his tract: "Though the following writing hopes to serve as a kind of brief admonition for those who have come into their last hours, it also is suitable for all Christians in general so that they may acquire the readiness and knowledge for how to die well."[28] This sentence says something important not only about the audience of the late medieval *Ars Moriendi* but also about the contents of its instruction. It only partly contains special instructions on how to behave at the deathbed of one's neighbor. Even more, the *Ars Moriendi* tried to convey a universal *scientia mortis*,[29] that is, a saving knowledge of the right attitude to have about dying and death. Its writings were intended for people who were not yet in the moment of death but who nevertheless still ought to learn about how to prepare for a blessed death and how to help others achieve it. In this sense Luther's sermon on dying — whose original addressee (Schart) died ten years later — followed the tradition of the late medieval *Ars Moriendi*, because he too aimed for a well-considered "readiness for dying,"[30] a preparation and readiness to die confidently in Christ. It is strik-

   25. Rudolf, *Ars moriendi*, 1040.
   26. Gerson, "De arte moriendi," 722f.
   27. Gerson, "De arte moriendi," 721f.
   28. Gerson, "De arte moriendi," 728.
   29. Within his "Opus tripartitum," Gerson gave his tract on dying the heading "Tertia pars huius opusculi de scientia mortis," in Gerson, "De arte moriendi," 728. Suso (see n. 7 above) had already given his work the heading "De scientia utilissima homini mortali, quae est scire mori"; *Horologium Sapientiae*, 526.12f.
   30. StA 1:232.2; LW 42:100.

ing that he concentrated *only* on the dying of Christian individuals and not on pastoral care at someone else's deathbed, but this could very likely be because Markus Schart had asked him for precisely that kind of work.[31]

In another quite traditional way, Luther visualized the hour of death through its two sides: threatening *Anfechtung* and saving comfort. In contrast to the *contemptus mundi* and *memento mori* literature of the eleventh to thirteenth centuries, *ars moriendi* literature between Suso and Luther focused on the hour of death and on individual judgment at the moment of death. To be sure, the waves of plague in the fourteenth and fifteenth centuries intensified the collective experience of death's terrifying nearness. Nevertheless, the pastoral strategy of late medieval teaching always assumed that its audience suppressed the idea of death, imagining it to be far away and living unprepared for its arrival.[32] The *ars moriendi* literature, in clear parallel to the popular "dance of death" images, viewed its basic task as the need to bring death into the midst of people's lives, holding the decisive deathbed moment before their eyes so that they would take pause, begin the journey to a blessed death, and also take seriously the task of helping others come to a good death. In this sense, the old antiphon *Media vita in morte sumus* ("In the midst of life we are in death") was updated for the later Middle Ages. Together with sin and hell, this unsettlingly near visualization of the hour of death remained a decisive element in how Luther expressed fear and comfort in his own version of the hymn "Mitten wir ym leben sind mit dem tod umbfangen." This was his 1524 revision of the medieval antiphon and, at the same time, a musical complement to his 1519 sermon on dying.[33]

The extreme finality of the hour of death, constantly arising as a

---

31. In contrast to Werner Goez, "Luthers 'Ein Sermon von der Bereitung zum Sterben' und die spätmittelalterliche ars moriendi," *Lutherjahrbuch* 48 (1981): 97-113. Goez's overstatement of the fact that Luther did not mention the pastoral care and accompaniment of the sick has already been challenged in Mennecke-Haustein, *Luthers Trostbriefe*, 49. See also n. 183 below.

32. Akerboom, "Only the Image," 250. See also Luther's "Sermon on Preparing to Die," *StA* 1:234.25-31; *LW* 42:102 (section 8): "Thus the evil spirit turns everything upside down for us. During our lifetime, when we should constantly have our eyes fixed on the image of death, sin, and hell — as we read in Psalm 51[:3], 'My sin is ever before me' — the devil closes our eyes and hides these images. But in the hour of death when our eyes should see only life, grace, and salvation, he at once opens our eyes and frightens us with these untimely images so that we shall not see the true ones."

33. WA 35:126-132.51; *LW* 53:274-76.

mental reminder of that decisive dramatic moment, was quite characteristic of the *Ars Moriendi*. The *Illustrated Ars* described the goal of its texts and pictures in precisely the same way: they should serve both the educated and the laity as a mirror *(speculum)* in which to see their past life and meditate upon the hour of their death as if it were at hand.[34] In this way the deathbed scene might gain a new quality of omnipresence.[35] Three great uncertainties in particular became essential: uncertainty about the time and manner of death, uncertainty about one's own state of grace, and uncertainty about the result of the judgment. Doing it right therefore depended on always being ready, not proudly assuming one's security but also not falling into despair. Instead, people should begin now (at the latest!) to die to the world with humility and hope, focusing their minds and efforts on the hereafter.

5. Two Conceptions of the *Ars Moriendi*: Salvation in Life and a Chance in Death

If there was a common conception of the *ars moriendi* before Luther, there were nevertheless great differences based on whether the accent fell more on God's strictness and the exertion of human efforts toward salvation or whether it fell on the side of God's immense mercy that opened the possibility of salvation to even the greatest sinners. The view of strictness corresponded to a broader concept in which the *ars moriendi* could be understood alongside the ability to change one's way of life. The hour of death then appeared as the conclusion of a process that ordinarily reached fulfillment only if everything before it had already been prepared for these last steps of the journey. This included a clear moment of "too late." At that point, whatever sanctification had been neglected in life could no longer be made up for in death. If people of sound mind missed the chance to turn to a pious life, then (apart from rare exceptions) they would no longer have the power to bring themselves to a true repentance when they were weak and oppressed by demons.[36] The constant visualization of the hour of death therefore was supposed to inspire people not to put off until their final hour anything that would serve their salvation. The source of this

---

34. Akerboom, "Only the Image," 251.
35. Akerboom, "Only the Image," 250.
36. Suso, "Büchleins der ewigen Weisheit," chap. 21 (cited in n. 7 above).

model of a life trajectory certainly lies in the earlier monastic tradition and its maxim of living in such a way that one daily dies to the world.[37] Examples from the Carthusian monks Dionysius von Rijkel[38] and Jacob von Paradies[39] or the Benedictine Bernhard von Waging[40] show how the lifelong preparation for death was propagated as the monastic norm around 1450. During the fifteenth century, this rigorous program of *ars moriendi* started to extend into the lives of secular laypeople. This recalls Suso's wide popular reception,[41] as well as the influence of people like Jacob the Carthusian, Johannes Geiler von Kayserberg,[42] and — at the end of the century — the Dominican preacher Girolamo Savonarola in Florence.[43]

In contrast, other *ars moriendi* authors placed particularly great emphasis on the fact that it was never "too late" for a blessed death, right up to one's last breath. They stressed that in dying itself rested the opportunity for a perfect repentance that wiped out all punishments for sin.[44] Because dying as the loss of life is the bitterest agony for all creatures on earth,[45] people can turn their inner acceptance and endurance of dying into an instrument of salvation, anticipating purgatory and letting it become the gateway to paradise.[46] The thief crucified at Christ's right hand served as

---

37. Haas, "Didaktik des Sterbens," 19f.

38. Dionysius the Carthusian, "De particulari judicio in obitu singulorum dialogus" (ca. 1450), art. 34 in *Opera Omnia* 41, 475f.

39. Jacob the Carthusian, *De arte bene moriendi* (ca. 1450), especially chap. 19. See also Dieter Mertens, *Iacobus Carthusiensis: Untersuchungen zur Rezeption der Werke des Kartäusers Jakob vom Paradies (1381-1465)* (Göttingen: Vandenhoeck & Ruprecht, 1976).

40. Bernhard von Waging, *Tractatus de morte necnon de praeparatione ad mortem seu speculum mortis* (before 1458?). See also Rudolf, *Ars moriendi*, 92-95. Similar examples can be found in Wolfgang Kydrer of Salzburg and Bernhard the Benedictine of the Tegersee Cloister. For more on the Benedictines, see Johannes von Kastl, *Scire bene moriendi* (1410), 68f., and Mertens, *Iacobus Carthusiensis*, 179f.

41. See n. 36 above. On the reception of Suso's lifelong catechetical model, see Mertens, *Iacobus Carthusiensis*, 183f., and Haas, "Didaktik des Sterbens," 30f.

42. Mertens, *Iacobus Carthusiensis*, 254-69.

43. Girolamo Savonarola, sermon in the Florence Cathedral (November 2, 1496), sermon 28 in *Opera di Girolamo Savonarola*, vol. 2, ed. Vincenzo Romano (Rome, 1962), 326-97.

44. This view was clearly influenced by Gerson throughout the fifteenth century; see "De arte moriendi," 729f. See also Akerboom, "Only the Image," 255.

45. A reference to Aristotle's *Nicomachean Ethics*, in *Aristoteles Latinus*, vol. 26/2, 37. See also Akerboom, "Only the Image," 250.

46. Paltz, "Collatio funeralis in exsequiis doctoris Theodorici Wissensee" (1486), in

an example of such an instrumental use of death. After a life lived in mortal sin, he realized this last chance to gain salvation and so perfectly sanctified his dying that Christ told him, "Today you will be with me in paradise" (Luke 23:43).[47] This thief was the paradigm for the consequent internalization of holiness in the late Middle Ages. In the *Illustrated Ars*, for instance, an angel gives the dying person the following words of comfort and inspiration: "Even if you had committed as many robberies, thefts and murders as there are drops in the ocean and grains of sand, even if you alone had committed all the sins in the world, never showed any regret, never confessed them, and now have no opportunity to confess, you should still never despair, for in such cases an inner contrition alone is sufficient" *(sola contritio interior).*[48] Therefore, the decision about whether the soul after death enters heaven, hell, or purgatory did not depend on the duration of one's path to salvation or on the number of merits earned during one's lifetime (though these were still relevant for determining the level of eternal bliss), but on whether the dying person succeeded in conforming his or her inner self to Christ. That was certainly a comforting perspective, but it set the whole weight and pressure of sanctification on the hour of death and on the need to constantly visualize this in meditation. "A person's entire salvation," said the *Illustrated Ars,* "consists in how life ends."[49]

6. Striving toward the Perfect Death

With this, we see again the commonality of all late medieval *Artes Moriendi,* regardless of whether they emphasized the sanctification of an entire lifetime or the unique opportunities presented in the hour of death.

Opusculum, 417.10-18 and, more broadly, 416.1–422.14. This Latin passage had appeared earlier in the German "Himmlischen Fundgrube," 242.11-27. He also discussed this material in the 1502 "Coelifodina," 204.14–210.19. See also the entire third section of "Coelifodina: De modo bene moriendi," 161-228.

47. Paltz, "Collatio funeralis," 417.19–421.30; "Himmlische Fundgrube," 243.1–248.23; "Coelifodina," 210.14–226.9. Paltz and his Erfurt teacher Johannes von Dorsten (d. 1481) borrowed the idea that death could serve as an "instrumentum" for the dying from Saint Augustine, *De civitate Dei* 13.4, in PL 41:380, as cited in "Collatio funeralis," 416.6-8, "Himmlische Fundgrube," 241.7-11, and "Coelifodina," 208.1-4.

48. Akerboom, "Only the Image," 254.

49. Akerboom, "Only the Image," 228.

In either case, the teachings, admonitions, and consolations strive for the perfection of a pious death. The critical preparation for the moment of death consisted in completing the Christian virtues and living according to an exquisitely crafted way of life, when the hour of death marks its highest success and its maximal amount of merit and satisfaction. Above all, this meant having Christian faith in the church's teaching; true love of God; real sorrow for sins; a readiness to forgive others and to ask them for forgiveness; gratitude for the abundance of God's riches; a desire for the gracious sacramental helps of the church; a willingness to leave earthly riches and the longing for heavenly blessedness; the endurance and even joyful acceptance of suffering and death in the pattern of Christ; the humble and hopeful entreaty for the protecting help from the Holy Trinity, Saint Mary, and the angels and saints during the dangerous crossing to the hereafter; and finally the trust in God's mercy so that dying people could commend their souls to God.[50] In the end, everything hung on the fact that the fear of punishment before God's righteousness retreated before the loving trust in God's boundless compassion and the assuring prayer for God's mercy.[51] The *Ars Moriendi* hoped to give dying people the serenity to stop worrying about their own sinfulness or holiness, to stop worrying about all earthly things, and to surrender themselves entirely to God's saving compassion with a confident hope.[52]

7. The Protective Blessedness That Comes *Extra Nos* and Its Relationship to the Formation of the Inner Person

The centrality of the dying person's fervent prayer for help, protection, and mercy clearly reveals how much the theologians of the later Middle Ages understood a blessed death as being embedded in the dynamic sphere of external protection. We might call it a "blessedness from beyond us" *(Extra-nos-Heiligkeit)*. Here the dominant position belonged to the substitutionary power of atonement of Christ's passion. As was stated in

---

50. As typified in Gerson, "De arte moriendi," 733. See also Rudolf, *Thomas Peuntners "Kunst des heilsamen Sterbens,"* 28.5-20.

51. If a person suddenly fell into mortal danger and did not have time for intense preparation, the person was supposed to trust and hope in God's mercy, saying, "O my God and creator! O Jesus Christ, my redeemer, have mercy on me and be gracious to me, a poor sinner." Rudolf, *Thomas Peuntners "Kunst des heilsamen Sterbens,"* 51.10-13.

52. Staupitz, *Werke,* 8of. and 88.8-10.

the frequently quoted chapter of admonishments in the "Anselmian Questions," the dying should wrap themselves entirely in the passion in order to have the chance of passing the divine judgment.[53] Not only Christ but also the whole heavenly and earthly *communio sanctorum* (communion of saints) would be interceding for the dying, including the supportive people gathered at the deathbed. This protective community approached the dying person as near and visible means of grace, who brought with them the sacrament of extreme unction and other rituals, sacraments, and sacred symbols (e.g., holy water, incense, a death candle, and the crucifix), and who read important devotional texts and prayers aloud, all the while showing comforting images, above all images of the Crucified and Saint Mary. The authors of *ars moriendi* literature thought it paramount that such visualizations of mercy reach and shape the dying person on the inside. External help and salvation would only work insofar as the prayer of a pious dying person was awakened or strengthened. The woodcuts of the *Illustrated Ars*, for example, strikingly portrayed how the heavenly powers of protection — with God the Father, Christ, and Saint Mary at their head — would stand beside the bed of the dying person[54] and put to flight the devils who wanted to drag the soul into their power through evil inspirations. Even so, this salvation would only be successful because an angel instills correspondingly virtuous inspirations and thereby helps achieve the proper inner attitude of dying: a humble, loving, devoted, and trusting heart.

The intense visualization of the hour of death, its devilish *Anfechtungen*, and the oppressive imminence of divine judgment[55] strengthened the tendency of fifteenth-century theology and piety to emphasize that

---

53. Anselm of Canterbury, *Admonitio morienti et de peccatis suis nimium formidanti*, in PL 158:686f.; Appel, *Anfechtung*, 67-71.

54. See pictures number 1 *(temptatio diaboli de fide)*, 2 *(bona inspiratio angeli de fide)*, 6 *(bona inspiratio angeli de patientia)*, 7 *(temptatio diaboli de vana gloria)*, and 8 *(bona inspiratio angeli contra vanam gloriam)*; as a symbol of Christ's saving passion, the crucifix is set up directly opposite the deathbed in pictures number 10 *(bona inspiratio angeli contra avaritiam)* and 11 (a concluding picture of the good death), in Akerboom, "Only the Image," 261-62, 266-68, and 270-71.

55. The image of a divine judgment of the individual immediately after death developed in the thirteenth century in contrast to a more distant universal judgment at the last day; see Hamm, "Theologie und Frömmigkeit im ausgehenden Mittelalter," in *Handbuch der Geschichte der evangelischen Kirche in Bayern*, ed. Gerhard Müller, Horst Weigelt, and Wolfgang Zorn (St. Ottilien: EOS, 2002), 1:192f.

weak human beings depended upon help, protection, and mercy. The *ars moriendi* literature documents this development. At the same time, it clearly shows that the intensified emphasis on external protection did not displace the soteriological significance of believers' inner virtues; instead, it had quite the opposite effect of making a certain kind of internalized virtue into something necessary for salvation. To get a sense of this, consider a richly expressive epitaph painting by Hans Holbein the Elder, in which God the Father as divine judge speaks the words, "I will show mercy to all those who leave this world with true repentance."[56] The key virtue of "true repentance" points to the basic attitude of humility in the inner person. This humility considers itself totally unworthy of heavenly reward because it does not count its own virtuous qualities, merits, and satisfactions but relies entirely upon substitution, intercession, and mercy. However, having this attitude becomes de facto the true virtue, merit, and satisfaction that is worthy before God.[57]

It is therefore characteristic of the *Ars Moriendi* that it first offered the helpful imminence of the means of grace and then made it possible for a person's inner conscience and attitude to reach a peak in the hour of death, thereby binding these two things tightly together. Here we recognize a variant of the traditional *cooperatio* model of how God interacts with people for the sake of their heavenly bliss, but this happens in such a way that the cooperation of the dying gets detached from the realm of outward action and is seen only as a loving and trusting attitude of inner acceptance. On this inward level, then, everything — especially the visualization of the protecting *extra nos* sanctification and the reception of extreme unction[58] — aimed at the perfection of Christian virtues and at masterfully and skillfully taking the form of Christ in the *imitatio passionis*,[59] us-

---

56. Holbein completed this painting in 1508 for the Augsburg wine merchant Ulrich Schwarz; it hangs in and belongs to that city's art gallery, Kunstsammlungen Augsburg, no. 3701. See also Bruno Bushart, *Hans Holbein der Ältere*, 2nd ed. (Augsburg: Verlag Hofmann-Druck, 1987), and Hamm, "Was ist Frömmigkeitstheologie?" 39-44.

57. On the medieval distinctions between the personal/subjective relationship to God (especially in prayer) and objective descriptions of that relationship, see chap. 3 above.

58. See section 20 of this chapter.

59. The idea that the dying person ought to imitate the pattern of Christ's passion and death (praying, crying, calling out for forgiveness, commending the soul to the heavenly Father, and accepting death) can be seen above all in the *Speculum artis bene moriendi* (n. 11 above). See also, Rudolf, *Ars moriendi*, 76, and Jacob the Carthusian, chap. 19.

ing the word *ars* (art) in the sense of an acquired skill and readiness. When viewed from that perspective, being able to die well was a personal disposition that came through becoming pious. Herein lay the condition for salvation. Those who could finally hand life and death over to God as a kind of voluntary sacrifice[60] would be received into blessedness by God. Without this "willing preparation," no one could become blessed.

The *ars moriendi* literature consistently differentiated between the situation of the healthy and those who were gravely ill. Things that a healthy person ought to actively work for and think about could be overlooked by someone who was dying.[61] In any case, the teachings about how to die were written for the healthy, insofar as their own death and the death of others were or should be already present to them. As the fundamental statement of this teaching, *Media vita in morte sumus* told them they must already possess the necessary knowledge about dying and already learn how to die and be ready to take their leave. Healthy people needed to know already what will or will not be important when they are at death's door. In that way, every teaching about how to die, even if it were only concerned with the final hour, was also teaching how to live every hour. To this extent, the school of internalization, the practice of repentance, humility, and thankfulness, of willed serenity and a loving desire for the heavenly home took special hold on those people still standing in the *vita activa*, since they, too, should at that very moment be aware of their total dependence on the protecting power of mercy. In this sense, *ars moriendi* meant that one's entire life should be directed to the hour of death and the salvific crossing from this world to the next. It is therefore only logical that all the *ars moriendi* authors of the fifteenth and early sixteenth centuries were committed church reformers, who pressed for an intensification and strict regulation of the Christian life in the cloister and in the world. The concentration of the hour of death shows no sign of having been accompanied by a "secularization of the spheres of life."[62] Rather than exhibiting signs of "secularization," the wider context of the *ars moriendi* presents the dynamic of an intensified Christianization un-

---

60. Paltz, "Himmlische Fundgrube," 245.25-27.

61. Note a somewhat different preparation for dying in Geiler von Kaysersberg, "Sterbe ABC" (n. 15 above).

62. This in contrast to Tenenti's thesis in Ruggiero Romano and Alberto Tenenti, *Die Grundlegung der modernen Welt: Spätmittelalter, Renaissance, Reformation* (Frankfurt am Main: Fischer-Bücherei, 1967), 100-103. See also Haas, "Didaktik des Sterbens," 26-29, and Grosse, *Heilsungewißheit*, 227f.

der the slogan "Turn away from worldly vanity to a better life of heavenly blessing!"[63] As far as we can recognize it, these writings were desired and read by people who eagerly thought about how to improve their pious living and their prospects in the hereafter.[64]

8. The *Ars Moriendi* within Late Medieval Institutionalization of the Hereafter

The *ars moriendi* was part of the large and multifaceted late medieval institutionalization of the hereafter, along with practices like buying indulgences and leaving endowments to benefit the beloved dead. What connects the *ars moriendi* to the other parts of the institutional apparatus is the *cooperatio* and *communio* model of giving and receiving, with respectively graded achievements and graces ranging from minimum to maximum. It is telling how the merchant's attitude of calculation, bargaining, and buying did not remain restricted to indulgences and endowments but spread into some of the teaching about dying. In Paltz, for example, death can become the currency of a dying man, which he can use to buy the riches of the heavenly kingdom like a wise merchant.[65] Paltz called this a *kaufschlagen*, making a deal with death,[66] an *ars prudenter negotiandi circa mortem propriam* (the clever skill of negotiating around one's own death),[67] and a "good trade."[68] This good deal would come by having the sick person accept death patiently and willingly. Here the merchant's urbane thoughts about profit intensely combined with the internalization of piety,[69] so that this institutionalization of the hereafter, with all its blunt calculations and account-

---

63. Johannes Busch, *Chronicon Windeshemense*, ed. Karl Grube (Halle: Hendel, 1886), chap. 47, pp. 372-75.
64. See section 3 of this chapter.
65. Paltz, "Himmlische Fundgrube," 242.1-10; "Collatio funeralis," 417.19–421.30; and "Coelifodina," 217.14-23.
66. Paltz, "Himmlische Fundgrube," 242.10 and 243.4.
67. Paltz, "Collatio funeralis," 417.24f.
68. Paltz, "Collatio funeralis," 421.13-17 *(felix negotiatio, felix commutatio, saluberrima mercantia)*. See also Hamm, *Frömmigkeitstheologie*, 293f.
69. For instance, see Jacob the Carthusian, chap. 20. On the theme of Christ as the heavenly merchant, see Hamm, "Theologie und Frömmigkeit," 207, and Hamm, "Den Himmel kaufen: Heilskommerzielle Perspektiven des 14. bis 16. Jahrhunderts," *Jahrbuch für biblische Theologie* 21 (2006): 239-75.

ing for the hereafter, nevertheless did not work without the prayer of a pious heart.

An indulgence or an endowment of a mass could only benefit those who had died in a state of love and true repentance. In that way, the *ars moriendi* and its emphasis on virtuously and internally learning how to die well could stand in the middle of the entire late medieval apparatus for securing one's place in the hereafter.

9. The Reformation's End to the *Ars Moriendi*: The Eschatological Finality of Justification

Beginning with Luther's sermon, however, we can see exactly how the Reformation's instructions about a blessed death meant the end of the traditional *ars moriendi*. The new Reformation view of justification turned away from thoughts about cooperation, satisfaction, and merit, as well as the principle of "artfully" forming interior virtues, which would then reach their peak in the hour of death. Even when Reformation authors borrowed individual elements from the late medieval *ars moriendi* literature, these gained an essentially different sense because of the Reformation view of salvation. There was still the theme of "preparation for dying,"[70] that is, of being ready in the midst of life and at its end, but this no longer taught the perfection of one's clever preparations for the journey to the next life. In that sense, there was no longer any Reformation *ars moriendi*.

From the medieval perspective, the decisive point for people's prospects in the hereafter was what they made out of their dying and whether their dying was successful. This pressure on or tension about a pious fulfillment was then — at least in the intention of the new teaching on death — removed from the hour of death. From a Reformation perspective, believers receive the certainty that in the midst of life they have received final salvation from God, which comes regardless of their being pious or striving for piety. That is the eschatological fullness of justification: it must not simply set in motion a way of sanctification through merit and satisfaction in order to achieve blessedness; rather it turns those who have freely received grace into heirs of blessedness, independent of their love, humility, repentance, endurance, serenity, or other virtues. Believers had already be-

---

70. See n. 30 above.

come *iustus et salvus* (justified and saved).[71] This soteriological finality of justification meant freedom from focusing on the hour of death and brought nonanxiousness for living and dying. With this, the medieval antiphon *Media vita in morte sumus* took on a new meaning. As Luther reworked it, faithful Christians experience being enveloped by death, assailed by the jaws of hell and demonic fear, and chased by their sins,[72] but in this distress the voice of the gospel tells them that the risen Christ has broken the power of death, sin, and hell so that now, replacing fear of death and hell, the joyful certainty of life and blessedness can enter in: "In the midst of death we are enveloped in life."[73] To be sure, the late medieval *ars moriendi* emphasized that too, with regards to the helping and saving powers of mercy that are close to threatened souls. But by breaking with the traditional *ars moriendi* theology more broadly and by connecting justification directly with the reception of salvation, the Reformation view gave the presence of the heavenly life a new character of personal assurance of salvation, freedom from any institutions related to the hereafter, and release from all the conditions that needed to be achieved or fulfilled for salvation. If damnable death is always present in the midst of life and if the sanctified life is always in the midst of death, then believers' last moments of life are also released from every special pious way of life, and death loses all that is demonic, gruesome, and dreadful to it. In death there no longer awaits that individual judgment by God, which weighs virtuous quality and morality.[74] God has already remitted all punishments out of pure grace, making purgatory irrelevant, too.

71. WA 54:183.27-29; *LW* 34:334: "I had also acquired the beginning of the knowledge of Christ and faith in him, i.e., not by works but by faith in Christ are we made righteous and saved." WA 40/I:662.7f.; *LW* 26:439: "to the extent that a Christian believes, to that extent he is in heaven." On a "realized eschatology" in Luther, see Ole Modalsli, "Luther über die Letzten Dinge," in *Leben und Werk Martin Luthers von 1526 bis 1546*, vol. 1, ed. Helmar Junghans (East Berlin: Evangel. Verl.-Anst., 1983), 338.

72. See the beginning of the first three verses of Luther's hymn "In the Midst of Life" (n. 33 above).

73. WA 40/III:496.16f.; *LW* 13:83: "The voice of the Law terrifies because it dins into the ears of smug sinners the theme: 'In the midst of earthly life, snares of death surround us.' But the voice of the Gospel cheers the terrified sinner with its song: 'In the midst of certain death, life in Christ is ours.'" See also, WA 12:609.17, "Ey mitten in dem todt wil ich das leben finden."

74. See n. 55 above. With the Reformation's rejection of the doctrine of purgatory, the reformers and later Protestant orthodox theologians de-emphasized the notion of individual judgment and reemphasized the universal judgment of Christ on the last day.

10. Death as Healing Medicine

Luther saw death as the culmination of both God's wrath and God's grace.[75] This corresponded to his idea that Christians are simultaneously sinner and justified. Under sin and the law, people experience physical death, through which the "jaws" of hell open as a terrifying punishment. As justified, however, Christians understand death as a healing medicine of the loving God who wants to call them home and heal them from sin.[76] That which death hides behind its walls becomes the promise of the gospel. Without regard to some special internal spiritual quality, Christians can die fearlessly, willingly, and full of desire for their heavenly home and the "dear last day."[77] In two hymns printed in 1524, Luther expressed this stealing of death's power and drama in such a way that he mocked it and called it "sleep." Christians can mock death because Christ's death and resurrection have swallowed it up: "The Scripture has published that — / How one death the other ate / Death is become a laughter."[78] At the same time, the Christian life until the time of death will be a joyful, peaceful passing away because the Christian no longer fears it; death has become sleep, a passing over into the life and salvation of Christ:

> In peace and joy I now depart,
> As God wants me.
> Content and still is mind and heart,
> He doth save me.
> As my God hath promised me,
> Death is become my slumber.[79]

---

75. Bernhard Lohse, *Luthers Theologie in ihrer historischen Entwicklung und in ihrem systematischen Zusammenhang* (Göttingen: Vandenhoeck & Ruprecht, 1995), 345-53; Paul Althaus, *Die Theologie Martin Luthers*, 5th ed. (Gütersloh: Gütersloher Verlagshaus Gerd Mohn, 1980), 339-54; Otto Hermann Pesch, *Theologie der Rechtfertigung bei Martin Luther und Thomas von Aquin: Versuch eines systematisch-theologischen Dialogs* (Mainz: Matthias-Grünewald-Verlag, 1967), 774-79; and Werner Thiede, "Luthers individuelle Eschatologie," *Lutherjahrbuch* 49 (1982): 18-20.

76. WA 10/III:76.1f. and WA 31/I:169.34–170.19.

77. WA Br 9:175.17, no. 3512, "Kom, lieber jungster Tag, Amen"; *LW* 50:219. WA 34/II:411.1f., "Es mus dahin komen, ut expectemus diem extremum und frolic warten."

78. *LW* 53:257; WA 35:444.10-12, *Christ lag in Todes Banden*, v. 4: "Die schrifft hat verkundet das, / wie eyn tod den andern fras. / Eyn spott aus dem tod ist worden."

79. *LW* 53:248; WA 35:438.14–439.2, *Myt frid und freud ich far do hyn*, v. 1: "Myt frid

11. Death as Peaceful Passing and as Dramatic Battle

When Luther emphasized Christian death as gentle and peaceful, free from fear and terror, "as if falling asleep and not dying,"[80] he stood entirely within the late medieval tradition of picturing the good death in the same way as those countless depictions of Mary's blessed death. According to the standards of the *ars moriendi*, Mary died the ideal death, surrounded by the prayers of the twelve apostles, her hands crossed or holding a crucifix, her face reflecting the peaceful and joyful journey of her soul into the heavenly hereafter.[81]

The last woodcut of the *Illustrated Ars Moriendi* quite similarly depicted death as a God-given passing.[82] The goal of all writings about preparing to die was a fearless, willing, and trusting departure, so that at the end the one who was dying could confidently answer the Anselmian question "Are you happy that you are dying in the Christian faith?" with "Yes, I am happy."[83] Of course, the *Illustrated Ars* also showed pictures of the moments before that closing scene, in which the final peaceful ending has come only through heavy *Anfechtungen*. The common idea of the later Middle Ages was that Satan never stops trying to bring Christian souls into his power, so that the battle between the heavenly and demonic powers actually peaks at the end. Just as Luther clearly took a burden away from dying, he just as impressively viewed the dying Christian as still also having a part in a dramatic battle. In Luther, this battle formed an even sharper contrast to the total composure and calmness of the peaceful

---

und freud ich far do hyn / ynn Gotts wille. / Getrost ist myr meyn hertz und syn, / sanfft und stille, / Wie Gott myr verheyssen hat: / Der tod is meyn schlaff worden."

80. WA 17/II:234.36-38, "Aber eyn Christen schmeckt odder sihet den tod nicht, das ist, er fulet yhn nicht, erschrickt nicht so dafur und gehet sanfft und still hynehn, als entschlieff er und sterbe doch nicht"; and WA 31/I:160.20.

81. Klaus Schreiner, "Der Tod Marias als Inbegriff christlichen Sterbens: Sterbekunst im Spiegel mittelalterlicher Legendenbildung," in *Tod im Mittelalter,* ed. Arno Borst et al. (Constance: Universitätsverlag Konstanz, 1993), 261-312, and *Maria: Jungfrau, Mutter, Herrscherin* (Munich: C. Hanser, 1994), 463-90.

82. Picture number 11 (see n. 54 above).

83. Anselm of Canterbury, *Admonitio morienti et de peccatis suis nimium formidanti,* in PL 158:685 and 688. Here is a question to be asked of a new initiate into the order: "Interrogatio: Laeteris, frater, quod in fide christiana moreris? Responsio: Gaudeo." Here is a question asked of a layperson: "Gaudes, quia in fide christiana moreris? Responsio: Gaudeo." See also, Appel, *Anfechtung,* 67 and 70.

passing. The 1519 "Sermon on Preparing to Die" shows especially clearly how close Luther still was to the late medieval dramatization of dying and how he outdid it through a significantly intensified understanding of *Anfechtung*.

12. Luther's "Sermon on Preparing to Die": Dying as a Birth out of Fear and into Joy

After Luther had spoken in the sermon's first two paragraphs about taking physical and spiritual leave of this world, he immediately in the next paragraph made his central theme the escalating tension between fear and joy. Completely within the tradition, he characterized dying here and in following passages as the pinnacle of fear, danger, and *Anfechtung*. And, just as in the theology of piety before him, he used the metaphor of a journey to show his readers that dying is a dangerous crossing into the hereafter: "Here we find the beginning of the narrow gate and of the straight path to life" (Matt. 7:14).[84] The narrow gate, which Luther especially emphasized, expressed the greatest danger and nightmarish fear. He underlined the event's drama by comparing it to the birth of a child (which, before modern obstetrics, was particularly dangerous and frightening), where everything is narrow and at the same time the emergence goes from narrowness into wideness, out of fear and into joy:

> Just as an infant is born with peril and pain from the small abode of its mother's womb into this immense heaven and earth, that is, into this world, so man departs this life through the narrow gate of death. And although the heavens and the earth in which we dwell at present seem large and wide to us, they are nevertheless much narrower and smaller than the mother's womb in comparison with the future heaven. Therefore, the death of the dear saints is called a new birth, and their feast day is known in Latin as *natale*, that is, the day of their birth. However, the narrow passage of death makes us think of this life as expansive and the life beyond as confined. Therefore, we must believe this and learn a lesson from the physical birth of a child, as Christ declares, "When a woman is in travail she has sorrow; but when she has recovered, she no longer remembers the anguish, since a child is born by her

---

84. *LW* 42:99 (3); *StA* 1:232.19.

into the world" (John 16:21). So it is that in dying we must bear this anguish and know that a large mansion and joy will follow (John 14:2).[85]

Luther stood within a tradition that understood human mortality as another kind of birth. He pointed to the medieval liturgical custom of celebrating the day of a saint's death as the saint's birthday.[86] Henry Suso had lifted up the joy with which one should welcome death as the moment of a new birth, of liberation from the burden of the body and the free entrance into eternal blessedness.[87] In contrast to Suso, however, Luther emphasized not only the joy about the birth but also the threatening crisis of narrowness and fear. For him, the metaphor of birth served a double function: it did not simply allow death to be seen as a passage opening into a completely different dimension of life, but it also illustrated the heightening of fear and its transformation into the greatest joy. This double-sidedness of fearful terror and comforting joy defines the composition of his sermon, just as it is characteristic of the overall structure of his theology then and later. For him, comfort always meant a "comforted despair."

13. Luther in the Tradition of an Interiorized Religious Iconography

Beginning his teaching about dying with biblical metaphors of birth, journey, gates, dwelling places, and mansions was not merely a stylistic tool Luther used for sermon illustrations. It comported rather closely to his theology of images and symbols, which characterized the wider argument of the sermon's thought and language, along with his aforementioned use of double-sided metaphors. By allowing his instruction to work by means of metaphors, he set himself within the tradition of a religiosity of internal seeing and the meditative powers of imagination and observation.[88] Like

---

85. *StA* 1:232.20-34 (3); *LW* 42:99-100.

86. Naming the day of death as a "birthday" began during times of Christian persecutions in the third and fourth centuries; see Alfred Stuiber, "Geburtstag," in *Reallexikon für Antike und Christentum* (Stuttgart: Anton Hiersemann, 1976), vol. 9, cols. 229-33.

87. Suso, "Briefbüchlein," letter 6 in *Deutsche Schriften*, 379.24–380.3.

88. Thomas Lentes, "Inneres Auge, äusserer Blick und heilige Schau: Ein Diskussionsbeitrag zur visuellen Praxis in Frömmigkeit und Moraldidaxe des späten Mittelalters," in *Frömmigkeit im Mittelalter: Politisch-soziale Kontexte, visuelle Praxis, körperliche Ausdrucksformen*, ed. Klaus Schreiner and Marc Müntz (Munich: Fink, 2002), 179-220,

the mystics and theologians of piety before him, Luther clearly held the opinion that people do not live primarily according to abstract ideas but according to images in their souls. Images of the outside world and the visual perceptions that come from our physical and inner eyes gain power over us. Whatever exercises power within us, whether it causes fear or gives comfort, depends on what we have "image-ined" and which images have the upper hand in us: for example, iconic representations of Christ judging harshly[89] with frightening demons and the terrifying torments of hell and purgatory, or images of the merciful Christ of the passion, of a graciously pardoning heavenly Father, the Madonna of the protective cloak, and assisting angels. The images gain power because people put themselves in the picture; that is, they allow them to rule over their imaginations, make an impression on their emotions, and direct their faith. People always live under this powerful influence of images — at least in Luther's opinion, which strongly followed the iconographic tradition of piety as seen in Suso. Especially when it comes to dying, everything depends on having and building the right images in one's soul: images that God wants to give us rather than those pictures with which the devil wants to lead us astray. Those who are dying live in this dilemma, which is why the late medieval *ars moriendi* attached so much importance on memorable sets of images and on the dying being surrounded by and filled with the right symbols and images.

---

and Lentes, "So weit das Auge reicht: Sehrituale im Spätmittelalter," in *Das "Goldene Wunder" in der Dortmunder Petrikirche: Bildgebrauch und Bildproduktion im Mittelalter*, ed. Barbara Welzel, Thomas Lentes, and Heike Schlie (Bielefeld: Verlag für Regionalgeschichte, 2003), 241-58. Note the similar visual imagery in Luther's "Meditation [Sermon] on Christ's Passion," WA 2:137.11 (4) and 137.22 (6); *LW* 42:8. For another example of Luther's visual language, note the following passage from a 1515 sermon: "So weys ich auch gewis, das Gott wil haben, man solle syne werck horen odder gedencken, so ist myrs unmuglich, das ich nicht ynn meym hertzen sollt bilde davon machen, den ich wolle odder wolle nicht, wenn ich Christum hore, so entwirfft sich ynn meym hertzen eyn mans bilde, das am creutze henget, gleich als sich meyn andlitz naturlich entwirfft yns wasser, wenn ich dreyn sehe"; WA 18:83.6-12. See also Schwarz, "Bild des Todes," 38f., and Mennecke-Haustein, *Luthers Trostbriefe*, 81.

89. Luther later reminisced about his earlier image of Christ, for instance in a sermon of November 1537, WA 47:275.33-36: "Ich hab mich im Bapstumb mehr fur Christo gefurcht dan fur dem Teuffel. Ich gedachte nicht anders, den Christus sesse im Himel als ein zorniger Richter, wie her den auch auff einem Regenbogen sitzendt gemahlet wirdet." Later in the same sermon, WA 47:277.8-10, he wrote, "Das machte alles der leidige Teuffel, de runs die schonen farben des herrn Christi aus den augen zeucht und schwartze farben druber gestrichen hat."

14. The Focus on Virtue in Late Medieval *Ars Moriendi* Iconography

The images, symbols, or signs around which Luther built his teaching about dying highlight the continuity as well as the essential differences with the traditional *ars moriendi*. Particularly revealing is the comparison with the *Illustrated Ars*. Its series of woodcuts is defined by the contrast between devilish *Anfechtungen* and divine counterforces (the same is true in the collection of images that accompanied Luther's text), so that five images of temptation are juxtaposed with five images of overcoming *Anfechtung*.[90] One may therefore think that Luther had allowed these images to work into the inner imagination of the soul, which would have been entirely within the spirit of how the woodcuts had been used for personal internalization. In fact, Luther did not speak of visual pictures *(picturae)* but of vivid mental images *(imagines)* that make their impression on people's ideas and feelings. Far more important is how Luther's images have entirely different contents from the *Illustrated Ars*, thereby presenting a fully different kind of *Anfechtung* and overcoming *Anfechtung*, of being set free from fear, and of consolation. Through images and texts, the *Illustrated Ars* depicts five *Anfechtungen* with which devilish spirits may try to divert the mortally ill from the path of virtuous dying: temptations to unbelief, despair, impatience, vainglory or arrogance, and greed, which clings to earthly possessions. Each of these is then contrasted to the good inspiration of angels who strengthen the dying in the five corresponding virtues: faith (the "basis of all salvation"),[91] hope (a "guide on the way to heaven"),[92] willing endurance (which is especially meritorious),[93] self-emptying humility,[94] and a voluntary poverty that can let go of life (for this "leads to heaven").[95] Here is the familiar program of preparation and perfection in the *ars moriendi* since the time of Gerson, which aimed for Christian virtue, merit, and worthiness,[96] for the sake of form-

---

90. Akerboom, "Only the Image," 261-70.
91. Akerboom, "Only the Image," 251.
92. Akerboom, "Only the Image," 251.
93. Gregory the Great, *Homiliae in evangelia*, CCSL 141:327.191f.; Akerboom, "Only the Image," 256.
94. Akerboom, "Only the Image," 258. On the late medieval connection between humility and certainty of salvation, see Hamm, "Theologie und Frömmigkeit," 192 and 195.
95. Akerboom, "Only the Image," 259.
96. In general scholastic doctrine, the dying only reach salvation when they are in a

ing and perfecting the inner person who, by imitating Christ step-by-step, becomes conformed to the loving, enduring, and joyful dying of the Son of God.

15. Luther's Realistic and Existential Images of Fear

In contrast to this, Luther's teaching on "preparing to die" does not point to either the hazards challenging one's inner virtue or the ways to strengthen it. In place of the five temptations, Luther's work contains three terrifying and fearful literary images of death, sin, and hell.[97] First, if these images take hold of dying people, then they dread an unprepared, evil death as proof of God's condemning wrath.[98] They then become disheartened because of the number and size of their sins, perceiving "that even all their good works have become sins."[99] Finally, in vain curiosity *(vana curiositas)*, they want to know if they have been elected by God,[100] only to end up hating God because they find no trustworthy evidence but instead see themselves delivered up to the eternal torments of hell.[101] While the traditional temptations lead the dying to believe something false, the three images of which Luther spoke placed before their eyes an existential reality in which all people do in fact find themselves: in mortality, in sinfulness, and having deserved just condemnation of their entire existence. It is good and necessary for each person to recall this reality while alive.[102] For this is precisely the terrible danger that may come if the images of this reality win great power over people and if the devil (the real master of internalization) implants these images so deeply in the soul of the dying that they, as Luther repeatedly says, "forget God,"[103] that is, they lose sight of the saving

---

state of saving grace *(gratia gratum faciens)*, which is a combination of God's divine love *(caritas)* and the ability to earn merit *(merita de condigno)*. Merit and worthiness, however, could certainly be based on different and easily relativized criteria. See Berndt Hamm, *Promissio, Pactum, Ordinatio: Freiheit und Selbstbindung Gottes in der scholastischen Gnadenlehre*, Beiträge zur historischen Theologie 54 (Tübingen: Mohr, 1977).

97. Sections 6-8 of the "Sermon on Preparing to Die"; *LW* 42:101-3.
98. *StA* 1:233.32–234.3 (6); *LW* 42:101.
99. *StA* 1:234.22 (7); *LW* 42:101.
100. *StA* 1:234.34-36 (8); *LW* 42:101.
101. *StA* 1:235.1-8 (8); *LW* 42:101.
102. *StA* 1:234.7-9 (6) and 234.24-31 (7); *LW* 42:101-2.
103. *StA* 1:234.4f. (6), 234.19 (7), and 235.21 (9); *LW* 42:101f.

counterreality of God's grace. The dying then might succumb to the devilish temptation to fixate on the question of personal worthiness or unworthiness before God, no longer able to recognize that the saving action of Jesus Christ is effective precisely for them, the perpetually unworthy.[104]

If those who are dying allow terrifying images to sink too deep inside, these will become devilish illusions that hide images of salvation. What can be a healthy fear during one's lifetime becomes a hopeless entanglement in doubt and anxiety when facing death. The way in which Luther describes the devilish power of these images of fear to take possession of a person certainly mirrors his own experience of *Anfechtungen* in the monastic school of internalization, especially when — in contrast to other earlier *ars moriendi* authors — he describes the oppressive doubts about predestination that allow a terrified person to fall into hatred of God, blasphemy, and longing for another God.[105] At the same time, however, Luther could address all those who demanded firm guarantees of grace and certainty of salvation when dying but who found no relief in the traditional methods of intensified piety and increased investments in the hereafter.

16. Christ as the Threefold Image of Nonanxious Salvation, *Extra Nos*

Following what I have just said about the essential features of a Reformation view of justification and dying, it is clear where Luther found dying people's escape from the problems of *Anfechtung*. People should already "in the midst of life" adjust themselves to the devil's fear tactics and know that they cannot by their own powers withstand evil thoughts about death, sin, and predestination. Instead, they need to let themselves receive the liberating external relationship to the reality of God's efficient grace. In this way, Luther directed his readers' attention to that protecting *extra nos* holiness of Christ and the *communio sanctorum*, just as many other *ars*

---

104. StA 1:240.19-29 (16); LW 42:105. See also n. 144 below.

105. See n. 101 above. Among *ars moriendi* authors before Luther, I found *Anfechtung* related to predestination only in Staupitz, chap. 7, 66.14-25: "Die acht anfechtigung ist in furbitzer [vorwitziger, zuviel wissen wollender] nachfrage der ewigen vorsehung. . . ." The basis for this finding likely lies in the fact that Staupitz, like his student Luther, held a strongly Augustinian view of predestination, unlike most pastoral or catechetical writers before the Reformation, who would have considered this teaching to involve more personal freedom.

moriendi writers had done before him, most recently Stephan Fridolin,[106] Johannes von Paltz,[107] and Johannes von Staupitz.[108] Luther continued this traditional line and took it to its end point by completely separating the saving effect of Christ's act of salvation from any question of human quality, for instance, the abilities to love or repent. If Staupitz could still warn of a "too presumptuous confidence in God's mercy" (that is, the devil makes "people who are dying more careless" by preventing the careful examination of their consciences and leading them to believe that no one becomes blessed by his or her righteousness and works but by God's mercy and grace alone),[109] Luther instead viewed the fundamental *Anfechtung* as not expecting salvation through God's mercy and the life and death of Christ alone.[110] He therefore couched the liberating turn from internal to external, from self-searching to an *extra nos* identity, in his admonition: "Seek yourself only in Christ and not in yourself and you will find yourself in him eternally."[111]

For Luther, the entire *ars moriendi* lay in this shift of perspective, inasmuch as he still used the term "art" in his "Sermon on Preparing to Die." "The one and only approach [*kunst*] is to drop [the three threatening images] entirely and have nothing to do with them," since they only want to chain people to their mortal, sinful, and degenerate condition. "But how is this done?" asked Luther. "It is done in this way: You must look at death while you are alive and see sin in the light of grace and hell in the light of heaven, permitting nothing to divert you from that view."[112] In other words, through the Christian faith, people are taught to see the transparency of these fearful pictures so that they can see through

---

106. See Petra Seegets, *Passionstheologie und Passionsfrömmigkeit im ausgehenden Mittelalter: Der Nürnberger Franziskaner Stephan Fridolin (gest. 1498) zwischen Kloster und Stadt* (Tübingen: Mohr Siebeck, 1998), 337.

107. See n. 16 above and Hamm, *Frömmigkeitstheologie am Anfang des 16. Jahrhunderts*.

108. See n. 17 above; Hamm, *Frömmigkeitstheologie*, 234-43; and Lothar Graf zu Dohna and Richard Wetzel, "Die Reue Christi: Zum theologischen Ort der Buße bei Johann von Staupitz," *Studien und Mitteilungen zur Geschichte des Benediktinerordens und seiner Zweige* 94 (1983): 457-82.

109. Staupitz, chap. 7.7 (on *Anfechtung*), 66.6-14.

110. *StA* 1:235.41–236.1 (10); *LW* 42:104: "For Christ is nothing other than sheer life, as his saints are likewise."

111. *StA* 1:237.11 (12); *LW* 42:106.

112. *StA* 1:235.27-30 (9); *LW* 42:103.

them[113] into those three comforting pictures that Christ himself reveals as the "three images" of life, grace, and heavenly blessedness.[114] Because death, sin, and hell are realities of my existence, I cannot simply look away from them and replace them with "positive" images that offer a friendly message; I cannot simply look at the Christ of the redemption. It depends far more on seeing through my own distress and recognizing that all dying, all the burden of sin, and all the damnation of being abandoned by God are found in the passion and *Anfechtung* of Christ.[115] That is when I realize that "Christ's life has taken your death, his obedience your sin, his love your hell, upon themselves and overcome them."[116] If I, in Christ, should find myself together with the three terrifying pictures[117] and see that he has deprived them of their power, then they can no longer frighten me. Only then do they fall away from me and disappear without distorting and disputing everything as before.[118] It is therefore essential to know that the realities of corruption and the counterrealities of life, grace, and heaven are bound together in each of the three images of Christ.

17. Images of Christ as Internal Images of Faith

Such is the view from faith. As soon as Luther introduced the images of Christ as images of faith, it became clear that this turn outward had everything to do with the inner person. From Luther's point of view, this liberating moment cannot be internalized enough. To that extent, he pushed not only the medieval logic of *extra nos* but also that of internalization further. For the threefold image of Christ can only really be comforting (i.e., give trust, certainty, rest, peace, and joy) when it pierces the innermost soul. Even there, where the frightening images threaten to become all-

---

113. *StA* 1:235.23 (9); *LW* 42:103.
114. *StA* 1:237.36 (13); *LW* 42:106.
115. *StA* 1:235.33-39 (10); *LW* 42:104: "you must not view or ponder death as such, not in yourself or in your nature, nor in those who were killed by God's wrath and were overcome by death. If you do that you will be lost and defeated with them. But you must resolutely turn your gaze, the thoughts of your heart, and all your senses away from this picture and look at death closely and untiringly only as seen in those who died in God's grace and who have overcome death, particularly in Christ and then also in all his saints."
116. *StA* 1:239.31-33 (15); *LW* 42:108.
117. See nn. 111 and 116 above.
118. *StA* 1:236.2-4 (10); *LW* 42:104. Cited below in note 121.

powerful, the person must view or imagine *(eynbilden)*[119] the images of life, grace, and salvation, engrave them within oneself *(ynn sich bilden)*,[120] or even better, "The more profoundly you impress that image [of Christ] upon your heart and gaze upon it, the more the image of death will pale and vanish of itself without struggle or battle. Thus your heart will be at peace and you will be able to die calmly in Christ and with Christ, as we read in Revelation [14:13], 'Blessed are they who die in the Lord Christ.'"[121] The concept of "imagining" in the sense of internally imprinting images on the soul corresponds to the "deconstruction" *(Entbildung)* of other images and comes from the terminology of Middle High German mysticism.[122] To describe the character of this turn within a person's inner foundation with his sermon on dying, Luther privileges the concept of faith. The crucial images that Christians should "imagine" in fighting against death, sin, and fear of hell are images of faith.

18. Luther's Newer Concept of Faith and Its Connection to Anthropological Inwardness and Christological Outwardness

Ever since his first Psalms lectures (1513-15), Luther raised the medieval concept of faith (then defined as an intellectual term) from the bottom rung on the ladder of virtues up to the central concept of the Christian life. At the same time, he removed it from the realm of virtue entirely, as if it were merely something to attain to reach salvation.[123] The intense combination of anthropological inwardness and christological outwardness forms an essential element in the new Reformation view of faith. People

---

119. *StA* 1:236.1 (10); *LW* 42:104.

120. *StA* 1:236.16 and 20 (11); *LW* 42:104.

121. *StA* 1:236.1-4 (10); *LW* 42:104.

122. See Jacob Grimm and Wilhelm Grimm, *Deutsches Wörterbuch*, vol. 3 (Leipzig: S. Hirzel, 1862), 149f., on "Einbilden." See also the use of the words *einbilden* and *bilden* in Meister Eckhart, *Die deutschen Werke*, ed. Josef Quint, 5 vols. (Stuttgart: W. Kohlhammer, 1958-76), 1:553 and 563; 2:812 and 847; 3:637; 5:572 and 584; and Suso, *Deutsche Schriften*, 565 and 585.

123. See chap. 3 above. See also Reinhard Schwarz, *Fides, spes und caritas beim jungen Luther, unter besonderer Berücksichtigung der mittelalterlichen Tradition* (Berlin: De Gruyter, 1962), and Matthias Kroeger, *Rechtfertigung und Gesetz: Studien zur Entwicklung der Rechtfertigungslehre beim jungen Luther*, Forschungen zur Kirchen- und Dogmengeschichte 20 (Göttingen: Vandenhoeck & Ruprecht, 1968).

who face their mortality and total sinfulness and come to faith are struck by the Spirit of God in their innermost being, that place where the existential move between anxiety and courage, fear and trust, doubt and certainty, despair and joyful assurance happens.

The strangest and most significant thing about this internal faith is that people's courage, trust, consolation, certainty, and joy cannot be explained or derived from inside, as if they more or less expressed various pious states of thinking and feeling. To be sure, the entire liveliness of this faith is internal, working cognitively and emotionally within the soul, above all when experienced as an intense trusting love of God and as lived out ethically in love of one's neighbor. Nevertheless, neither faith's enduring source of certainty and trust nor its essential and saving righteousness comes from within. Rather, it only comes *extra nos* in Christ.[124] Faith liberates people in their living and their dying solely as a purely receptive experience.[125] When sinners who have been driven into a corner by frightening images look away from themselves, see the crucified and risen Christ, and set their firm hope of their faith on him, then the comforting, trustworthy images of life, forgiving grace, and election to eternal salvation reach their innermost being as images of Christ. People can confront and overturn these internal images of fear precisely because this faith has come entirely from outside themselves.

In view of the contrast between sin and grace, Luther formulated this fundamental move from outer to inner and the "imagining" of the threefold image of Christ thus:

> You must . . . look at sin only within the picture of grace. Engrave that picture in yourself with all your power and keep it before your eyes. The picture of grace is nothing else but that of Christ on the cross and of all his dear saints. How is that to be understood? Grace and mercy are there where Christ on the cross takes your sins from you, bears it for you, and destroys it. To believe this firmly, to keep it before your eyes and not to doubt it, means to view the picture of Christ and to engrave it in yourself [*das gnaden bild ansehen und ynn sich bilden*].[126]

---

124. Karl-Heinz Zur Mühlen, *Nos extra nos: Luthers theologie zwischen Mystik und Scholastik*, Beiträge zur historischen Theologie 46 (Tübingen: J. C. B. Mohr, 1972).

125. Friedrich Gerke, "Anfechtung und Sakrament in Martin Luthers Sermon vom Sterben," *Theologische Blätter* 13 (1934), "Hier liegt der tiefste Sinn der Lutherschen *sanctitas passiva*."

126. StA 1:236.12, 15-20; LW 42:104-5.

In the late medieval *ars moriendi* up through Staupitz, following and imitating the Christ of the passion played a crucial role in the formation of people preparing to die.[127] This disappeared entirely from Luther's teaching about dying.[128] For him, the dying person's christological gaze aims not at *imitatio* of Christ or at *imitatio* of the robber to Christ's right,[129] but solely at Christ's place as substitute: through his dying and rising for us, Christ has taken death, sin, and damnation upon himself and has overcome them.[130] To people who labor under fear of death and who suffer for sins, faith alone provides the saving external connection to the *Christus pro nobis*, thereby delivering them from their legalistic self-obsessions.

19. The Human Inability to Know and the Personal Certainty of Salvation through Faith in Christ

In the same way, faith frees people from fears about predestination, doubts about being chosen by God, and hellish images of eternal damnation. That

---

127. See n. 59 above and Staupitz, chap. 6, 62:15.1–19.21, 23-28, "So dann in diser erforschunge gesucht, wie man wol sterben solle und mogen tzu gewinne des weigen lebens, abwaschung der sund und betzalung aller schuldt, ist baldt geantworth: Stirb, wie Christus starbe, ßo stirbst du ann [ohne] allen tzweyfel selick und wol!" "Er is allein der, dem alle menschen folgen kunnen, in dem alles guts leben, leiden und sterben allen und ytzlichen vorgebildet, also, das nymant recht thuen, recht ledien, recht sterben kan, es geschehe dann gleichformig dem leben, dem leiden, dem sterben Jesu Christi, in welchs todt aller andere todt vorschlunden ist [1 Cor. 15:54]."

128. One might say that Luther turned the *imitatio Christi* into an *imitatio hominis*, in which he lets the dying Christ and the dying person remain the same in their *Anfechtung*: "He was assailed by the images of death, sin and hell just as we are," *StA* 1:238.10f. (14); *LW* 42:107. This comparison of Christ to us is exactly the point of imitation that Luther emphasized in this sermon: just as Christ silently bore these three images, we should also let them fall away and only "cling to God's will" (*StA* 1:239.1f.; *LW* 42:108). Luther then immediately drops the language of imitation, as he drops the traditional teaching about *imitatio* as a virtue and a perfection of "doing enough" and bearing enough suffering. In his view, faith does not mean becoming equal to the exemplary Christ but being taken into the *Christus pro nobis*. Insofar as there may be a secondary practical effect of *imitatio*, see his 1519 "Meditation on Christ's Passion," *LW* 42:3ff.

129. In comparison to late medieval *ars moriendi* literature, it is striking that the thief next to Christ on the cross does not appear at all in Luther's sermon. This means that the most important personal paradigm in *ars moriendi* instruction is missing, who only a few years earlier had defined Paltz's instructions for dying. See n. 47 above.

130. *StA* 1:237.36–238.6 (13); *LW* 42:106-7.

is, it frees them from the terrible dilemma of the human desire to know things for sure and of the human inability to know for sure.[131] Luther said,

> After all, you will have to let God be God and grant that he knows more about you than you do yourself. So then, gaze at the heavenly picture of Christ, who descended into hell [1 Pet. 3:19] for your sake and was forsaken by God as one eternally damned when he spoke the words on the cross, "Eli, Eli, lema sabachthani!" — "My God, my God, why hast thou forsaken me?" [Matt. 27:46]. In that picture your hell is defeated and your uncertain election is made sure. If you concern yourself solely with that and believe that it was done for you, you will surely be preserved in this same faith.[132]

Here Luther struck the tense bowstring between forbidden knowledge and gracious certainty of salvation. If you fall into yourself, he says, you will not find anything good.[133] This means that living and dying human beings find no basis or certainty of salvation in themselves, certainly not in any form of the *ars moriendi* or in their own repentance or humility, willingness or endurance in suffering, love or thankfulness, as desirable and important as these may be as effects of faith.[134] Instead, Luther connected the question of knowing to the question of being, an "ontology of the person."[135] The question of being has to do with the essential reason for our election and salvation: this does not lie in our piety, merit, or disposition at the time of death; it lies solely in Christ, the one abandoned and condemned by God, who has "conquered hell through his omnipotent love" and "gives this to us all if we but believe."[136] Because of this, no knowledge of salvation or certainty of election comes from either reflecting upon one's own condition or speculating about God's counsels. Those kinds of self-assurance and certainty about God's salvation are denied to humans. Neither sinking into oneself nor making some kind of ascent to God frees

---

131. See nn. 100 and 101 above.

132. *StA* 1:237.3-10 (12); *LW* 42:105-6.

133. *StA* 1:237.15-17; *LW* 42:106: "However, if you do not adhere solely to this but have recourse to yourself, you will become adverse to God and all saints, and thus you will find nothing good in yourself."

134. See section 25 below.

135. Wilfried Joest, *Ontologie der Person bei Luther* (Göttingen: Vandenhoeck & Ruprecht, 1967).

136. *StA* 1:238.3-6 (13); *LW* 42:107.

The Early Luther

a person from anxiety about predestination. Only Christ's descent into the God-forsakenness of hell and his resurrection from death and damnation can do that. Through faith, for all who are struggling, Christ will certainly be present as the conqueror of hell and witness of God's saving love.[137] In the process, of course, internal faith becomes totally external. It puts an end to individualistic searches for worthiness and signs of the divine will and finds the personal certainty of salvation *extra nos* solely in Christ's overcoming of the forces of evil. Those who seek themselves only by looking to Christ and relying on him will be sure of finding salvation; they can even be sure of it already.[138] In this way, being and knowing have been joined together.

20. The New Function of the Sacrament of Extreme Unction in Luther's Sermon

Luther's sermon overcame all fears and doubts with respect to God and humanity through its Christology. Between instruction and consolation, the new view of faith brought a complete outward turn, from the internal dimension focused on personal qualities to the external dimension of Christ's sheltering grace. Luther strengthened this turn by assigning an important preparatory role to the sacraments in ministering to the dying. After spending paragraphs 6 through 14 describing the theme of frightening and comforting images, paragraphs 15 through 17 address the "holy sacraments" in detail. He had earlier made a little nod to their importance for dying people in paragraphs 4 and 5. Given the background of the late medieval *ars moriendi*, it was natural to deal thoroughly with the sacramental means of grace in such a tract. Here, too, Luther stayed within the traditional framework when at this time (autumn 1519) he accepted extreme unction, alongside Holy Communion and confession, as a sacrament for the dying. Even so, he discussed only communion and absolution with any concreteness. Of course, the way he introduced the sacraments already fully harmonized with his new doctrine of salvation.

In the late Middle Ages, extreme unction (sometimes called "last rites") offered protective aid to empower, intensify, and complete a person's virtuous, meritorious, and satisfactory preparation for dying. Its sa-

---

137. *StA* 1:238.4 (13); *LW* 42:107.
138. *StA* 1:237.7-11 (12); *LW* 42:105-6.

credness served the *ars moriendi* ideal of a final climb toward holiness in a person's life.[139] Therefore, some authors stressed that this sacrament for the dying might often turn an imperfect and angst-ridden repentance *(attritio)* into true loving repentance *(contritio)*.[140] In Luther, however, the sacraments worked the other way around. They should give afflicted sinners the certainty that their salvation does not depend on any requirements of personal quality, virtue, holiness, or merit. Gained through the indulgence controversy, this new view of the sacraments in the first half of 1518 was reflected in his turning from making a true act of repentance to having faith in the sacraments' promises.[141] Consequently, he did not speak here of human virtues but only of the "virtue of the sacrament" to work against sin and the human lack of virtue.[142] Luther pointedly placed this kind of virtue in seeing the sacraments as applicable and useful[143] in opposition to traditional reflections on the worthiness or unworthiness of the dying person about to receive the sacrament: "God gives you nothing because of your worthiness, nor does he build his Word and sacraments on your worthiness, but out of sheer grace he establishes you, unworthy one, on the foundation of his Word and signs. Hold fast to that and say, 'He who gives and has given me his signs and his Word, which assure me that Christ's life, grace, and heaven have kept my sin, death, and hell from harming me, is truly God, who will surely preserve these things for me.'"[144] Luther continued by making this divine reliability concrete through an example from the sacrament of confession: "'When the priest absolves me, I trust in this as in God's Word itself. Since it is God's Word, it must come true. That is my stand, and on that stand I will die.' You must trust in the priest's absolution as firmly as though God had sent a special angel or apostle to you, yes, as though Christ himself were absolving

---

139. Gerson, "De arte moriendi" (observation number 1), 735.

140. On this widespread and predominantly Scotist teaching of the fifteenth century, see Berndt Hamm, "Wollen und Nicht-Können in der spätmittelalterlichen Bußseelsorge," in *Spätmittelalterliche Frömmigkeit*, ed. Berndt Hamm and Thomas Lentes (Tübingen: Mohr Siebeck, 2001), 127f.

141. Oswald Bayer, *Promissio: Geschichte der reformatorischen Wende in Luthers Theologie*, Forschungen zur Kirchen- und Dogmengeschichte 24 (Göttingen: Vandenhoeck & Ruprecht, 1971).

142. *StA* 1:233.14 (5) and 233.23f. (6); *LW* 42:100-102.

143. *StA* 1:239.6f.; *LW* 42:108: "we now turn to the holy sacraments and their blessings to learn to know their benefits and how to use them."

144. *StA* 1:240.27-32 (16); *LW* 42:110.

you."[145] After this passage follow four different aspects of Luther's sacramental theology (in paragraphs 21-24) that need to be emphasized in light of his teaching about dying.

21. The Sacramental Visualization and Substantiation of Christ in the Images of Faith

First, it is important that Luther defined the sacraments in the traditional way as a combination of sign and word, whereby the symbolic element was absorbed entirely into the verbal character of the sacrament. The symbol becomes a visible word or a spoken sign.[146] Luther became even clearer when he spoke of "signs," "promise," or "contract."[147] As long as the discussion is only about the images of Christ (i.e., the saving reality of Christ *extra nos* that needs to become an internal image of faith for life, grace, and salvation), the question remains open as to how this long-ago act of redemption might become a present reality and consolation to a dying person. Luther addressed this question by accentuating the gospel's direct effect on the spoken, performative form of the sacraments and then connecting the soul's images of faith to these external symbols and words of promise. Unlike the *ars moriendi* literature, he did not speak of actual pictures that should be shown to the dying. Instead, he concentrated the external, physical element and the need to visualize salvation completely on the sacraments, in which the visible and audible were combined into *one* action.[148] In giving comfort, trust, and certainty of salvation to a frightened, dying person, he considered this to

---

145. StA 1:240.32-36 (16); LW 42:110.

146. See the following quotation from Augustine, which was important for Luther, PL 35:1840: "Accedit verbum ad elementum, et fit sacramentum, etiam ipsum tamquam visibile verbum."

147. StA 1:239.14 (15), LW 42:108: "a sign and testimony"; StA 1:240.2 (16), LW 42:109: "nothing but God's words, promises, and signs"; StA 1:241.3 (17), LW 42:111: "signs and promises"; and StA 1:241.23f., LW 42:111: "In the sacraments we find God's Word — which reveals and promises Christ to us."

148. StA 1:239.19-25 (15); LW 42:108-9: "It follows from this that the sacraments, that is the external words of God as spoken by a priest, are a truly great comfort and at the same time a visible sign of divine intent. We must cling to them with a staunch faith as to the good staff which the patriarch Jacob used when crossing the Jordan [Gen. 32:10], or as to a lantern by which we must be guided, and carefully walk with open eyes the dark path of death, sin, and hell, as the prophet says, 'Thy word is a light to my feet' [Ps. 119:105]."

be the most important aid, since — especially in the bread and wine — it showed the afflicted inner person an external visible symbol of Christ's healing and spoke a word of promise.[149] Thus, the accent on the sacramental symbol and word corresponded to the basic movement of Luther's teaching about dying (as in all his theology) from the outer dimension of Christ and his *promissio* to the inner dimension of having faith in Christ.[150]

22. Personal Assurance of Faith through the Sacraments

Through the sign and promise of the sacraments comes the personal assurance or affirmation of faith. In them, Christians have absolutely certain symbols and assurances, which God has made fully binding and which can be trusted without reservation.[151] To use the sacraments properly "involves nothing more than believing that all will be as the sacraments promise and pledge through God's Word. Therefore, it is necessary not only to look at the three pictures in Christ and with these to drive out the counter-pictures, but also to have a definite sign which assures us that this has surely been given to us. That is the function of the sacraments."[152]

This formulation allows us to see clearly where for Luther the "more" of the sacraments rests in comparison with the iconographic messages of the story of God's salvation. On the general level, the holy images of Christian proclamation show the victory over death, sin, and hell in Christ; the signs and words of the sacraments, however, lead from the general to *pro me* (for me). They do not simply show salvation but rather turn it into individual assurance through their personal promise and application "that

---

149. The emphasis on the real presence in the bread and wine became focused in Luther's thought later in his encounters with Karlstadt and Zwingli. In 1519-20 his view was more on the promise given through the sacrament.

150. The move from outward to inward is expressed in the words "Nothing is more pleasing and desirable to the ear than to hear that sin, death, and hell are wiped out. That very thing is effected in us through Christ if we see the sacraments properly. The right use of the sacraments involves nothing more than believing that all will be as the sacraments promise and pledge through God's Word," in *StA* 1:241.25-28 (17); *LW* 42:111, as well as *StA* 1:239.4f. (14); *LW* 42:108: "Only Christ's image must abide in us." See also Oswald Bayer, *Martin Luthers Theologie: Eine Vergegenwärtigung* (Tübingen: Mohr Siebeck, 2003), 41-61.

151. *StA* 1:240.14f. (16); *LW* 42:110: "Faith must be present for a firm reliance and cheerful venturing on such signs and promises of God."

152. *StA* 1:241.27-31 (17); *LW* 42:111.

your sin, your death, and your hell are also vanquished and wiped out and that you are thus redeemed."[153] Thus the faithful answer of afflicted people lies not only in their inner circumspection but also in the unwavering trust and the sure confidence that can be given to the divine promise. Here the metaphor of image gives way to the visible word. Luther's *promissio* theology, packed into the sacraments, leads beyond the piety of meditating on images without thereby abandoning it. For him, theological concentration on the spoken word of salvation and the context of the pious contemplation of images are always connected to one another.[154] In that way, Luther's "Sermon on Preparing to Die" is characteristic of the total structure of his Reformation theology.

23. God's Voluntary Pledge through the Sacraments' Promise of Salvation

When Luther spoke of the sure, certain, and binding[155] character of the verbal and symbolic nature of the sacraments, especially in the priestly absolution and the eucharistic gift of Christ's body, he always had God's voluntary pledge in mind, through which God has forever promised to be present in the sacramental promises and symbols. In this sense Luther talked about something being impossible for God due to God's own faithfulness and truthfulness: "The sign, the promise of my salvation will not lie to me or deceive me: 'It is God who has promised it, and he cannot lie either in words or deeds.'"[156] And again, "it will and must therefore be true that the divine sign does not deceive me. I will not let anyone rob me of it. I would rather deny all the world and myself than doubt my God's trustworthiness and truthfulness in his signs and promises. Whether worthy or unworthy of him, I am, according to the text and the declaration of the sacrament, a member of Christendom."[157] By looking away from one's personal

---

153. *StA* 1:240.8f. (16); *LW* 42:109. The full sentence reads: "What will it profit you to assume and to believe that sin, death and hell are overcome in Christ for others, but not to believe that your sin, your death, and your hell are also vanquished and wiped out and that you are thus redeemed?"

154. This is rightly emphasized in Martin Nicol, *Meditation bei Luther* (Göttingen: Vandenhoeck & Ruprecht, 1984), in contrast to Oswald Bayer.

155. See n. 152 above and *StA* 1:241.43; *LW* 42:112.

156. *StA* 1:239.33-35 (15); *LW* 42:109.

157. *StA* 1:241.5-8 (17); *LW* 42:111.

qualities for salvation, the certainty of salvation through faith arises solely from this unconditional reliability and God's own healing words of comfort and promise to the afflicted.

24. God's Real Presence in the Sacraments

It is truly God who comes near to me in the sacraments as "my God,"[158] and who thus becomes the inner assurance of faith. This is the center point of Luther's comfort for the dying, in which "God himself" is always present as *Christus pro me* (Christ for me): "In the sacraments your God, Christ himself, deals, speaks, and works with you through the priest. His are not the works and words of man. In the sacraments God himself grants you all the blessings we just mentioned in connection with Christ. God wants the sacraments to be a sign and testimony."[159]

The comforting nearness of grace reaches its peak for the one who is dying in the formulaic title "God Christ himself." With this phrase, Luther re-formed the *ars moriendi* tradition and its special emphasis on the nearness of the heavenly means of grace for the dying, changing, for instance, the way the woodcuts of the *Illustrated Ars* show the merciful God standing at the deathbed.[160] In Luther, this nearness of the sheltering salvation *extra nos* culminated not in pictures but in the word event of the personal pledge, namely, "God's word itself."[161] He understood the comforting character of the sacraments entirely from the perspective of their being word events.[162] As the saving words and verbal signs of the sacraments make clear, Luther found in them the merciful faithfulness, truthfulness, and omnipotence of God on which his faith could totally depend so that dying could become a "cheerful venture."[163] Only in this way does the *extra nos* become a cheerful, trusting confidence in one's conscience; only so do the comforting images of Christ reach a person's innermost soul.

---

158. *StA* 1:241.5-8 (17); *LW* 42:111.
159. *StA* 1:239.11-14 (15); *LW* 42:108.
160. See n. 54 above.
161. See n. 145 above.
162. See n. 148 above.
163. See n. 151 above; *StA* 1:240.14f. (16); *LW* 42:110.

25. Visualizing the Sheltering *Communio Sanctorum*

In good medieval fashion, Luther integrated the visualization of the entire *communio sanctorum* into the sacramentally given presence of God and Christ to the dying (especially at the end of his sermon in paragraphs 18 and 19). If the body of Christ is given to the dying through the Lord's Supper, then this is a sign, promise, and assurance to faith that they are accompanied by the protective aid and defense of the community of all angels, saints, and Christians.[164] "There is no doubt, as the Sacrament of the Altar indicates, that all of these in a body run to him as one of their own, help him overcome sin, death, and hell, and bear all things with him. In that hour the work of love and the communion of saints are seriously and mightily active."[165] Whoever does not believe this has not taken seriously "the communion, help, love, comfort, and support of all the saints in all times of need" promised in the body of Christ.[166] In this way, Luther integrated the late medieval concept of intercession into the *communio* idea of the body of Christ in his Reformation teaching about how to die. Together with the crucified Christ, the saints of all times in their suffering and dying take our sins upon themselves, bear them, overcome hell, and intercede for us before God.[167] This community is always at hand to help. Therefore, people who have faith should humble themselves and accept the help of the heavenly powers of protection; that is, they should call upon all the holy angels, particularly their own guardian angel, the Mother of God, all the apostles and the beloved saints, especially the ones God has given them for special reverence.[168] Such instructions by Luther do not signify any relativizing weakening of Christ's mediation of salvation but signify the extension of Christology to the members of Christ who in the effective event at Golgotha could become Christ for those who

---

164. This view of the communion of saints is true in paragraph 17 concerning the Lord's Supper (*StA* 1:241.1-5; *LW* 42:110-11); it is expressed again in paragraph 18, as the presence "of the dear angels, of the saints, and of all Christians" (*StA* 241.36; *LW* 42:112).

165. *StA* 1:241.36-40 (18); *LW* 42:112.

166. *StA* 1:241.41-44 (18); *LW* 42:112. The full sentence reads, "He who doubts this does not believe in the most venerable Sacrament of the Body of Christ, in which are pointed out, promised, and pledged the communion, help, love, comfort, and support of all the saints in all times of need."

167. *StA* 1:236.20-23 (11), 239.16-19 (15), 241.2-5 (17), 241.36-39 (18), and 242.34-36 (19); *LW* 42:104, 108, 111, and 113.

168. *StA* 1:242.27-33; *LW* 42:113.

need help.[169] In this sense, Luther had already extended the three images of Christ (life, grace, and salvation) to the saints.[170] Whoever looks to Christ also sees those who "die with you in Christ, bear sin, and vanquish hell."[171]

Within this *communio* motif, Luther reversed the direction of the view in the closing sections. Where he had spoken earlier of what the faithful should see, he now emphasized the passivity of the redemptive being seen and sustained. Even when dying people have taken leave of the world and all its people, they are not alone at the end; instead, the multitude of heavenly helpers are watching them[172] and sustaining their soul. "If you remain in that faith, all of them will uphold you with their hands. And when your soul leaves your body, they will be on hand to receive it, and you cannot perish."[173]

With this picture of the soul being received and borne up on high by the protecting powers of the hereafter, Luther also stayed in the realm of the traditional.[174] Yet he adapted all the traditional elements into a new general concept of preparation for death. The relationship between faith and the divine promise especially shows this. Strictly speaking, it is not faith that bears the dying but rather the *communio* of the triune God, the angels, saints, and all Christians, to whom the dying belong through faith.

---

169. See *The Freedom of a Christian*, StA 2:298.12-16; LW 31:366: "Although the Christian is thus free from all works, he ought in this liberty to empty himself, take upon himself the form of a servant, be made in the likeness of men, be found in human form, and to serve, help, and in every way deal with his neighbor as he sees that God through Christ has dealt and still deals with him"; and StA 2:305.1-11; LW 31:371: "I should lay before God my faith and my righteousness that they may cover and intercede for the sins of my neighbor which I take upon myself and so labor and serve in them as if they were my very own."

170. StA 1:235.39 (10), 236.1 (10), 236.17, 20-23 (11), and 237.12f. (12); LW 42:104 and 106.

171. StA 1:242.3f. (18); LW 42:108. See also StA 1:243.22f. (20); LW 42:114: "[God] commands his angels, all saints, all creatures to join him in watching over you, to be concerned about your soul, and to receive it."

172. StA 1:241.32-34 and 241.45–242.1 (18); LW 42:112: "in the hour of his death no Christian should doubt that he is not alone. He can be certain, as the sacraments point out, that a great many eyes are upon him"; and, later in the same, God's "eyes rest upon him" and "If God looks upon you, all the angels, saints, and all creatures will fix their eyes upon you."

173. See n. 171 above.

174. See picture number 11 in n. 54 above.

But this is only possible because this sheltering community has been firmly fixed through Christ's promise, which is the source of faith's certainty. When Luther stressed the supporting protection, security, and assurance of this community in this way, he actually strengthened the late medieval notion of the hidden and saving *extra nos* salvation of the *communio sanctorum*. He reinforced this idea primarily because he disconnected the *communio sanctorum* from the qualitative aspect of one's own piety and merit by centering everything on the Christ event. In the summarizing final section of his sermon, it is striking how Luther, as before, described the attitude of dying Christians in words that bring to mind the repertoire of virtues in the traditional *ars moriendi*. The dying do not fear death but accept it willingly, and their hearts are filled with joy, praise, humility, devotion,[175] love of God, and thankfulness for God's goodness.[176] But for Luther these are self-evident effects of faith's certainty rather than the last stage of a program of preparing to die, the purpose of which is to pay off punishments for sin, preserve people from impending time in purgatory, and enable the best possible and most meritorious place in salvation. Thus, the blessed effects of faith described by Luther were not conditions for salvation but the consequences of a salvation already received. In this sense, Heinrich Bullinger would later write in his instructions for dying in 1535, "Here everything with which one earlier heavily burdened the dying — namely how they must make satisfaction and pay for each and every sin — falls away."[177]

26. Luther's Sermon as a Groundbreaking Evangelical Profile of "Preparing to Die"

As different as the periods were, the relationship between the Reformation and the Middle Ages must be acknowledged simultaneously as a continuation and as a break. On one side, the Reformation handled death in conti-

---

175. StA 1:243.29-35 (20); LW 42:114-15.
176. StA 1:242.27-33 (19); LW 42:113.
177. Heinrich Bullinger, *Bericht der krancken: Wie man by den krancken und sterbenden menschen handlen, ouch wie sich ein yeder inn siner kranckheit schicken unnd zum sterben rüsten sole*... (Zurich: Christoph Froschauer, October 1535), fol. C5r. See also, Andreas Mühling, "Welchen Tod sterben wir? — Heinrich Bullingers 'Bericht der Kranken' (1535)," *Zwingliana* 29 (2002): 55-68. I am grateful to Dr. Mühling for making the first edition of Bullinger's piece available to me.

Luther's Instructions for a Blessed Death

nuity with late medieval teachings and pastoral care, picking up and intensifying the very pointed theology of mercy, grace, and comfort and taking these to their logical conclusions. On the other side, Luther's sermon started that decisive break from the late medieval *ars moriendi* model of cooperation and virtue, founding instead a new Reformation type of instruction for dying, namely, an "anti-art" of blessed dying. Decisive and groundbreaking elements are visible already in 1519, even if later Reformation writings on consolation for the dying and instructions for pastoral care of the sick and dying went in different directions.[178] The essential application of the new theology of justification to the deathbed scene is there, along with the message that the dying person "only" needs to believe in order to receive through pure mercy all that is necessary for salvation for Christ's sake. The weight falls entirely on basing the salvation of the dying exclusively on Christ's crucifixion and on the confident faith that is certain of its redemption because it gazes at *Christus pro me* and no longer needs to worry about a proper and worthy preparation for dying.

Luther's sermon showed how this theology rolled away the heavy stone that was placed on the hour of death, relinquishing the extreme finality of the late medieval instructions for dying. The traditional notion of a battle of otherworldly powers at the deathbed was certainly theologically sharpened and surpassed; it remains characteristic of Luther's theology that a sinner's location between law and gospel means that the relationship to death is stamped by a lifelong conflict between fear and comfort.[179] But it was already clear in 1519 that faith was the only way to prepare for dying and that one became certain of salvation by trusting God's victory over death, sin, and hell. "If you concern yourself solely with that and believe

---

178. See the bibliography for works on this topic by Luise Klein, "Die Bereitung zum Sterben: Studien zu den frühen reformatorischen Trost- und Sterbebüchern" (Diss. theol., Göttingen, 1958); Claudia Resch, *Trost im Angesicht des Todes: Frühe reformatorische Anleitungen zur Seelsorge an Kranken und Sterbenden* (Tübingen: Francke, 2006); and Austra Reinis, *Reforming the Art of Dying: The "Ars Moriendi" in the German Reformation (1519-1528)* (Burlington, Vt.: Ashgate, 2007). See also Franz, *Huberinus — Rhegius — Holbein: Bibliographische und druckgeschichtliche Untersuchung der verbreitetsten Trost- und Erbauungsschriften des 16. Jahrhunderts;* Moeller, "Sterbekunst in der Reformation"; and Konrad Hammann, "'Die Allerseligste Vorbereitung zum seligen Sterben': Kontinuität und Wandel lutherischer Frömmigkeit und Sterbekultur vom 16. bis zum 18. Jahrhundert im Spiegel der Göttinger Leichenpredigten," *Jahrbuch der Gesellschaft für niedersächsische Kirchengeschichte* 101 (2003): 117-64.

179. See sections 10, 12, and 13 above.

that it was done for you, you will surely be preserved in this same faith";[180] and "your heart will be at peace and you will be able to die calmly in Christ and with Christ."[181] Therefore, to be ready to die is a subject for one's entire life. There are always devilish *Anfechtungen*. Overcoming them always depends on being certain that as people baptized into the faith of the gospel, believers receive salvation without respect to any works, worthiness, or unworthiness. People who believe and pray in this way are always prepared for a blessed death, even if death should come unexpectedly.[182] Particular deathbed rituals or spiritual preparations were no longer necessary. For this reason, Luther's "Sermon on Preparing to Die" does not mention the role of the deathbed helper. Instead, by referring to the generous *communio sanctorum* that he so clearly stressed at the sermon's end, Luther did not mean the people around the deathbed but heavenly "benevolent powers."[183] For, since no one can come to faith by his or her own strength but, rather, God creates and sustains it in the soul,[184] being ready means nothing other than to "implore God and his dear saints our whole life long for true faith in the last hour, as we sing so very fittingly on the day of Pentecost, 'Now let us pray to the Holy Spirit for the true faith of all things the most, that in our last moments he may befriend us, and as home we go, he may tend us."[185] In a very principled and typical Reformation sense, Luther's teachings about how to die and how to live fall together.

For Luther, the sacraments were essential personal appropriations of the gospel for the assurance of faith. This sacramental focus in "Sermon on Preparing to Die," however, entirely disappeared in many other Reformation authors' works about dying, even in those written by Luther's immediate circle.[186] This simply confirms how varied the Reformation literature

---

180. *StA* 1:237.8-10 (12); *LW* 42:105-6.

181. *StA* 1:236.3f. (10); *LW* 42:104.

182. Luther confirmed this view in later critiques of *ars moriendi* literature, for instance, in a sermon of 1536 (WA 41:669, 13-24).

183. See section 3 above, especially n. 31. Luther more sharply expressed himself on this topic in the famous Invocavit Sermons of March 1522 in *StA* 2:530.5-7; *LW* 51:70: "every one must himself be prepared for the time of death, for I will not be with you then, nor you with me." On the fact that this did not mean there would no longer be pastoral care at the deathbed, see Mennecke-Haustein, *Luthers Trostbriefe*, 49.

184. *StA* 1:242.27-29 (19); *LW* 42:113.

185. *StA* 1:243.5-8 (19); *LW* 42:114. Here Luther cited a well-known medieval hymn, the full text of which can be found in *LW* 53:263-64.

186. For instance, see Kaspar Güttel, "Ein Tröstlicher Sermon" (1523). Güttel was a

on "preparing to die" became. Still, the basic tenor of this teaching about dying lies in the intense connection among *sola fide*, personal certainty of salvation, the fundamental *solus Christus*, and a programmatic liberation from fear and relief for the dying. The faithful can meet their last hour and divine judgment without fear, with a peaceful confidence, and free from any strategies about taking precaution or attaining perfection, since there is no purgatory and Christ has wiped out the punishments of hell, opened heaven, and appointed believers as heirs of salvation.[187]

---

fellow monk and a friend of Luther, who was similarly influenced by Staupitz. One fruit of this sermon is its writing about death; the second section (on how to overcome *Anfechtung*) follows Luther's 1519 sermon closely but does not mention the sacraments. This is reminiscent of Staupitz, whose 1515 writing on the subject similarly left out the sacraments. See Austra Reinis, "Evangelische Anleitung zur Seelsorge am Sterbenden 1519-1528," *Luther* 73 (2002). On Güttel in Zwickau, see Bernd Moeller and Karl Stackmann, *Städtische Predigt in der Frühzeit der Reformation: Eine Untersuchung deutscher Flugschriften der Jahre 1522 bis 1529* (Göttingen: Vandenhoeck & Ruprecht, 1996), 87f.

187. Some insecurity might certainly remain among the living, for instance, if they wondered if they would stay faithful to Christ in their time of *Anfechtung*. For this reason, Lazarus Spengler, the Lutheran town clerk in Nuremberg, worked out a kind of advance directive. In three versions (1527, 1529, and 1533), he made a personal confession of faith and had it notarized. He explained first that he wanted to remain in the faith until his death. Next, he said that any fear or anxiety during his dying that caused him to disavow his faith could only be the work of the devil, so that people could be confident of his willing faith. Spengler took his confession word for word from Luther's 1528 "Confession concerning Christ's Supper," WA 26:499.2-10 and 509.24-27; *LW* 37:163 and 371. In these confessions, Luther and Spengler were clearly acting within late medieval traditions; see Berndt Hamm, *Lazarus Spengler (1479-1534): Der Nürnberger Ratsschreiber im Spannungsfeld von Humanismus und Reformation, Politik und Glaube* (Tübingen: Mohr Siebeck, 2004), 299-308.

CHAPTER 6

Luther's Discovery of Evangelical Freedom

Because of its programmatic objectives, the Reformation in Germany and Switzerland can be characterized as a liberation movement. The concept of freedom was the strikingly dominant role in Reformation writings, at least until the end of the Peasants' War. It became a catchphrase, contrasting the liberating power of God's word to the enslaving powers of the papal church and its attendant theological, social, and economic systems. This concept signaled the beginning of a new era because it tried to express how people have been freed once and for all, thereby empowering a new authority, which was actually not new but had rather been buried for centuries. People of the time greeted this liberating historical break as a release from the yoke of Egypt, an exodus into the Promised Land, deliverance from the Babylonian captivity, and the breaking of the morning dawn after a long night. Such experiences of liberation and declarations of freedom, including those of Zwingli and his Swiss and upper German spheres of influence, received their first impulses from Luther. This freedom was kindled by his mastery of clear biblical interpretation, which was admired by all parties, and by his

---

On Luther's understanding of freedom, see the following works in the bibliography: Maurer, *Von der Freiheit eines Christenmenschen*; Joest, *Gesetz und Freiheit*; Iwand, "Die Freiheit des Christen und die Unfreiheit des Willens"; Pesch, "Freiheitsbegriff und Freiheitslehre bei Thomas von Aquin und Luther"; Ebeling, "Frei aus Glauben"; Hamm, *Promissio, Pactum, Ordinatio*; Jüngel, *Zur Freiheit eines Christenmenschen*; Moeller and Stackmann, *Luder — Luther — Eleutherius*; Jacobi, "Christen heißen Freie"; Rieger, *Von der Freiheit eines Christenmenschen*.

Luther's Discovery of Evangelical Freedom

outspoken engagement in the face of ecclesiastical authority (in Augsburg in 1518 with Cajetan), the scholarly world (in Leipzig in 1519 with Eck), and the emperor and empire (in Worms in 1521). And it was precisely Luther who through his writings defined the era and his contemporaries' shared views of reformation over against the papacy by means of the concept of Christian freedom, *libertas Christiana*. In both *The Babylonian Captivity of the Church* and *The Freedom of a Christian* (1520), he gave reform-minded people the vocabulary for achieving separation from the priestly papal church and its system of good works. Luther's new language of liberation gained the interest of everyone from princes to peasants for different reasons, which led to its being recast with very significant consequences and finally spun off into a multiplicity of Reformation theologies and institutions. Nevertheless, the critical observation remains the fact that the liberation movement of the Reformation had its roots in Luther's theology of liberation. A look at the events surrounding this Wittenberg monk and at an entire era's impulse toward freedom leads us therefore to the question: What was that Christian freedom that Luther discovered and that gained such illuminating power among his contemporaries?

What was new about Luther's understanding of freedom (and which simultaneously reveals to us the center of his Reformation theology) can only be comprehended by looking at it from the background of medieval theology. There, too, "freedom" was a main theme, kept in perpetual motion, even, by a comprehensive theology of liberation. Medieval theology considered freedom to be preservation from the temptations of the devil, the world, and one's own body. It was deliverance from sinful corruption and from the guilt and punishments of sin. It was liberation into the righteousness of a new spiritual life and the glory of eternal life.

Within this sphere of traditional pious hopes about freedom in the hereafter, medieval thinkers focused especially on the theological and psychological problem of the freedom of the will, that is, the relationship between God's efficient grace and the human ability to make free decisions *(liberum arbitrium)*. On this point, scholastic theologians from the twelfth to the beginning of the sixteenth century offered two fundamentally different possibilities: the freedom of the will was viewed as either a freedom working against grace or a freedom coming from grace. From this differentiation, I will now characterize the two opposing views, within which the scholastic theology of grace developed numerous modifications and an abundance of partial solutions. Without some necessary simplifications, it is impossible to find a way through this labyrinth of doctrinal opinions. Taking a look at the most sharply stated opposing positions, however, outlines at least the width of the spectrum and reveals common basic tendencies.

The ancient Greek idea of the rational being's freedom to choose stands behind the notion of freedom with respect to grace; like Hercules at the crossroads, one has to choose between the arduous path of virtue and the easy road of vice. With their free wills, people can decide for or against God's justifying grace, either opening or closing themselves to it. Naturally, they can only be saved through the gift of this new quality of grace, but whether or not they receive this grace depends on their decision. Here, in the realm of morality, there is no all-powerful necessity. This is the freedom of autonomous individuals who determine their own fate with respect to grace, which we find above all in the thought of William of Ockham (d. 1347) and his followers.

In contrast, a quite different understanding of freedom can be found in those scholastic theologians who set themselves firmly on the theology of grace characterized by the Pauline theology of the late Augustine. Examples of this would include Thomas Aquinas (d. 1274) in his *Summa theologiae* and Luther's superior in the order, his teacher and pastor Johannes von Staupitz (d. 1524). For these theologians, freedom in the theological sense was not freedom to decide about grace but a freedom that first comes from grace; this is a freedom and a certainty of will poured out through grace. This means that God's grace, working in people and reversing the direction of their wills, empowers them to voluntarily do what is good from within their innermost drive, so they can thereby fulfill the true intention of God's law. Freedom is the graciously given ability to love willingly and spontaneously. Here freedom's opposite is not the concept of necessity *(necessitas)*, as in Ockham's view, but of coercion *(coactio)*. That is, according to God's predestination, the change created by grace certainly occurs by necessity, but God always lets this necessary consequence of gracious election happen in such a way that people experience it not as coercion but as an affirmation that comes from inner willingness and joy. For Thomas Aquinas, for instance, this meant that God determines a person's direction through the supernatural habit of grace only by moving the person's will in a manner consistent with the person's own human nature. God's movement transforms itself into a spontaneous self-movement of the person; the person moves toward the goal of eternal life as an active subject while at the same time being moved and directed by God.[1] The Au-

---

1. See especially Thomas Aquinas, *Summa theologiae* I-II, q. 113, art. 3.

gustinian students of the Middle Ages called this grace-filled participation the freedom of a free will, the *liberum arbitrium*.

As clear as the differences between these two lines of thinking about freedom in the medieval tradition are (a difference between Greek philosophy and Saint Paul), a deep similarity is nevertheless remarkable: both are psychologically oriented, so that consideration of the human soul and its freedom of the will mirror each other. This was quite true in the strict Augustinian tradition, as well. For its entire interest was dedicated to reflecting upon how divine grace becomes active in humans, how the external working of the Holy Spirit becomes the deepest life principle within people, and how people might achieve this in themselves through a lifelong process in which human identity discovers the reason for its creation. In this, freedom enters the realm of the theology of grace only in the dynamic of freely chosen love and the good works that come from it. These things are then seen as conditional requirements: the final goal of eternal life cannot be given, unless Christians are on the path of good works, which has been made possible by justifying grace.[2] Christian freedom is therefore an inner quality within people whom God has pardoned; it is the necessary requirement for passing through the final judgment.

This overview of the medieval theology of grace also leads us to the conclusion that a dominant concept of freedom focused on what humans were able to achieve, even when that achievement would completely wither under the perspective of divine gift. It is only mentioned in passing that a similar limitation had been established regarding the medieval view of the church. The "freedom of the church" had become a slogan of church politics since the investiture controversy of the eleventh century, when priestly power and legal and economic privileges were defended against the encroaching laity. Announced by reformers of the time as a sign of integrity among the clergy that featured hierarchical organization, disciplined submission, and a ritually purified way of life, the weighty monastic system sought to guarantee the transfer and administration of salvation. That's how the ideal argument went, at least. The interest in salvation was also critical here. If the theology of grace focused on the psychology of the free will, this notion of the freedom of the church similarly concentrated on institutional-

---

2. Johann von Staupitz, *De exsecutione aeternae praedestinationis*, §45: "nequaquam igitur sine bonis moribus et operibus sanctis"; §50: "sine talibus operibus numquam." See also the idea of merit in §37 and the unfolding of the thought of freedom in §§170-77 (§170: "sine qua nulli adulto salutem concedit").

izing the sacred nature of the divine presence. In both cases, freedom meant the expansion of the human opportunities to gain grace, whether this was of a subjective/personal nature or of an objective/institutional nature.

Martin Luther entered the Erfurt cloister of the Augustinian hermits in 1505, and this medieval system of achievement led the young brother into deep doubt. He did not find any free spontaneity of pure love of God and neighbor in himself, but only the poison of selfishness and a subtle hatred of a God who punishes sinners with a far-off righteousness. Luther's quest for a merciful God was a futile quest for a quality of his own heart that might pass the judgment of his critical self-analysis and become the basis for God's giving grace to free him entirely from the guilt of sin and to effect grace in him.

In the fall of 1512, having sprouted up academically into a doctor of theology, Luther succeeded Staupitz as professor of biblical interpretation in Wittenberg. It is incredibly fortunate that all Luther's early lectures (beginning in 1513) have been preserved. Most of those are in Luther's own handwriting, while some are the students' transcripts. There were his lectures on the Psalms (1513-15), Romans (1515-16), Galatians (1516-17), and — beginning in the same winter semester as the Ninety-five Theses — Hebrews (1517-18). These outlines of a biblical theology give us a clear glimpse into how Luther's Reformation theology came into being. They show us how he sought a way out of the agonizing discrepancy between the late medieval religious demand for achievement and his experience of radical sin. Step-by-step, they show us how he found theological and existential clarity through the interpretation of the Bible.

The decisive departure from the tradition that ushered in a new epochal understanding of freedom started already in the Psalms lectures and was completed in the Romans lectures. Here, out of all the complex and controversial problems surrounding Luther's "Reformation turn," we can simply sketch one line of development. When Luther began his interpretation of the Psalms in 1513, he had already experienced the collapse of his monastic striving for piety. He could then work out that experience through the idea that people can never be good "in themselves," for God alone is *bonus in se ipso*.[3] Instead, people remain sinners before God all their lives.[4] In this apparently hopeless situation, how can there be a positive relationship between God and sinners? Luther found a way out of that

---

3. WA 4:210.25f.; *LW* 11:347.
4. WA 3:289.6f.; *LW* 10:237.

question through the idea of truth. Saving righteousness only reaches those who come to God in truth. Luther thus found the starting point for truth to be that place where people accept the real diagnosis of their situation; that is, they recognize themselves to be sinners, confess it, and do not try to build a house of lies about their own righteousness. Insofar as people find only sin in themselves, which accuses and condemns them, they fall into an accurate judgment, which is identical to God's judgment about them. But that is precisely what changes one's standing before God entirely. Instead of being condemned, such a person is pronounced righteous, for God no longer condemns those who have condemned themselves and who have thereby participated in God's truth.[5] In this, God overrules the sentence of condemnation that the sinner had accepted as true by means of a saving judgment that allows the sinner to be counted as righteous. The main thing is that salvation or condemnation is not determined by an objective, visible condition of a person's moral nature. Viewed theologically (not according to the perspective of bourgeois morality), a person's condition is always sinful. But much more decisive is the perspective of the judgment: self-judgment and God's judgment.

This point already reveals a fundamental feature of Luther's entire theology: Luther's interest was not primarily in natural categories or the nature of things as they exist in themselves *(In-sich-Sein)*, but in the personal relationships that take a nature out of itself and beyond itself. A reorientation of human existence thus meant for him not a natural or qualitative change but a new decree that comes externally through one's relation to judgment. Those who have condemned themselves see themselves with new eyes: God has placed them under the new verdict of "acquitted." Incidentally, Luther appears to have come to this concept not simply through his fearful personal experience of corrupt human nature but also through his education in the nominalist philosophy and theology of the University of Erfurt. The late medieval nominalist worldview (in opposition to Thomism, for instance) characteristically sought to derive general concepts not from the nature of things in themselves but from the relationship between the discerning mind and its subject.

In this way, Luther also placed the humble self-accusations of sinners into an external relationship, since he viewed even that as the working of a prevenient grace given by the merciful God.[6] This new personal judgment

---

5. WA 3:287.20–293.21, especially 289.31–290.6; *LW* 10:237-39.
6. WA 4:446.31-34.

is the way that God's justifying grace comes to people. At the same time, Luther's view remained focused on the God who judges and on those who judge themselves. This particularly shows itself in a certain conditional way of looking at things: the judgment of sinners in their self-accusation and confession of sins is the *condition* and the necessary preparation (*dispositio, praeparatio*) for the final acceptance of the sinner in God's judgment, even when it is God alone who fulfills this condition by opening the sinner's eyes. Still closely connected to the medieval theology of grace and judgment, this conditional structure in Luther's early theology of humility[7] is also the reason why Luther did not pointedly apply the concept of freedom in his first lectures on the Psalms, except in a very unspecific, traditional sense and usually when prompted by the vocabulary of the Latin text of the Bible (e.g., the grace of God that frees from sin and unrighteousness).[8] Luther was not yet freed from looking at himself, from looking at that subtle achievement that existed precisely in admitting the inability to achieve anything.

In this respect, the lectures on Romans (1515-16) revealed a further key development in Luther's theology, even if the transition was fluid and the idea of the "precondition" had not yet been completely abandoned.[9] The manuscripts of Luther's lectures show how he was released from the negative obsession with the self and the judging God, opening up a new insight about God's generosity. Luther already knew that people live by God's gift of grace. But his image of the merciful God and God's justifying righteousness was totally eclipsed by the concept of God's judging righteousness: God justifies through judgment. When people judge themselves, they are justified.[10] The grace of God working in sinners must change their fundamental outlook about judgment in such a way that they

---

7. Examples in Berndt Hamm, *Promissio, Pactum, Ordinatio: Freiheit und Selbstbindung Gottes in der scholastischen Gnadenlehre*, Beiträge zur historischen Theologie 54 (Tübingen: Mohr, 1977), 377-85.

8. WA 3:119.15f. and 453.4-24; LW 10:395-96.

9. We ought to note that Luther kept the conditional manner of formulation as long as he lived. Later, he could occasionally say "*If* (or *because*) people believe, they will be justified by God" or "God justifies the person *because of* his faith," as in *The Freedom of a Christian*, §11, WA 7:25.18-20 (German) and 54.23 (Latin); LW 31:351. Here Luther speaks simply from the human point of view and without making faith *theologically* a *requirement* for grace and salvation. What appears from a human point of view to be a condition is, as God sees it, a consequence.

10. WA 3:461.20–467.4; LW 10:403-8.

can endure God's righteous judgment. This reorientation of God's mercy and grace with respect to God's judging righteousness overcame Luther, so that he gained a new idea about *iustitia Dei*, the righteousness of God.

As Luther reported in several later reminiscences, the Reformation meaning of *iustitia Dei* revolved around a certain understanding of Romans 1:17: "The righteousness of God is revealed through the gospel." With the explication of this passage, right at the very beginning of his Romans lectures, the new interpretation of righteousness greets us: "by the righteousness of God we must not understand the righteousness by which He is righteous in Himself but the righteousness by which we are made righteous by God. This happens through faith in the Gospel."[11] Luther no longer understood the righteousness of God revealed in the gospel as the diagnosing, punishing, or rewarding righteousness of a heavenly judge; it was also no longer a static personal trait that forced people to obsess over their own sinful or spiritual being, as if judgment only came through this kind of process. Instead, righteousness became identical with the event of divine mercy given as a gift. It is a righteousness that shares itself, in which God incorporates sinful beings into God's own righteous being in order to justify them. This justifying righteousness of God no longer appears simply as one aspect of God's judging righteousness but is now the comprehensive saving reality of righteousness. On the sinner's side, the negative attitude of humility in self-judgment is circumscribed by the positive foundation of a believing and hoping trust.

The break with scholasticism first becomes visible when we notice *which* understanding of justification this dynamic concept of righteousness entails. For the dynamic of a self-sharing righteousness of God could be viewed in a thoroughly Catholic way: as the arrival of a supernatural grace and a new quality of love, which then ultimately and meritoriously evolve into the reward of eternal life.

That is exactly the view of justification that Luther rejected in his Romans lectures. In contrast to it, Luther presented his new theology of relationship — the personal relationship of judging and being judged —

---

11. WA 56:172.3-5; *LW* 25:151. Already in his *Dictata super Psalterium* Luther occasionally allowed the concept (by no means alien to scholastic theology) that God's righteousness is *also* a justifying righteousness that is bestowed upon the sinner as the *iustitia Christi* (see WA 4:19.30, 37-39; *LW* 11:172-73); but he did not draw out the consequence of this, which could soon be seen in the unmistakable words in the lectures on Romans: "*non* ea debet accipi, qua ipse iustus est in se *ipso*" (including the interpretation of the *iustitia Dei* and the *iustitia Christi* as a *iustitia externa* that justifies the believer).

which he was developing even further than he had in his Psalms lectures.[12] How does the righteousness of God reveal itself to be a justifying power? How does God bridge the chasm of sin and death created by the devil that separates God from humans? By means of judgment alone. God justifies people not on the basis of their inner moral qualities but rather externally, *ex sola Dei reputatione,* that is, solely on the basis of God's judgment that has declared sinners to be righteous even though in themselves they remain sinful.[13] The decisive point here is how Luther gave the category of judgment a new positive foundation based on Christ. He did this through the concept of "imputation" *(reputatio, imputatio),* thereby overcoming the concept of righteousness' negative dependence on ideas about judgment.[14] For that righteousness that God gives to sinners through God's own self-disclosure is the righteousness of Jesus Christ — God made flesh — who has been revealed to us in his vicarious suffering and death and who came for our benefit. The merciful God the Father reckons Christ's righteousness to be our righteousness, accepting it as the righteousness of sinful people. With this, the person and work of Christ coincide with the mercy and righteousness of God. God's righteousness is therefore mercy, because as the righteousness of Christ it becomes the righteousness of the human being.[15] Luther called this righteousness of ours a *iustitia externa* or *iustitia aliena* (an external, foreign, or alien righteousness), because it is not our property but always remains the righteousness of Jesus Christ imputed to us, which connects us with God only through the relationship of judgment.[16]

In the lectures on Romans, Luther was already describing this process of justification as an "exchange," as a trade between Christ's righteous-

---

12. Luther spoke specifically of *relatio* in the Romans lectures in WA 56:269.8 and 13; *LW* 25:257. The Aristotelian category of relation stands here in antithesis to the categories of *qualitas* and *habitus;* see chap. 9, n. 21 below.

13. WA 56:268.26–273.3, especially 269.2; *LW* 25:257-60.

14. In the lectures on the Psalms (WA 3:175.9-11; *LW* 10:146), Luther already used the expression *reputare iustitiam,* specifically in the interpretation of Ps. 32:2 ("Beatus vir, cui non imputavit dominus peccatum") and referring to Rom. 4:3 and 5 (of Abraham: "reputatum est illi ad iustitiam," "reputatur fides eius ad iustitiam"); yet here the *reputatio* is not so emphatically connected with the idea of the "external" righteousness as from the beginning in the lectures on Romans.

15. Sermon of February 24, 1517, WA 1:140.8-12; *LW* 51:29; and Luther's letter to Georg Spenlein on April 8, 1516, WA Br 1:35.15-36, no. 11; *LW* 48:12.

16. WA 56:158.10–159.24; *LW* 25:136-37.

ness and human sin.[17] Also, just as in his later tract *The Freedom of a Christian* (1520),[18] the theme of the "happy exchange" has as its goal the saving gift of freedom. As Luther put it, the heart of the believer turns from self-accusation to Christ, saying:

> Whence shall we take thoughts to defend us? Only from Christ, and only in Him will we find them. For if the heart of a believer in Christ accuses him and reprimands him and witnesses against him that he has done evil, he will immediately turn away from evil and will take his refuge in Christ and say, "Christ has done enough for me. He is just. He is my defense. He has died for me. He has made His righteousness my righteousness, and my sin His sin. If He has made my sin to be His sin, then I do not have it, and I am free. If He has made His righteousness my righteousness, then I am righteous now with the same righteousness as He. My sin cannot devour Him, but it is engulfed in the unfathomable depths of His righteousness, for He Himself is God, who is blessed forever." Thus we can say, "God is greater than our heart" (1 John 3:20). The Defender is greater than the accuser, immeasurably greater. It is God who is my defender. It is my heart that accuses me. Is this the relation? Yes, yes, even so![19]

With these sentences, Luther described his fundamental experience of freedom as being the remission of sin. For him, the gate to freedom was the ability to accept oneself as an unholy and ruined sinner and — simultaneously — to see oneself in the light of Christ's righteousness. In the Romans lectures, Luther announced this new perspective of "simultaneously" in the famous formula *simul iustus et peccator* (simultaneously justified and sinner).[20] This does not mean that a person is part sinner, part justified. It means that a person is entirely justified in God's judgment *(ex reputatione Dei)* and simultaneously entirely a sinner due to the reality of sinful human nature.[21] To put this in terms of an eternal salvation yet to

---

17. See the passage in the letter mentioned in n. 15, particularly lines 35-37; *LW* 48:12: "'Lord Jesus, you are my righteousness, just as I am your sin. You have taken upon yourself what is mine and have given to me what is yours. You have taken upon yourself what you were not and have given to me what I was not.'"

18. WA 7:25.26–26.12 (German) and 54:315–55.36 (Latin), §12; *LW* 31:351.

19. WA 56:204.14-25; *LW* 25:188.

20. WA 56:272.17-19; *LW* 25:260.

21. WA 56:272.17-19 and 271.29f.; *LW* 25:260.

come: the entire person remains a sinner throughout earthly life, even as a new righteous existence of obedience to God begins to appear.[22] But because God promises sinners a future liberation from this radically sinful existence,[23] the fullness of righteousness is already present for people now through the hope of faith. They have become *iustus ex promissione*[24] (justified by the promise) or *iustus in spe* (justified through hope).[25] The basis for this possibility of actualized promise and hope comes through the presence of the imputed righteousness of Christ.

Being simultaneously in total sin and in total righteousness, in accusation and in acquittal, is the point at which Luther ultimately broke with the medieval religion of achievement and its conditional concept of freedom. In scholastic thought, justification and the acceptance into salvation fall away from each other, separated by the bumpy stretch of road where liberated humans cooperate with grace. Freedom thus becomes a requirement for the ultimate acceptance into salvation. For Luther, on the contrary, freedom is itself the unconditional acceptance into salvation. This epochal break in the understanding of freedom and this key resolution of the traditional system of salvation-oriented self-achievement became possible by reevaluating the righteousness of God as that judging sentence of righteousness given in Christ that can be claimed as one's own righteousness. As Luther recalled one year before his death, this was the discovery in which he felt "altogether born again and had entered paradise itself through open gates."[26] Justification "simultaneously" opens the gates of paradise, because God does not pronounce the sinner righteous because of good works or in anticipation of them; rather, until the Last Judgment, God justifies without respect to works, thereby unconditionally receiving sinners into blessedness.

Along with his new perspective on unconditional justification, Lu-

---

22. WA 56:272.20; LW 25:260. On this change in existence that begins and develops within the Christian, Luther could use the expression *partim peccator, partim iustus*, as in WA 56:442.21f.; LW 25:434. But this partial aspect of *partim* is encompassed by the total aspect of *simul*. According to Luther, what a person has not yet achieved must always be regarded as total sinfulness.

23. On connecting the concepts *promissio/promittere* and *liberatio/liberare*, see WA 56:271.28, 31 and 272.8; LW 25:260.

24. WA 56:272.18; LW 25:260.

25. WA 56:269.30; LW 25:258: "peccatores in re, iusti autem in spe," and 272.4f.; LW 25:260: "in spe promissae sanitatis."

26. WA 54:186.8f.; LW 34:337.

ther's lectures on Romans and the following lectures on Galatians addressed the theme of freedom very pointedly and with sharper distinctions between the theology and piety of the medieval church.[27] In this, he emphasized two sides of Christian freedom, which then become the outline of his 1520 tract on freedom, namely, that the Christian is a free lord over all things and a servant in all things. On one hand, freedom is the freedom of the conscience from the law,[28] the fulfillment of which is now no longer a condition for the salvation of the faithful; rather it is always continuously given through Jesus Christ's fulfilling of the law. On the other hand, Luther understood freedom to be a spontaneous willingness to love, which dedicates itself to serving the neighbor.[29]

Freedom is liberation. Freedom is servitude. These two sides of Christian freedom correspond to Luther's concept of faith as he was developing it in the years 1515 to 1517 through his discovery of the gracious righteousness of God. Faith was then not only the negative fixation on the sinner's humble self-remorse but simultaneously the positive focus on trust in the God who saves. Here it becomes clear that Luther's fundamental perspective of a liberating judgment from God — the imputation and the acquittal — is by no means an "as if" judgment, as if it were a narrow rationalist perspective lacking any reality in the created world. For Luther, the righteousness of God that has been communicated through judgment always included the arrival of an effective change, too. God not only gives sinners God's own righteousness through Jesus Christ; God also, as the Holy Spirit, gives them a readiness to receive the gift. Faith is the effective arrival of the Holy Spirit. It is nothing other than sinners looking away from themselves and covering themselves in the righteousness of Christ. Luther also defined faith as a human judgment analogous to God's. Its place is in the conscience, which is nothing other than that basic attitude that people have about themselves, where they see themselves between the judgments of God and the devil, either accusing or defending themselves.[30] In faith, the conscience claims for

---

27. See Bernd Moeller and Karl Stackmann, *Luder — Luther — Eleutherius: Erwägungen zu Luthers Namen* (Göttingen: Vandenhoeck & Ruprecht, 1981), 193-96.

28. WA 56:424.16f.; *LW* 25:416.

29. Luther called such service the *summa libertas* and the *libertas optima et propria christianorum*, in WA 56:481.24-26; *LW* 25:474.

30. See the definition of conscience in the later tract *On Monastic Vows* (1521), WA 8:606.32-35; *LW* 44:298: "For conscience is not the power to do works, but to judge them. The proper work of conscience (as Paul says in Romans 2[:15]), is to accuse or excuse, to make guilty or guiltless, uncertain or certain."

itself God's judgment, which sees the whole person in the totality of sin and acquits it of all guilt and punishment. Also analogous to God's judgment, this judgment of faith is an effective reality and the highest vitality, out of which endlessly flow good works, honor to God, and benefits to neighbors. These are the two sides of Christian faith, the two sides that correspond to Christian freedom: the liberating freedom of judging faith and the bound freedom of a faith active in love.

The vocabulary of this second aspect — freedom as willingness to love — shows its great similarity with that view of freedom through grace visible in the strict Augustinian tradition of the Middle Ages.[31] But the critical point here is that Luther released this Pauline idea of willing service from the conditional context of the medieval theology of grace. Works of love do not ultimately culminate in a person winning salvation.[32] Instead, they flow naturally from the gift of salvation. For this reason alone they are truly free; that is, they are voluntary works of freedom. They do not need to build anything up before God but can focus themselves totally on the world's needs. This view of works is bound very closely to the fact that Luther, unlike medieval theologians, did not stress the subjective existence of the active person or the person's conversion of divine action into independent and spontaneous human cooperation.[33] Luther was not interested in that. Quite the opposite, he was interested in the creative efficacy of God alone and the pure passivity of the justified with respect to God. For him, then, a person's individuality did not indicate the continual movement of one's effort but indicated that person's inclusion in God's movement, in being swept away *(raptus)* and driven along, to the exclusion of any notion of merit, no matter how subtle. Luther's critique therefore validated a strict Augustinian interpretation of the *liberum arbitrium*.

From this two-sided understanding, a new kind of ecclesiastical critique using the language of freedom started to grow in these same years of 1516-17.[34] The freedom of the believing conscience from the law meant not

---

31. Commentary on Galatians (1519), WA 2:559.32–560.37; LW 26:325. See also Staupitz, *De exsecutione*, §§122-32, under the heading *De allevatione oneris legis*.

32. Staupitz, *De exsecutione*, §52: the *finis* (end) of the *opus christianum* (Christian work) is "glorification seu magnificatio, quae gratiae sunt effectus."

33. On the free election of persons, see also Staupitz, *De exsecutione*, §§170-72, and sermons 12 (111:40-42) and 27 (214:26-35). Staupitz wrote the Tübingen sermons (on Job 1:1–2:10) in 1498.

34. See especially the central excursus on freedom near the end of the Romans lectures, WA 56:493.15–498.12; LW 25:486-92.

only freedom from God's law but, even more, freedom from all the statutes and traditions of the church, which had inserted themselves as conditions for salvation or as aids to salvation that could bridge sinful misery and heaven's majesty. Luther called for a reform of canon law and a reduction of ceremonies, insofar as those things made Christians focus on their religious effort and established a spiritual hierarchy. He simultaneously made it clear, however, that his own critique did not have to do with changing the nature of the church itself but with liberating consciences in a way that went beyond external church structures to get to the true inner judgment of faith. If the conscience can be freed from its manic upside-down attempts to achieve salvation and could be grounded instead in the gospel's word of acquittal, then it could bear all possible forms of law and praxis — even tyrannical ones — as it would be led by love of the neighbor, consideration for those with weak consciences, and a concern for orderly social structures. Freedom thus proved itself to be both liberation and restraint in the realm of church critique, too, showing how Luther remained true to his fundamental perspective of judgment on this point, as well. Freedom does not depend on the nature of things in themselves. Everything — for salvation or condemnation — depends on the true or false judgment about things. This was the position from which Luther voiced his critiques of both the radical and conservative parties in the following years. Luther tracked the deepest roots of the church's "captivity" down to how humans stand before God. From that point, though, he gained a relativizing tranquility with respect to external changes, compared to which the impatience of revolutionaries looked like a new legalism.[35]

As the Lutheran concept of freedom developed further from 1517 to 1522, Christian freedom went from being only occasionally mentioned at the time of the indulgence controversy and the Ninety-five Theses (October 31, 1517) to the central expression of Luther's theology. The new programmatic weight that this concept received is illuminated by a very personal event. Beginning with a letter of November 11, 1517, and continuing in twenty-seven more letters, Luther wrote his name in a way that shined a light on his new self-understanding, signing as "Martin Eleutherius" (Martin the Liberated or Freed One), along the lines of 1 Corinthians 7:22.[36] This

---

35. Luther's Invocavit Sermons in 1522: WA 10/III:20.18-31; *LW* 51:78.

36. Letter to Johannes Lang (November 11, 1517), WA Br 1:222.56, no. 52. The reference to 1 Cor. 7:22 (*apeleutheros, eleutheros*) can be seen in the connection of Eleutherius and *dulos*: "F(rater) Martinus Eleutherius, imo dulos et captivus nimis." The translation

reflected the fundamental change in Luther's situation: the autumn of 1517 was when his critiques of scholastic theology and the papal church first entered the public arena.[37] Open conflict with the dominant academic and ecclesiastical authorities exposed Luther to a growing pressure about his own legitimacy, which he countered with an increasing self-awareness, namely, his own awareness of freedom. He found the new basis for legitimacy in Holy Scripture, which he had already valued as his sole source of truth up to that point. Now, however, he regarded it for the first time both as the exclusive source of legitimacy and as his court of appeals against the church and its traditions.[38] From this, he derived the *right* of Christian freedom: the *ius Christianae libertatis*.[39] This is the divine right of the gospel, which overrides the legal claims of human authorities and thereby opens the gates of its liberating message. Still, Luther did not declare scriptural freedom and its liberation from human rules to be some abstract "scriptural principle." Far more, he gained this freedom from, and grounded it on, the heart of Scripture itself, the "word of God, which teaches all freedom."[40] This, of course, included freedom from the enslaving legalism of canon law.

---

of Eleutherius as "the [liberated by God and therefore] free one" in Moeller and Stackmann (*Luder — Luther — Eleutherius*, 198) is certainly correct. Admittedly, the scanty lexical occurrences of *eleutherius* speak rather for the active "the liberator," but the plentiful examples of *eleutherios*, "the free one," leave the passive interpretation open. In any case, the classical examples mean little for the meaning in Luther. The self-description as a liberator (like that of a Reformer) was totally foreign to Luther and also had no biblical connection. He saw himself as the one cast out from God and driven by him, as in Heiko A. Oberman, *Luther: Mensch zwischen Gott und Teufel* (Berlin: Severin und Siedler, 1982), 223-25. On the connection of the new self-description, Eleutherius, with the almost simultaneously executed change of name from Luder to Luther (in the letters for the first time on October 31, 1517), see Moeller and Stackmann.

37. The publication of the *Disputatio contra scholasticam theologiam* (September 4, 1517) and the *Disputatio pro declaratione virtutis indulgentiarum* (October 31, 1517).

38. As in the sermon "Von dem Ablaß und Gnade," which was probably written shortly after the Ninety-five Theses but only printed in March 1518; WA 1:246.27-30.

39. *Resolutiones disputationum de indulgentiarum virtute* (Spring 1518), WA 1:530.4; LW 31:83. See also, *Ad dialogum Silvestri Prieriatis de potestate papae responsio* (August 1518); WA 1:647.33f.

40. See Luther's open letter to Pope Leo X, which he placed as the preface to his tract *The Freedom of a Christian* (dated September 6, 1520, but written at the end of October 1520), WA 7:9.29-31 (German), 7:47.28-30 (Latin); LW 31:341: "I acknowledge no fixed rules for the interpretation of the Word of God, since the Word of God, which teaches freedom in all other matters, must not be bound [2 Tim. 2:9]."

Such a new legitimacy based on the authority of Scripture brought a freedom from illegitimate human claims to authority. At the same time, as Luther made clear in the indulgence controversy, this view brought his attention to Scripture's own power to speak to its readers. Having already discovered freedom to be the gift of God's righteousness, Luther knew concretely in 1518 that the external, physical word of the preached gospel is what addresses sinners with the promise of forgiveness and righteousness. The timeless relationship with God's judgment "embodies" itself in the historical relationship of human language. In this way, the external dimension of Christ's righteousness corresponds to the external dimension of the word. In *The Freedom of a Christian*, therefore, Luther described the freedom that comes through Christ as a freedom given voice through the word of God.[41] For Luther, then, freeing the church from its Babylonian captivity under the papacy meant nothing other than opening the church up to the liberating promise of the gospel, which also meant releasing the church from the medieval focus on its own priestly dignities. Thus, in 1518, Luther united the two medieval traditions about freedom (as expressed in the theology of grace and in church politics, respectively) into a single reestablishment of Christian and ecclesiastical freedom that came from the gospel.[42] Only after making this connection, after integrating evangelical

---

41. WA 7:24.5–25.4 (German) and 52.37–53.33 (Latin), §§9 and 10; *LW* 31:351.

42. As important as the changes in Luther's vocabulary were in 1518, these do not define his "Reformation" theology. Quite apart from the desire of systematic theology to grab on to something that can be called a "Reformation" theology, narrowing a definition about what is or is not a "Reformation" view around a particular vocabulary is wrong for three historical reasons.

First, it contradicts Luther's own memories, which do not have to do with the appropriation of a promise through the preached word but above all revolved around a new understanding of *iustitia Dei*.

Second, the comparison with the many medieval theologies of grace — especially the use of Augustine's anti-Pelagian writings, which most starkly emphasize God's omnipotence and are seen clearly in writers like Gregory of Rimini and Johannes von Staupitz — has revealed the following. The break from existing traditions and systems did not come from a change in vocabulary that Luther discovered in 1518. Instead, it came from a theology of justification, which we can see in the Romans lectures and even in the early lectures on the Psalms. It is important to note that the break here does not represent the full transformation of Luther's theology but is instead a qualitative leap in a long process of development that included many discoveries. There is much to commend a use of the word "Reformation," which highlights what changed and challenged existing systems (especially in comparison to medieval theologies) and which cannot simply be described as a varia-

The Early Luther

freedom into the new exclusive authority of Scripture and the *verbum externum*, did the teacher of Reformation theology become the Reformer of the church.

I hope that my overview of Luther's early theology has made the nature of Luther's discovery of evangelical freedom clear. It was the discovery of people's freedom from themselves.[43] This freedom is simultaneously

---

tion among many options in medieval theology. After all, such relatively novel but thoroughly "Catholic" positions were held by Gregory of Rimini and Johannes von Staupitz.

Third, a use of the word "Reformation" based on later Lutheran terminology contradicts the shared consciousness about what Reformation meant at the time. Said differently: Anyone who used Luther's assertion about the saving efficacy of the *verbum externum* as the measure of a Reformation theology would not be able to name another real Reformation theologian besides Luther. Based on such a narrow definition, Karlstadt, Zwingli, Bucer, and probably even Calvin would not be considered "Reformation" theologians. Such a narrow definition reveals itself to be the product of a later theological construct that neither describes what the majority of greater or lesser reformers of the time thought was "reforming" about their work nor expresses what the Roman Catholic Church would have attacked as the false teaching of the reformers. In the question of Luther's Reformation origins, the concept of "Reformation" should always remain open enough to be applied to those movements that went in different directions from Luther.

That my pre-1517 dating of Luther's "Reformation turn" (that is, the beginnings of his Reformation theology) does not contradict Luther's famous recollection from the 1545 preface to volume 1 of his Latin works is shown in Rolf Schäfer, "Zur Datierung von Luthers reformatorischer Erkenntnis," *Zeitschrift für Theologie und Kirche* 66 (1969). To avoid misunderstanding, I should say that for me this issue has less to do with a fixed moment when Luther subjectively experienced something that he would later describe as a breakthrough and more to do with finding objective, historical, and theological signs of a break with respect to medieval views of freedom. On the difference between a "Reformation turn" and "Reformation breakthroughs," see Otto Pesch, "Zur Frage nach Luthers reformatorischer Wende: Ergebnisse und Probleme der Diskussion um Ernst Bizer, 'Fides ex auditu,'" in *Der Durchbruch der reformatorischen Erkenntnis bei Luther*, ed. Bernhard Lohse (Darmstadt: Wissenschaftliche Buchgesellschaft, 1968), 498-500. One might certainly admit, too, that both concepts were closely connected in Luther's life: many "turns" suggest many more "breakthroughs." Testimonies to a subjective awareness of a breakthrough arise in the time of the Romans lectures in WA 56:274.2-11; *LW* 25:261 and WA Br 1:35.22f., no. 11; *LW* 48:12 (in connection with the theme of exchange between Christ's righteousness and human sin). When I apply the concept of "discovery" to Luther, I mean first of all the discovery of a fact, which would not necessarily (but certainly might) include some simultaneous and subjective awareness of that discovery.

43. WA 7:22.31f., §6 (German); cf. *LW* 31:348: "Damit du aber aus dir heraus und von dir los, das heißt: aus deinem Verderben heraus, kommen kannst. . . ." See also WA 7:38.8f., §30; *LW* 31:371, "By faith he is caught up beyond himself into God."

freedom *from* the law and freedom *for* God and *for* neighbors. People need to be released from the need to fulfill the law, which always forces sinners to focus on themselves; only then are believers opened up *for* God and their neighbors. For Luther, such liberation only becomes real through the mode of judgment, which unconditionally acquits sinners when the effective word of the gospel pronounces upon them the righteousness of Christ.

Luther's central idea of freedom is that Christian freedom is the unconditional acceptance into salvation without respect to any works. The story of how it changed the world is not simply a story of unintentional misunderstandings or intentional transformations; it is a story that enjoys fundamental agreement across a wide variety of Reformation viewpoints. Melanchthon, Zwingli, Bucer, and Calvin, to name only the leading theologians, were united with Luther in this unconditional understanding of freedom. To be sure, they viewed the life of the justified differently because of a positive and instructional function of God's law. This was not a condition for salvation, however, but the consequence of the hidden wholeness of Christ's fulfillment of the law and righteousness, which is always and already passed on to sinners. This reveals the heart of a shared Reformation theology, even if much of what developed in the sixteenth century as the Reformation was put into practice through programs, propaganda, and processes took some different directions. Though such movements may not have been entirely stamped by Luther's theology, they would have been inconceivable without the impetus that Luther gave them.

CHAPTER 7

Freedom from the Pope and Pastoral Care to the Pope: The Compositional Unity of *The Freedom of a Christian* and Its Dedication Letter to Pope Leo X

The goal of this chapter is to arrive at a better overall understanding of Luther's tract *The Freedom of a Christian* by observing its close connection to the letter to Pope Leo X. My conclusion is that these two often separated writings are unified in that they express a simultaneous freedom from the pope and pastoral care to the pope.

The publication of Luther's famous tract on freedom is connected with five texts, all of which he wrote after October 12, 1520, and were printed around November 20. Two pairs of texts make up the primary substance of this volume: the dedication letter *Epistola ad Leonem decimum summum pontificem*[1] with the attached *Tractatus de libertate Christiana*,[2] and the two corresponding German texts, the *Sendbrief an Papst Leo X*[3] with the tract or sermon *Von der Freiheit eines Christenmenschen*.[4] In this

---

1. WA 7:42-49; LW 31:333-41.
2. WA 7:49-73; LW 31:333-75; see also, StA 2:264-309.
3. WA 7:3-11; see also *Luthers Werke in Auswahl*, ed. Otto Clemen, vol. 2, 6th ed. (Berlin: De Gruyter, 1967), 2-10 (henceforth cited as Cl).
4. WA 7:20-38; Cl 2:11-27; StA 2:265-305. Luther described *The Freedom of a Christian* (in the dedication to the German edition to Hermann Mühlpfort discussed below) as a "little tract and sermon" (see n. 14 below). To be sure, the designation of the genre of the Latin version as a "tract" points to a discursive discussion of a doctrinal problem. And yet

---

This essay first appeared as a lecture at the 2006 Sixteenth Century Conference in Salt Lake City. I thank my colleague Dr. Timothy Wengert for his further suggestions, which appeared in an English version of this essay in *Lutheran Quarterly* 21 (2007): 249-67.

chapter, I will not be addressing the subtle and theologically significant differences between the Latin and German editions or the question of their compositional histories, as my further argument will not be affected by it. The matter of their publication can easily be established. The German texts were printed first. Since the industrious printer in Wittenberg, Johann Grünenberg, published the *Sendbrief* separately immediately after it was completed, Luther wrote a brief new dedication for the German tract on freedom (which had probably not been part of the original plans) to Hermann Mühlpfort, a town magistrate in Zwickau.[5] Luther's original plan was to keep the dedication letter to the pope and the tract on freedom together, offered in two languages.[6]

The thesis of the following study is that Luther wrote the open letter to Leo X and the tract on freedom as a compositional unity. Therefore, the two texts should be interpreted closely together, which means that the tract contains the understanding of the letter and, conversely, the letter reveals the intent of the tract on freedom. The letter is clearly not just a dedication for the following tract, because it is more than half as long, with its own literary, theological, and political significance. That is, it is practically a separate short sermon by Luther on his position with respect to the pope and the papacy. But both texts are related to each other and correspond to one another. Also, Luther published these as a twofold pamphlet with an eye on their public effectiveness. In their unity, they were supposed to convey a programmatic message to the Latin- and German-speaking public, to scholars and nonspecialists, to clergy and laity.

---

the diminutive form "little tract" in connection with the term "sermon" is a clear indication that Luther is not classifying this on the level of learned scholastic tractates; rather the Latin and German versions of *Freedom of a Christian* have a place in the chain of his early new High German sermons of the years 1518 to 1520. These sermons are short, simple, edifying writings that mediate the essentials of his theology in catechetical and elementary ways with a pastoral impetus.

5. WA 7:20; *LW* 31:333; Cl 2:10; StA 2:263. The letter is falsely addressed to "Hieronymus" Mühlpfort. (For the first English translation of the German text of *Freedom of a Christian*, see Philip D. W. Krey and Peter D. S. Krey, eds., *Luther's Spirituality* [Mahwah, N.J.: Paulist, 2007], 69-90.)

6. Compare especially Luther's agreement with Karl von Miltitz in the Antonine Praeceptory Lichtenburg on the Elbe on October 12, 1520, about which he reported on the same day in a letter to Georg Spalatin: ". . . magna spe statuimus, ut ego ad summum pontificem epistolam edam utraque lingua, praefixam parvulo alicui opusculo, in qua narrem historiam meam et quam non unquam personam eius appetierim, totum pondus in Eccium versurus." WA Br 2:197.6-9, no. 342; *LW* 48:179-81.

In what follows, I begin with a brief survey of the prehistory of the texts. They are set in the context of peace initiatives between the Saxon nobility and the papal chamberlain, Karl von Miltitz, who was endeavoring to find a peaceful settlement to the conflict between Luther and the Roman curia. For that reason, on August 28, 1520, he consulted Luther's order. Thereupon the old and the new vicars-general of the Observant Order of Augustinian monks in Germany, Johannes von Staupitz and Wenceslas Linck, journeyed to Luther in Wittenberg. Around September 6, he declared himself willing to address a letter privately to the pope in which he assured him truthfully that he never intended any personal harm to him.[7] As yet, there was no mention of a theological writing to the pope in the sense of the later tract on freedom. This plan to place the letter to the pope before a supplementary little work *(parvulo alicui opusculo)* appeared for the first time on October 12, 1520, as a result of a meeting between Luther and Miltitz.[8] What had happened?

On October 10, the papal bull of excommunication, *Exsurge domine,* reached Wittenberg. It demanded that Luther recant its forty-one recriminations within sixty days, inform the curia of this either personally or in writing, and then burn the documents that contained his errors. If he did not do so before the deadline for recantation had passed, Luther was to be considered excommunicated.[9] The bull therefore demanded total submis-

---

7. See Luther's letter to Georg Spalatin from September 11, 1520: ". . . ut R[everendus] P[ater] Staupitius et novellus Vicarius Wenceslaus ad me profecturi orarent me, ut literas privatim ad Romanum Pontificem scriberem, contestans, nihil me in personam suam unquam fuisse molitum, sperans hoc consilio rem bene habituram. . . . Scribam itaque, id quod res est, nihil unquam in me fuisse, quod in personam Pontificis raperetur. Quid enim et facilius et verius scribere possum? Caeterum, sedem ipsam et causam ne atrocius tractem, inter scribendum cavendum erit mihi; aspergetur tamen sale." WA Br 2:184.7-10, 12-15 (no. 337). I translate the second section thus: "Therefore I will write to the Pope what the situation really is, that nothing ever occurred to me that could be construed as attacking the person of the Pope. For what can I write more clearly or truly? Moreover, I must be careful in writing that I do not assail the papal see and the case before it too severely. Nevertheless, it will be strewn with its own salt [meaning: sharply criticized]." Already here, then, Luther had both senses of his statement in view, according to which he will then construct his letter to Leo X (see nn. 21-24 below): the friendly and humble diction in connection with the person of the pope and the vehemently critical tone in connection to the papal office, the Roman See.

8. See n. 5 above.

9. See the depiction of the events and the content of the bull of excommunication in Martin Brecht, *Martin Luther: Sein Weg zur Reformation, 1483-1521* (Stuttgart: Calwer,

sion to the infallible authority of the papacy. Only by submitting totally could Luther remain a member of the church's community of salvation. This document presupposed the papal doctrine formulated in the bull *Unam sanctam* of 1302 and confirmed by Leo X at the Fifth Lateran Council in 1516, that subservience to the Roman pontiff was necessary for the salvation of every human being.[10]

Luther answered the arrival of the bull of excommunication with an intensified awareness of freedom. On October 11, he notified Georg Spalatin of the arrival of the bull with the words, "Already I am much freer because I have finally received the certainty that the Pope is the Antichrist and has been publicly exposed as the seat of Satan. May God preserve His own so that they may not be led astray by his most godless pretence [of holiness]."[11] In the spring and early summer of 1520, Luther had already reached the conclusion that the pope was the Antichrist, that is, that the papacy was an unholy, satanic power raging against Christendom and thus heralding the approach of the last days.[12] When he thus spoke of his own increased freedom after the arrival of the bull and the confirmation of this

---

1981), 371-84; there also is a discussion of the history of the origin of the letter to Leo X and the tract on freedom, 385-88.

10. "Porro subesse Romano Pontifici omni humanae creaturae declaramus, dicimus, diffinimus omnino esse de necessitate salutis." The papal bull *Unam Sanctam*, by Boniface VIII, dated November 18, 1302, in *Enchiridion Symbolorum*, ed. Henricus Denzinger and Adolfus Schönmetzer, 36th ed. (Freiburg: Herder, 1976), 281 (no. 875). *Unam Sanctam* was confirmed by Pope Leo X at the eleventh session of the Fifth Lateran Council on December 19, 1516, in the bull *Pastor aeternus gregem*. See *Enchiridion Symbolorum*, 355.

11. "Iam multo liberior sum, certus tandem factus papam esse Antichristum et satanae sedem manifeste inventum. Tantum servet Deus suos, ne seducantur eius impiissima specie." WA Br 2:195.22-24 (no. 341).

12. See Reinhard Schwarz, *Luther* (Göttingen: Vandenhoeck & Ruprecht, 1986), 80f., and Luther's tract from August 1520, *The Babylonian Captivity of the Church*. Already at this time Luther had in view the impending arrival of the papal bull of excommunication, and he reacted to its call to recant in a quite unusual way, in that he stylized his writing from the beginning as a kind of recantation. Earlier, when he had contested the divine right of the papacy, he had conceded to a human right via Rom. 13. "But now I know and I am certain that the papacy is the kingdom of Babylon" ("scio nunc et certus sum papatum esse regnum Babylonis"), that is, symbolizing with the name "Babylon" the sphere of evil, in which Satan rules through his human vice-regent, the Antichrist. "Esse papatum aliud re vera nihil quam regnum Babylonis et veri Antichristi." WA 6:498.4f. and 537.24f.; *LW* 36:11 and 72.

certainty about the Antichrist, what he was saying was this: as a teacher of divine truth, I am being attacked by Satan himself; in this situation of extreme superhuman threat, I know that I am freed from all fainthearted regard for human power and help and am entrusted solely to the protection of God. The more terribly the satanic powers behave, the more I am free and the more I am sheltered in the grace of God through faith.[13]

Against this background, it is understandable why on October 12, the day after the letter to Spalatin, Luther gave Karl von Miltitz the aforementioned promise to add a theological tract to the already-planned conciliatory letter to the pope. From Luther's perspective in these dramatic days, it was logical that this *opusculum* (short work) could be nothing other than a programmatic writing about freedom. In view of the papal demand for submission, this document would openly explain from Holy Scripture the basis of the total freedom and religious independence that placed him even above the papacy.[14] The chronology of this series of events in the autumn

---

13. In the letter to Spalatin, Luther stressed his great joy at this, that he, as an unworthy person before God, had been made worthy of such a "holy persecution" *(sancta vexatio)* by the Antichrist. This is a recurring leitmotif in Luther: precisely the servants of God's Word will be afflicted especially terribly by Satan, because through them he sees his power as "prince of this world" threatened. Luther's declaration of freedom (mentioned above) is directly connected to this announcement of joy. He pursued this further in connection with the prognosis, received from Erasmus, not to place any hope in Emperor Charles V. Luther explained that this should also not be really surprising, and he cited Ps. 145:2 (Vulgate): "Do not put your trust in princes nor in human children, in whom there is no salvation." WA Br 2:195.20-27 (no. 341). See also the letter to Michael Muris written shortly thereafter, cited in n. 50 below.

14. In the short dedicatory letter to Hermann Mühlpfort in the German version (see n. 4 above), Luther explicitly mentioned that his tract is intentionally directed at the papacy: he has "dedicated this little tract and sermon to you [Hermann] in the German version, which in the Latin I dedicated to the Pope so that it may indicate to everyone the cause (not unproven, I hope) for my teaching and writing on the papacy" ("diß tractatell unnd Sermon euch wollen zuschreyben ym deutschen, wilchs ich latinisch dem Bapst hab zugeschrieben, damit fur yderman meyner lere und schreyben von dem Bapstum nit eyn vorweyßlich, als ich hoff, ursach angetzeygt"), WA 7:20.19-22; *LW* 31:333. With these words, Luther was saying that with his tract on freedom (which he described as a small tract or sermon) he has laid out before everyone, in complete openness, the cause, that is, the legitimation, for his teaching and his writing about the papacy — an explanation that, as he hopes, is not unproven, that is, one, based as it is on arguments from Holy Scripture, that cannot be proven false. Thus, Luther hopes that those who read in *The Freedom of a Christian* about how Christian freedom is grounded in the theology of justification understand why he rightly attacked the bases of a papal understanding of the church.

of 1520, with its mixture of personal and literary events, clearly shows how in the development of his theology Luther not only followed the dynamic of his own thought, which pressed him to further conclusions, but simultaneously responded to the increasing and escalating pressure of his ecclesiastical opponents, so that he saw himself as "one driven forward."[15]

In the two-part pamphlet containing the letter and the tract on freedom, Luther took his past several years' growth in his awareness of freedom and reflections about freedom to their logical conclusions. Here, the theologies of church, normative doctrine, and authority were closely and even inseparably connected to Christian freedom and its personal theology of justification.[16] To the increasing pressure that the papal party and the Roman authorities exerted upon him from the spring of 1518 up to the publication of the bull threatening excommunication in June 1520, Luther responded with a progressively intense and critical radicalization, which deepened and widened his understanding of freedom beyond his initial attack on scholastic theology and the practice of selling indulgences in the autumn of 1517.[17] In the summer of 1520, he reached the final stage of the total break with the medieval structure of church, theology, and piety. By then, Christian freedom meant seeing himself and all believing Christians as liberated from all juridical, dogmatic, and sacramental principles of the papal church, insofar as they did not receive their legitimacy from the norm of Holy Scripture. The fundamental attack on the sacramental struc-

---

15. See Heiko A. Oberman, *Luther: Mensch zwischen Gott und Teufel* (Berlin: Severin und Siedler, 1982), 223-25.

16. See Thorsten Jacobi, *"Christen heißen Freie": Luthers Freiheitsaussagen in den Jahren 1515-1519* (Tübingen: Mohr Siebeck, 1997); Berndt Hamm, "Martin Luthers Entdeckung der evangelischen Freiheit," *Zeitschrift für Theologie und Kirche* 80 (1983): 50-68.

17. With the publication of his theses against scholastic theology from September 4, 1517, and his Ninety-five Theses of October 31, 1517, Luther entered into open conflict with the academic and ecclesiastical authorities of Christendom. Directly connected to this is the fact that between November 11, 1517, and early 1519 he signed a total of twenty-eight letters as "Martinus Eleutherius" (Martin the Liberated or Freed One) and, connected to this, changed the spelling of his family name from Luder to Luther (first in the cover letter to the Ninety-five Theses to Archbishop Albrecht of Mainz on October 31, 1517). See Bernd Moeller and Karl Stackmann, *Luder — Luther — Eleutherius: Erwägungen zu Luthers Namen* (Göttingen: Vandenhoeck & Ruprecht, 1981); Jacobi, "Christen heißen Freie," 139-49. This name change and its meaning primarily show how Luther met the growing pressure for legitimation with a growing awareness of authority, that is, an awareness of freedom. Exactly this kind of reaction also appeared in October 1520.

ture of the medieval church, combined with the absolute demonization of the papacy, was the final step. Luther did this in his tract of August 1520, *The Babylonian Captivity of the Church*, in which he proclaimed that Christian freedom based on baptism was in effect a confession: "I cry out for this freedom and this awareness [of freedom], and I cry with confidence."[18] By sending a thematically condensed tract on freedom (built upon the earlier "captivity" writing) together with the weighty letter to the pope, Luther was gathering the theological and ecclesiastical harvest of the previous months and years. At the same time, it is characteristic that he took this logical next step only when the pressure of threatened excommunication reached its climax with the arrival of the bull.

But amid this (in his view) diabolical escalation, how could Luther strike the promised conciliatory tones by combining the tract on freedom with a letter to Leo X? In fact, his letter does reveal this aim, which has constantly caused confusion in research on Luther. The dedication letter has been viewed as a dubious document full of contradictions,[19] oscillating between harshest tones of uncompromising criticism of the pope and a humble obsequiousness ("So now I come, Holy Father Leo, and lying before you I beg . . ."),[20] which Luther could not really have meant seriously. However, a careful analysis of the letter — taking into account its connection with the tract on freedom — does indeed reveal that it is quite theologically coherent in its construction and formulation.

---

18. "Pro hac duntaxat clamo libertate et conscientia, clamoque fidenter." WA 6:537.12; *LW* 36:72. With *conscientia* Luther meant *conscientia libertatis (nostrae)*, emphasized in this section of text; that is, the awareness of freedom that is awakened in a person through God's gospel (WA 6:537.8f. and 15; *LW* 36:72).

19. See the uncritical citation of this in *StA* 2:260f. On this letter, see Erwin Iserloh, "Die protestantische Reformation," in *Handbuch der Kirchengeschichte*, vol. 4, *Reformation, Katholische Reform und Gegenreformation*, ed. Josef Glazik and Hubert Jedin (Freiburg im Breisgau: Herder, 1967), 75, uncritically cited in *StA* 2:260f. Against this, see Brecht, *Martin Luther*, 388, which still does not explain the two-sided nature of the letter. On the intricacies of the debate over the character of this letter, see Matthieu Arnold in his introduction to the French translation of the letter in Marc Lienhard and Matthieu Arnold, eds., *Luthers Oeuvres*, vol. 1 (Paris: Gallimard, 1999), 1468f.; Scott H. Hendrix, *Luther and the Papacy: Stages in a Reformation Conflict* (Philadelphia: Fortress, 1981), 112-17; Volker Leppin, *Martin Luther* (Darmstadt: Wissenschaftliche Buchgesellschaft, 2006), 160f.

20. "Alßo kum ich nu, H. V. Leo, und zu deynen fuessen liegend bitte. . . ." WA 7:9.25. See also the Latin version: "Ita venio, Beatissime pater, et adhuc prostratus rogo. . . ." WA 7:47.25; *LW* 31:341.

From his earliest lectures up to the last years of his life, Luther's theology was characterized by the basic differentiation between faith and love or doctrine and life, between the dimension of the truth of the word of God received in faith and the ethical dimension of life, its sinfulness or sanctification.[21] Both dimensions are inextricably bound together in Christian existence. To this fundamental theological differentiation, the letter reveals two apparently contradictory but in fact closely related levels of pronouncement. On the personal level of "brotherly love,"[22] Luther emphasized that he had never attacked the pope as a person with respect to his lifestyle but that he always thought of him most respectfully and considered him "a sheep among wolves," wishing him the very best — especially spiritual salvation — and praying for him.[23] On the transpersonal level of doctrine and truth,[24] however, he launched an undiplomatic and uncompromising attack against the office, doctrine, and jurisdiction of the papacy, that is, against the official role of the pope as an opponent of the divine truth sitting on the Roman throne. Luther expressly equated the Roman Church, including its supposedly Petrine succession, with those corrupting powers of hell, against which Christ protects his own. In this, the papacy appears as the center of Satan's power over the world.[25] Thus Luther differen-

---

21. See Berndt Hamm, "Toleranz und Häresie: Martin Bucers prinzipielle Neubestimmung christlicher Gemeinschaft," in *Martin Bucer zwischen Luther und Zwingli*, ed. Matthieu Arnold and Berndt Hamm (Tübingen: Mohr Siebeck, 2003), 85-106, here 102f. On the corresponding passages in Luther, see also Gerhard Ebeling, *Lutherstudien*, vol. 3 (Tübingen: Mohr Siebeck, 1985), 145f., with nn. 55-57. See Luther's tract from October 1520, *Von den neuen eckischen Bullen und Lügen*, particularly WA 6:581.7-19.

22. WA 7:10.39f.: "... biß ich bruederlicher liebe pflicht außricht." See also the Latin version in WA 7:48.29; *LW* 31:343: "... dum officium charitatis implevero."

23. For the German version of the letter: WA 7:3.12-15, 3.22–4.16, 4:37–5.2, 5.32f., 6.34–7.2, 10.31–11.13; for the Latin: WA 7:42.14-16; 43.6-19; 43.33-36; 44.19f.; 45.13-17; 48.22–49.3; *LW* 31:334-36, 338, 342f.

24. On the difference between the "life" (*mores*) of his ecclesiastical opponents (including the person of the pope) and the "doctrine" or the "truth" of God's word, see the German, WA 7:4.17-19 (*lere — leben*) and 4.37–5.4 (*person/leben — des gottlichen wortis warheyt*); Latin, WA 7:43.20f.; *LW* 31:335 (*mores — doctrina*) and 43:33-37 (*persona/mores — verbum veritatis*).

25. See the German, WA 7:5, 8-13; 5.23-31; 5.37f.; 6.21-32; 6.37; 10.22-24; Latin, WA 7:44.3-6; 44.12-18; 44.23f.; 45.3-11; 45.14f.; 48.16f.; *LW* 31:336-38, 342. See particularly WA 7:6.27-29: "das es war ist, Rom sey vortzeyten gewest eyn pfort des hymels, und ist nu eyn weyt auffgesperreter rache der helle, unnd leyder eyn solcher rache, den durch gottis tzorn niemand kan zu sperrenn."

tiated not only between the person of the pope and his "unchristian" dependence on the Roman curia, but also — much more importantly — between his person, the authority of his papal office, and the abundance of power that came with it. Leo's own Roman See, the *cathedra Petri*, was the worst "dungeon" in which he, as a person, could be imprisoned.

In the letter, Luther thus focused the diabolical character of the papacy on the problem of the pope's authoritative and juridical position of being considered lord over this world and the hereafter, with "power in heaven, in hell, and in purgatory," so that everyone must be subservient to him in order to achieve spiritual salvation.[26] Even more, to Luther the height of iniquity and the epitome of the satanic Antichrist lay in the fact that papal doctrine elevated the pope to lordship over the holiest thing on earth, the Holy Scriptures. The holiness of his office had claimed for itself normative supremacy over the word of God.[27] For Luther, the fundamental perversion of the papal church showed itself to be its captivity to the fiction that the pope is not simply a human person but is *mixtus Deus* (mingled with God), commanding and demanding "all things."[28] When Luther focused his reckoning with the papacy through this question of the quasi-divine lordship over all things, even over all the people of Christendom,[29] he arrived at the main theme of his tract on freedom, since for him the teaching of Christian freedom in this sense meant nothing other than revealing the right Christian relationships of power and subordination.

The observation that the two levels of pronouncement that I have mentioned in the letter correspond exactly to the tract on freedom helps clarify this. The tract differentiates between the two aforementioned dimensions of existence for the believing Christian. In faith, that is, in the inner relationship to the liberating truth of the gospel, a Christian is "a free lord over all things" and thus has access to eternal salvation, free of all di-

---

26. "Laß dich nit betriegen, die dyr liegen und heucheln, du seyest eyn herr der welt, die niemant wollen lassen Christen seyn, er sey den dyr unterworffen [an allusion to the formulation in the papal bull *Unam Sanctam* (see n. 9 above)], die do schwetzen, du habst gewalt ynn den hymel, yn die hel und ynß fegfewr." German, WA 7:10.3-6; Latin, WA 7:48.2-4; *LW* 31:341.

27. See the German, WA 7:10.8-16; Latin, WA 7:48.6-11; *LW* 31:342.

28. "... du seyest nit eyn lautter mensch, sondernn gemischt mit gott, der alle ding zu gepieten und tzu foddern habe." German, WA 7:9.40–10.1; Latin, WA 7:47.36f.; *LW* 31:341.

29. See n. 26 above, and WA 7:10.9; the rule of the pope over all Christendom ("gemeyne Christenheyt"); Latin, WA 7:48.7; *LW* 31:342.

vine and human laws. In this respect, Christians are subject to no earthly lord, including the tyranny of the pope. But with respect to brotherly love, when it is not a question of one's salvation but of the physical and spiritual need of the neighbor, these same Christians become "willing servant[s] of all things" and are subject to anyone who needs help, maybe even including the pope or other "terrible prelates."[30] This voluntary readiness for submission and service is circumscribed by obedience to the word of God.[31]

With this, the two-sidedness of the tract on freedom reveals the coherence of the divergent tones within the letter. Viewed in light of the tract on freedom, it is literally necessary and theologically consistent that in the dedication letter Luther adopt not only the harshly critical tone against the Roman Church and its demands for submission but also the conciliatory note of brotherly submission and pastoral care. On the one hand, Luther observed his total freedom from the pope when he pointed out that Christ alone, not the pope, was Lord of the church.[32] The subservience necessary for salvation can only be claimed by Christ and the proclamation of his divine word, not by the pope. Because the pope raises this claim, he makes himself the Antichrist and an idol.[33] On the other hand, however, under the auspices of "brotherly love," Luther stressed the pastoral care service that he owed to the pope and wanted to show to him as a neighbor in extreme danger.[34]

---

30. Near the end of the tract (paragraph 28), Luther speaks about this service "out of love and freedom" and how it can be accommodated to the innumerable commands and laws of the "mad prelates" and "of the pope, the bishops, the monasteries, the foundations, the princes and lords," so long as it does not transpire under the opinion that through it one becomes righteous and holy. German, WA 7:37.2-13; Latin, WA 7:68.3-13; LW 31:370. In the letter, Luther displays this kind of subjection (out of "brotherly love") over and against the pope. "Ich mag nit schmeycheln ynn solcher ernster, ferlicher sache [that is, in the face of the great danger in which the soul of the pope was situated], ynn wilcher szo mich ettlich nit wollenn vorstehen, wie ich deyn freund und mehr denn unterthan sey, szo wirt er sich wol finden, der es vorsteht." German, WA 7:10.40–11.3; Latin, WA 7:48.29-31 ("plusquam subiectissimus"); LW 31:343.

31. See paragraph 28, German, WA 7:37.14f.; Latin, WA 7:68.13f.; LW 31:369f.

32. See the letter, German, WA 7:10.13-25; Latin, WA 7:48.10-18; LW 31:342.

33. See the letter, German, WA 7:10.23f. ("eyn Endchrist und Abtgott"); Latin, WA 7:48.17 ("Antichristus et Idolum"); LW 31:342.

34. See the letter, German, WA 7:10.31–11.3; Latin, WA 7:48.22-31; LW 31:342f. It is noteworthy how Luther stresses in this section the "true care" and care-filled attentiveness of brotherly love, which perceives the neighbor's endangerment, emergency situa-

Luther put this pastoral care into practice publicly via a pamphlet. That means that it not only applies to the pope personally, and to his person *coram Deo* (before God), but to all Christians who have been led astray and endangered on their way to salvation. Looked at even more closely, this pastoral care happens in two ways. In the letter, it appears above all in Luther's discussion of the destructive law and of the crucial norm of Christ's truth; in the tract on freedom, however, this appears through the words about the gospel that builds up. In the letter, Luther wanted to serve the pope and Christianity by inviting and allowing them to accept the unmasked truth that the papacy was not simply a human construct but, on a metaphysical level, had become the Antichristian dominion of Satan, which had fallen under God's condemning judgment. In the tract on freedom, Luther the poor mendicant wanted to provide the pope, the "most holy father in God"[35] (and simultaneously all Christians), with the riches of spiritual treasure, that is, with the liberating truth of the divine promise of salvation, thereby serving his real salvation.[36] The key point is that, as Luther understood it, the loving service of pastoral care consisted in the very fact that one opens up the biblical truth of faith to one's neighbor, be

---

tion, and need for help — concretely, that of the pope — and so obligates even the most humble Christian to ignore the high rank of the pope and to be subject to him in humble readiness to help. Thereby Luther incorporates here the train of thought and concepts from the tract in paragraphs 26-28 (German, WA 7:34.23–37.15; Latin, WA 7:64.13–68.14; *LW* 31:364-70). The pastoral care of the pope is service to the neighbor "out of free love," which attends wholly to what is "necessary, useful and salutary for him" (paragraph 27).

35. Thus the address at the beginning of the Letter in WA 7:3.1-4, "To the most holy father Leo the 10th, Pope in Rome, all blessedness in Christ Jesus our Lord. Amen. Most holy in God the Father. . . ." In the Latin version, Luther uses the simple title "ad Leonem . . ." and "Leoni. . . ." In the German Luther enhances the customary address "Holy Father," which he uses quite often in the letter. This is not just a concession to the actual office and dignity of the pope in the Roman Church, but, rather, in my opinion, this is a very seriously thought-out theological statement that the pope, as a person, is called to greatest holiness, that is, to eternal blessedness before God. To this end Luther closes the letter with the words: "Da mit ich mich d[einer] H[eiligkeit] befilhe, die yhm behalt ewig Jhesus Christus, Amen." In the Latin, Luther rightly translated *Heiligkeit* with "beatitude," WA 7:49.3; *LW* 31:333.

36. At the end of the letter to Leo X, Luther wrote about his tract: "Ich byn arm, hab nit anders damit ich meyn dienst ertzeyge, so darffstu auch nit mehr den mit geystlichen guttern gepessert werdenn." This follows the sentence about the *Heiligkeit* or *beatitudo* cited at the end of the previous note (cf. *LW* 31:333).

the neighbor pope or peasant. This should be done through the humiliating and sharply deconstructive judgment of the law and in the uplifting message of the gospel, which is so full of promise. Viewed from this perspective, the apparent two-sidedness of the letter and the tract fades into a higher unity concerning the Christian witness. The service of love really does take place in such a way that those who love bear witness in word and deed to their neighbor for the sake of the neighbor's salvation; the freedom of faith that liberates from false powers is itself sovereign "over all things." Looking back on his conflicts with the National Socialist state and the governing body of his own church, the Franconian Lutheran Karl Steinbauer (1906-88) named this form of love to one's neighbor that is related to truth and faith as "providing witness to each other." Luther expressed this same view in the letter to Pope Leo through his words, "Truly, I tell you the truth, for I wish you well."[37]

The compositional interrelatedness of the letter and the tract reveals not only that the tract proves to be a key to understanding the letter but also, conversely, that the letter is a key to understanding the tract. Ignoring the letter and the conflicts of 1520, one can certainly read the tract entirely correctly as a tract on justification and salvation that deals with existential, Christian, and biblical fundamentals. As we know, this is the particular preference of systematic theologians. But if we carry out Luther's movement from dedication letter to doctrinal tract, then the tract on freedom can be seen through its context as an ecclesiastical manifesto against the power of the Roman papacy and against every form of bureaucratic lordship. Its pointed statements (along with several scriptural passages cited for the same purposes) about Christian authority, dignity and honor, royal sovereignty and the priesthood of all Christians[38] are directed against an ecclesiastical tyranny, a *terrifica tyrannis,* which put itself above the Christian faith, the interpretation of Holy Scripture, and the admission of

---

37. See the German, WA 7:6.19f.; Latin, WA 7:45.3; *LW* 31:337: "veritatem enim tibi dico, quia bona tibi volo." Luther maintains here the scholastic definition of Christian charity as "alicui bonum velle" (to desire good for the other). For example, see Thomas Aquinas, *Summa theologiae* II/II, q. 23, art. 1, resp. On Karl Steinbauer (1906-88), see his four volumes of memoirs, *Einander das Zeugnis gönnen,* vols. 1-4 (Erlangen: Selbstverlag, 1983-87), and Christian Blendinger, *Nur Gott und dem Gewissen verpflichtet: Karl Steinbauer — Zeuge in finsterer Zeit* (Munich: Claudius, 2001).

38. See the tract, paragraphs 14-17, German, WA 7:26.32–28.37; Latin, WA 7:56.15–58.22; *LW* 31:353-56. See also paragraph 18; German, WA 7:29.17-20 ("wie wir könig und priester seyn, aller ding mechtig"); Latin, WA 7:59.3-6; *LW* 31:357.

Christians into salvation.[39] Read in this way, this tract on the word of God, faith, love, communion with Christ and the neighbor, along with its mystical ingredients, shows itself to also be an essential contribution to the discourse about church authority, lordship, and norms that Luther had been publicly conducting since the autumn of 1517. In contrast to the legal structures of the Roman Church, the tract lays out guidelines for a "right of Christian freedom" given by God's gospel to the church of Jesus Christ.[40]

Following his experience of the papal church's "satanic lordship," Luther articulated Christian existence in general as freedom from all spiritually based authority, so that Christian existence meant free sovereign lordship over all things. "And this has as a result that a Christian is raised so high above all things through faith that he will be spiritually a lord of all; for nothing can harm his salvation. Indeed, all things must be subject to him and help for salvation, as St. Paul teaches in Romans 8[:28], 'All things must help the elect for their good,' be it life, death, sin, piety, good and evil, however one desires to name it."[41] "This is a really high, noble honor and a truly omnipotent lordship, a spiritual kingdom, since nothing is so good or so evil but that it must serve me for my good if I believe and have need of nothing, but my faith is sufficient for me. See, is this not a priceless free-

---

39. See the tract, paragraph 17, German, WA 7:28.36–29.6; Latin, WA 7:58.23-30 (with the formulation: "in tantam pompam potestatis et terrificam quandam tyrannidem"); *LW* 31:356; paragraphs 28-29, German, WA 7:37.4-27; Latin, WA 7:68.3-28; *LW* 31:370; see also the addition to the Latin version, WA 7:69.33-37; 70.29–71.1; 71.8-10, 15-26, 35-39; 73.8-12; *LW* 31:372, 373, 374f., 377.

40. In 1518 Luther spoke of the "right of Christian freedom" *(ius christianae libertatis)* in the explanation of the Ninety-five Theses (WA 1:530.4-8; *LW* 31:83) and in the *Responsio ad dialogum Silvestri Prieriatis de potestate papae*. See Jacobi, "Christen heißen Freie," 155-64; Hamm, "Entdeckung," 65. Luther derived the normative quality of the Holy Scriptures, which grounded such a right, from the content of the biblical Word of God, that it "teaches all freedom" ("alle freyheyt leret"), German, WA 7:9.29-31; Latin, WA 7:47.28-30 ("quod libertatem docet omnium aliorum"); *LW* 31:341. This statement of the letter to Leo X finds its development in all those numerous "all" statements of the *Freedom of a Christian*, which state that a Christian is a lord above *all* things. See also the following paragraph.

41. "Und das geht also zu, das ein Christen mensch durch den glauben ßo hoch erhaben wirt ubir alle ding, das er aller eyn herr wirt geystlich; denn es kan yhm kein ding nit schaden zur seligkeit. Ja es muß yhm alles unterthan seyn und helffen zur seligkeyt, wie S. Paulus leret Ro. 8.: 'Alle ding müssen helffenn den außerwelten zu yhrem besten', es sey leben, sterben, sund, frumkeit, gut und bößes, wie man es nennen kan." In paragraph 15, German: WA 7:27.21-26; Latin (with changes), WA 7:57.2-8; *LW* 31:354.

dom and power which Christians possess! *(Ecce haec est Christianorum inaestimabilis potentia et libertas!)*."[42]

In these sentences, Luther formulated the "autarky" or self-sufficiency of faith in its connection to Christ, namely, its complete independence of every actual and conceivable thing, satanic or godly, which claims to stand as an impediment, mediation, or condition between Christians and their salvation, whether these be the sinful or upright condition of hearts and actions, the divine commandments of Holy Scripture, or the human statutes of the papal church. For those who believe, all these powers have been subjugated. Believers can deal with them without pressure, since such powers can do them no spiritual or mental harm but must instead serve them and be helpful,[43] without being necessary for salvation.[44] This even holds true for God's holy law, because the acceptance of a person into salvation no longer depends on the requirement of fulfilling God's commandments. Faith alone, being taken into full saving communion with Christ, is sufficient for receiving blessedness from God.

It is remarkable that in the tract on freedom Luther always speaks of the lordship and dominion of believers over "things" but never of a superiority that believers have over other people. In faith, that is, as an inner person and in a spiritual respect, when it is a question of the Christian's relationship to truth and salvation, a Christian is "subject" to "no one," to no

---

42. "Das ist gar ein hohe, ehrliche wirdickeit und eyn recht almechtige hirschafft, ein geystliche königreych, da keyn ding ist ßo gut, ßo böße, es muß mir dienen zu gut, ßo ich glaube, und darff seyn doch nit, sondern meyn glaub ist mir gnugsam. Sihe, wie ist das ein köstlich freyheyt und gewalt der Christen!" Paragraph 15, German, WA 7:28.1-5; Latin (with changes), WA 7:57.18-23; *LW* 31:355.

43. See n. 40 above and paragraph 15, WA 7:27.32-28.1-5: ". . . das ist, ich kann mich on [an or in] allen dingen bessern nach der seelen, das auch der todt und leyden müssen mir dienen und nützlich seyn zur seligkeyt." Latin, WA 7:57.16-18; *LW* 31:355: ". . . in omnibus possum lucrum facere salutis, adeo ut crux et mors cogantur mihi servire et cooperari ad salutem."

44. To explain the citation above (together with n. 42), faith alone is fully sufficient for salvation, that is, the pure trust in the unbreakable validity of God's promise of salvation. So when Luther, following Rom. 8:28, wrote that all things — even suffering and death — benefit a person and help a person toward salvation (see nn. 40 and 41 above), he meant that these things do not remove one's faith but rather can only strengthen and increase faith, because the believer recognizes in all these things the merciful will and compassionate devotion of God. Luther spoke repeatedly about the increase and amplification of faith in the tract. See, for example, paragraph 20, German, WA 7:30.13; Latin, WA 7:59.39; *LW* 31:358, and paragraph 27, German, WA 7:35.21f.; Latin, WA 7:65.28; *LW* 31:366f.

individual on earth, and certainly to no "thing."⁴⁵ In this respect, however, the Christian cannot be a lord over others, for Christ alone is Lord over people through his word and Spirit. In faith, however, that Christian is with Christ "a free lord over all things" *(omnium dominus liberrimus)*, that is, over everything people otherwise raise up as conditions, means, or obstacles to salvation. These include qualities, virtues, works, institutions, laws, traditions, achievements, and the like. Simultaneously, the Christian, like Christ through his incarnation, is "subject" to "everyone" in a serving, voluntary love. Thus, as a matter of principle, every person is "subject" to his or her fellow human beings, but thereby also subject with inner consent to the dictates and sufferings of the "things."⁴⁶

Following the line of thinking found in the letter, we can see the underlying clash with the papal power of the keys, which is hidden in the sentences just quoted from the tract.⁴⁷ Therefore they should be read in this way: As a believer, every Christian stands above the papacy — but not above the person of Leo X. Even in his capacity as Antichrist, as an incarnate adversary of God, the pope cannot harm believers in any way. Without their needing it, he must serve them in all submissiveness and "be helpful for their salvation."⁴⁸ For the more he attacks the faithful with his "tyranny," the more they take refuge in faith in Christ and the more confident they become about their freedom from human and satanic powers. This is exactly the same sense that Luther had after the arrival of the bull threatening excommunication, when — shortly before he began working on *The Freedom of a Christian* — he wrote to Spalatin on October 11: "Al-

---

45. See the first principle at the beginning of the tract: "Eyn Christen mensch ist eyn freyer herr über alle ding und niemandt unterthan" and "Christianus homo omnium dominus est liberrimus, nulli subiectus." German, WA 7:21.1f.; Latin, WA 7:49.22f.; *LW* 31:344.

46. See the second principle: "Eyn Christen mensch ist eyn dienstpar knecht aller ding und yderman unterthan" and "Christianus homo omnium servus est officiosissimus, omnibus subiectus." German, WA 7:21.3f.; Latin, WA 7:49.24f.; *LW* 31:344. On the matter of being subjugated to the "things" of this earthly life, see paragraph 15 (German, WA 7:27.28-31; Latin, WA 7:57.11-14; *LW* 31:354): ". . . quando ipso vitae usu videmus nos omnibus subiici, multa pati atque adeo mori, immo quo Christianior quisque est, hoc pluribus subiectus est malis, passionibus et mortibus, ut in ipso principe primogenito Christo et omnibus fratribus suis sanctis videmus." On the example of Christ who, although he was free, "doch umb unßer willenn ein knecht wordenn [ist]," see paragraph 26, German, WA 7:35.9-19; Latin, WA 7:65.5-25; *LW* 31:366.

47. See nn. 40 and 41 above.

48. See nn. 42 and 43 above.

ready I am much more free,"⁴⁹ or a few days later to Michael Muris: "I beg you: Teach the men to disdain boldly! Christ himself says [Matt. 10.17], 'Beware of men!' It is a great thing to have a merciful God and to trust in him."⁵⁰

Viewing the compositional unity of the letter and the tract in this way and keeping them together as a double pamphlet, it is clear why right at that time and never so adamantly either before or after, Luther saw himself challenged and compelled to express — or even to confess — the Christian freedom and service he shared with all believers in a theologically coherent and publicly accountable way *(coram publico)*.⁵¹ The arrival of the bull gave the final impetus to this project. In this escalating confrontation with the "seat of Satan," he considered it imperative to write to the pope in such a way as to send him a tract that clearly expressed his basic position on questions of church authority, dominion, and submission, answering the questions: Who is lord over people and things? Who serves whom? By explaining the meaning of Christian freedom and service, he pulled the rug out from under papal ideas of superiority and submission, along with all their normative, juridical, and soteriological consequences. Simultaneously, however, he showed in what sense he still remained subject to the pope and how he wanted to be helpful to the pope and other representatives of the church hierarchy through a loving concern for the salvation of their souls. He wanted them to truly become "Christ's vicars" through a servant love.

The extent to which the thought process and terminology within *The Freedom of a Christian* were influenced by the ecclesiastical confrontations during 1520 can be seen by comparing it with the "Sermon on Two Kinds of Righteousness," printed in early 1519.⁵² This comparison is especially

---

49. See n. 10 above.

50. October 20, 1520, letter to Michael Muris, a Cistercian from Altcella who was studying in Leipzig, WA Br 2:202.35-37, no. 345: "Rogo te, disce homines fortiter contemnere, dicente Christo: 'Cavete ab hominibus!' Magna res est, Deum habere propitium et in eo confidere." See also *Wider die Bulle des Endchrists*, WA 6:617.2-5, which was written at the same time as the letter and the tract on freedom: "Ich byn von gottis gnadenn frey, darff unnd wil mich der dinger keyniß widder [weder] trosten noch entsetzen. Ich weyß wol, wo mein trost und trotz stehet, der mir wol sicher steht fur [vor, coram] menschen und teuffeln."

51. See n. 14 above, for the words with which Luther listed the objectives of the freedom tract in his dedication letter to Hermann Mühlpfort.

52. WA 2:143, 145-52; LW 31:297-306.

convincing, because the sermon stands very close thematically to *The Freedom of a Christian* and anticipates much of it. The similarity in the overall structure is especially striking, for the sermon already made the basic distinction between Christ's justifying righteousness received in faith and the righteousness of the good works that flow from that. Both writings employ the motif of the "happy exchange" between a bridegroom and a bride to illustrate how Christ's righteousness becomes human righteousness.[53] They also both use a christological interpretation of Philippians 2:5-8 to anchor the duty of active righteousness in service to the neighbor, following Christ's example.[54] Although ideas of servitude, obedient submission, and service are all present in the Christ hymn of Philippians 2,[55] Luther had not yet in 1519 recognized the tension between a Christian servitude and a free Christian lordship over all things. He had not yet connected justification by faith with the declarations about the kingly rule and the priestly power of all Christians, nor with the provocative antipapal thesis that in faith a Christian is servant to no one.[56] This corresponds to the fact that in the "Sermon on Two Kind of Righteousness" Luther had not yet mentioned Christian freedom, to say nothing of making it into that work's theme and central concept.[57] Nor had he yet taken the question of Christian lordship to its final conclusions. All this changed through the escalation of the conflict with the papal church in 1520, climaxing with the arrival of the papal bull of excommunication.

In this way, one can read the entire tract on freedom as Luther's particular and universal processing of his basic conflict with the Roman papal

---

53. Compare the *Sermo de duplici iustitia*, WA 2:145.14-21 and 146:8-16; *LW* 31:297 and 298, with the tract on freedom, paragraph 12, German, WA 7:25.26–26.12; Latin, WA 7:54.31–55.36; *LW* 31:352.

54. The *Sermo de duplici iustitia* is for the most part dedicated thematically to Phil. 2:5-11, the first part of the Christ hymn (WA 2:145.1-6; *LW* 31:297). However, it is first in the second part, when dealing with the "second righteousness" of the Christian walk in good works, that Luther returns to his theme from Philippians, WA 2:147.36ff.; *LW* 31:301. He proceeded similarly in the freedom tract, the second part of which reaches its high point in the christological argumentation based on Phil. 2:5-8. This text set the course of his thought from paragraph 26 to paragraph 28, German, WA 7:34.33–35.19 and 35.25-27; Latin, WA 7:64.38–65.9 and 65.32-35; *LW* 31:365 and 366.

55. See *Sermo de duplici iustitia* (WA 2:148.12-21 and 32f.; 149.5f. and 15f.; *LW* 31:301f., and n. 45 above).

56. See n. 44 above.

57. He cited the Vulgate of Ps. 31:2 ("In iustitia tua libera me") and spoke of the freedom of Christ (WA 2:146.21 and 148.2f. and 16; *LW* 31:299, 302).

church. Since the tract ties together various aspects of freedom that had entered Luther's thought and actions from 1515 to 1520, one could and surely ought to read it in many other ways, for instance, as a mystical tract.[58] The complex structure of this tract explains the variety of ways in which it has been interpreted, all those varied and even controversial interpretations, which were also certainly determined by its readers' different contexts. Although the tract on freedom could be understood and translated into concrete situations in varying ways, it would — to say the least — be enormously reductive of its wide perspective to omit consideration of the thematic roots and emphases that came from the ecclesiastical conflicts of 1520. As a result of such a consideration, however, this means that *The Freedom of a Christian* is not a purely theological work. Instead, it belongs to sixteenth-century discourse about lordship, power, and authority. It has thus not been a matter of simple misunderstanding that many readers have read it as a tract against an illegitimate lordship that had rejected God's law.

---

58. See chapter 8, "How Mystical Was Luther's Faith?"

CHAPTER 8

How Mystical Was Luther's Faith?

1. The Question in Light of New Research

Over the past forty years, few topics in Luther research have been as intensely, controversially, and productively discussed as the theme of "Luther and mysticism."[1] The discussion is by no means concluded or exhausted but remains in progress. One might even say that it has presently entered a phase of objective clarity. This new objectivity has a confessional and historical dimension.

On the one hand, a typical Protestant fear of touching anything mys-

1. A certain break characterized the essays and discussions on this theme at the third international Luther Congress (1966 in Järvenpää, Finland). See the conference publication, Ivar Asheim, ed., *Kirche, Mystik, Heiligung und das Natürliche bei Luther* (Göttingen: Vandenhoeck & Ruprecht, 1967), especially the essays by Oberman, "Simul gemitus et raptus," and Iserloh, "Luther und die Mystik." Oberman's essay was later published in his collection of essays *Die Reformation*. I find Iserloh's study to be the most noteworthy contribution to the theme of all recent research, because, as a Catholic Luther scholar, he read the sources in new and refreshing ways and — without the qualms of Protestant scholarship — could speak of Luther's mysticism. This is quite in opposition to the essay by Hägglund in that volume, which pointedly said, "Die Mystik ist katholisch, wird von einem Gottesgedanken oder einem religiösen Leitgedanken beherrscht, der dem Luthertum fremd ist. Deshalb kann zwischen Luther und der Mystik kein wirklich positives Verhältnis bestanden haben" (86). Since that conference, the academic study of Luther's mysticism has been an "on the one hand . . . on the other" kind of topic. See Volker Leppin, "Luther-Literatur seit 1983, Teil II," *Theologische Rundschau* 65 (2000): 439-42.

tical is in the process of disappearing. Because of confessional perspectives, there was a hardening of the idea that mysticism was essentially Roman Catholic (as in Adolf von Harnack, a typical voice of Albrecht Ritschl's liberal school)[2] or that evangelical faith and mysticism were like fire and water (as in Karl Barth and his dialectical theology).[3] Those times appear to be over. A very different concept of mysticism has opened up the possibility of even interpreting the Reformation view of faith as a kind of evangelical mysticism. Above all, however, this has opened the possibility of not only understanding those reforming spiritualists whom Luther derided as "enthusiasts" to be mystical theologians but also of seeing Luther as the founder of an evangelical mysticism and as someone at home in a Protestant mystical spirituality.

There follows also a fully changed historical perspective on the subject. In the past forty years, we have learned to no longer see the Middle Ages as a monolithic era of Roman Catholicism but as a period containing deep breaks, tensions, and volatility, out of which have grown both modern Roman Catholic Christianity and Protestant Christianity.[4] This now means, though, that we can no longer view Luther's enormous innovations simply as a protest against certain outward forms of medieval ecclesiology, theology, and piety, but above all as a creative extension of a typically late medieval dynamic of reform and therefore as the continuation of a certain kind of Christian mysticism.[5]

---

2. Adolf von Harnack, *Lehrbuch der Dogmengeschichte III*, 4th ed. (Tübingen: J. C. B. Mohr, 1910), 433f.

3. Walther von Loewenich, *Luthers theologia crucis*, 5th ed. (Witten: Luther-Verlag, 1967), 170-73. Loewenich agreed with the judgments of Karl Barth, Friedrich Gogarten, and Emil Brunner, coming to the conclusion, "Darum verhalten sich Glaube und Mystik zueinander wie Feuer und Wasser" (172). Compare that, however, to Loewenich's more cautious view in the afterword of the fourth edition (1954) and the fifth edition, 205f.

4. On the concept of polarity in the Middle Ages, especially of opposites in the late Middle Ages, see Volker Leppin, "Von der Polarität zur Vereindeutigung," in *Frömmigkeit — Theologie — Frömmigkeitstheologie*, ed. Gudrun Litz et al. (Leiden and Boston: Brill, 2005), 299-315. See also Berndt Hamm, "Die Stellung der Reformation im zweiten christlichen Jahrtausend," *Jahrbuch für biblische Theologie* 15 (2000): 198-205.

5. Berndt Hamm, "Wie innovativ war die Reformation?" *Zeitschrift für historische Forschung* 27 (2000): 481-97.

2. Late Medieval Theological Reform as Sounding Board for a Diffusive Mysticism

To mention only one example, I would like to describe a thread of continuity found in the devotional, practical, and pastoral theology of the fifteenth century that has the following traits: first, a concentration on internalization, prayers of the heart, meditation, lifelong repentance, humility, and imitation of Christ's suffering; second, a stress on human poverty, weakness, and sinfulness compared to the immensity of divine mercy, which is open even to the greatest sinners and which comes to them through Christ's incarnation and passion; third, a strong accent on the soul's deep communion of love with the humbled and risen Christ, whose saving presence all Christians should experience as a reality for and in themselves, *pro me* and *in me*. This christocentric and intensely grace-based theology of experience found its primary audience outside the universities. It had a strong monastic stamp, because it drew above all from the writings of Augustine and Bernard of Clairvaux that were mediated through the monasteries.[6] Especially characteristic of the decades just before the Reformation was the way these theological impulses for reform also influenced educated laypeople beyond the cloister, giving their religious interests a new focus on self-observation, spiritual comfort, and personal formation. For the young brother Martin Luther, the most important proponent of this "theology of piety"[7] was his superior in the order, his pastor and teacher, Johannes von Staupitz.[8] Staupitz should not be viewed in isolation. Rather, in his thoroughly original way (both before and after 1500), he advocated the kinds of theological reforms without which one cannot understand the genesis of Luther's own theology.

By objectively viewing the deep roots of Luther's new theology in

---

6. On this kind of theology (in connection with the intensive reception of Bernard of Clairvaux), see Ulrich Köpf, "Monastische Theologie im 15. Jahrhundert," *Rottenburger Jahrbuch für Kirchengeschichte* 11 (1992): 117-35, and "Monastische und scholastische Theologie," in *Bernhard von Clairvaux und der Beginn der Moderne*, ed. Dieter R. Bauer and Gotthard Fuchs (Innsbruck: Tyrolia, 1996), 96-135.

7. Berndt Hamm, "Was ist Frömmigkeitstheologie? Überlegungen zum 14. bis 16. Jahrhundert," in *Praxis Pietatis: Beiträge zu Theologie und Frömmigkeit in der Frühen Neuzeit, Festschrift für Wolfgang Sommer*, ed. Hans-Jörg Nieden and Marcel Nieden (Stuttgart: Kohlhammer, 1999), 27f.

8. Berndt Hamm, "Staupitz, Johann(es) von," in *Theologische Realenzyklopädie* (Berlin: De Gruyter, 2001), 32:119-27.

the soil of the late medieval reforming theology that I have described above (that is, without worrying whether Luther's distinctive theological profile and the evangelical faith might somehow vanish), we will be able to perceive how strongly Luther's theology is rooted in particular mystical traditions. It was, in fact, characteristic of numerous advocates of this pre-Reformation pastoral theology to draw from mystical sources and to integrate instructions about mystical experience into their theological program. The theology of piety became the basis of a diffusive mysticism.[9] An example of this piety in the early fifteenth century was the famous *Imitatio Christi (The Imitation of Christ)*.[10] Even more impressively, though, Staupitz presented the architecture of his theology as a specific form of Christian mysticism. This theology was entirely based upon the spiritual path of living in God's love, as preached in Advent 1516 from the pulpit of the Augustinian church in Nuremberg.[11] Before that, he had passed it on to Luther, his brother in the order, in the lecture room and in personal dialogue.[12] It not only integrated mystical concepts, themes, and experiences, but was — as I shall soon show — basically mystical in its teaching on salvation. Against this background, the question pointedly arises as to the mystical character of Luther's Reformation theology, a question that looks beyond the common consensus of current Luther research.

---

9. Berndt Hamm, "'Gott berühren': Mystische Erfahrung im ausgehenden Mittelalter: Zugleich eine Klärung des Mystikbegriffs," in *Gottes Nähe unmittelbar erfahren*, 113.

10. Thomas à Kempis, *Imitatio Christi*. This work includes a critique of high-flying, speculative, visionary, and self-indulgent mysticism. Instead, it offers a daily encounter with the suffering Christ and a promising program of mysticism based on humility, love, and Christ's passion, which culminates in a mystical Christian freedom from worldly entanglements as an anticipation of heavenly blessing.

11. In early 1517, Staupitz turned this Advent sermon into the Latin tract *De exsecutione aeternae praedestinationis*. Both the German and Latin versions are available in Staupitz, *Libellus De exsecutione aeternae praedestinationis*, ed. Lothar Graf zu Dohna et al. (Berlin: De Gruyter, 1979).

12. After his parents and later his wife, Katharina von Bora, no one had a bigger influence on Luther than his "spiritual father" Johannes von Staupitz. See WA TR 1:245.12, no. 526; LW 54:97: "Staupitz is the one who started the teaching [of the gospel in our time]." See also Richard Wetzel, "Staupitz und Luther," in *Martin Luther*, ed. Volker Press and Dieter Stievermann (Stuttgart: Klett-Cotta, 1986).

3. The Thesis: The Mystical Nature of Luther's Theology

Among researchers, it is uncontested that during his early years in the monastery and while he was developing his new theology Luther learned and used various traditions and motifs of medieval mysticism.[13] He thought highly of mystical theologians such as Bernard of Clairvaux, Jean Gerson, and especially Johannes Tauler, and the so-called Frankfurter with his *Theologia Deutsch*,[14] even occasionally extolling them in poems of praise.[15] There is also no doubt among researchers that Luther's turn against scholasticism opened a new door for the experiential and emotional dimensions of mystical spirituality and that his Reformation theology contained significant individual moments and aspects that one can, with all prudence, describe as mystical. This becomes provocative and controversial, however, when one asks about the grand scheme of Luther's new theology and about the center of his Reformation views of salvation and revelation. The notion that the origin of this theology, its transformation or "turn," could be understood in its nature as the formation of a new kind of mysticism would surely encounter more hostile skepticism than agreement in contemporary Luther research and especially in Lutheran churches. Research, however, lives in its readiness to experiment, that is, in its being open to test unfamiliar ways of thinking that go beyond contemporary consensus. I would like to take this risk as I try to establish the following thesis on the basis of the historical sources.

Luther's mature theology, the one that can be described in the fullest

---

13. As a biblical scholar, Luther very early (no later than during his first Psalms lectures) became familiar with mystical terms and concepts and included them in his exegetical work. See Heiko A. Oberman, "Simul gemitus et raptus: Luther und die Mystik," in *Die Reformation: Von Wittenberg nach Genf* (Göttingen: Vandenhoeck & Ruprecht, 1986), 73-82. Oberman's phrase "exegetical mysticism" soon became standard in Luther research. Even before that period, however, Luther would have also learned mystical views and concepts through his diligent study of Gabriel Biel's works *Collectorium* and *Expositio canonis missae*, so that his later critiques of scholasticism could come from these engagements with it.

14. Andreas Zecherle, "Die 'Theologia deutsch': Ein spätmittelalterlicher mystischer Traktat," in *Gottes Nähe unmittelbar erfahren*, 1-95.

15. The high point of these mystical panegyrics came in Luther's praise of Tauler (see n. 147 below). Luther spoke of no other theologian in such exclusively positive terms as Tauler. On Luther's more critical use of Bernard, see Theo Bell, *Divus Bernhardus: Bernhard von Clairvaux in Martin Luthers Schriften* (Mainz: P. von Zabern, 1993), and Bernhard Lohse, "Luther und Bernhard von Clairvaux," in *Bernhard von Clairvaux: Rezeption und Wirkung im Mittelalter und in der Neuzeit*, ed. Kaspar Elm (Wiesbaden: Harrassowitz, 1994), 271-301.

sense of the word "Reformation" theology, not only has a mystical side or dimension to it, and not only receives traditional mystical themes, images, and concepts, but also reveals mystical traits in its compositional entirety. If my title asked, "How mystical was Luther's faith?" then I should like to say that his understanding of faith was mystical in such a way that the essential connections within his theology (for instance, between divine righteousness and human sin, between Christ and the soul, or between the divine and human natures in Christ) can be described as "modes of communication" and as a kind of mystical synapse.

4. The Concept and Definition of "Mysticism"

With this, I propose a distinct view of mysticism that does not apply the term diffusively to all possible forms of spiritual piety at the end of the Middle Ages. A spirituality and theology that valued the affects of experience, the moment of faith's experience, and a personal relationship to Christ in love, trust, meditation, and heartfelt prayer should not be named "mystical," although all these factors are important ingredients in a mystical relationship to God. If "mysticism" is more than this and if we want to admit this unique form of mysticism to be fundamental to Luther's view of salvation, then we can do so only if we actually open up the concept of mysticism. It would be methodologically fatal to fix the concept of mysticism too narrowly to certain kinds of medieval traditions. Then we would only be able to conclude that since Luther viewed God's relationship to humans differently, he must not have been a mystical theologian. Conversely, we would then have to admit that we meet a new kind of mysticism in Luther, a Reformation mysticism of faith, just as in the Middle Ages there were frequent and astonishing new outbreaks of mysticism.[16] But what can we gather about this from his writings?

It only makes sense to advance this question when I now reflect upon how the concept of mysticism can be used more meaningfully, not restricting it unnecessarily but also not letting it widen too diffusely. I prefer to start with the vocabulary, based on those sources within the Western Christian tradition that disciplined historians can broadly describe as "mystical."

---

16. See the splendid study by Susanne Köbele, "*Heiligkeit durchbrechen:* Grenzfälle von Heiligkeit in der mittelalterlichen Mystik," in *Sakralität zwischen Antike und Neuzeit,* ed. Berndt Hamm et al. (Stuttgart: Steiner, 2007), 147-69.

Above all, these would be the writings of Pseudo-Dionysius the Areopagite, Bernard of Clairvaux, Angela de Foligno, Mechthild of Magdeburg, Meister Eckhart, Johannes Tauler, Henry Suso, and Jan Ruysbroeck, and not only the works themselves but also the peculiar ways in which these traditions were transmitted and received. If we keep our eyes on this varied spectrum of ways to have a mystical relationship with God and choose a definition that does not immediately exclude evangelical approaches to mysticism, then we can reach the following conceptual boundary: where a mystical relationship of God to humanity is invoked, it always has to do with the personal, direct, and holistic experience of a blessed nearness to God that reaches its goal through an inner union with God.[17]

Once again, allow me to emphasize the essential elements within this definition. The Christian mysticism of the premodern West continually aimed for a holistic personal encounter with God that seized all of a person's spirit, intellect, will, imagination, feelings, and physical senses. With this experience should come an immediate and direct relationship to God, an immediacy that knocks down all the disruptive factors and situations that get between God and the soul. This direct contact brings spiritual communion with God, touching the innermost soul and experienced by the soul as the comforting, joyful, and blessed presence of God, nearness to God, and union with God. In many different variations, this *unio mystica* (mystical union) comes to mean a loving perception and a perceiving love. In the Middle Ages, a theology that focused on this kind of experience of God's nearness, reflected upon it, and sought to teach it as a way of life was called a "mystical theology" *(theologia mystica)*, in contrast to the scholastic theology of the universities and the monastic orders.[18] Was Luther in this sense a "mystical

---

17. Insofar as I use the mystical concept of "nearness" or "imminence" *(Nähe)* to mean an immediate experience of God, I agree with McGinn's view of mysticism as being defined by an immediate awareness of being in God's presence; see Bernard McGinn, *The Presence of God: A History of Western Christian Mysticism*, vol. 1 (New York: Crossroad, 1992). To me, the idea of "nearness" describes mystical intensity and directness better than the word "presence" *(prescence)*, because nearness includes a relationship and connection that is characteristic of love. In fact, people in medieval times spoke of this experience of nearness — especially the experience of union *(unio)* — to emphasize a relationship instead of some consciousness or experience of being in the presence of God.

18. On the vocabulary of fifteenth- and early-sixteenth-century mysticism, especially the *theologia mystica* of Pseudo-Dionysius and Gerson, see Johannes Altenstaig, *Lexikon Theologicum* . . . (1517; 1619), ed. Johannes Tytz (New York: George Olms, 1974), 909f.: "Theologia mystica [as an affective theology, in contrast to speculative theology],

theologian," who as a teacher and reformer of the church sought to faithfully live out a mystical relationship with God? One clue to answer this could be that, according to his own vocabulary, the *theologia mystica* represented the highest, truest, and most desirable form of Christian theology.[19]

5. Luther's Protection against a Mysticism Exclusively for Exceptional People

Here we should add a caveat: Luther was no proponent of an elitist mysticism. He neither referred to certain mystical raptures, ecstatic experiences, revelations, visions, or angel choirs, nor did he care to give instructions for such.[20] He also opposed a speculative mysticism that, as in Pseudo-Dionysius the Areopagite (ca. 500), strove for the ascent of the perceptive spirit into the mysterious darkness of divine being.[21] He did not write for spiritual mountain climbers or virtuosi. For that reason, he was averse to the traditional image of a heavenly ladder upon which the soul climbs on its mystical upward journey to union with God.[22] For him there was no

---

etsi sit suprema atque perfectissima notitia, tamen potest haberi a quolibet fideli, etiamsi sit muliercula vel idiota." Luther stood in this tradition of Gersonian "democratic" mystical theology.

19. In a conventional way, Luther differentiated *theologia mystica* as a *sapientia experimentalis* from the discursive *theologia rationalis* or *theologia doctrinalis*. See his *Randbemerkungen* on Tauler (1516) in WA 9:98.20f. and the lectures on Hebrews (1517-18) in WA 57/III:179.6-11 and 197.15-20; LW 29:179 and 200. Here Luther agrees with Biel and Staupitz on the theological importance of mystical theology for the *homo spiritualis*.

20. WA 40/III:657.11-18 and 32-36.

21. Luther could use the *theologia negativa* of Pseudo-Dionysius quite positively in his process of externalization. See Karl-Heinz Zur Mühlen, "Mystische Erfahrung und Wort Gottes bei Luther," in *Mystik: Religion der Zukunft — Zukunft der Religion*, ed. Johannes Schilling (Leipzig, 2003), 48-52, and Paul Rorem, "Martin Luther's Christocentric Critique of Pseudo-Dionysian Spirituality," *Lutheran Quarterly* 11 (1997): 291-307. See also nn. 111 and 113 below.

22. On the medieval tradition of the heavenly ladder, see Christian Heck, *L'échelle céleste: Une histoire de la quête du ciel*, 2nd ed. (Paris, 1999), and Gottfried Seebass, *Die Himmelsleiter des hl. Bonaventura von Lucas Cranach d.Ä. Zur Reformation eines Holzschnitts* (Heidelberg: C. Winter, 1985). Luther addressed this topic in a sermon of January 1525, WA 17/I:438.22-25: "Es ist viel davon geschrieben, wie der mensch soll vergottet warden; da haven sie leytern gemacht, daran man gen hymel steyge und viel solchs dings. Es ist aber eytel partecken [armseliges, jämmerliches] wreck; hie [Eph. 3:19] ist aber der

special virtue or deed, experience, or knowledge, through which a pious person could climb to God. When he spoke of grace, he never meant it as a special endowment graciously given to a mystical elite, who went beyond the normal plane of Christian life in order to take part in extraordinary experiences of salvific and blessed nearness to God. No, for him grace in all its divine fullness and power was a movement that embraced all believing Christians. This certainly happened in a suitable way for each believer, but also in a common way and without any ranking of qualitative order. With this, Luther was advancing a development that had been growing in influence since the thirteenth century and can be described as a tendency to open the gates of mysticism, to "democratize" or popularize it.[23] In the fifteenth century, this transformation had already gone far. By that time, the majority of mystical texts aimed not for the limits of ecstasy or for exceptional experiences but for a simple love of Christ, which yields to the way of the cross in everyday life, and there experiences innermost connection to the incarnate God.[24]

---

rechte und nehiste weg, hyman zu komen, angezeygt." WA TR 5:295.21-25, no. 5658a, and the autobiographical note in a 1527 Christmas sermon, WA 23:732.8f., "Ich bin auch auff der selben treppe gewest, ich hab aber ein bein druber zubrochen." For more on how Luther interpreted Jacob's ladder of Gen. 28, see nn. 33 and 34 below. For the sense in which there was room in his incarnational theology and theology of the cross for talk about a ladder, see nn. 105, 113, and 114 below.

23. On the "democratization of mysticism," especially with respect to the *Devotio moderna* and Gabriel Biel, see Heiko A. Oberman, *Der Herbst der mittelalterlichen Theologie*, trans. Martin Rumscheidt and Henning Kampen (Zurich: EVZ-Verlag, 1965), 318-22. On the use of the term "democratization of mysticism," see McGinn, *The Presence of God: A History of Western Christian Mysticism*, vol. 3 (1999), 37-40.

24. On the transformation of mysticism in the fifteenth century, see Werner Williams-Krapp, "'Dise Ding sint dennoch nit ware zeichen der Heiligkeit': Zur Bewertung mystischer Erfahrungen im 15. Jahrhundert," in *Frömmigkeitstile im Mittelalter*, ed. Wolfgang Haubrichs (Göttingen: Vandenhoeck & Ruprecht, 1990), 61-71, and Williams-Krapp, "Frauenmystik und Ordensreform im 15. Jahrhundert," in *Literarische Interessenbildung im Mittelalter: DFG-Symposion 1991*, ed. Joachim Heinzle (Stuttgart: Metzler, 1993), 301-13; Hamm, "Theologie und Frömmigkeit im ausgehenden Mittelalter," in *Handbuch der Geschichte der evangelischen Kirche in Bayern*, ed. Gerhard Müller, Horst Weigelt, and Wolfgang Zorn (St. Ottilien: EOS, 2002), 170-72 and 204-6; Barbara Steinke, "'Den Bräutigam nehmt euch und habt ihn und verlasst ihn nicht, denn er verlässt euch nicht': Zur Moral der mystik im Nürnberger Katharinenkloster während des 15. Jahrhunderts," in *Gottes Nähe unmittelbar erfahren*, 139-64.

6. Luther's Statements about the Soul's Inner Unity with Christ in the One Body of the Christian Congregation

In carrying out this dynamic change into everyday and common Christian practice, Luther placed the entire emphasis on what a living faith gives to all Christians. Remarkably, though, the mystical factor in his theology by no means disappeared because of this Christian egalitarianism. To the contrary, what I have characterized as "mysticism" gained a surprising intensification and sharpening in Luther. This can be seen at first glance — from his first lectures through his late lectures on Genesis — in how pointedly and repeatedly Luther focused on the unification of Christians with the incarnate God, Jesus Christ. He described the intimate communion of the faithful with Christ by following Johannine and Pauline texts about Christ's being in us and our being in Christ, a union *(unio)* and a "being one" *(unum esse)* of the believing soul with Christ.[25] In light of medieval mystical traditions on the theme of the bride and marriage (inspired above all by Bernard of Clairvaux's interpretation of the Song of Solomon), it was natural that Luther expressed the holistic communal character of this connection by using the image of marriage.[26] Thus, in his famous tract on freedom of 1520, he said that faith unites the soul with Christ like a bride with a bridegroom. The two become one, "one body," as Luther (following Eph. 5:31) went on to say, continuing the christological interpretive tradition about the story of the creation of man and woman.[27] With this reference to Ephesians (5:32), Luther had in view not only the believing individual but also the entire congregation of Jesus Christ. Christ's body is the church, the *corpus Christi mysticum*, within which all Christians are joined together with Christ and with one another into a single body. Luther could illustrate the intensity of this union even further by combining the symbolism of the body with the image of a cake. Together with Christ, we the faithful are a cake, in which we are all equally mixed up and baked together.[28]

---

25. Reinhard Schwarz, "Martin Luther (1483-1546)," in *Große Mystiker: Leben und Wirken*, ed. Gerhard Ruhbach and Joseph Sudbrack (Munich: C. H. Beck, 1984), 192-200.

26. On the language of marriage in mysticism, see Reinhard Schwarz, "Mystischer Glaube — die Brautmystik Martin Luthers," in *Von Eckhart bis Luther: Über mystischen Glauben*, ed. Wolfgang Böhme (Karlsruhe: W. Böhme, 1981), 20-32.

27. WA 7:25.26-30; *LW* 31:351: "The third incomparable benefit of faith is that it unites the soul with Christ as a bride is united with her bridegroom. By this mystery, as the Apostle teaches, Christ and the soul become one flesh [Eph. 5:31-32]."

28. Sermon on John 17:20f. (1528), WA 28:184.13f.: "'Unum,' id est unum corpus,

The Early Luther

In his 1531 lectures on Galatians, Luther went so far as to sharpen the point individually by speaking of a personal unity: "Faith constructs from you and Christ as it were one person, so that you cannot be separated from God but are closely bound to him."[29] With this formulation, Luther interpreted Galatians 2:20, "It is no longer I who live but Christ who lives in me." As he continued to interpret Paul, Luther made it clear that he understood the personal unity of Christ and the sinful human in the sense of a mutual self-identification. The sinner says, "'I am as Christ.' And Christ, in turn, says: 'I am as that sinner who is attached to Me, and I to him. For by faith we are joined together into one flesh and one bone.' Thus Eph. 5:30 says: 'We are members of the body of Christ,' of His flesh and of His bones: in such a way that this faith couples Christ and me more intimately than a husband is coupled to his wife."[30]

7. The Union of Both Natures in Jesus Christ and the Communion between Christ and the Soul in the "Happy Exchange"

What is the best way to understand such mystical expressions of union and unity made by Luther? These expressions were woven out of biblical threads, especially the classical citation about *unio mystica* from 1 Corinthians 6:17: "But anyone united to the Lord becomes one spirit with him."[31] The appropriate understanding of Luther's mystical union can only be taken from the Christology that provided the framework for all his

---

res, Kuch, non tanum de concordia dicit, quia mundus etiam concors." Sermon on John 20:17 (1529), WA 29:300.12f.: "Si ipse ad patrem fährt, da wird ex patre, Christo et fratribus ein Kuch." Sermon on Maundy Thursday (1523), WA 12:488.7-11: "So fasset er widerumb mein sunde auff sich, meyn todt, meyn hell, und backen also ynn einander, und werden eyn brot und eyn kuchen mit einander. Und so wyr denn mit Christo eyn kuchen sind, so wirckt das selbige soviel, das wyr auch unter einander eyn ding werden."

29. WA 40/I:285.5f.; LW 26:168.

30. WA 40/I:285.26–286.17; LW 26:168.

31. WA 57/III:187.15–188.3; LW 29:188: "But this righteousness is the righteousness about which it is written in Rom. 1:17 that it is from faith, as is stated that in the Gospel 'the righteousness of God is revealed from faith to faith.' This is erroneously explained as referring to the righteousness of God by which He Himself is righteous, unless it were understood in such a way that faith so exalts man's heart and transfers it from itself to God that the heart and God become one spirit and thus in a way are the divine righteousness, the 'formative' righteousness, as they call it, just as in Christ the humanity, through the union with the divine nature, became one and the same Person."

statements about believers' communion with Christ. It was in the classical doctrine of the two natures, Christ's true divinity and true humanity, that Luther found his basic model for the union of Christ; one could even call this the "original sacrament."[32] He repeatedly based the justified sinner's saved status on the union of the divine and human natures in one person, Jesus Christ. If one indeed might speak of a mystical ladder to heaven, then that should only be the ladder by which the most exalted Godhead in infinite mercy descended to take on earthly human nature, binding to itself the humble and despised person of Bethlehem and Golgotha.[33] The incarnate Christ alone is the ladder: *Scala Christus est, quia Christus est via* — "Christ is the ladder, because Christ is the Way" (John 14:6).[34] This is how Luther interpreted Jacob's ladder in Genesis 28, finding in it a type of and a foundation for the union of the sinful person with Jesus Christ, who alone is righteous. Just as two natures come together in the one person of Jesus Christ without dissolving indiscriminately into each other, so does the internal personal communion of the soul and its bridegroom, Christ, happen in a unity that does not simply conflate the two essences.[35]

For Luther, though, the main reason for this unification lay in what he described in various ways as a "happy exchange" or a blessed trade between the eternal righteousness of the incarnate God, Jesus Christ, and the sinfulness of the human being.[36] In the Christmas event of the incarna-

---

32. On this connection between Christology and soteriology, see Wilhelm Maurer, *Von der Freiheit eines Christenmenschen: Zwei Untersuchungen zu Luthers Reformationsschriften 1520/21* (Göttingen: Vandenhoeck & Ruprecht, 1949), 36-40 and 51-60, and Notger Slenczka, "Christus," in *Luther Handbuch*, ed. Albrecht Beutel (Tübingen: Mohr Siebeck, 2005), 384f.

33. Christmas sermon (1524), WA 16:143.34–144.21: "er kömet zu dir und hat eine Leiter, einen Weg und Brücken zu dire gemacht." Luther views this *descensus* of Jesus Christ as a descent and humiliation in two ways: (1) as a connection of divine majesty with humanity, and (2) as the submission of the human Jesus of Nazareth to human nature and its suffering, dying, and hellish fates. See also his words on Gen. 28, WA 43:579.40–580.1; *LW* 5:219, and a sermon on John 14 (1520), WA 9:494.24f.: "Scala stat in terra, id est natura Christi descendit ac tetigit, immo adsumpsit formam contemptissimam pauperis pueri."

34. WA 9:494.17.

35. On Luther's interpretation of Jacob's ladder, see n. 33 above and WA 43:582.15-29.

36. Luther also called this a "blessed struggle and victory," WA 7:25.34; *LW* 31:351. See also Berndt Hamm, "Den Himmel kaufen: Heilskommerzielle Perspektiven des 14. bis 16. Jahrhunderts," *Jahrbuch für biblische Theologie* 21 (2006): 264-68, and Thomas Hohen-

tion, the Godhead humbled itself, maintaining in the human nature of Jesus the closest exchange of divine and human characteristics, the so-called *communicatio idiomatum* (the communication of properties), a wonderful interplay of the two natures in the one person of Jesus Christ.[37] In the same way, the event of justification brings the wondrous exchange of properties between the righteous bridegroom, Christ, and the "poor, despised, wicked little whore," as Luther called the sinful soul in his tract on freedom.[38] Christ takes a person's sins upon himself, and, in return, the person is given the gift of Christ's righteousness.

The decisive point about this exchange of properties is the victorious triumph that Luther cited from 1 Corinthians 15:54: "Death is swallowed up in victory."[39] Because Christ has made our sins his own, as if he had committed them himself, he also took upon himself the consequences of sin, death, and hell. His life ended with Golgotha and the descent into hell. But all this was triumphantly "swallowed up" into his divinely incarnated being: sin was swallowed up in his righteousness, death was swallowed up in his resurrection, and hell was swallowed up in his blessedness.[40] When

---

berger, *Lutherische Rechtfertigungslehre in den reformatorischen Flugschriften der Jahre 1521-22* (Tübingen: J. C. B. Mohr, 1996), 117-20.

37. WA 43:579.34-36 and 580.2-24. See also Notger Slenczka, "Communicatio idiomatum," in *Religion in Geschichte und Gegenwart*[4] 2 (Tübingen: Mohr Siebeck, 1999), cols. 433-34, and Oswald Bayer, ed., *Creator est creatura: Luthers Christologie als Lehre von der Idiomenkommunikation* (Berlin: De Gruyter, 2007).

38. WA 7:26.4-7 and 25.34f.; *LW* 31:351. Already in the Romans lectures (1515-16), Luther had connected the communication of attributes and the sinner's status as *simul iustus et peccator,* in WA 56:343.18-23; *LW* 25:332: "For in this way there comes about a communication of attributes, for one and the same man is spiritual and carnal, righteous and a sinner, good and evil. Just as the one and the same Person of Christ is both dead and alive, at the same time suffering and in a state of bliss, both working and at rest, etc., because of the communication of His attributes, although neither of the natures possesses the properties of the other, but are absolutely different, as we all know."

39. See n. 36 above.

40. On the vocabulary of "swallowing up" *(Verschlingens, absorbere),* see WA 7:55.11-17; *LW* 31:352: "By the wedding ring of faith he shares in the sins, death, and pains of hell which are his bride's. As a matter of fact, he makes them his own and acts as if they were his own and as if he himself had sinned; he suffered, died, and descended into hell that he might overcome them all. Now since it was such a one who did all this, and death and hell could not swallow him up, these were necessarily swallowed up by him in a mighty duel; for his righteousness is greater than the sins of all men, his life stronger than death, his salvation more invincible than hell."

the poor, sinful human bride, who is destined for death and hell, is given the gift of her heavenly bridegroom's righteousness, then she has been given everything. For with righteousness (that is, being accepted and loved by God) come eternal life, preservation from hell, and heavenly blessing. Through the "bridal ring" of faith she receives these benefits;[41] she is always sure of them through faith. The basis of this faith, however, is the incarnation of God's Son and the fully divine, fully human Jesus Christ, whose intimate communication in his two natures establishes the blessed communication between Christ and the soul. Only as God incarnate could Christ triumphantly swallow sin, death, and hell and give himself to the believing soul with his righteousness, life, and eternal bliss. This is how the *unio mystica* provides the foundation between Christ's divinity and humanity. It is that wondrous unity between God's glory and human misery and that mystical exchange between Christ and the soul in his *corpus mysticum* (mystical body). This is the same incarnational theology of the *communicatio idiomatum* through which Luther saw the basis for Christ's bodily presence in the Lord's Supper, a mystic moment of unification between God and creature.[42]

8. Luther's Mysticism: The Foundational Experience of Salvation and the Resulting Active Sanctification in Life

The personal union and the holistic unification of Christ and the soul is nothing other than the foundational experience of salvation for the entire Christian life; it is the justification of the ungodly. In essence, this is communion with Christ, in which every kind of communication is a work of the Holy Spirit.[43] This is the Spirit of Jesus Christ that sets hearts aglow, fills them with living faith (that is, with trust, love of God, and the certainty of hope), and then makes it possible for all good works of love to neighbors to flow out of liberated consciences. With this begins an all-

41. See n. 40 above.
42. See n. 128 below.
43. In terms of the *filioque* of the West, Luther integrated the Holy Spirit's work so much with the activity of the risen Christ that he made no mention of the Holy Spirit's power to inspire on its own. But that does not lessen the eminently pneumatological nature of the soul's communion with Christ. See Bernhard Lohse, *Luthers Theologie in ihrer historischen Entwicklung und in ihrem systematischen Zusammenhang* (Göttingen: Vandenhoeck & Ruprecht, 1995), 248-56.

inclusive sanctification of life, which Luther thematized as Christian discipleship and as a lifelong conformation to Christ's self-dedication, his way of the cross, and his overcoming of the world.[44] Because, by the working of the Holy Spirit, God dwells in the soul and impels it to follow Christ, it is in no way unfounded to speak with the Finnish School of Luther research about a mystical "deification" of believers,[45] so long as — like Luther — one keeps in mind the infinite, irrevocable distance between Creator and creation, as well as the persistent stain of sin that always remains in the life of the justified person.[46]

In Luther's view, one cannot say emphatically enough that true Christian faith is a divine life-changing power in the spirit of love for God and the neighbor. Even more important is to discriminate with Luther between the foundational experience of being saved and the effect of this foundation. The fundamental event occurs when the saving story of Jesus — from his incarnation to his cross and resurrection — becomes effective for me personally, when I experience what Luther calls the "happy exchange" of Christ — by grace alone, without my cooperation — who joined himself to my misery, took my corruption upon himself, and gave me all his favor, life, and blessing. That is mysticism in its purest sense: a personal and perfect union of God and person,[47] which has at its center the immediate, total, and intimate experience of blessed nearness to God, freeing the heart, consoling it and lifting it up to joyful certainty. This kind of mysticism forbids every thought of conditions and prior achievements that might pin the gift of salvation to some quality, disposition, or human contribution. When we

---

44. Luther emphasized imitation of Christ on one hand as imitation in *Anfechtung* and, on the other, as love given freely to the neighbor. On the first, see his meditation on Christ's passion, WA 2:141.8–142.2 (15); *LW* 42:13-14. On the second, see *The Freedom of a Christian*; WA 7:34.23–38.5 (26-29); *LW* 31:358-64.

45. See Miikka Ruokanen, ed., *Luther in Finnland — Der Einfluß der Theologie Martin Luthers in Finnland und finnische Beiträge zur Lutherforschung* (Helsinki: Luther-Agricola-Gesellschaft, 1984); Simo Peura and Antti Raunio, eds., *Luther und Theosis: Vergöttlichung als Thema der abendländischen Theologie* (Erlangen: Martin-Luther-Verlag, 1990); and Simo Peura, *Mehr als ein Mensch? Die Vergöttlichung als Thema der Theologie Martin Luthers von 1513 bis 1519* (Mainz: P. von Zabern, 1994).

46. For a critique of the Finnish School of Luther research led by Tuomo Mannermaa, see Albrecht Beutel, "Antwort und Wort: Zur Frage nach der Wirklichkeit Gottes bei Luther," in *Protestantische Konkretionen: Studien zur Kirchengeschichte* (Tübingen: Mohr Siebeck, 1998), 28-44.

47. WA 7:25.32f. (12), *LW* 31:351; WA 7:28.19-21 (16), *LW* 31:356; WA 7:30.11f. (20), *LW* 31:358; WA 7:35.22f., 30-32 (27), *LW* 31:366-67; WA 7:37.31f. (29), *LW* 31:371.

see it in this way, we see that Luther intensified the mystical immediacy and gracious presence of God. No human virtue or deed can come between the pure mercy of God and my total unworthiness. Here there are no rungs that connect the gap between God and humanity; there is only direct contact between the richness of God's salvation and the sinner's lack of salvation. In pure passivity, the soul receives all of God's gifts of salvation.

That is enough for justification as the foundation of salvation. The effect of this primary mystical relationship between God and people is that all the active holiness that the Holy Spirit creates in believers becomes an inner vitality of the loving heart and is expressed under the form of good works. These traits, however, while remaining directly connected in life and experience to the total holistic experience of salvation, can make no contribution to the acquisition or assurance of salvation. What is remarkable and unique in Luther's mysticism can therefore be described in a first summary like this: Luther rejected the traditional model of a process or steps for the mystical ascent to complete union with God. Instead he placed the soul's perfect union with Christ at the beginning of every faith-filled Christian relationship to God, as the union that cannot be surpassed in this life and endures to the end. It is this unconditional gift of salvation, this being taken up into Christ's saving body, that carries and protects believers through *Anfechtungen*, sin, and death. Instead of a person going upward to become ever holier, Christ moves downward to the unholy sinner in a radical mysticism of descent.[48] Where the merciful Christ finds people in their deepest misery, there the most intense *unio* can arise, which Luther described in images of marriage, exchange, and being swallowed up, and which he intensified in the concept of Christian freedom. Here is the *unio* in which both righteousness and holiness are given to people, thereby giving a freedom "which surpasses all other freedom as heaven surpasses the earth."[49]

9. Staupitz's Marriage Mysticism in the Incarnation and the Happy Exchange

With this position against the Pseudo-Dionysian and Platonizing tradition of a spiritual ascent to heaven, Luther picked up another medieval mystical

---

48. There are many examples of Luther equating the majesty of Christ's coming with his descending to human misery. See nn. 33 and 35 above.
49. See n. 106 below.

tradition from before his time that had already emphasized the descent of God to the pitiful human being in the saving event of the incarnation and passion.[50] A conception like Luther's was already in the air around 1500. The young brother could especially encounter this way of thinking in his own order. My attention turns especially to the aforementioned Johannes von Staupitz. He was quite close to Luther personally — not only as father confessor but also as his theology teacher[51] and predecessor in the chair at Wittenberg — and Luther highly valued his three tracts published in 1515, 1517, and 1518, without a doubt reading them exhaustively.[52] Among these tracts, the one written at the end of 1516, *De exsecutione aeternae predestinationis (On the Fulfillment of Eternal Predestination)*, was particularly important.[53] This is no less than an elaborately composed and systematically thick collection of the Augustinian superior's biblical theology. Built around Romans 8:30-32, it described the arc from God's predestining election in grace to the fulfillment of the divine plan for salvation in Christ's incarnation, the justification of sinners, and the various manifestations of the Holy Spirit in the life of the justified.[54]

Here is a strikingly high measure of agreement with Luther's general view of a mystical theology. Like Luther, Staupitz described the central experience of salvation for every Christian as a mystical union of God and person in one body. In Staupitz, too, Ephesians 5:30-32 and its metaphor of a marital union for describing the relationship between Christ and the church served a key purpose, so that Staupitz here equated *ecclesia sive anima* with a personal intensity, equating the church with the soul.[55] The chapter entitled "On the Marriage between Christ and the Christian" *(De*

---

50. Eric L. Saak, *High Way to Heaven: The Augustinian Platform between Reform and Reformation, 1292-1524* (Leiden: Brill, 2002), 467-583.

51. One thinks especially of the time from 1508 to 1509, when Luther first studied with Staupitz in Wittenberg for an extended period of time; Martin Brecht, *Martin Luther: Sein Weg zur Reformation, 1483-1521* (Stuttgart: Calwer, 1981), 98.

52. In addition to the tract *De exsecutione aeternae praedestinationis*, see also "Ein büchlein von der nachfolgung des willigen sterbens Christi" (1515) and "Von der lieb Gottes" (1517-18), in *Johann von Staupitzens sämmtliche Werke*, vol. 1, *Deutsche Schriften*, ed. Joachim Karl Friedrich Knaake (Potsdam: Krausnick, 1867), 50-119.

53. See n. 11 above.

54. On the structure of the tract, see Staupitz, *De exsecutione*, 29-34.

55. Staupitz, *De exsecutione*, 144. See also, Berndt Hamm, *Frömmigkeitstheologie am Anfang des 16. Jahrhunderts: Studien zu Johannes von Paltz und seinem Umkreis*, Beiträge zur historischen Theologie 65 (Tübingen: Mohr, 1982), 234-36.

matrimonio Christi et Christiani) is the centerpiece of Staupitz's whole tract.[56] But it is particularly noteworthy that in his understanding of spiritual marriage Staupitz already saw a close connection between the incarnation, Christ's two natures, and the event of individual justification. The primary marriage event in salvation took place in Christ's incarnation, when the Son of God took human nature and thus bound himself into one body with the church of elected souls. What Staupitz stressed here, in precisely the same sense as Luther's later thought, is the point about the radical descent of God that reconciles absolute differences, about Christ's coming down into the God-forsaken realms of human life, which he described in his own words as "the joining together *(coniunctio)* of the greatest mercy with the greatest misery."[57] This was an event of such immediacy that "the *summa misericordia* descends directly upon the *summa miseria.*"[58] This could not have been expressed more emphatically. Like Luther, Staupitz here freed the christological doctrines of the "two natures" and the *communicatio idiomatum* from their metaphysical abstraction and revealed their soteriological intent.[59] In this way, the incarnation and the wonderful exchange of the divine and human qualities of Christ gained the character of a mystical saving event in which everything was aimed at union, intimate communication, and an exchange between God and people.[60] Closely connected, as Staupitz explained it, the justification of the sinner also took on the character of a Christ mysticism, which was nothing other than a consistent development of the communication between the two natures. Here,

56. Staupitz, *De exsecutione,* 142-49.

57. Staupitz, *De exsecutione,* 150/152: "Ego admirer coniunctionem summae misericordiae cum summa miseria. Admiror, inquam, et gratias ago, quia inde venit salus peccatori, inde processit gloria maxima salvatoris; inde deus suavis nobis factus est, inde peccator deo acceptus. Gratias igitur habeo et misericordias domini in aeternum cantabo." See also the heading of chap. 10, "De correspondentia summae misericordiae cum summa miseria."

58. Staupitz, *De exsecutione,* 154: "Amor enim iste sponsalis summa misericordia est et super summam miseriam directe cadit, de exstinctione peccati prae cunctis sollicitus."

59. See the comments in the introduction to the volume (n. 54 above) on Staupitz's use of the *communicatio idiomatum.*

60. Staupitz, *De exsecutione,* 148: "Ex his omnibus consequens est, quod omnia, quae habet Christus, verbum incarnatum, per assumptionem humanae naturae nostra fecit, ad salutem nostram omnia donavit, dicente scriptura: 'Qui proprio filio non pepercit, sed pro nobis omnibus tradidit illum, quomodo non etiam cum illo omnia nobis donavit.'" On the concept of "all," which Staupitz here picked up from Rom. 8:32, see n. 47 above.

looking at the individual soul and its misery, the statements on the spiritual marriage and on the mystical union into one body[61] reach their peak and — as later in Luther — have as their goal the "happy exchange" between the qualities of the two partners in the marriage.[62] In communication with one another, they find their identity in the other, so that Christ says about his sinful bride, "I am the Christian"; conversely, the bride says, "I am Christ."[63] These are formulations that make us think immediately of Luther's statements (quoted above) on the personal unity of Christ and the self.[64] Staupitz explained the result of this mystical marital "transfer" *(Übertragung)*[65] of the "I" to the "You" and from the "You" to the "I" by allowing the bride to say to Christ, "Thus you are mine and everything you have, you have for me. I am yours and all that is in me belongs to you. And because we are one, what is yours is mine in such a way that it still remains yours; and what is mine is yours in such a way that it still remains mine. Thus I am righteous through your righteousness and through my own sin I am a sinner; and through my guilt you are a sinner and through your own righteousness you are righteous."[66] The sinful soul thereby receives the total forgiveness of sins and the perfect righteousness of the Son of God, which is the basis for its acceptance into heavenly bliss and its certain hope of salvation.[67] As Staupitz made clear, all this is a generous movement of divine mercy to the pitiful human being. Through pure grace, people will be taken

---

61. See Staupitz, *De exsecutione*, 142/144, for Staupitz's discussion of Eph. 5:29-32.

62. See Staupitz, *De exsecutione*, paragraphs 64f., 76f., 78, 82, and 102-5, for Staupitz's praise of the wonderful trade *(admirabile commercium)*.

63. Staupitz, *De exsecutione*, 146: ". . . ut sic Christus dicat: 'Christianus est meus, christianus est mihi, christianus est ego'; et sponsa: 'Christus est meus, Christus est mihi, Christus est ego.'" This language of *meus, mihi,* and *ego* is developed further in paragraphs 57-62.

64. See section 7 above.

65. Staupitz, *De exsecutione*. The heading for chapter 11 is "De translatione peccati nostri in Christum."

66. Staupitz, *De exsecutione*, 158: "Ideo tu es meus, et universa quae habes mihi habes. Ego suum tuus, et quidquid in me est tibi est. Et quia sumus unum, tua ita mea sunt, quod maneant tua; mea sic tua sunt, quod etiam maneant mea. Sum igitur sic ego tua iustitia iustus et mea culpa peccator; tu es mea culpa peccator et tua iustitia iustus." See also 156: "[Christus] nostra peccata sua facit, quatenus sicut christianus Christi iustitia iustus, Christus christiani culpa iniustus sit et peccator."

67. On Staupitz's certainty of salvation being a certainty based on hope, see n. 63 above and *De exsecutione*, 138: "in istis [meritis Christi] fundamus collocamusque firmam spem sue certe fundatam cognoscimus," and 234f. *(vera spes)* and 286f. *(certa spes)*.

up into the marriage-like community of salvation with Christ, that is, into the church's body of the predestined, without being able to contribute anything to it by their own ability and action.

10. Staupitz and Luther: A Mystical Basis of Salvation for All Christians

As with Luther, the mystical doctrine of salvation also occupied a central theological place for Staupitz. The blessed union of a soul with its bridegroom is not the result of spiritual development; rather, this *unio* forms the basis of the whole Christian life, the merciful gift of being that is above all human quality, morality, and activities. In its essence, this union is nothing other than being taken into the saving communication of the body of Christ. The personal, holistic, and perfect union of God and person happens right at the beginning of Christian existence, at that moment when the sinful soul is justified. Like Luther, Staupitz expressed the completeness of this *unio* using the words *omnia* and *universa*:[68] when Christ unites himself with sinners, he gives them all his gifts of salvation. The most important agreement between Staupitz and Luther lies in this basic mysticism for all Christians, because it affects the foundation of their theology. Here is a thoroughly mystical polarity, since for both theologians the union between the righteous Son of God and the sinful soul is the only thing necessary for salvation in the Christian life. In this way, they take traditional bridal mysticism to unprecedented heights in the theology of grace and justification.

Of course, it is also necessary for salvation that the soul become conscious of this gift of communion with Christ, committing its salvation to Christ in full trust; in this way, the Holy Spirit allows the *unio* to become a fundamental personal experience of God's presence. But for Staupitz, every additional spiritual experience that follows from this — those diverse manifestations of the Holy Spirit that accompany the living out of a Christian life that were so important for mystics in the Middle Ages — retreats into the subordinate status of what is not necessary for salvation, and perhaps not even relevant to salvation.[69] Intimately blessed, priceless, "sweet,"

---

68. See nn. 47, 60, and 67 above.
69. Staupitz, *De exsecutione*, 186f. Staupitz differentiates here between what is necessary for salvation and the gifts of the Holy Spirit that God gives beyond that. Love re-

and inspiring experiences of the love of God that fill the heart and are thus direct effects of the marriage-like communion with Christ are bestowed upon the soul beyond what is necessary and common to all Christians. In contrast to traditional mysticism's basing salvation on God's mercy and human misery coming together, Staupitz developed a mystical theology of the gifts of the Spirit.[70] He characterized these as ways of experiencing a foretaste of heavenly salvation *(praegustus salutis)*[71] in different degrees of intensity.[72] As precious as these life-changing spiritual gifts of receiving and sharing love were to him, he clearly differentiated them from the more fundamental saving relationship that everybody has when Christ gives them his righteousness. In this respect, Staupitz prefigured Luther's style of christocentric mysticism in essential ways.[73] In saying this, though, I do not mean that Staupitz's tract must have served as a direct literary model for Luther. Rather, one might say that in his early years in the cloister, Luther had already grown familiar with a kind of christocentric mysticism through Staupitz and probably some other impulses in his order, which had their roots in the earlier patristic and medieval traditions and eventually became the soil for Luther's own mystical theology.[74] In any case, it is striking that in the lectures on Romans (1515-16) he could already describe the process of justification in a way that comes very close to his later descriptions of the "happy exchange."[75]

---

mains preeminent in Staupitz's soteriology. See Adolar Zumkeller, *Johannes von Staupitz und seine christliche Heilslehre* (Würzburg: Augustinus-Verlag, 1994), 176-83, and Hamm, *Frömmigkeitstheologie,* 240-42.

70. The first half of Staupitz's tract provides the basic mysticism behind his view of salvation. The second half covers the mystical theology that comes from the gifts of the Holy Spirit.

71. Staupitz introduces the second half of the tract with a chapter entitled "De praegustu salutis" ("A Foretaste of Salvation").

72. Staupitz, *De exsecutione,* 192-97. Here Staupitz develops four steps of love, peaking with the sexual imagery of the naked Christ and the naked soul being bound in the most intimate and faithful love. This is no longer a basic mystical step for the salvation of all Christians but an experience for elite mystics. The fourth step was only experienced by Mary, Christ's mother.

73. Wetzel, "Staupitz und Luther," 86f. Wetzel shows how Luther developed the idea of the happy exchange from Staupitz.

74. On the theological origins of the happy exchange, see Wetzel, "Staupitz und Luther," 86.

75. See especially WA 56:204.14-25; *LW* 25:188: "Whence shall we take thoughts to defend us? Only from Christ, and only in Him will we find them. For if the heart of a be-

11. Luther's Transformation of Traditional Mysticism in the Union of Word and Faith

Despite Luther's and Staupitz's remarkable agreement as sketched here, Luther's basic view of the relationship between Christ and the soul in justification gains a quite different profile when contrasted to the mystical theology of his fatherly mentor and friend. We can grasp the difference best when we observe that (unlike Staupitz and all previous mystical texts) Luther described the event of the sinful soul's union with its heavenly bridegroom as a relationship between word and faith.[76] As soon as he wanted to explain the marriage-like union and communion of salvation between the sinful soul and the protecting righteousness of the Son of God, he pointed to the saving word of God. Haunted by God's law, the sinner encounters this liberating word of salvation in the Bible's gospel promises, found in both the Old and New Testaments. In these promises, Christ himself enters into direct contact with pitiful people and gives them everything they need: God's favor, his liberating forgiveness of sin, and acceptance into eternal salvation, all summed up together in the concepts of "righteousness" *(iustitia, frumkeyt)* and "justification." Because this assuring word of the *promissio Dei* is a living word, the effective presence of Christ and his Holy Spirit,[77] it not only brings all these saving gifts close to hand but also gives people the inner readiness to receive such gifts. This is the faith given

---

liever in Christ accuses him and reprimands him and witnesses against him that he has done evil, he will immediately turn away from evil and will take his refuge in Christ and say, 'Christ has done enough for me. He is just. He is my defense. He has died for me. He has made His righteousness my righteousness, and my sin His sin. If He has made my sin to be His sin, then I do not have it, and I am free. If He has made His righteousness my righteousness, then I am righteous now with the same righteousness as He. My sin cannot devour Him, but it is engulfed in the unfathomable depths of His righteousness, for He himself is God, who is blessed forever.' Thus we can say, 'God is greater than our heart' (1 John 3:20). The Defender is greater than the accuser, immeasurably greater. It is God who is my defender. It is my heart that accuses me. Is this the relation? Yes, yes, even so! [*Sic, sic, etiam sic!*]."

76. Zur Mühlen, "Mystische Erfahrung und Wort Gottes bei Luther," and Gerhard Müller, *Die Mystik oder das Wort: Zur Geschichte eines Spannungsverhältnisses* (Stuttgart: F. Müller, 2000).

77. Oswald Bayer, *Promissio: Geschichte der reformatorischen Wende in Luthers Theologie*, Forschungen zur Kirchen- und Dogmengeschichte 24 (Göttingen: Vandenhoeck & Ruprecht, 1971), and *Martin Luthers Theologie: Eine Vergegenwärtigung* (Tübingen: Mohr Siebeck, 2003), 46-61.

to the despondent sinner through God's word and Spirit: faith as the certain assurance that what God promises really happens to me. Without merit or worthiness, out of pure divine mercy, I am God's beloved child and heir of salvation.

If we take seriously the fact that for Luther the gospel is not simply a *signum*, a powerless sign, but is *res*, the thing itself as an active and promised word in which Christ gives himself to the sinner, then we can understand why in his 1520 tract on freedom he could insert the mystical union of the soul with Christ and the marital exchange of properties into the relationship between word and faith. Discussing the divine promises and their wholly unifying power, he wrote, "Since these promises of God are holy, true, righteous, free, and peaceful words, full of goodness, the soul which clings to them with a firm faith will be so closely united with them and altogether absorbed by them that it not only will share in all their power but will be saturated and intoxicated by them. . . . This, then, is how through faith alone without works the soul is justified by the Word of God, sanctified, made true, peaceful, and free, filled with every blessing and truly made a child of God."[78] The word of God plays the active and effective part in this union; the receptive part is played by the faith of the child of God. A few lines later, Luther transferred the old mystical image of the union of fire and iron[79] to the *unio* between word and faith: "No good work can rely upon the Word of God or live in the soul, for faith alone and the Word of God rule in the soul. Just as the heated iron glows like fire because of the union of fire with it, so the Word imparts its qualities to the soul. It is clear, then, that a Christian has all that he needs in faith and needs no works to justify him; and if he has no need of works, he has no need of the law; and if he has no need of the law, surely he is free from the law. . . . This is Christian liberty, our faith."[80]

Through the metaphor of red-hot iron (which he also used elsewhere),[81] Luther articulated the most intense union of God and humans within the context of his theology of justification and of the word. Like the two substances of fire and iron,[82] the contact of faith with the word of God

---

78. WA 7:24.22-29; *LW* 31:349.

79. This image goes back to Origen and Cyril of Alexandria. For a discussion of its use from Bernard of Clairvaux to Luther, see Hamm, "Gott berühren," 118.

80. WA 7:24.31–25.2; *LW* 31:349.

81. *StA* 2:189 n. 111.

82. See *The Babylonian Captivity of the Church* (1520), WA 6:510.4-8; *LW* 36:32.

so completely binds them together that the divine properties belonging to the word also become those of the soul, which becomes full of all of God's goodness, holiness, and righteousness.[83] At the same time, it is also clear that the substances or natures are not changed into one another. Although the iron is red hot, it does not become fire but remains iron. In the same way, the entire perfection of Christ's saving righteousness is given to people so that it becomes their own, but without being transformed into human nature, substance, and quality; human existence is also not changed into divine being. Whatever God's gospel and Spirit change within the believing person remains human, fragmentary, creaturely; it cannot be equated with the saving gift of the divine word and its qualities of perfection. More will be said on this from the perspective of the external righteousness of Christ.

12. Luther's Faith Mysticism: The Faithful Soul's Direct Connection to the Gospel

In view of this internal mystical relationship between faith and the liberating word of God, one can say that Luther transferred the typical mystical focus on immediacy and directness (mentioned earlier in the attempt to define mysticism)[84] to an immediacy of the word. The unmediated relationship of the soul to God became for him the immediate relationship to the living word of God. This immediacy was twofold. First, it was related to the irrelevance of the personal quality and morality of the active person. That is, the liberating relationship of the believer to God's gospel happens without any mediation through human virtues and good works.[85] When a person answers the promise of grace with childlike confidence, saying, "Dear Father!" then — as Luther put it in his interpretation of Galatians — "Father and son come together, and a marriage is contracted without any ceremony or pomp. That is, nothing comes in the way [between the marriage partners]: no Law, no work is demanded here."[86] Second, immediacy is ecclesiological. The soul's relationship to God's graciously given word excludes any kind of priestly mediation of salvation. With Volker

---

83. See the citation corresponding to n. 78 above.
84. See section 4 above.
85. See section 8 above.
86. WA 40/I:593.21-25; LW 26:390.

Leppin, I see in Luther's doctrine of the common priesthood of all baptized believers a certain simplified transformation of mystical ideas about the immediacy between God and people.[87] In this twofold way (directly through the word and without priestly mediation), Luther advocated a new kind of immediacy between God and people, which would have been considered typically heretical according to previous categories.

To be sure, the biblical word of proclamation is an earthly, sensory linguistic medium. For Luther, though, it was an equally unmediated medium because God — Father, Son, and Holy Spirit — comes near to people through the gospel in a way that is otherwise unparalleled on earth, becoming one with people because it is in the gospel's promise that God's favor is bestowed upon sinners. For this reason Luther could also say that those who understand God's word correctly have it "without a medium" from the Holy Spirit in a direct experience, taste, and feeling.[88] When Luther transformed the immediacy of traditional mysticism into an immediacy of the word, faith simultaneously became the central concept of the Christian life for him: faith is the confident reception of the gospel. However, this meant that Luther surrendered the traditional centrality of love, which had still remained the decisive point for Staupitz.[89] In Luther, the medieval "love mysticism" became the Reformation's "faith mysticism." It is hardly possible to express more emphatically the radical break that Luther's theology brought to the history of Western mysticism. But what did he mean by making this leap from love to faith?

13. Luther's Journey from the Inside to the Outside of *Anfechtung*: The External Righteousness of Christ and the External Word

The magnitude of this break makes sense only by starting with the basic situation of *Anfechtung* in Luther's life. This characterized the whole structure of his new theology and his new mysticism as well, while the topic of *Anfechtung* did not play any meaningful role in Staupitz's mystical theol-

---

87. Hamm and Leppin, *Gottes Nähe unmittelbar erfahren*, 183-85.
88. See Luther's commentary on the Magnficat (1521), WA 7:546, 24-27; LW 21:299: "No one can correctly understand God or His Word unless he has received such understanding immediately from the Holy Spirit. But no one can receive it from the Holy Spirit without experiencing, proving, and feeling it."
89. See chap. 1 above.

ogy but remained on the periphery. Staupitz stood solidly in that scholastic and mystical tradition that viewed the justification of sinners as the shift from lovelessness into a new ability to love.[90] For him, too, the essential element of God's saving relationship to people lay in this shift.[91] The sinful soul is raised out of an egocentric orbit and brought into orbit around God, a gravitational field of God's love for its own sake. Thus the mystical theology of the late Middle Ages focused primarily on the soul's blessed union in love with its heavenly bridegroom. But this mystical and monastic ideal about the pure love of God was so completely shattered for young brother Luther that he fell into a desperate crisis of *Anfechtung*. In his innermost being, he could not find the ability to love that he sought and instead had to realize the total nothingness of his efforts to become holy before God. Commended to him by the internalizing agenda of mystical theology as a way to reach the deepest level of perception and love, the journey inward was not for him the road to the intimate experience of the blessed nearness of God but the road to the confrontation with his own basic sin: that total unworthiness, absolute separation from God, and even the terrifying wrath of God, who judged him and condemned him.

Stricken by this *Anfechtung* that was devastating his sense of self and God, his conscience (his innermost religious awareness) was in danger of drowning in obsessive and fearful visions of the Last Judgment, sin, death, and hell. That is when Luther found the liberating way out through the radical turn outward. This was his guiding light to the external righteousness of Christ, which covered the sinner like a sheltering cloak or like the wings of a mother hen protecting her threatened chicks from a bird of prey.[92] Through faith, of course, the terrified soul does internally apply

---

90. In addition to many passages in *De exsecutione*, see also "Von der lieb Gottes" (n. 52 above).

91. For Staupitz, this essential, life-changing coming of the love of God (in both its active and passive senses) in the human heart is nothing other than the temporal consummation of God's eternal predestination. To that extent, human salvation therefore depends on God's election from eternity.

92. On the image of the cloak, see the Romans lectures, WA 56:278.1-7; *LW* 25:265: "He is covered, I should add, through Christ who dwells in us, as Ruth in a figurative sense says to Boaz: 'Spread your coat over your maidservant, for you are next of kin' (Ruth 3:9). 'And she uncovered his feet and lay down' (Ruth 3:7), that is, the soul lays itself down at Christ's humanity and is covered with His righteousness. Likewise, Ezek. 16:8: 'I spread my garment over you and covered your nakedness.' And in Ps. 63:7: 'In the shadow of Thy wings I sing for joy.'" On the image of the hen and chicks, see WA 10/I:1:280.11–285.9.

iustitia Christi to itself, but in its saving perfection this is never the same thing as an internal personal quality or a spiritual ability to love. Completing this outward turn also had the consequence for Luther of finding a guiding light in the external biblical word of the gospel, which comforts people with an abundance of righteousness and salvation that comes from outside themselves and can never be found as long as people look inside themselves.[93] Precisely because the word of salvation and the Holy Spirit bound to it come entirely from the outside, they can touch sinners in their innermost being and there, in their afflicted consciences, direct them entirely to the liberating external dimension of *Christus pro me*. This focus, however, belongs to faith, which in its essence does not look at the self, its inner substance, or good works, but instead attaches itself entirely to the word of promise and Christ's assurance, finding there alone its blessed confidence.[94]

14. Faith, Not Love, as the Central Concept of the Union with Christ That Justifies

It is of profound theological consequence that, due to his disillusioning experience of *Anfechtung*, Luther no longer devoted himself to the concept of love as the best way to articulate the saving relationship between the sinful soul and a merciful God.[95] To find a basic mystical vocabulary for this, Luther chose the concept of faith, of all things, which in traditional theology was the weakest emotion and the least pious dimension within Christian life; for according to medieval Catholic thought, it was not faith but rather the ability to love that saved people. When Luther tied the justification of the ungodly to faith and the faith-filled hearing of the word, he wanted to say that — however much the assurance of faith might inspire love of God[96] — people are not justified and saved by spiritual feelings or by pi-

---

93. On the origins of this *extra nos* dimension of Luther's early theology, see Karl-Heinz Zur Mühlen, *Nos extra nos: Luthers theologie zwischen Mystik und Scholastik*, Beiträge zur historischen Theologie 46 (Tübingen: J. C. B. Mohr, 1972).

94. Bayer, *Promissio*.

95. On this move from love to faith, see chap. 3 above.

96. To be theologically precise, we must say that faith, according to Luther, is the heart's trust in God's saving goodness. This is always a kind of radical love of God. That is, it really is a kind of love, which expects and receives all things from God. But faith does not justify through its active ability to love or through its sparks of feeling but rather only

ous emotions like the love of God or penitential love. They are saved instead only by a passive reception from the outside in. For him, faith is the way of pure receiving, of the sinner's conscience being given the gift of Jesus Christ's righteousness. This is bestowed upon believers when they trust the gospel; that is, they know themselves to be nothing, but they trust everything to the saving acts of God. The point of this "evangelical" faith lies in its "only": you need "only" to believe, for "when you believe, you have";[97] you need not and dare not reflect on your own ability to love, your repentance, or your works of obedience to God, because these are all irrelevant for your salvation.

15. Mystical Rapture: The Ecstatic Nature of Faith

The mystical character of this faith, which allows the soul to become one with the gospel and thereby with Christ himself, was developed by Luther when he applied the traditional mystical concept of *raptus* (rapture) — that ecstasy of being lifted up and being transported — to faith and faith alone. "Nos ergo per fidem rapimur et efficimur una caro cum ipso [Christo]" ("Therefore we are carried along by faith and become one flesh with him").[98] Staupitz also applied the concept of rapture to the basic mystical experience of all Christians, knowing that it did not belong only to those few people who had been especially blessed with ecstatic experiences.[99] The difference, though, is that, like the mystical tradition before him, he connected this "being taken up out of oneself" with the ecstatic nature of love, which pulls sinners out of their self-centeredness.[100] What is completely

---

through its passive receiving. Not the loving person but the sinful person will be pronounced free at life's end. This is what Luther meant to say with precision when he named faith rather than love as the saving relationship between God and humans.

97. WA 7:24.13; *LW* 31:348-49.

98. WA 43:582.21f.; *LW* 5:223. See also, Oberman, "Simul gemitus et raptus"; Iserloh, "Luther und die Mystik," 71f.; Zur Mühlen, *Nos extra nos*, 51-66 and 104; Miikka Ruokanen, "Luther und Ekstase," *Kerygma und Dogma* 32 (1986); and Athina Lexutt, "Luthers Verhältnis zur Mystik. Ein kirchengeschichtlicher Lösungsversuch zur Frage: Mystik und Protestantismus — Himmlisches Paar oder Duo infernale?" *Der evangelische Erzieher* 49 (1997): 19-40.

99. Staupitz, *De exsecutione*, 194 and 200, the latter of which reads, "[The law of Christ] rapit totum hominem sibimet et totaliter extra se ipsum ponit."

100. Staupitz, *De exsecutione*, 202f.

new in Luther comes in his connecting rapture and faith. For Luther, one can even say that faith naturally moves toward rapture, to an existential otherworldliness, since it pulls people out of all that is visible, experiential, sensory, and knowable in this life and sets them in the entirely different, truly divine reality of the word of Christ, that is, in the transcendent reality of Christ's righteousness and eternal blessedness.[101] Looked at in this way, the faithful have their being outside of themselves, *extra nos*. At the end of his tract on freedom, Luther said that a Christian "lives not in himself."[102] "By faith he is caught up beyond himself into God. By love he descends beneath himself into his neighbor. Yet he always remains in God and in his love, as Christ says in John 1[:51], 'Truly, truly, I say to you, you will see heaven opened, and the angels of God ascending and descending upon the Son of man.'"[103] Here again we encounter the image of Jacob's ladder from Genesis 28. It is clear how far behind Luther left the mystical motif of the ladder up to heaven.[104] A person does not ascend to God on high on the rungs of his powers of knowledge and love but is snatched out of misery by God's word. All our life, this upward movement of faith remains connected to the downward movement of Christ to us in his word.[105]

16. "Being Taken Up" *(Raptus)* as the Soul's Way of the Cross

For Luther, the *raptus* and *extra nos* of faith bring not only the liberation of Christian freedom[106] but also the harsh bitterness of the cross.[107] The in-

---

101. Lectures on Hebrews, WA 57/III:144.10-12; *LW* 29:149: "Therefore faith in Christ is an exceedingly arduous thing, because it is a rapture and a removal from everything one experiences within and without to the things one experiences neither within nor without, namely, to the invisible, most high, and incomprehensible God."

102. See the following footnote, and WA 7:22.31–23.1; *LW* 31:371.

103. WA 7:38.6-12; *LW* 31:371.

104. See nn. 22 and 34 above.

105. See nn. 113 and 114 below and n. 34 above.

106. After the words about *raptus* and *extra nos* near the end of the tract on freedom (corresponding to n. 103), Luther immediately wrote, "Enough now of freedom. As you see, it is a spiritual and true freedom and makes our hearts free from all sins, laws and commands, as Paul says, I Tim. 1[:9], 'The law is not laid down for the just.' It is more excellent than all other liberty, which is external, as heaven is more excellent than earth"; WA 7:38.12-14; *LW* 31:371.

107. WA 57/III:185.2-4 and 6-8; *LW* 29:185: "For faith causes the heart to cling fast to celestial things and to be carried away and to dwell in things that are invisible. For patience

tense interweaving of his mystical theology and his theology of the cross reveals itself here, as he theologically processed his experience of *Anfechtung*. Against the background of Luther's own monastic *experientia*, *Anfechtung* means — both at its most terrifying and at its most salvific — that all internal personal securities are destroyed, especially the confidence in one's own being, abilities, knowledge, and action, so that people experience death and hell and are thereby conformed to the Christ of the passion.[108] This is the sense in which Luther interpreted the image of the bride's embrace of Christ,[109] as he said in his second set of lectures on the Psalms (1519-21): "These embraces, however, are death and hell."[110] In the same interpretation of the Psalms, he spoke of the mystical experience of *raptus*, which leads the soul through the word into the loneliness of the marital bedchamber (of Christ), but he did so to make it clear that this kind of "being taken out of oneself" is not a pleasure but the bitterest suffering in communion with the Crucified One. This is the total deprivation, dying, and going to hell of all the things people get used to having and of all the supports that people cling to. Luther understood this process as a critical correction of the mystical theologians of the Middle Ages who, influenced by Pseudo-Dionysius the Areopagite and his *theologia negativa*, said that the soul ascended to the darkness of God beyond all positive ideas of existence. For Luther, on the contrary, the journey of withdrawal from the world into divine darkness is not an *actio* of spiritual virtue but the *passio* of faith, a passive experience of being led along Christ's way of the cross. Here, therefore, let this line of thinking crest in the sentence, "The cross alone is our theology."[111] For him, this is where mysticism's real *theologia negativa* lies: in the ruin and destruction of all human existence and ability before God.

---

is necessary in order that by it the heart may be sustained not only in its contempt for the visible things that attract but also in its endurance of those that rage. For this is how it happens that the believer hangs between heaven and earth, and, as Ps. 68:13 says, 'sleeps among the sheepfolds,' that is, that in Christ he is suspended in the air and crucified."

108. On Luther's experience of *Anfechtung* during his early years in the cloisters of Erfurt and Wittenberg, see chap. 2 above.

109. Hamm, "Gott berühren."

110. WA 5:165.18-27.

111. WA 5:176.16-33.

17. The Redemptive *Raptus* of Faith: From Hidden Salvation to Certainty of Salvation

Because of the marriage-like connection to Christ, the liberating nature of the mystical "being taken out of oneself" and "being raised on high" also comes immediately back into view. Through communion with the suffering Christ, the *raptus* of faith becomes salvation from *Anfechtung*, sin, death, and damnation. In the liberation from all false confidence in earthly assurances, the believing soul is led to its true life and salvation. "For just as Christ, by reason of His union with immortal divinity, overcame death by dying, so the Christian, by reason of his union with the immortal Christ — which comes about through faith in Him — also overcomes death by dying. And in this way God destroys the devil through the devil himself and accomplishes His own work by means of an alien work."[112] What Luther said here about victory over death in his early lectures on Hebrews (1517-18) is likewise valid for the victory over hell through salvation, the victory over the power of sin through forgiveness of sins, and the victory over the soul's *Anfechtungen* through its certainty of salvation. This is all a soteriological application of Christology's two natures united in Christ, which now also joins Christians to Christ. In this way, Luther could positively use the otherwise problematic image of the ladder, saying of the crucified Christ, "he is the ladder by which we come to the Father."[113] Qualified in this sense by the theology of the cross, a kind of mysticism of ascent develops out of the mysticism of descent: there is an *ascendere* that comes from faith in God's mercy.[114]

As Luther understood it, it is characteristic of faith that it is not a new kind of vision and it does not become the basis for supersensory experiences of the transcendent. As believers, Christians remain bound to this world's evidence of sin, suffering, and death. Because of this, they never in this lifetime meet God the Father and Christ in their uncreated being, in the *nuda divinitas* (naked divinity) of their unveiled majesty, but only under the opposite form of earthly misery. This kind of Christian mysticism, which Luther posited in sharp contrast to any variety of

---

112. WA 57/III:129.21-25; LW 29:136.

113. WA 6:562.12-14; LW 36:109.

114. WA 9:494.32f. and 495.16f. and WA 43.582.24-26; LW 5:223: "In this way we ascend into Him and are carried along through the Word and the Holy Spirit. And through faith we cling to Him, since we become one body with Him and He with us."

speculative and "enthusiastic" *(schwärmerisch)* Pseudo-Dionysian mysticism, can never break through the hiddenness of God in the passion and soar upward to a direct vision of the eternal.[115] It always remains a mysticism of the cross, which means that given the hiddenness of salvation, it is a mysticism of *Anfechtung*. At the same time, this is also a mysticism of the word, which, as we have seen, allows the believer to become one with the proclaimed word of the gospel.[116] This word gives the troubled sinner the revelation of what is hidden. As "word" it participates in the earthly hiddenness of God and the means of salvation: it is "only" a word and not an all-revealing vision. But to those who hear it, whose inner ears have been opened by the Holy Spirit, it reveals with a liberating and unmistakable clarity the saving truth behind the cloaked reality: behind the concealing humanity of the martyred Jesus is the divinity of Christ; behind his death is the resurrection; behind guilt is the forgiving word of pardon; and behind the self-evidence of hell and condemnation is eternal blessing.

In this way, the *raptus* of faith becomes certainty of salvation. From the burdensome uncertainty about one's own ability to love and the agonizing hiddenness of the divine desire to save, the gospel plucks believers up into a certainty that cannot be deduced from any earthly experience. In this personal certainty of salvation, Luther's mystical turn to the outside reached its conclusion.[117] In his view, this understanding transcended all the medieval mystical nearness of God. For though the traditions before Luther — including Staupitz — offered a "foretaste" of eternal salvation when the soul might delight in the "sweet" experience of getting close to divine love,[118] even offering a personal certainty of salvation in the soul's affective ability to hope,[119] the medieval texts offered no personal assurance

---

115. WA 39/I:389.10–391.20.

116. See sections 11-14 above, and n. 111.

117. In a sermon from Maundy Thursday 1523, Luther combined the happy exchange, the gift of communion in the Lord's Supper, and the metaphor of the cake to explain the basis for certainty of faith: "Darumb byn ich sicher und gewiß, das mir Christus alle gueter schencket, die er hat, und alle seine kraft und macht." "Wen nun mit Christo ein küchen bist, was wiltu mehr haben? Du hast alles uberschwengklich, was dein hertz begeret, unnd sitzest nun ym paradeyß"; WA 12:486.8-487.26.

118. See n. 71 above. Already on the first step (n. 72 above), those who love God enjoy the delicious word that they will not die, as Christ speaks to their hearts, "Today you will be with me in paradise" (Luke 23:43); Staupitz, *De exsecutione*, 149.

119. See n. 67 above.

The Early Luther

of salvation through faith's knowledge of the truth.[120] For Luther, however, the fullness of the graciously given presence of God and the life-giving nearness of God's salvation revealed itself to be this certainty of faith. This gave him the feeling of being born again and the impression of heaven having been opened: he "entered paradise itself through open gates."[121] Thus, in a sermon of 1523, he spoke of the happy exchange between Christ's righteousness and our unrighteousness: "See! When you enter there, what more do you want? There you are already blessed and in paradise."[122]

18. The Brokenness of Luther's Mysticism and Its Power to Bless

The unique way that Luther combined the mystical themes of *raptus, exstasis,* and *excessus* (going beyond) with a life of Christian faith reveals an idiosyncratic brokenness in the overall character of his Christ mysticism. This is why traditional Luther research understandably holds great reservations about applying the concept of mysticism to Luther's theology and his view of faith. Luther let the union of the soul to the Godhead experience several fractures: in sinners' deep experience of *Anfechtung,* in the reality of the crucified Christ's passion, in the hiddenness of God's presence under the opposite form of a terrifying divine distance, and in the binding of the communion of God to word and faith. For Luther, therefore, there is no longer any Christian possibility for the innermost soul to gain immediate mystical contact with the hidden secrets of God.

In this critical relationship to the mystical tradition, however, one can see an extension and transformation of mysticism, in the sense of these new conceptions and formulations, which remain quite characteristic within the history of Western mysticism.[123] The fractures in the human relationship to God did not prevent Luther from asserting that all Christians may have an intimate union of their soul with Christ, in which the fullness of the Godhead connects the pitiable soul to the blessed certainty of faith. Where outer and inner come together in the indwelling of Christ's Spirit and in the *raptus* of faith, there arises a new unity of God and person. This can evolve into a unique power of unification, because the cer-

---

120. On the difference between the late medieval certainty based on hope and Luther's certainty of faith, see chap. 3 above.
121. WA 54:186.8f.; *LW* 34:337.
122. WA 12:487.1-3 and n. 117 above.
123. See n. 16 above.

tainty of salvation does not require an attempt at some human sanctification[124] but, in the midst of its brokenness in the human relationship to God and in the terrifying distress of divine distance, instead becomes a liberating reality. Thus the brokenness of mysticism and its power to bless create an immediacy within human life.

19. Luther in the Tradition of Late Medieval Passion Mysticism

With this new mysticism, Luther did not merely cut himself off from medieval mysticism but, in his own way, inherited, continued, and intensified it. This is seen most impressively in the example of Johannes von Staupitz. Together with Staupitz, Luther stands in a mystical tradition that, especially since the time of Bernard of Clairvaux, found its central perspective in God's coming down to human misery.[125] For this kind of mysticism, the union of the soul with Christ always meant being placed into Christ's *unio* with human flesh and blood, participating in his incarnation and passion, and being marked by his cross. The image of the soul that finds a refuge and home in Christ's wounds is characteristic of this context.[126] This physical concept of *unio* certainly affected Luther's understanding of the Lord's Supper, in which sinners and the humbled Christ come together in an intimate communion of physical/sacramental eating and drinking. This is why the physical "real presence" of Jesus Christ in the Supper was so important for Luther, because here, as a believing communicant, he found

124. See nn. 85 and 86 above.
125. See n. 50 above.
126. Thomas Lentes, "Nur der geöffnete Körper schafft Heil: Das Bild als Verdoppelung des Körpers," in *Ausstellungskatalog: Glaube Hoffnung Liebe Tod*, ed. Christoph Geissmar-Brandi and Eleonora Louis, 2nd ed. (Vienna: Graphische Sammlung Albertina, 1996), 152-55; Petra Seegets, *Passionstheologie und Passionsfrömmigkeit im ausgehenden Mittelalter: Der Nürnberger Franziskaner Stephan Fridolin (gest. 1498) zwischen Kloster und Stadt* (Tübingen: Mohr Siebeck, 1998); Ulrich Köpf, "Die Passion Christi in der lateinischen religiösen und theologischen Literatur des Spätmittelalters," in *Die Passion Christi in Literatur und Kunst des späten Mittelalters*, ed. Walter Haug and Burghart Wachinger (Tübingen: M. Niemeyer, 1993), 21-41, and "Passionsfrömmigkeit," in *Theologische Realenzyklopädie* (Berlin: De Gruyter, 1997), 27:722-64. As his pastor, Staupitz advised Luther when in *Anfechtung* about predestination to meditate on the wounds of the crucified Christ and to seek comfort nowhere else; Berndt Hamm, "Johann von Staupitz (ca. 1468-1524) — spätmittelalterlicher Reformer und 'Vater' der Reformation," *Archiv für Reformationsgeschichte* 92 (2001): 32f.

himself gathered into the saving event of mystical union. Here he was gathered into the descent of God "im unser armes fleysch und blut" ("in our poor flesh and blood"),[127] the physical union of God and humanity, the holy body of Christ's two natures, and the happy exchange, which physically takes place in our bodies between the saving innocence of the Crucified One and our guilt.[128]

The brokenness of the theology of the cross in Luther's mysticism and its characteristic structure of God's saving presence *sub contrario* (under the form of opposites) are thus rooted in a late medieval spirituality that — rather than making a speculative ascent to the heights — invites the soul searching for God into an intimate familiarity with the pitiful, incarnate, martyred Christ. Luther extended this passion mysticism of humility from the fifteenth and early sixteenth centuries into his theology of the cross, shaping his mysticism of word and sacrament.

20. Luther's Encounter with the *Anfechtung* Mysticism of Johannes Tauler

What Luther could not find in Staupitz was a deeper view of the abyss of his experiences of *Anfechtung*. As his father confessor and theologian, Staupitz did refer him to the comforting treasures of salvation in the Son of God's incarnation and passion, especially to the direct connection between God's loving mercy through his vicarious passion and the sinner's intimate loving confidence of being saved. Because of Luther's terrifying experience of God's distance and wrath, however, Staupitz's words did not fully resonate with him, because such extreme spiritual feelings about being so totally wrong to God and himself took him far from Staupitz.[129] But

---

127. A citation from Luther's Christmas hymn "Gelobt seist du, Jesu Christ," verse 2: "The Father's only son begot / In the manger has his cot / In our poor dying flesh and blood / Doth mask itself the endless good / Kyrioles," in WA 35:435.7-11; *LW* 53:241.

128. In this sense, the image of one body and one cake, in which Christ and believers are baked together (so to speak), simultaneously condenses a theology of justification, ecclesiology, and the sacraments into one three-dimensional mystical meaning; see nn. 28 and 117 above.

129. On Staupitz's perplexity in the face of Luther's *Anfechtungen*, which he could no longer address through the familiar language of scrupulosity or a tightly wound conscience, see WA TR 1:62.1f., no. 141; 1:240.12-15, no. 518 (*LW* 54:94-95); 2:26.4-6, no. 1288 (*LW* 54:133); 2:403.19-22, no. 2283; 6:106.32–107.3, no. 6669.

in traditional late medieval mysticism there was a thread that focused on precisely this extreme position of absolute God-forsakenness, feeling like nothing, and great hopelessness, which even placed these things in the center of the spiritual life.

Luther encountered this branch of mysticism relatively late, that is, not during his theological studies and also not before he began lecturing. Instead, his encounter first came in 1515 or 1516 while he was working on his Romans lectures, after he had already laid the foundations for his new understanding of justification.[130] Even then, it was tellingly another member of the Augustinian Order who helped him: not Staupitz himself, but Staupitz's pupil and friend Johannes Lang from the Erfurt cloister. Within Staupitz's circles, shaped by his christocentric mysticism of love, it was evidently natural to occupy oneself with mystical German texts such as those of Johannes Tauler (d. 1361),[131] who had been a Dominican pastor in Strasbourg. Lang gave Luther a 1508 edition of Tauler's sermons,[132] to which Luther then provided marginal notes in 1516.[133] For Luther, the encounter with Tauler made for an electrifying reading experience. A similar thing happened a few months later when he read the tract of a late medieval author strongly influenced by Tauler, the so-called Frankfurter. This work was first published in an incomplete edition under the title "A German Theology" in 1516, then published in its entirety in 1518.[134] Luther read this at first as one of Tauler's authentic works. The spark of enthusiasm for Tauler also infected other reforming theologians like Andreas Bodenstein von Karlstadt and Thomas Müntzer. In this way, Luther and his Wittenberg circle[135] became pioneers in the richly varied Protestant reception of late medieval mystical texts, which continued for many years to the time of Johann Arndt (1555-1621), and beyond him into Pietism.[136] Luther found in Tauler and in the Tauler-like spirit of "A German Theology" a new para-

---

130. Brecht, *Martin Luther*, 137-44.

131. WA Br 1:160.8-14, no. 66.

132. "Sermones: des hochgeleerten in gnaden erleüchten doctoris Johannis Thauleri . . ." (Augsburg: Otmar, 1508). See Henrik Otto, *Vor- und frühreformatorische Tauler-Rezeption: Annotationen in Drucken des späten 15. und frühen 16. Jahrhunderts* (Gütersloh: Gütersloher Verlagshaus, 2003), 53, 69, 175-77, 317-20.

133. WA 9:95-104; Otto, *Tauler-Rezeption*, 183-214.

134. Zecherle, "Die 'Theologia deutsch'"; Otto, *Tauler-Rezeption*, 177-80.

135. Otto, *Tauler-Rezeption*, 175-254, especially 175-77.

136. Volker Leppin, "Tauler, Johannes (ca. 1300-1361)," in *Theologische Realenzyklopädie* (Berlin: De Gruyter, 2001), 32:745-48.

digm for mystical theology, in which the mysticism surrounding the incarnation and cross was further developed into a practical teaching about what to do when feeling far from God.

21. Structural Affinities between the Mysticism of Tauler and Luther

The difference between three stages of life on the mystical path to God is typical of Tauler.[137] In the first stage, pious people turn away from created things in order to receive a refreshing nearness to God, the joy of God's boundless riches, and the pleasure of God's loving embrace.[138] In the second step, this spiritual discovery of sweetness and everything they previously felt and knew about God are taken away. God withdraws into complete hiddenness, throwing people into such an agonizing loneliness and darkness that life seems to be a hell, even "more than hell."[139] In this distance from God, pitiful people become aware of their total nothingness and experience a personal "annihilation."[140] Their lives have fallen out of the realm of meaning.[141] When they reach this deepest point, they arrive at the third stage of existence: God descends to them, streaming the blessed abundance of God's Spirit into their emptiness, and lets these riches become the basis for a spiritual birth in God, which lifts people high above themselves[142] into union with divine being. Here then occurs the deifica-

---

137. John Tauler, *Die Predigten Taulers*, ed. Ferdinand Vetter (Berlin: Weidmann, 1910), 154-62.

138. Tauler, *Die Predigten Taulers*, 160.24-26: "Und so wirt er von unserm herren mit grosser süssikeit begobet, und wirt im ein innerlich umbevang in bevintlicher vereinunge."

139. Tauler, *Die Predigten Taulers*, 161.24f.: "Möchte helle gesin in disem lebende, so duchte si das me denne helle: sere minnen und des geminten gütes darben."

140. Tauler, *Die Predigten Taulers*, 162.14-17: "Kinder, in disem in der worheit ze sinde, das ist der tiefster grunt gerechter demütkeit und vornichtkeit den man mit sinnen nut begriffen enmag in der worheit. Wan in disem ist das aller worseste bekentnisse sines eigenen nichts."

141. On these worst *Anfechtungen*, see Bernd Moeller, "Die Anfechtung bei Johann Tauler" (Diss. theol., Mainz, 1956), 46-48; Christine Pleuser, *Die Benennungen und der Begriff des Leides bei J. Tauler* (Berlin: E. Schmidt, 1967), 198-200; and Otto, *Tauler-Rezeption*, 192-201.

142. On being taken beyond or out of oneself, see Tauler, *Die Predigten Taulers*, sermons 37 (n. 143), 39 (162.4f.), 53 (245:13f.), and 54 (252.16-19). See also Volker Leppin,

tion of people's inner humanity, so that through God's grace they become what God's being is by nature.[143] The deeper they previously sank in that agonizing distance from God and the annihilation of the self, the higher they will now be raised out of themselves through this mystic *raptus* and through this spiritual ecstasy.[144]

What especially fascinated Luther about Tauler's experiential theology was, on one hand, the dominant theme of passivity: people do not move actively and single-mindedly toward God, but rather, God removes all support, leading to the overwhelming "calmness" that comes entirely from the healing work of God. On the other hand, Tauler became Luther's teacher of desperate *Anfechtung* and comforted doubts. He showed him a mysticism that released him from the bitterest experiences of the absence of God and offered him a preparation for blessed union with God in the hell of God-forsakenness. This dialectic of terrifying distance from God and comforting nearness to God corresponded to Luther's monastic experiences and the line of thinking he was pursuing in his first lectures.[145]

After a moving description of the wretched moment that robs the person of all knowledge of God, Luther could read in one of Tauler's sermons: "In such anguish the poor soul cannot believe that this unbearable darkness could ever become light."[146] Luther took this same exact tone in his *Resolutiones* on the theses on indulgences (1518) when, after praising Tauler, he said that Tauler offered more true and pure theology than all the scholastic teachers in all the universities; this judgment matches his many

---

"Externe Personenkonstitution bei Johannes Tauler," in *Selbstbewusstsein und Person im Mittelalter*, ed. Günther Mensching (Würzburg: Königshausen & Neumann, 2005), 55-64.

143. On this repeated theme in Tauler's thought, see Tauler, *Die Predigten Taulers*, sermons 26 (109.23f.) and 37 (146.21-27): "In disem wirt die sele alzemole gotvar, gotlich, gottig. Si wirt alles das von gnaden, das Got ist von nature, in der vereinunge mit Gotte, in dem inversinkende in Got, und wirt geholt uber sich in Got. Also gotvar wirt si do: were das si sich selber sehe, si sehe sich zemole fur Got. Oder wer si sehe, der sehe si in dem kleide, in der varwe, in der wise, in dem wesende Gotz von gnaden, und wer selig in dem gesichte, wan Gott und si sint ein in diser vereinunge von gnaden und nut von nature."

144. On this mystical rule in Tauler ("the deeper . . . the higher"), see Tauler, *Die Predigten Taulers*, sermons 39 (162.17f.) and 53 (245.14-18 and 25-29).

145. Bernd Moeller, "Tauler und Luther," in *La Mystique Rhénane*, ed. Jeanne Ancelet-Hustache (Paris: Presses universitaires de France, 1963), 160-62; Otto, *Tauler-Rezeption*, 192-201; see also chap. 2 above.

146. Tauler, *Die Predigten Taulers*, sermon 39 (161.31-33): "Das ist der armen selen in dem qwellende als ungelöiplich, das das unlidelich vinsternisse iemer ze liechte muge komen."

other positive comments about Tauler.¹⁴⁷ Luther followed this with a dramatic report of his own agonizing *Anfechtung*, in order to then say with Tauler, "In this moment (strange to say) the soul cannot believe that it can ever be redeemed."¹⁴⁸ Luther had the feeling that Tauler understood him. In fact, one can rightly speak with Bernd Moeller of a "structural affinity in their thinking."¹⁴⁹ Each in his own way developed a mystical theology that not only recognized the poles of extreme God-forsakenness and innermost nearness to God; they also connected the two poles so tightly together that one single existential movement results: blessed communion with Christ comes through the hell of God's hiddenness.

22. Luther's Distance from Tauler and His Founding of a New Type of Western Mysticism

The comparison with Tauler also clearly reveals Luther's chronological and theological distance. He picked up the logic of Tauler's thought and gave it a turn, signifying a break with this mystical tradition, as well as with every other variety of medieval mysticism. The difference announced itself already in the view of *Anfechtung*. For Luther, the seed of *Anfechtung*'s terror did not rest simply in the hiddenness of God and the God-forsaken darkening of existence but also in the exact opposite: in the pole between the healing nearness of God's grace and the oppressive nearness of God's wrath.¹⁵⁰ As a hostile attacking power, God is elusive; as the relentlessly demanding, judging, and condemning One, God is also terribly close to the sinner. Here was an example of a mystical experience of the closeness of the negative *(e negativo)*. The key difference concerning blessed union with God hangs directly upon this. For Tauler, the liberation of a soul's ag-

---

147. WA 1:557.25-32; *LW* 31:129. See Moeller, "Tauler und Luther," 158f.; and Otto, *Tauler-Rezeption*, 211-14.

148. WA 1:558.1-3; *LW* 31:129. This entire paragraph shows striking parallels to Tauler's sermon 39 (*Die Predigten Taulers*, 161.8-33), which Luther did not make notes on in his *Randbemerkungen*. That he knew this passage well is suggested by a citation of 1539, WA 39/I:456.7f., in which he wrote, "Talis enim est doctrina legis, ut, si vere tangat cor, so wirt einen die weite welt zu enge." Compare to Tauler (161.18f.): "das im alle dise wite welt ze enge wirt." A similarly noteworthy parallel appears in the *Resolutiones* (with a reference to Tauler), WA 5:203.10-16.

149. Moeller, "Tauler und Luther," 167.

150. Iserloh, "Luther und die Mystik," 70.

ony is an elevation of the inner person into the deifying *unio mystica*. This mystic *raptus* occurs when people are swept up in their innermost being so that the birth of God takes place in the innermost soul. Thus the movement upward is simultaneously a movement into the depths. "Height and depth," said Tauler, "are one and the same here."[151]

Luther, on the other hand, experienced his *Anfechtung* as such a crisis of the inner, spiritual self, such a fearful awareness of radical sin in the depths of his heart, that he could no longer find the way to a liberating certainty about God and salvation by following the mystical path inward.[152] Because it was very important for him that Christian freedom affected a person's innermost being (the conscience), it grew critical that this freedom only came to the inner person from the outside, through the promise and the reception of the external, alien righteousness of Jesus Christ. Through faith, the inner person set inside this external promise of the gospel, only there finding intimate union with Christ and a firmly anchored certainty of salvation.

By connecting with and then dissenting from Staupitz's and Tauler's paradigms, Luther founded a new type of mysticism. Luther picked up the characteristic brokenness of late medieval mysticism as we encounter it in exemplary fashion in Staupitz's theology of humiliation and Tauler's theology of *Anfechtung*, but he radicalized their respective medieval insights about the immediacy of God's presence and human brokenness. He widened the distance between God's holiness and the sinner's ungodliness, the chasm between the exalted divinity of Christ and the pitiful humanity of Jesus, to its most extreme conclusion: God alone can bridge this infinite gap through merciful communication and the "happy exchange."

23. Luther's Intensification of Mysticism

We now discuss the unique intensity of Luther's mysticism as a characteristic of his entire theology. No theologian or mystic before him had stressed the gap between God and the creature as sharply as he did. Likewise, no one else had seen God and humans bound so tightly to each other through the incarnation, or had made the sinful person's healing communion with God so naturally free of any requirements or conditions. In con-

---

151. Tauler, *Die Predigten Taulers*, 162.18: "Wan hoch und tief ist do ein."
152. Moeller, "Tauler und Luther," 163-65; Otto, *Tauler-Rezeption*, 201-11.

trast to the mystical texts of the Middle Ages that were relevant to him, Luther excluded every kind of qualitative disposition of the soul and every hierarchical way to receive salvation. In this way, bridging the chasm and stressing God's blessed communication with human misery became the unprecedented high point of the absolutely wonderful, graciously given riches of grace. Luther's Christmas and Easter hymns give a lively impression of this. God opens heaven, giving divinity itself through Christ and Christ himself through the gospel, and makes this gracious movement without respect to any human quality and worthiness. In Luther's view, this movement brings an intense *unio* and *communio* between divine and human that is more intense, trustworthy, intimate, comforting, refreshing, and blessed than anything else on earth. As he emphasized, the sinner is given the gifts of full salvation, God's presence, the nearness of grace, communion with Christ and the community of the faithful.[153] These are received through God's promises, that is, through Holy Scripture, the preaching of the gospel, baptism, and the Eucharist.

Luther's view of *extra nos*, which characterized his understanding of the gospel and faith, seems at first glance to be incompatible with real mysticism. It is only incompatible with mysticism, though, if one has tied the concept of mysticism to a particular ideal of inwardness and an ontologically substantial relationship between God and human, refusing to recognize that there were already strong impulses in medieval mysticism that pointed to the external dimension of grace and salvation through Christ, in contrast to a more Platonizing ontology of spirit and identity.[154] In this way, Luther can be understood as continuing medieval developments within mysticism. In any case, he himself viewed the decisive basis for personal certainty of faith as coming from outside: the arrival "from the outside in" of the word of grace and the Holy Spirit. Late medieval mysticism before Luther was always striving for the ideals of security, certainty, and the peace of the soul. "Fly safely into the embraces of the bridegroom!" Jean Gerson cried out at the end of his famous treatise on mystical theology.[155] For the greatly afflicted Luther, however, the certainty of salvation

---

153. See Luther's use of the word "all" in the passages cited in n. 47 above.

154. Steinke, "Den Bräutigam nehmt euch," especially 163f., and McGinn, *The Presence of God*, vol. 3.

155. Jean Gerson, *De mystica theologia*, in *Ioannis Carlerii de Gerson de mystica theologia*, ed. André Combes (Lugano: Thesaurus Mundi, 1958), tract 2, 216.130f.: ". . . tunc vola secures in amplexus sponsi!" See also Sven Grosse, *Heilsungewißheit und Scrupu-*

through faith provided the key moment for experiencing God's gracious nearness and uniting with Christ. Whatever people were trying to reach on the mystic ladder of salvation was already ultimately and insurmountably present for Luther through faith's certainty of salvation, which can only be surpassed by the vision of heavenly majesty after death. If we can see how Luther's entire theology sought to give the conscience this comforting hiddenness and certainty and how this held the most intimate and immediate communion with Christ for him, then we can acknowledge him as one of the outstanding representatives of Western mysticism.

24. Why It Makes Sense to Label and Understand Luther as a "Mystical Theologian"

In conclusion (and in anticipation of possible critiques), I would like to ask why we should encumber ourselves with the problematic vocabulary of labeling Luther as a "mystical" theologian and of labeling his theology as "mystical." What is gained in that classification? Strong historical reasons have informed my decision to use this vocabulary. Luther had picked up a core concern of the Western tradition that we generally label "mystical." That concern was the desire to express the blessed experience of God's coming near to pitiful human beings and to articulate the intimate union with God as seen in light of God's infinite superiority to, distance from, and hiddenness in the world. Luther placed himself particularly in the tradition of the bride and marriage mysticism and in the tradition of the dark mysticism of *Anfechtung*. He added christological depth to each tradition, exploring a new dimension of the soteriological binding of the soul to Christ. On the basis of his own biographical experience and by means of his Reformation break, Luther made the tensions between the deepest fear of God's hiddenness and the unprecedented experience of comfort in the saving nearness of grace and security in God[156] (both so characteristic of Western mysticism since the thirteenth century) into the structural principle of his entire theology. From this it becomes clear that Luther's Reformation reorientation happened not only on the rational level of discursive

---

lositas im späten Mittelalter: Studien zu Johannes Gerson und Gattungen der Frömmigkeitstheologie seiner Zeit (Tübingen: J. C. B. Mohr, 1994), 128f.

156. On the new mysticism of the thirteenth century and following, see Hamm, "Gott berühren," 129-32 and 136f.

scholastic theology but also on the affective level of experiential mystical theology. This reorientation can therefore also be understood as a qualitatively new form of mysticism.

Most of all, however, the application of the vocabulary of mysticism offers us the chance to understand Luther's Christology and theology of justification not only in their forensic sense (as in the tradition of Anselm of Canterbury) but also in their holistic relevance to life, experience, and piety. It shows the historical context of Luther's theology and spirituality, in which there were different variations on three main points: the status of the person who needs and receives salvation from a heaven that has been opened up by God; the immense gracious nearness of God as a "deifying" communion with Christ in the body of Christ; and the growing awareness of a personal certainty of salvation that, at the same time, also infinitely transcends individuality. Luther had a critical corrective attitude to these three inherited perspectives, even as he intensified them. In my estimation, to describe this Reformation intensification adequately, the concept of mysticism — with its rich and various tensions — is indispensable. All who are determined to judge that Luther does not represent a mystical theology must ask themselves whether their concept of mysticism is wide enough, whether they are too strongly attached to older conventional concepts within historical theology (especially to the ontological legacies of a Pseudo-Dionysian or Eckhartian mysticism), or whether they can resist the broad phenomenological and terminological spectrum offered by the more recent research on mysticism from the time of the early church writers until modern Protestantism.[157]

---

157. Anselm Steiger, *Fünf Zentralthemen der Theologie Luthers und seiner Erben: Communicatio — Imago — Figura — Maria — Exempla, mit Edition zweier christologischer Frühschriften Johann Gerhards* (Leiden: Brill, 2002).

CHAPTER 9

Justification by Faith Alone: A Profile of the Reformation Doctrine of Justification

1. The Theology of Grace in the Late Middle Ages

That people are justified by faith alone and not by works is a slogan that evangelical Christians consistently used from the beginning to explain their religious and ecclesiastical identity. Most of all, the exclusive concept of "alone" made this formula a rallying point against everything that one perceived as belonging to the opponents in the Roman papacy and their justification by works. Conversely, the traditional Catholic believers also used "faith alone" and faith's exclusive connection to the saving word of the gospel to describe most clearly the foreign, new, and heretical nature of the so-called evangelicals. Supporters of the Reformation, however, were of the firm conviction that it was not they but the "papists" who were new and untraditional, viewing themselves as the truest interpreters of Holy Scripture and especially the apostle Paul. From across the centuries of decay and corruption, they saw themselves as biblical interpreters who had relatively contemporary and immediate access to the apostle's original Christian proclamation.[1] On this basis, Luther dared to add the decisive little word "alone" to his interpretation of the key passage of Paul's writing in Romans 3:28, because only in this way could the apostle's true intention

---

1. WA 30/II:635.8–643.13, especially 640.33–641.13 and 643.1-10.

The following chapter is based on a lecture given on November 28, 2009, at Coburg Castle, with revisions appropriate to a written format.

be authentically preserved in the German language of the early sixteenth century: "So we hold that a person is justified by faith alone, without respect to works of the law."[2]

Luther's emphasis on *sola fide* (faith alone) famously stands in immediate relationship to the other *solus* formulations in his view of justification: sinners are given salvation through God's grace alone *(sola gratia)*; they experience salvation only on account of Christ and in communion with Christ *(solus Christus)*; justifying faith is based on and received through the word of God alone *(sola verbo)*; and this divine word is contained in Holy Scripture alone *(sola Scriptura)*. To the present day, one rightly looks upon these exclusive formulas with a normative focus as that which founded communal understandings of the Reformation and represented the break with the late medieval church. In this way, however, most people overlook just how much the Reformation's exclusive focus on *solus* and its view of justification also inherited the medieval tradition. To say it more precisely, the Reformation owed its view of justification to a specific late medieval tradition of the previous years and decades.

Just as there had already been heated conversation about indulgences before Luther, so did Luther and other reforming theologians enter a highly volatile debate about justification and true repentance. To begin with, I will turn to an important commonality within late medieval theology, in which I ascertain that the pure nature of grace in justification had already formed the heart of the church's teaching about the sinner's way to heaven before the Reformation.[3] I mean the word "heart" quite literally:

---

2. "So halten wyrs nu, das der mensch gerechtfertiget werde on zuthun der wreck des gesetzs alleyn durch den glawben." From the first edition of Luther's translation of the New Testament, Wittenberg, September 1522 (the so-called September testament), cited from "Das Newe Testament Deutzsch" (Leipzig, 2005). Luther changed the text to read "So halten wir es nu, das der Mensch gerecht werde on des Gesetzes wreck alleine durch den Glauben," in a new edition of "Die ganzte Heilige Schrifft Deudsch," Wittenberg 1545 (Munich: Volz/Blanke, 1972), and in later editions.

3. To speak of the "pure nature of grace" *(puren Gnadencharakter)* in justification according to the medieval Catholic sense would be to say that God alone is the dispenser of the imputed and justifying grace that liberates people from the mortal condemnation of sins and makes them just and pleasing to God again *(gratia gratum faciens)*. That the majority of medieval theologians taught that sinners had the ability to decide to receive this justifying grace and to achieve a *dispositio ad gratiam* does not change the fact that grace first gives justification and all its benefits to sinners ("by God alone") on account of Christ's passion.

the heart of a sinful person, which orbits only around itself, is so transformed by the influx of divine grace that it now revolves around God, can love God and neighbor wholly, and can become capable of a truly heartfelt repentance for its sins and begin a truly lifelong process of confession. It is good Catholic teaching to say that, in terms of justification, the life of a Christian is a path of good works, whose purpose is to pay back the penalties of sin and earn the heavenly reward. But this view of works ought not to cover up the fact that theologians of the fifteenth century had already made justification by grace alone and on account of Christ alone the fulcrum or the hub of the turning point that results in a life's salvation.[4] Justification never happened by works but always *sola gratia*, which then became the origin of good works. The saving work of Christ's passion and the communion of believers with Christ as founded by the Holy Spirit make God's gift of grace effective in the heart, so that justification can grow into a life of salvation, together with all good works of the inner and outer person, as the good fruits of the good tree. Without grace there would be no human ability to love, no fulfillment of God's commandments, and no ethically meritorious works.

It is therefore entirely within the meaning of medieval Catholicism to emphasize that when the judging God rewards good works, God is rewarding himself, because God alone allows the work to become good, in the sense of its being a goodness that conforms with God's intent. Many theologians, including the late scholastic theologian Gabriel Biel of Tübingen, who was so important for Luther, could go even further and say that the qualitative goodness of the work has nothing at all to do with making it meritorious but that God accepts a work as meritorious through God's covenantal faithfulness alone and God's immense liberality alone *(sola liberalitas)*.[5] What comes from the self as unworthy, God — in God's endless goodness — validates as meritorious and rewards out of pure

---

4. On the boom in *solus* slogans in the decades before the Reformation and their ability to be stretched alongside other "alone's," see Berndt Hamm, "Reformation als normative Zentrierung von Religion und Gesellschaft," *Jahrbuch für biblische Theologie 7* (1992): 252f., and "Von der spätmittelalterlichen *reformatio* zur Reformation: Der Prozess normativer Zentrierung von Religion und Gesellschaft in Deutschland," *Archiv für Reformationsgeschichte* 84 (1993): 37-41.

5. On the slogans *ex sola liberalissima voluntate [Dei], ex sola acceptantis liberalitate*, and *ex nuda liberalitate* among Ockhamists including Gabriel Biel, see Berndt Hamm, *Promissio, Pactum, Ordinatio: Freiheit und Selbstbindung Gottes in der scholastischen Gnadenlehre*, Beiträge zur historischen Theologie 54 (Tübingen: Mohr, 1977), 372f.

mercy *(sola misericordia)*. Thus I can hold fast to this first assertion that the Reformation accent on "alone" *(solus)* had a fascinating forerunner in late medieval *solus* formulations, which in various ways emphasized the primacy of God's grace and mercy and Christ's liberating and saving work.[6] Even the distinctive *sola fide* of justification "by faith alone" can appear among this ensemble of Catholic *solus* formulations,[7] as long as one means by it the faith in Christ's vicarious suffering and rising *pro nobis*, which alone is the basis for all love, hope, spiritual growth, and good works of a Christian life.

There is now, however, a next step to mention, which is why the justification of sinners was highly debated by late medieval theologians, even though all of them clearly emphasized the nature of pure grace. There was in particular a wide mainstream to which the aforementioned Gabriel Biel and Luther's later opponent Johannes Eck belonged. It taught that, despite the weakness of their natural abilities to perceive and to will, sinners still had the freedom to decide whether they were for or against God's saving, life-changing justifying grace. This does not change the fact that justification remains an experience of grace. But it does mean that reaching this grace is within a person's hands, so that a person is self-empowered through the ability to decide and through the *liberum arbitrium* (free will), just like the ancient hero Hercules at the crossroads. Quite different, however, was the teaching of a minority of late medieval theologians that one can describe as Augustinian. Almost all of them belonged to Luther's order, the Augustinian Order, including Luther's monastic superior, teacher, and faith confessor Johannes von Staupitz. These theologians understood themselves as the true students of the later Augustine in his fights against the heretic Pelagius. That meant that they denied that sinful people have any freedom of choice with respect to God's effective grace. The reception of God's justifying grace, together with everything that belongs to it (like salvation and a person's abilities to love and serve), is not grounded in the sinner's prepared disposition but in predestination alone, God's eternal gracious election *(sola praedestinatio)*. Those whom God elects to blessed-

---

6. Erich Meuthen, "Gab es ein spates Mittelalter?" in *Spätzeit: Studien zu den Problemen eines historischen Epochenbegriffs*, ed. Johannes Kunisch (Berlin: Duncker und Humblot, 1990), 115.

7. Berndt Hamm, "Von der spätmittelalterlichen *reformatio* zur Reformation," *Archiv für Reformationsgeschichte* 84 (1993): 39: "... das uns got durch kein ander mitel hat wollen rechtfertigen den allein durch den gelauben in das plutvergin Jhesu Christi, in dem allein all unßer gerechtikeit ist . . ." (citing from Fridolin at the end of the fifteenth century).

ness without respect to their qualities, God also calls, justifies, and sanctifies, giving meritorious and satisfactory power to their good works. On account of Christ, God unfailingly leads these who were chosen in eternity to blessedness, with a necessity that the elect themselves do not experience as compulsion but as freedom from the power of sin. Thus they see themselves as willing and spontaneous subjects, just as Luther expressed it in his 1520 tract on freedom: believers perform good works of love out of inner spontaneity and a totally uncoerced willingness.[8] In this, Luther assumed himself to be a faithful student of the strict Augustinian and anti-Pelagian tradition of his order, saying that God gives faith and steadfastness in faith only to those who have been elected from eternity for salvation. Just as among the reformers, the dominance of grace for these late medieval theologians had become a prime part of predestination. As Staupitz wrote in the year before Luther's Ninety-five Theses, they understood the entire life of salvation that comes from the rebirth of justification as *exsecutio aeternae praedestinationis* (the fulfillment of eternal predestination).[9]

With this, I have defined the area in which the strikingly new and paradigm-shifting Reformation message of "justification by faith alone" can be explained. I have made this task very challenging on purpose by emphasizing more than usual the tendency of the later Middle Ages to lift up the mercy and grace of God. Seen in this way, the Reformation view of justification is embedded in a theology of grace, which clearly peaked in the decades before Luther's arrival. In particular, the Reformation tied its *solus* principle to very specific traditions of the Middle Ages, which in various ways highlighted the centrality of deliverance through Christ and the efficacy of the Holy Spirit, thereby preparing the way for the forceful, central, and exclusive vocabulary of *"solus, solus, solus."* When we recognize this astounding continuity and understand the Reformation as the extension of a specific medieval tradition, our view is simultaneously sharpened to see what was new about the Reformation, why Luther's view of justification broke away from the contentious spectrum of late medieval doctrines, and why traditional Catholics viewed the Reformation's "justification by faith alone" as intolerable and heretical.

---

8. StA 2:285.35–305.11, paragraphs 20-29.

9. Staupitz, *De exsecutione aeternae praedestinationis* (1516-17). Around the same time there appeared the German translation of a work by the Nuremberg official Christoph Scheurl, "Ein nutzbarliches büchlein von der entlichen volziehung ewiger fürsehung."

In what follows, I will try to summarize this paradigm-shifting newness as succinctly as possible in eight points.[10]

2. Luther's View of Justification: Salvation as an Unconditional Gift of God's Love

2.1 The Finality of Justification and the Certainty of Faith for Believers

From the perspective of all medieval teachings, including those of the most faithful students of Augustine, nothing is eschatologically final about sinners' justification, which pulls them out of the damnable and God-forsaken condition of mortal sin. In their view, the real justification of sinners happens when God justifies through the gift of grace, which comes first after death and then in the verdict of final acceptance into eternal life. Between these two points — justification during life and the acceptance into salvation — lies a path of needing to remove sin from one's life, becoming sanctified, practicing love and fulfilling the law, earning merit and "doing enough" to become worthy of heavenly reward. God's acceptance of humans into salvation therefore does not happen unconditionally, but rather requires a total change in the quality and morality of the person who has been freed from mortal sins to now be able to love.

In contrast, by the time of his 1515-16 lectures on Romans at the latest, Luther had grown convinced that the final acceptance of sinners into salvation happens precisely in justification, as an unconditional acceptance of a person without respect to any quality or morality of sanctified living. In the midst of their own sinfulness, people receive God's acquittal: "You are righteous and holy to me on account of Christ. You are not righteous now and holy later, but right now — before you have or do any good and without your needing to be able to achieve or earn anything — I give you my entire good pleasure and I accept you into blessedness. Let this be told to you and trust in it!" For Luther, "faith" is nothing other than this: letting this final word be said and trusting in this astounding promise of God. Luther said, "If you have faith, you have everything."[11] By this he

---

10. Berndt Hamm, "Was ist reformatorische Rechtfertigungslehre?" *Zeitschrift für Theologie und Kirche* 83 (1986): 1-38.

11. StA 2:273.2; LW 31:348: "If you believe, you shall have all things." See also the first

meant, "You have more than everything. You have what is final and unsurpassable. This cannot be taken away after death but will come out of hiddenness into the revelation of glory."

Why would a person's acceptance into salvation through the justification of the ungodly turn into an unsurpassable moment in the present? Because, by giving grace, the Lord does not give a "something" but gives himself and his entire undivided love; and God is unsurpassable. In faith, therefore, sinners already receive a personal certainty of salvation, which medieval theologians fundamentally denied that people could have.[12] They emphasized that people could never gain assurance before death about that final certainty or security *(certitudo, securitas)* of whether they were worthy of salvation. With Luther, however, the conditions for salvation that come from a prepared worthiness fall away, because people are and always remain unworthy of salvation. Therefore Luther could proclaim the unconditional certainty of salvation as a direct consequence of the unconditional favor of God.

2.2 The Freedom of a Christian

Among the early sermons of Luther that became popular, there are no writings about justification.[13] There are, however, works about the freedom of a Christian and about the captivity of the church, respectively.[14] That is fully consistent with how Luther abandoned the traditional meaning of *iustificatio,* "justification." He had made this term unusable in its previous form and had to explain it constantly through other concepts to avoid being perpetually misunderstood. "Justification" was then no longer one part within a larger concept about personal qualities, describing a kind of midpoint on the path to the mountaintop. Instead, it became a comprehensive concept of relationship, which indicated the entire gift of salvation and a fundamentally reorienting certainty within life about be-

---

Psalms lectures, WA 3:180.26, "tantum habes, quandum credis," and the explanation of the Ninety-five Theses, WA 1:541.7f.; *LW* 31:100: "you will have peace only as long as you believe in the word of that one who promised."

12. Medieval theology considered personal certainty of salvation to be a certainty of hope but not a certainty of faith. See chap. 3 above.

13. Luther intended but never completed a booklet to be entitled *De iustificatione* (WA 30/II:643.12f.).

14. See chaps. 6 and 7 above.

ing totally accepted.[15] Luther connected this gift of God, certainty in life and certainty of faith, with the new central concept of Christian freedom or the freedom of the conscience. He was especially concerned about liberation from the damnable curse of God's unfulfilled law. This was really also liberation from the perspective of "achieving" some saving norm, which — beginning with the command to love — a person needed to fulfill to inherit salvation.

For Luther, the basic problem of his existence was certainty that he saw himself as oppressed by God's holiness, which claimed the total devotion of his life and love. He also simultaneously perceived a radical evil within himself; he was not filled with a pure love of God and neighbor but with the poison of selfishness.[16] In this miserable circumstance, he found the door to freedom, the "gate to paradise," in the gospel, which he had learned to hear in an entirely unusual way.[17] The gospel was telling this professor of Holy Scripture, "You are allowed to know yourself bluntly and realistically as an unholy and corrupt sinner, even for your entire span of life. At the same time, you are also allowed to see yourself always in the light of the saving righteousness of Christ." This message made it possible for him to fall upon a new and liberating path based on the certainty of faith, hope, and salvation.

2.3 "The Happy Exchange" — "Simultaneously Justified and Sinner"

In the early Romans lectures of 1515-16, Luther had already expressed this fundamental experience of liberation as an "at the same time" kind of event, as a simultaneous totality of accusation and defense. There he said that sinners who have applied the accusation of the living God to themselves then turn from the self-accusing path of despair to Christ, saying,

> Christ has done enough for me. He is just. He is my defense. He has died for me. He has made His righteousness my righteousness, and my

---

15. On the difference between the categories of *qualitas* and *relatio* in the process of justification, see n. 21 below.

16. On this kind of "impending doom" *(nahen Zorn)*, see chap. 2, sections 4 and 5 above.

17. This is how Luther described his breakthrough about the meaning of *iustitia Dei* (Rom. 1:17) in 1545; see nn. 107 and 108 of chap. 2 above.

sin His sin. If He has made my sin to be His sin, then I do not have it, and I am free. If He has made His righteousness my righteousness, then I am righteous now with the same righteousness as He. My sin cannot devour Him, but it is engulfed in the unfathomable depths of His righteousness, for He Himself is God, who is blessed forever. Thus we can say, "God is greater than our heart" (1 John 3:20). The Defender is greater than the accuser, immeasurably greater. It is God who is my defender. It is my heart that accuses me. Is this the relation? Yes, yes, even so! [*Sic, Sic, etiam Sic!*]¹⁸

This threefold *"Sic, Sic, etiam Sic!"* is certainly the most emphatic place in all of the Romans lectures. It is the christological confession of an experience of salvation, which Luther then about four years later described as the "happy exchange" or trade in his tract on freedom.¹⁹ Individual components of this "exchange" theme were already visible in the early church and in the Middle Ages. What was totally new, however, was how Luther set two wholes or totalities in relationship to each other. Christ makes the totality of my sin his, even though he himself remains sinless, thereby stripping the power away from unholy evil. In return, I simultaneously get the fullness of his righteousness from him, receiving my final defense right now through faith. To be sure, in my present reality I remain a sinner, because I am never able to live with the self-surrender that God's law demands of me. But my sins no longer have any power to condemn me, because Christ has stepped in for me with his endless, vicarious, protecting, and sheltering divine wholeness. This is exactly what Luther meant with his famous formula "simultaneously justified and sinner," which first arose in the Romans lectures²⁰ and which the Catholic doctrine of justification still struggles with. In this phrase, Luther was saying above all that people — when viewed relationally — are judged as entirely righteous before God. That is because God accepts them as children and heirs of salvation. In a disturbing simultaneity, however, people — when viewed qualitatively — are entirely sinful in the reality of their nature.²¹

18. WA 56:204.17-25; *LW* 25:188.
19. See chap. 8, section 7 above.
20. WA 56:272.17-19; *LW* 25:260.
21. Luther at the doctoral examination for Joachim Mörlin (1540), WA 39/II:141.1-6: "Christianus est dupliciter considerandus, in praedicamento relationis et qualitatis. Si consideratur in relatione, tam sanctus est quam angelus, id est imputatione per Christum, quia deus dicit se non videre peccatum propter filium suum unigenitum, qui est velamen

2.4 Renovatio *and* Imputatio: *The Different Effects of the Renewed Sanctification and the Imputed Righteousness of Christ*

What I have just said about the reality and totality of sin might sound off-putting to some. That is because Luther viewed the justification of the ungodly not only as an external relationship between people and Christ but also as an effective appropriation of Christ's efficacy, which changes people on the inside. God not only awards forgiveness of sin through the gospel on account of Christ but he also binds this word event of forgiveness to the work of the Holy Spirit, which creates faith in the heart and thereby gives people a fundamental reorientation of trust. Through faith, which delivers itself entirely passively into God's mercy,[22] the heart becomes the workshop of the Holy Spirit, who fills it with the highest spiritual activity: the activity of a most joyful gratitude, innermost love of God, and a love of the neighbor that is ready to dedicate itself in service to other people and not falter in helping them in their daily troubles and needs. Quite spontaneously and without any pressure to fulfill the law, the faithful then live into God's law. Still, these good works that Luther could praise so highly never have the sinless purity and perfection that would make them worthy of heavenly blessing. Measured against the wholeness that God's holy will requires of us, our earthly existence and all the things that we do remain empty, unholy, and saturated by sin. Thus the last words that Luther wrote down before his death were "We are beggars. That is true."[23] We stand before God with empty hands, without any qualities or activities that might support us.

For this reason, the renewal of our life through faith, love, hope, and the good works these generate can never be the basis for our justification and for our having been given saving mercy. The basis has to rest in a perfectly total removal of sin, which always lies just outside the Christian life of faith. This is where — already in the Romans lectures — the key concept of *reputatio* or *imputatio* (imputation) comes into play for Luther: God

---

Mosi, id est legis. Sed christianus consideratus in qualitate est plenus peccato." On the veil of Moses, see 2 Cor. 3:12-18. On the contrast between a relationship of judgment *(imputatio, reputatio Dei)* and a quality *(qualitas, esse rei)*, see Luther's lectures on Rom. 4:7, WA 56:287.16-24; *LW* 25:274. See also chap. 3, n. 13 above.

22. On the meaning of this expression (the connection between total passivity and the activity of handing oneself over), see sections 2.5 and 2.6 below.

23. "Wir sein pettler. Hoc est verum." See chap. 2, n. 63 above.

imputes the perfection of Christ's righteousness to sinners and counts it as good, while not holding their sins against them but instead forgiving them.[24] Luther described this imputed righteousness of Christ as a "foreign" and "external" righteousness *(iustitia aliena, externa).*[25] As we have seen, this gets truly and very effectively applied to us. Nevertheless, when this perfect wholeness is credited to us, it never exists as an inner personal quality within us. As limited and broken creatures because of sin, people receive this "solely" as a reality *extra nos*,[26] that is, in the manner of being totally accepted and as an effect of God's final word of absolution.

Luther repeatedly emphasized this event with the image of the hen and her chicks. When the bird of prey attacks, the weak chicks take refuge under the wings of the hen, who shelters and protects them. In the same way, oppressed sinners take refuge from Satan with the assurance of faith under the sheltering protection of Christ's righteousness.[27]

> Faith, if it is true faith, is such that it does not rely on itself, on its believing, but it holds on to Christ and shelters itself under his righteousness; it lets this righteousness be its shelter and shield, even as the chick does not rely on its life and speed, but seeks shelter under the mother-hen's body and wings. To survive before God's judgment seat, it is not enough for one to say: I believe and have received grace; for everything within him is unable to protect him sufficiently. Rather he holds up to this judgment Christ's own righteousness; he lets it deal with God's judgment and it stands up for him forever with all honors, as Psalms 111[:3] and 112[:3, 9] say: "His righteousness endures forever." Under this righteousness he creeps, snuggles, and crouches; he trusts

---

24. See Luther's exposition of Rom. 4:7 (Vulgate: "Beati, quorum remissae sunt iniquitates et quorum tecta sunt peccata. Beatus vir, cui non imputavit Dominus peccatum"), WA 56:268.26–291.14; *LW* 25:257-78, especially WA 56:287.15-24; *LW* 25:274, a paragraph that ends with the sentence "Therefore we are all born in iniquity, that is, in unrighteousness, and we die in it, and we are righteous only by the imputation of a merciful God through faith in His Word." See also Sybille Rolf, *Zum Herzen sprechen: Eine Studie zum imputativen Aspekt in Martin Luthers Rechtfertigungslehre und zu seinen Konsequenzen für die Predigt des Evangeliums* (Leipzig: Evangelische Verlagsanstalt, 2008).

25. WA 56:158.10–159.24; *LW* 25:136.

26. Karl-Heinz Zur Mühlen, *Nos extra nos: Luthers theologie zwischen Mystik und Scholastik*, Beiträge zur historischen Theologie 46 (Tübingen: J. C. B. Mohr, 1972).

27. Sermon on Saint Stephen's Day (1522), especially the interpretation of Matt. 23:37, WA 10/I:1:280.11–285.9; *LW* 52:92ff.

and believes and does not doubt that it will keep him protected. Then it also comes to pass that way, and he is preserved through this same faith, not for the sake of faith, but for the sake of Christ and his righteousness, under whose protection he is living.[28]

Luther's interpretation of the hen and chicks illustration directly expresses how — in the theologically concise meaning of justification — faith itself does not protect and save a person, nor does "what is in a person" save. Instead, all who entrust themselves to Christ through faith are sheltered by his external righteousness.[29]

Luther could illustrate this same message through the image of a cloak. Just as in the biblical story of Ruth, where Ruth tells Boaz, "Spread your cloak over your servant, for you are next-of-kin" (Ruth 3:9), so does the human soul throw itself at the feet of Christ's humanity and get covered by his righteousness.[30]

The images of the hen and the cloak clearly show that the personal growth in Christians' lives and the sanctification of their lives never becomes identical with the fullness and wholeness of Christ's righteousness, which covers them from the outside. That also means that believers do not find their Christian identity within themselves but that — apart from themselves — it comes from outside through Christ and God's mercy.[31]

---

28. WA 10/I:1:281.11–282.2; LW 52:96.

29. The protecting and saving righteousness of Christ reaches sinful people through the interactive mediation of the word of the gospel, the Holy Spirit, and the believer's faith. On this interaction, see section 2.7 below.

30. WA 56:278.1-5; LW 25:265: "He is covered, I should add, through Christ who dwells in us, as Ruth in a figurative sense says to Boaz: 'Spread your coat over your maidservant, for you are next of kin' (Ruth 3:9). 'And she uncovered his feet and lay down' (Ruth 3:7), that is, the soul lays itself down at Christ's humanity and is covered with His righteousness." Luther emphasized the aspect of relationship in the biblical text as a way of highlighting Christ's human nature: we humans can take refuge in his righteousness, because he became human. Luther based the acquittal from guilt and the protection of Christ's righteousness in the words "through Christ who dwells in us." This means that effectiveness belongs to Christ, whose *iustitia externa* and *aliena* benefit sinners; this is for Luther something that always happens within the community of Christ's faithful, who are called by and preserved through the Holy Spirit, the Spirit of Christ.

31. This sense of believers "being taken out of themselves" to mean something truly external is where Luther deviated from traditional medieval concepts of *raptus;* see chap. 8, sections 15-17. See also Wilfried Joest, *Ontologie der Person bei Luther* (Göttingen: Vandenhoeck & Ruprecht, 1967).

Seen this way for Luther, God's mercy and love are then nothing other than God's righteousness, which is given entirely in Christ. To put it the other way around: the Pauline concept of "the righteousness of God" *(iustitia Dei)*, which had initially terrified him, when viewed in light of Christ became for him the key concept for understanding divine mercy.[32]

2.5 Giving and Giving Back, Activity and Passivity

The entire late medieval view of salvation was characterized by a fundamental duality. For instance, when God leads sinners step-by-step into salvation, it is not only God who is active and giving but also each person who participates as a coworker. A person's own activity under the form of good works and using one's own gifts (as in giving alms or charity) was therefore relevant for salvation. This process not only involved a person's external works but more primarily included the activity of the soul: the inner activities of love and repentance and a willing self-sacrifice to God and neighbor. As participating subjects, people needed to contribute something of themselves to reach salvation, even if (as many pastoral theologians emphasized before the Reformation) this was only a minimum amount of wanting or doing. They needed a minimal amount of repentance and, in case there were not any works of satisfaction, at least the purchase of an indulgence.

Martin Luther's new view of justification leaped out of this duality. It said that a minimal religious step was really no step. He had discovered a new "nothing": I can contribute absolutely nothing to my salvation; I need not do that anyway, and certainly not some minimum amount. When Luther connected justification with acceptance into salvation, he emphasized with unprecedented radicality the character of salvation as entirely constituting a gift that no one could adequately reciprocate in any relevant way for salvation. There was no longer any purchasing of grace or holiness for sinners, so that an entire system of providing for salvation, which included indulgences, collapsed. This is so astonishing, because thereby Luther usurped a highly powerful and logical force within religious history, one that possessed both ancient origins and contemporary resonance. This

---

32. Compare Luther's 1545 preface to his Latin works, WA 54:185.12–186.24; *LW* 34:336-37, with his interpretation of Rom. 1:17 in his first lectures on Romans, WA 56:171.26–172.15; *LW* 25:151-53. See also chap. 6.

said that there is no goodness that comes without conditions, no forgiveness without punishment, and no remission without propitiation.[33] The relationship between God and humanity must also therefore conform to the rules of gift, giving back, and reciprocal action.[34]

Luther, Zwingli, and Calvin cut across this timeless logic of religious history, as they offered a surprising implausibility by invoking Jesus and Paul. They taught faith in unconditional love from the beginning to the end, a divine majesty of pure giving, and a sovereign grace that cannot be repaid. This was explained and taught through the aforementioned image of the exchange or trade.[35] Luther obviously seized upon the traditional religious themes of gift and giving back, but he did so by pushing this argument *ad absurdum*. For what the soul brings to its bridegroom Christ as a dowry is nothing other than its sin, which is the absolute antigift.

It is then interesting how the reformers, beginning with Luther, lifted up faith's total passivity in justification[36] and, with it, the nature of the pure gift of salvation without human reciprocity in order to simultaneously and vigorously emphasize the spiritual activity and generosity of reborn believing Christians. We have already discussed this.[37] The personal traits found in people who actively believe, will, think, feel, give of themselves, and give good gifts to others were not taken less seriously in the Reformation than among their traditional counterparts, with the decided difference in the Reformation perspective that all these activities and gifts of a life of faith do not justify and therefore have absolutely no effect on salvation. The "I" of living faith does not exist or work in the realm of

---

33. Arnold Angenendt, "*Deus, qui nullum peccatum impunitum dimittit*: Ein 'Grundsatz' der mittelalterlichen Bußgeschichte," in *Und dennoch ist von Gott zu Reden: Festschrift für Herbert Vorgrimler*, ed. Matthias Lutz-Bachmannpp (Freiburg im Breisgau: Herder, 1994), 142-56.

34. On this issue in light of Luther research, see Bo Kristian Holm, *Gabe und Geben bei Luther: Das Verhältnis zwischen Reziprozität und reformatorischer Rechtfertigungslehre* (Berlin and New York: De Gruyter, 2006); Bo Kristian Holm and Peter Widmann, eds., *Word — Gift — Being: Justification — Economy — Ontology* (Tübingen: Mohr Siebeck, 2009); and Veronika Hoffmann, ed., *Die Gabe: Ein "Urwort" der Theologie?* (Frankfurt am Main: M. Lembeck, 2009).

35. See section 2.3 above.

36. Sebastian Degkwitz, *Wort Gottes und Erfahrung: Luthers Erfahrungsbegriff und seine Rezeption im 20. Jahrhundert* (Frankfurt am Main: Lang, 1998); Philipp Stoellger, *Passivität aus Passion: Zur Problemgeschichte einer "categoria non grata"* (Tübingen: Mohr Siebeck, 2010).

37. See section 2.4 above.

subjective self-possession. People are children of God, heirs of salvation, and captives released by Jesus Christ before and without any consideration of their ability to do or to give. What they then do and give from the wellspring of faith, however, is both an individual activity and the working of the Holy Spirit in their hearts. They were always able to do evil all by themselves. But God starts to do good first against their will, then through them and with them. They become God's partners in giving care, grounded in God's love, justification, salvation, and redemption, but never bearing God's creative and re-creating fruits on their own. Thus Luther posited the thesis in the Heidelberg Disputation of April 1518: "The love of God does not find, but creates, that which is pleasing to it."[38]

2.6 Faith, Love, Repentance

There is a classical model of an *ordo salutis* in Lutheranism, that is, a proper sequence for the Christian path through life, which goes like this. The start of Christian reorientation comes under the terrifying awareness of God's commandment, which can be characterized as attrition, a repentance based in fear. With the pain of repentance, people perceive themselves before God as sinners, recognizing their total inability to be justified by the divine commandment. Despairing of their own religious ability, they beseech God: "God, have mercy on me, a sinner!" At this, they receive in faith the gospel's liberating, comforting, and blessedly certain message that God has received them in grace and forgiven all their sin. They respond to this justifying liberation with joyful gratitude and active love, the fruits of repentance. In this way now, their entire life becomes one of practicing penitential love, in contrast to penitential fear. This classical model allows the three main elements of penitential despair, justifying faith, and active love to flow out of one another.

This schema thoroughly matches Luther's intent. With Luther, however, one would have to introduce two corrective comments that resist such easy schematization. The first emphasis is that the painful, humiliating, and contrite awareness of our own sinful nothingness and absolute inability to earn salvation not only precedes justifying faith but always exists as faith's

---

38. Heidelberg Disputation, thesis 28 (*StA* 1:212.2f. and 216.13f.; *LW* 31:41): "The love of God does not find, but creates, that which is pleasing to it. The love of man comes into being through that which is pleasing to it."

dark flip side. The hiddenness of God's grace strengthens and deepens the recognition of our own corruption and sorrow for sin,[39] so that this kind of disillusioned self-perception and humility is no longer surrounded by anxious and bitter doubts but by loving trust in God's mercy. For this reason, however, faith is never possible with the simultaneous repentance that comes from love. This was true even after 1518 when Luther clearly distinguished bright joyful faith from dark and painful repentance.[40]

With this, I come to a second important correction of the order of salvation sketched above, concerning the relationship between received faith and active love. For Luther and the other reformers, could there really be a faith that is not love *eo ipso*, in its innermost essence?[41] As Luther said over and over again, faith is a heartfelt trust in God's saving goodness, in God's unconditional mercy on account of Christ. Can this faith then be understood as the warming of the conscience through the power of the Holy Spirit and, therefore, as a fully trusting love, which is a real love that expects and receives everything from God? In fact, this seems to be precisely the case. Faith no longer has only a cognitive dimension but is simultaneously a kind of loving feeling, even the most radical ingredient in life, because it gives itself to God alone. But here's the decisive point: what justifies and saves sinners is not their ability to love, neither their emotions nor the affective sparks and warmth of faith, for these matter just as little as the cognitive power of faith. Instead, people are justified and saved by faith's purely passive receiving. The concept of faith binds and integrates an aware and loving activity with pure passivity. The same is also true for the concept of reception: the Holy Spirit effectively creates the faithful reception within people, both the passive experience of being a new creation and the active responsibility of an aware, loving, thankful trust. Still, faith and its reception only justify passively, that is, in the passive way that faith receives the perfect and promised righteousness of Christ. God's creative and creating work thus justifies by liberating not loving and love-worthy lives, but sinful and damnable lives, not active but passive people.[42] At the same time (and without creating a new necessary sequence), this always kindles love in the sinner. If it were otherwise, justification would be

---

39. See chap. 4, n. 79 above.
40. See chap. 4, section 12 above.
41. On this question, see also chap. 1 above.
42. For Luther's pointed thesis that the love of God is not to be found among the love-worthy but rather creates worthiness, see n. 38 above.

bound up in faith's loving activity, which would then force people to reflect constantly on their ability to love in order to be certain of salvation. With that, people would be back permanently on the unholy path of being confronted with their sinful and broken ability to love. Then they would live their entire lives without the certainty of salvation.

This relationship between prior justification on account of Christ and the simultaneously internal and external activity of the faithful through the power of the Holy Spirit matches how Luther always integrated pneumatology into Christology. He explained the life-changing work of the divine Spirit as a sign of Christ's liberating work of salvation and of the justifying communion with Christ that is promised to sinners. Luther adjusted every theology that fixated on the Spirit's ability to change the inner person by going back to the *extra nos* of Christology. For Luther, this is the sense in which the Holy Spirit is always and decidedly the Spirit of Christ *pro nobis* and *in nobis*.

In summary, we can say this about the relationship between faith and love. Although Luther viewed love as belonging inextricably to the nature of faith worked through the Holy Spirit and although the penitential love that then comes from the heart is a similarly inextricable true evangelical repentance, Luther nevertheless released the justifying relationship between gospel and faith that defines the entire Christian life from any consequent love, contrition, or human action. Calvin was even more systematic on this point. For Luther, Christian repentance had an oscillating role to play: on one hand, it was an entryway to faith, which could almost be a condition for receiving faith;[43] on the other, it came as an effect of faith. Calvin, however, conceptually grounded repentance neither as an entryway for justifying faith nor as justification itself. Instead, he put it entirely in the realm of the salvation that comes through faith.[44]

2.7 The Saving Communication between Internal and External

We can rightly describe Luther's view of justification as a path of radical internalization. Through the work of the Holy Spirit, faith arises in people's hearts, where their most subtle pride makes its nest and where they

---

43. See chap. 2, section 3 above.
44. John Calvin, *Institutio christianae religionis* (1559), 3.3, which contains the heading "Fides nos regenerari; ubi de poenitentia."

most deeply experience their own accusations, insecurities, afflictions, and failures. When Luther fleshed out this inner experience of spiritual *Anfechtung* in his first lectures, he saw himself standing very close to the late medieval *Anfechtung* mysticism of Johannes Tauler, which similarly gave access to the bitter experience of the dark night of the soul and one's own nothingness.[45] Unlike Tauler's mysticism, however, Luther added an opposite dynamic to the desolate internalization that pulled people down ever deeper into the vortex of despairing fear. That was the liberating external dimension of the gospel. In this way, we can describe Luther's gradual restructuring of the doctrine of justification between 1510 and 1520 as stages on a path leading outward. For him, this was the path for discovering new biblical perspectives about going outward rather than going inward to his own conflicted and unholy self.

Still, it appears important to me that this intensified interiorization and the forced exteriorization remain in constant communication with each other. The biblical word of the commanding and accusing law, through which God's holy will drives sinners into a corner, afflicts them with their internally corrupted and unholy selves. The gospel then steps precisely into this most internal heart of a person, which Luther called "conscience." This can be purely good news for sinful people because it turns the conscience entirely outward, instead of going further inward to people's habitual — and failed — attempts to be virtuous. Precisely because the saving word and its Holy Spirit come entirely from the outside, they can meet sinners in their innermost being and can totally redirect their agonized consciences to the liberating external dimension of *Christus pro me*.

This completes the circle, which I described earlier as the sinner's receiving from God the "external righteousness" of Jesus Christ. During the course of the indulgence controversy, it became important for Luther that people heard the gospel's justifying, liberating word of salvation not as an internal word. The word cannot climb out of the depths of the soul, because it would get mixed up in all the soul's inscrutable and untrusting doubts that threaten to drown it. In that case, the ultimate certainty of salvation that liberates the heart from all its self-doubts would remain impossible. This saving word can only be liberating, certain, and established on faith because it comes to the inner person from the outside. Beginning in 1518,[46] this meant for Luther not only that this word came from God in

---

45. See chap. 8, sections 20 and 21 above.
46. See chap. 4, section 12 above.

the power of the Holy Spirit but that it also was a physically external word, a word spoken orally or in writing, which comforts, promises, and addresses afflicted sinners with the decisive message of salvation. It says, "I proclaim you free from your sins. Your sins are forgiven you. You are a child of God on account of Christ and an heir of salvation." This word of gift happens orally through the means of preaching, sacraments, congregational singing, through a private word of assurance from a fellow Christian, and in writing through the means of the Bible and other Bible-soaked texts like the catechism or certain kinds of personal letters. The external word of the gospel that saves, comforts, and gives assurance can also meet afflicted people through images of proclamation.[47] In freedom, God bound himself to physical means of grace, in which the Holy Spirit awakens and preserves faith. God's gospel only wants to pull me up from my fatal inwardness through the mediation of the external word, which reckons *iustitia externa* (external righteousness) to me as an effective promise, as a performative word of action. This grounds the believers' certainty of salvation in an externality, which is free of all internal instabilities.

Luther's *Anfechtung* in the cloister and his intense biblical study led him in fevered steps to break with a specific medieval culture of internalization. This culture had been in continuity with older traditions, especially with Augustine and his Neoplatonic roots, which since the twelfth century had placed the essential points for justification and absolution in the internal person and in the genuineness of a person's repentance and love. With this program of internalization came a devaluation of everything outward and physical that did not have the ability to reach up to the higher spiritual nature of the soul. In the metaphysics and hermeneutics of the time, the insufficient external word could only have the function of serving as a sign of the internal and immediate contact between God and the soul.[48] In a certain sense, Luther continued this dynamic of internal-

---

47. See the succinct summary of Luther's understanding of images in Gudrun Litz, *Die reformatorische Bilderfrage in den schwäbischen Reichsstädten* (Tübingen: Mohr Siebeck, 2007), 21-27.

48. In the tradition of internalization, the internal word could lift up the soul as the insistent word of the Holy Spirit. This stood in contrast to the external word's efficacy in the sacraments, as in the words of baptism, the transforming words of institution in the Eucharist, and the words of absolution in the sacrament of confession, in which the spoken words matched the priestly means of salvation. On the general theme of externalization in the late Middle Ages, in which the most weight fell on Christian devotion to the guarantees of grace and salvation of the sacraments and the hierarchical mediation of

ization when conscience and faith became central points for the relationship with God. Understood as the freedom of faith, the term "freedom of conscience" is therefore his invention.[49] At the same time, however, he connected the inwardness of justification, faith, conscience, and freedom in an unprecedented way on the outward dimension of the external righteousness of Christ and the external physical word of saving proclamation. For him, Christian freedom was therefore not only a freedom of the inner person but also something very external, institutional, and juridical, especially when it came to the freedom to proclaim the unadulterated biblical word of God and freedom from the power of the pope.[50]

Understood in this way, justification did not mean for Luther that people do not find the gracious God when they find themselves and God in their innermost being. Instead, God encounters people outside of themselves as the unconditionally loving one; God also gives them this new gift in themselves and in their fellow creatures. In God, people can discover themselves, their fellow humans, and creation anew. In this, people and their fellow creatures are given themselves anew.

2.8 The Overall Structure of a Theology of Communication between God and the World

Luther's idea about the justifying communication between internal and external had a place within the overall structure of a theology of communication between God and the world. On the path between the earliest years of

---

those means of grace, see Berndt Hamm, *Frömmigkeitstheologie am Anfang des 16. Jahrhunderts: Studien zu Johannes von Paltz und seinem Umkreis*, Beiträge zur historischen Theologie 65 (Tübingen: Mohr, 1982), 222-47.

49. Although at least two examples can be found in the Middle Ages, the concept of "freedom of conscience" *(Freiheit des Gewissen* or *libertas conscientiae)* was discovered by Luther in 1521. Through him it became a great theme of the Western world. See Gerhard Ebeling, "Einfalt des Glaubens und Vielfalt der Liebe: das Herz von Luthers Theologie," in *Lutherstudien*, vol. 3, *Begriffsuntersuchungen — Textinterpretationen — Wirkungsgeschichtliches* (Tübingen: Mohr, 1985), 108-25 and 385-89 (especially 285). On the examples from the Middle Ages *(conscientiae libertas* by Boethius [d. 524] and *libertas conscientiae* by Pierre de Celles [d. 1183]), see Joseph Lecler, "Die Gewissensfreiheit," in *Zur Geschichte der Toleranz und Religionsfreiheit*, ed. Heinrich Lutz (Darmstadt: Wissenschaftliche Buchgesellschaft, 1977), 334.

50. See chap. 7 above.

his Reformation reorientation and the theology of his last years, this is where he made his intense connection between the doctrines of God, Christology, pneumatology, justification, ecclesiology, and the Lord's Supper. With respect to the Holy Trinity, he emphasized the particular individuality of the three persons at the same time that they share the most intimate communication of love. This provided the basis for his Christmas theology of the incarnation: God gets tangled up in the world's creatureliness out of pure mercy, communicating with the world's misery and humanity's sinful distress through the person of Jesus Christ. Christologically, Luther used the classical language of Christ's two natures — fully divine and fully human — so that in him everything belonging to the noblest divinity is connected to earthly human nature: here is that most humble, despised person of Bethlehem and Golgotha, here are the crib and the cross. This event provided Luther with the load-bearing foundation for the justifying union of Christ with the sinful soul in the "happy exchange." Because of the exchange of human and divine properties in Christ in the *communicatio idiomatum*,[51] and because through this the Godhead gained the victory in the resurrection, there can also exist the wondrous exchange of properties between Christ and the soul, in which the saving and justifying God has likewise won the victory.

Here arises a means of communication in which the most intimate exchange and clear distinctions belong together. The blessed communication among the persons of the Trinity also assumes their respective threefold distinctiveness. In Christ, the two natures are bound to each other, but without blending indistinctly into each other. In the same way, too, a unity exists amid the personal communion of the soul with its "bridegroom" Christ, in which neither is conflated into the other. Divine righteousness becomes the soul's possession, without somehow becoming the soul's own substance or quality. The *extra nos* of Christ's righteousness does not thereby abrogate one's interior life. God's word and the Holy Spirit shine through the soul like fire in iron (an old mystical image, which Luther picked up),[52] in such a way that the iron does not become fire, nor does the person through faith turn into the Holy Spirit or the word of God. In the Lord's Supper, too, the presence of Christ's body and blood is closely connected with the bread and wine, but without the physical elements being substantially changed.

This overall structure of a theology of communication had impor-

---

51. Oswald Bayer, ed., *Creator est creatura: Luthers Christologie als Lehre von der Idiomenkommunikation* (Berlin: De Gruyter, 2007).

52. See chap. 8, section 11 above, with nn. 79 and 80.

tant consequences for Luther's understanding of the church and its means of grace. With entirely the same view of the incarnation, Luther emphasized that in the community of Jesus Christ, God connects justifying grace and the work of the Holy Spirit with the efficacy of the external and physical word in order to liberate people in their innermost beings. In the same way, the two sacraments of baptism and the Lord's Supper bear the task of bringing Christ and his salvation near to each individual in the assembly of believers and of delivering these gifts to him or her. Also included in this communication of justification is the relationship that Christians have with each other, since the love received by all whom Christ has set free can now continue to flow to their neighbors.

In *The Freedom of a Christian*, Luther led this communications principle about love and devotion to the point where Christ becomes the substitute for the punishments of sin.

> See, according to this rule the good things we have from God should flow from one to the other and be common to all, so that everyone should "put on" his neighbor and so conduct himself toward him as if he himself were in the other's place. From Christ the good things have flowed and are flowing into us. He has so "put on" us and acted for us as if he had been what we are. From us they flow on to those who have need of them so that I should lay before God my faith and my righteousness that they may cover and intercede for the sins of my neighbor which I take upon myself and so labor and serve in them as if they were my very own. That is what Christ did for us. This is true love and the genuine rule of a Christian life. Love is true and genuine where there is true and genuine faith.[53]

Pushing this substitutionary Christology into a similar christologically rich substitutionary ethic did not mean a relative weakening of Christ's role as the only mediator. Instead, it widened Christology to include the members of Christ, who can likewise become Christ through the effective work of Golgotha and in giving Christ's body to those in need.[54] Because

---

53. StA 2:303.28–305.9; LW 31:371. See also Reinhold Rieger, *Von der Freiheit eines Christenmenschen: De libertate Christiana* (Tübingen, 2007), 322.

54. StA 2:299.11f.; LW 31:368: "Surely we are named after Christ, not because he is absent from us, but because he dwells in us, that is, because we believe in him and are Christs one to another and do to our neighbors as Christ does to us."

all Christians are set free by God's grace alone, are accepted into salvation on account of Christ alone, and receive the gifts of faith and love through God's Spirit alone, they can share this communicated salvation with others, without affecting their own state of grace or salvation. This is very different from the Catholic view of salvation, in which the praxis of sharing love brings about an increase in merit and, consequently, a higher degree of heavenly blessedness.

3. The Profile of a Reformation Theology of Justification

In eight points, I have tried to present Luther's view of justification, namely, what is meant by the compact slogan "justification by faith alone." In conclusion, the question arises of how representative this doctrine of salvation is for the Reformation as a whole.

It is essential to note that while all the main streams of the Reformation certainly trace their starting points back to Luther, Lutheranism is only one of those streams. Other streams of the Reformation followed other impulses, which released them from the authority and influence of Luther, resulting in differing views of justification, salvation, and other main points. It is therefore obvious that my sketch of several key facets of Luther's theology of justification (for instance, its connection between the incarnation and justification) does not apply to other Reformation theologians or their spheres of influence; other streams may have fundamentally different characteristics or use different vocabularies. On the other hand, one can say the following without hyperbole. Beyond simply those things that are characteristic of the Lutheran changes in the views of justification or salvation in contrast to traditional Catholic systems of religiosity, all the decisive components of a Reformation,[55] evangelical, or Protestant profile

---

55. In my view, the concept of "Reformation" is most appropriate when seen through the concept of a "system crash" or paradigm shift. What belongs to the Reformation is that which was systemically new in ecclesiology, theology, and piety, looking primarily to the Bible for guidance and finding intolerable the wide variations possible within medieval theology, piety, legal structures, reform models, and interpretation of Holy Scripture. This helps us answer the question of how to establish a Reformation profile for the doctrine of justification in the sixteenth century, because a view of justification in this or that theologian begins to lose its Reformation character wherever the themes of virtuous qualities or the actions of the natural or spiritual person start to be discussed in terms of what a sinner can or ought to do in order to be justified and stand before God's

can be found in Luther's early publications before the 1521 Diet of Worms. This profile was permanently shaped by the high degree of effectiveness of Luther's early publications.[56]

Normative views came even as the Reformation moved in different directions, especially in those circles influenced by Wittenberg, Zurich, Strasbourg, and Geneva. The particularly important teachings of Luther were the following: (1) the authoritative basis for justification by faith is Holy Scripture alone and its gospel of Jesus Christ; (2) all Christians directly receive God's mercy for the comfort of their conscience, free from all hierarchical church authority and without any mediation through Mary and the saints; (3) through justifying faith (which became the central concept of the Christian life), all Christians receive not only the forgiveness of sin but also acceptance into eternal life; (4) in this unconditional justification by grace alone, they are adopted as children of God and heirs of salvation and freed from all the guilt and penalties of sin, including temporal penalties; (5) they are saved on account of Christ alone, independent of the renewal of their lives, inner spiritual activity, or any external good works; (6) because God's gift of salvation comes entirely independent of human quality or worthiness, personal certainty of salvation through faith is possible; (7) good works of love to God and neighbors are the fruits of a living faith, consequences of and not conditions for justification, and therefore they are never a matter of

---

judgment. For precisely this question of "standing" and an effectively unconditional basis for standing remained the sensitive point in the exchanges between traditional Catholic believers and reformers when it came to justification and salvation. There were also church reformers and writers who, on the basis of the Reformation's biblical theology, were active against the Roman Catholic Church and its authority without ever having developed clear Reformation teachings that went much beyond the traditional ways of describing justification. Based on this, it is not historically accurate to limit what belongs to the Reformation to a particular teaching of justification, if that means excluding the church critiques that derived directly from that doctrine.

56. On this question of how the early writings of Luther were received (a highly relevant question when it comes to theologies of justification), see Bernd Moeller, *Luther-Rezeption: Kirchenhistorische Aufsätze zur Reformationsgeschichte*, ed. Johannes Schilling (Göttingen: Vandenhoeck & Ruprecht, 2001); Bernd Moeller and Karl Stackmann, *Städtische Predigt in der Frühzeit der Reformation: Eine Untersuchung deutscher Flugschriften der Jahre 1522 bis 1529* (Göttingen: Vandenhoeck & Ruprecht, 1996); and Thomas Hohenberger, *Lutherische Rechtfertigungslehre in den reformatorischen Flugschriften der Jahre 1521-22* (Tübingen: J. C. B. Mohr, 1996). On the influence of Luther's doctrine of justification on the Reformation in Zurich, see Berndt Hamm, *Zwinglis Reformation der Freiheit* (Neukirchen-Vluyn: Neukirchener Verlag, 1988).

"doing enough" to satisfy the penalties for sin or offering the meritorious effect of increasing reward; (8) attempts to reach salvation in this life by calling upon the saints, by funding masses or charities, by buying indulgences, by following the instruction of the *ars moriendi*, or — after death — by going through the penalties and purifications of purgatory all become obsolete; and (9) lifelong Christian repentance, which corresponds to the fact that sin remains in the justified, is no longer subject to questions whether it is a satisfactory repentance and whether it will ultimately lead to salvation and instead enters life wholly as a sign of the free gift of salvation and the thankful joy of sinners who have been gifted with grace.

In their varied patterns, Luther's writings communicated standards for the theology of justification that remained decisive for all churches of the Reformation, even in places where they received different accents than he gave them. As the example of Andreas Osiander shows, no supporter of the Reformation could backslide from these principles about justification or formulate them in unclear or ambiguous ways without evoking the corrective intervention of colleagues from the various Protestant camps.[57] With Luther, the Reformation undid the entire traditional understanding of salvation and its historical religious logic of gift and giving back. In place of the two-way medieval Catholic path of gradual cooperation between God and humanity that leads to salvation, there entered the new theme that God alone is effective. God's merciful goodness no longer exists in relationship to a humanity that is more or less receptive to God, or which is more or less on the path to salvation. Instead, people experience unconditional goodness in the child of Bethlehem and in the Crucified One. In total passivity, as absolute beneficiaries, they — the poor and the pitiful — receive a heaven, a salvation, and a blessedness that have been prepared for them by God alone.[58]

---

57. On the view of justification in the Nuremberg and Königsberg reformer Andreas Osiander the Elder (1496-1552), see Claus Bachmann, *Die Selbstherrlichkeit Gottes: Studien zur Theologie des Nürnberger Reformators Andreas Osiander,* Neukirchener Theologische Dissertationen und Habilitationen, vol. 7 (Neukirchen-Vluyn: Neukirchener, 1996).

58. This "total passivity" always coexists (as I showed in sections 2.5 and 2.6 above) with a spiritual activity in believing people, although this activity never has any bearing on justification and salvation. People are given salvation as a gift not only without it being based on their being in a state of good or evil (because God's mercy is given without such a basis), but far more they are given salvation in such a way that God alone also has the opposite power to reckon sins to people, thereby taking away the devil's power through the power of forgiveness. In this way, people are doubly passive in justification: passive as created beings and as sinners.

Bibliography

Abelard, Peter. *Commentariorum super S. Pauli epistolam ad Romanos*. In PL 178:783-978.

———. *Ethica seu liber dictus scito te ipsum*. In PL 178:634-78 (English title: *Peter Abelard's "Ethics,"* ed. David E. Luscombe [Oxford: Oxford University Press, 1971]).

———. *Petrus Abaelardus (1079-1142): Person, Werk und Wirkung*. Edited by Rudolf Thomas. Trierer theologische Studien 38. Trier: Paulus-Verlag, 1980.

Akerboom, Dick. "'. . . Only the Image of Christ in Us': Continuity and Discontinuity between the Late Medieval *Ars Moriendi* and Luther's *Sermon von der Bereitung zum Sterben*." In *Spirituality Renewed: Studies on Significant Representatives of the Modern Devotion*, edited by Hein Blommestijn, Charles Caspers, and Rijcklof Hofman, 209-72. Leuven: Peeters, 2003.

Altenstaig, Johannes. *Lexikon Theologicum . . .* (1517). Edited by Johannes Tytz. New York: George Olms, 1974.

Althaus, Paul. *Die Theologie Martin Luthers*. 5th ed. Gütersloh: Gütersloher Verlagshaus Gerd Mohn, 1980.

Angenendt, Arnold. "*Deus, qui nullum peccatum impunitum dimittit*: Ein 'Grundsatz' der mittelalterlichen Bußgeschichte." In *Und dennoch ist von Gott zu Reden: Festschrift für Herbert Vorgrimler*, ed. Matthias Lutz-Bachmann, 142-56. Freiburg im Breisgau: Herder, 1994.

———. *Das Frühmittelalter: Die abendländische Christenheit von 400 bis 900*. 2 vols. 2nd ed. Stuttgart: W. Kohlhammer, 1995.

———. *Geschichte der Religiosität im Mittelalter*. Darmstadt: Primus Verlag, 1997.

Anselm of Canterbury. *Admonitio morienti et de peccatis suis nimium formidanti*. In PL 158:686f.

———. *Cur deus homo. Warum Gott Mensch geworden*. Latin/German version. Edited by Franciscus Salesius Schmitt. Darmstadt: Wissenschaftliche Buchgesellschaft, 1967.

Appel, Helmut. *Anfechtung und Trost im Spätmittelalter und bei Luther.* Leipzig: M. Heinsius nachfolger, 1938.

Aristotle. *Ethica Nicomachea.* Edited by Renatus Antonius Gauthier. Leiden: Brill, 1972-74.

Arnold, Matthieu. "Les sermons de 1518-1519." In *Luther et la réforme: Du Commentaire de l'Épître aux Romains à la Messe allemande,* edited by Jean-Marie Valentin, 149-67. Paris: Ed. Desjonquères, 2001.

Asheim, Ivar, ed. *Kirche, Mystik, Heiligung und das Natürliche bei Luther.* Göttingen: Vandenhoeck & Ruprecht, 1967.

Auer, Johann. *Die Entwicklung der Gnadenlehre in der Hochscholastik mit besonderer Berücksichtigung des Kardinals Matteo d'Acquasparta.* Part 1, *Das Wesen der Gnade.* Freiburg im Breisgau: Herder, 1942.

Augustine. *Opera omnia.* In PL 32-47; also in CCSL 29-50A.

Bachmann, Claus. *Die Selbstherrlichkeit Gottes: Studien zur Theologie des Nürnberger Reformators Andreas Osiander.* Neukirchener Theologische Dissertationen und Habilitationen, vol. 7. Neukirchen-Vluyn: Neukirchener, 1996.

Bagchi, David. "Luther's Ninety-five Theses and the Contemporary Criticism of Indulgences." In *Promissory Notes on the Treasury of Merits: Indulgences in Late Medieval Europe,* edited by Robert N. Swanson, 331-55. Boston: Brill, 2006.

Barteau, Francoise. *Les romans de Tristan et Iseut.* Paris: Larousse, 1972.

Barth, Hans-Martin. "Leben und sterben können: Brechungen der spätmittelalterlichen 'ars moriendi' in der Theologie Martin Luthers." In *Ars Moriendi: Erwägungen zur Kunst des Sterbens,* edited by Harald Wagner and Torsten Kruse, 45-66. Freiburg im Breisgau: Herder, 1989.

Barth, Ulrich. "Die Geburt religiöser Autonomie: Luthers Ablassthesen von 1517." In *Aufgeklärter Protestantismus,* 53-95. Tübingen: Mohr Siebeck, 2004.

Basse, Michael. *Certitudo Spei: Thomas von Aquins Begründung der Hoffnungsgewißheit und ihre Rezeption bis zum Konzil von Trient als ein Beitrag zur Verhältnisbestimmung von Eschatologie und Rechtfertigungslehre.* Göttingen: Vandenhoeck & Ruprecht, 1993.

Baumgartner, Charles, and Paul Tihon. "Grâce." In *Dictionnaire de spiritualité ascétique et mystique* (1967), 6:701-50.

Bayer, Oswald. *Martin Luthers Theologie: Eine Vergegenwärtigung.* Tübingen: Mohr Siebeck, 2003.

———. *Promissio: Geschichte der reformatorischen Wende in Luthers Theologie.* Forschungen zur Kirchen- und Dogmengeschichte 24. Göttingen: Vandenhoeck & Ruprecht, 1971.

———. "Die reformatorische Wende in Luthers Theologie." *Zeitschrift für Theologie und Kirche* 66 (1969): 115-50.

———, ed. *Creator est creatura: Luthers Christologie als Lehre von der Idiomenkommunikation.* Berlin: De Gruyter, 2007.

Bibliography

Becker, Hansjakob, ed. *Geistliches Wunderhorn: Große deutsche Kirchenlieder.* Munich: C. H. Beck, 2001.
Bekenntnisschriften der evangelisch-lutherischen Kirche, Die. Hrsg. im Gedenkjahr der Augsburgischen Konfession 1930. 12th ed. Göttingen: Vandenhoeck & Ruprecht, 1998.
Bell, Theo. *Divus Bernhardus: Bernhard von Clairvaux in Martin Luthers Schriften.* Mainz: P. von Zabern, 1993.
Benton, John F. "Consciousness of Self and Perceptions of Individuality." In *Renaissance and Renewal in the Twelfth Century,* edited by Robert L. Benson and Giles Constable, 263-95. Cambridge: Harvard University Press, 1982.
Berger, Placidus. *Religiöses Brauchtum im Umkreis der Sterbeliturgie in Deutschland.* Münster: Regensberg, 1966.
―――. "Die sogenannten Anselmischen Fragen: Ein Element spätmittelalterlicher Sterbeliturgie." *Trierer Theologische Zeitschrift* 72 (1963): 299-306.
Bernard of Clairvaux. *Sämtliche Werke.* Latin/German version. Edited by Gerhard B. Winkler. 10 vols. Innsbruck: Tyrolia, 1990-99.
―――. *Sancti Bernardi opera.* Edited by Jean Leclercq, Charles H. Talbot, and Henricus M. Rochais. 8 vols. Rome, 1957-77.
―――. *Sermones super Cantica canticorum.* In *Sancti Bernardi opera,* vols. 1-2. Edited by Jean Leclercq. Rome: Editiones Cistercienses, 1957-58.
Beutel, Albrecht. "Antwort und Wort: Zur Frage nach der Wirklichkeit Gottes bei Luther." In *Protestantische Konkretionen: Studien zur Kirchengeschichte,* 28-44. Tübingen: Mohr Siebeck, 1998.
Beyschlag, Karlmann. *Grundriß der Dogmengeschichte.* Vol. II/2. Darmstadt: Wissenschaftliche Buchgesellschaft, 2000.
Biel, Gabriel. *Canonis misse expositio.* Edited by Heiko A. Oberman and William J. Courtenay. 4 vols. Wiesbaden: Franz Steiner, 1963-67.
―――. *Collectorium circa quattuor libros Sententiarum.* Edited by Wilfrid Werbeck and Udo Hofmann. 5 vols. Tübingen: Mohr Siebeck, 1973-84.
Bizer, Ernst. *Fides ex auditu.* Neukirchen-Vluyn: Verlag der Buchhandlung des Erziehungsvereins, 1958.
Blendinger, Christian. *Nur Gott und dem Gewissen verpflichtet: Karl Steinbauer — Zeuge in finsterer Zeit.* Munich: Claudius, 2001.
Böhme, Wolfgang, ed. *Von Eckhart bis Luther: Über mystischen Glauben.* Karlsruhe: W. Böhme, 1981.
Bollmann, Anne. "'Apostolinne van Gode gegeven': Die Schwestern vom gemeinsamen Leben als geistliche Reformerinnen in der Devotio moderna." In *Frömmigkeit — Theologie — Frömmigkeitstheologie: Contributions to European Church History, Festschrift für Berndt Hamm,* edited by Gudrun Litz, Heidrun Munzert, and Roland Liebenberg, 131-44. Leiden: Brill, 2005.
Bollmann, Annette Maria. "Frauenleben und Frauenliteratur in der Devotio moderna: Volkssprachige Schwesternbücher in literarhistorischer Perspektive." Ph.D. diss., Groningen, 2004.

Bibliography

Bornkamm, Heinrich. "Iustitia Dei in der Scholastik und bei Luther." *Archiv für Reformationsgeschichte* 39 (1942): 1-46.

Brandenburg, Albert. *Gericht und Evangelium: Zur Worttheologie in Luthers Erster Psalmenvorlesung*. Paderborn: Verlag Bonifacius-Druckerei, 1960.

Brecht, Martin. "Luthers neues Verständnis der Buße und die reformatorische Entdeckung." *Archiv für Reformationsgeschichte* 93 (2002): 281-91.

———. "Luthers reformatorische Sermone." In *Fides et pietas, Festschrift für Martin Brecht*, edited by Christian Peters and Jürgen Kampmann, 15-32. Münster: Lit, 2003.

———. *Martin Luther: Sein Weg zur Reformation, 1483-1521*. Stuttgart: Calwer, 1981 (English title: *Martin Luther: His Road to Reformation, 1483-1521* [Philadelphia: Fortress, 1985]).

Briesemeister, Dieter. "Ars moriendi." In *Lexikon des Mittelalters*, vol. 1, cols. 1041f. Munich: Artemis Verlag, 1999.

Bullinger, Heinrich. *Bericht der krancken: Wie man by den krancken und sterbenden menschen handlen, ouch wie sich ein yeder inn siner kranckheit schicken unnd zum sterben rüsten sole . . .* Zurich: Christoph Froschauer, October 1535.

Bumke, Joachim. *Höfische Kultur: Literatur und Gesellschaft im hohen Mittelalter*. Vol. 2. 3rd ed. Munich: Deutscher Taschenbuch Verlag, 1986.

Burger, Christoph. "Gottesliebe, Erstes Gebot und menschliche Autonomie bei spätmittelalterlichen Theologen und bei Martin Luther." *Zeitschrift für Theologie und Kirche* 89 (1992): 280-301.

———. "Gregor, Hugolin und der junge Luther." *Augustiniana/Louvain* 52 (2002): 335-51.

Busch, Johannes. *Chronicon Windeshemense*. Edited by Karl Grube. Halle: Hendel, 1886.

Bushart, Bruno. *Hans Holbein der Ältere*. 2nd ed. Augsburg: Verlag Hofmann-Druck, 1987.

Calvin, John. *Opera selecta*. Vol. IV. Edited by Peter Barth and Wilhelm Niesel. 3rd ed. Munich: Kaiser, 1968.

Corpus Christianorum. Series Latina. Vols. 1-. Turnhout: Brepols, 1953ff.

Corpus iuris canonici. Edited by Aemilius Ludovicus Richter, Emil Friedberg, et al. 2 vols. 2nd ed. Leipzig: Tauchnitz, 1879/81.

Corpus Reformatorum. Edited by Karl Gottlieb Bretschneider et al. 101 vols. Halle, 1834ff.

Coyle, John Kevin. *Augustine's "De Moribus Ecclesiae Catholicae": A Study of the Work, Its Composition, and Its Sources*. Fribourg: University Press, 1978.

Dalferth, Ingolf U. "Mere Passive: Die Passivität der Gabe bei Luther." In *Word — Gift — Being*, edited by Bo Kristian Holm and Peter Widmann, 43-71. Tübingen: Mohr Siebeck, 2009.

Degkwitz, Sebastian. *Wort Gottes und Erfahrung: Luthers Erfahrungsbegriff und seine Rezeption im 20. Jahrhundert*. Frankfurt am Main: Lang, 1998.

Denzinger, Heinrich. *Enchiridion symbolorum, definitionum et declarationum de rebus fidei et morum*. Latin/German edition. Edited by Peter Hünermann. 41st ed. Freiburg im Breisgau: Herder, 2007.

Bibliography

Dinzelbacher, Peter. *Die letzten Dinge: Himmel, Hölle, Fegefeuer im Mittelalter*. Freiburg im Breisgau: Herder, 1999.

―――. "Liebe II. Mentalitäts- und literaturgeschichtlich." In *Lexikon des Mittelalters*, 5:1965-68. Munich: Artemis-Verlag, 1999.

―――. *Vision und Visionsliteratur im Mittelalter*. Monographien zur Geschichte des Mittelalters 23. Stuttgart: Hiersemann, 1981.

Dionysius the Carthusian. *Opera omnia*. Vol. 41 [= Opera minor, vol. 9 (Tournai: 1912)].

Dohna, Lothar Graf zu. "Staupitz und Luther: Kontinuität und Umbruch in den Anfängen der Reformation." *Pastoraltheologie* 74 (1985): 452-65.

Dohna, Lothar Graf zu, and Richard Wetzel. "Die Reue Christi: Zum theologischen Ort der Buße bei Johann von Staupitz." *Studien und Mitteilungen zur Geschichte des Benediktinerordens und seiner Zweige* 94 (1983): 457-82.

Dörfler-Dierken, Angelika. "Luther und die heilige Anna: Zum Gelübde von Stotternheim." *Lutherjahrbuch* 64 (1997): 19-46.

Ebeling, Gerhard. "Des Todes Tod: Luthers Theologie der Konfrontation mit dem Tode." In *Wort und Glaube*, 4:610-42. Tübingen: Mohr Siebeck, 1995.

―――. "Einfalt des Glaubens und Vielfalt der Liebe: Das Herz von Luthers Theologie." In *Lutherstudien*, vol. 3, *Begriffsuntersuchungen — Textinterpretationen — Wirkungsgeschichtliches*, 126-53. Tübingen: Mohr, 1985.

―――. "Frei aus Glauben: Das Vermächtnis der Reformation." In *Lutherstudien*, 1:308-29. Tübingen: Mohr, 1971.

Eckermann, Willigis. "Buße ist besser als Ablaß: Ein Brief Gottschalk Hollens an Lubertus Langen." *Analecta Augustiniana* 32 (1969): 323-66.

Eckhart, Meister. *Die deutschen Werke*. Edited by Josef Quint. 5 vols. Stuttgart: W. Kohlhammer, 1958-76.

Elert, Werner. *Morphologie des Luthertums*. Vol. 1, *Theologie und Weltanschauung des Luthertums hauptsächlich im 16. und 17. Jahrhundert*. Munich: Beck, 1931.

Elze, Martin. "Das Verständnis der Passion Jesu im ausgehenden Mittelalter und bei Luther." In *Geist und Geschichte der Reformation: Festschrift für Hanns Rückert*, edited by Heinz Liebing and Klaus Scholder, 127-51. Arbeiten zur Kirchengeschichte 38. Berlin: De Gruyter, 1966.

Fabisch, Peter, and Erwin Iserloh, eds. *Das Gutachten des Prierias und weitere Schriften gegen Luthers Ablaßthesen (1517-1518)*. Münster: Aschendorff, 1988.

Falk, Franz. *Die deutschen Sterbebüchlein von der ältesten Zeit des Buchdruckes bis zum Jahre 1520*. Cologne: Bachem, 1890; Amsterdam: Rodopi, 1969.

Fischer, Balthasar. "Ars moriendi: Der Anselm von Canterbury zugeschriebene Dialog mit einem Sterbenden — Ein untergegangenes Element der Sterbeliturgie und der Sterbebücher des Mittelalters." In *Im Angesicht des Todes: Ein interdisziplinäres Kompendium*, vol. 2, edited by Hansjakob Becker et al., 1363-70. St. Ottilien: EOS Verlag, 1987.

Flörken, Norbert. "Ein Beitrag zur Datierung von Luthers Sermo de indulgentiis pridie Dedicationis." *Zeitschrift für Kirchengeschichte* 82 (1971): 344-50.

Franz, Gunter. *Huberinus — Rhegius — Holbein: Bibliographische und druck-

geschichtliche Untersuchung der verbreitetsten Trost- und Erbauungsschriften des 16. Jahrhunderts. Nieuwkoop: De Graaf, 1973.

Fridolin, Stephan. "Lehre für angefochtene und kleinmütige Menschen." Edited by Petra Seegets. In *Spätmittelalterliche Frömmigkeit*, edited by Berndt Hamm and Thomas Lentes, 189-95. Tübingen: Mohr Siebeck, 2001.

Genazino, Wilhelm. *Der gedehnte Blick*. Munich: C. Hanser, 2004.

Georges, Karl Ernst. *Ausführliches lateinisch-deutsches Handwörterbuch*. 2 vols. 8th ed. Darmstadt: Wissenschaftliche Buchgesellschaft, 2003.

Gerke, Friedrich. "Anfechtung und Sakrament in Martin Luthers Sermon vom Sterben." *Theologische Blätter* 13 (1934): 193-204.

Gerson, Jean. "De arte moriendi, lateinisch ediert, kommentiert und deutsch übersetzt von Fidel Rädle." In *Literatur — Geschichte — Literaturgeschichte: Beiträge zur mediävistischen Literaturwissenschaft, Festschrift für Volker Honeman*, edited by Nine Miedema and Rudolf Suntrup, 721-38. Frankfurt am Main: Lang, 2003.

———. *De consolatione theologiae*. In *Oeuvres complètes*, edited by Palémon Glorieux, 9:185-245. Paris: Desclée, 1973.

———. *De mystica theologia*. In *Ioannis Carlerii de Gerson de mystica theologia*, edited by André Combes. Lugano: Thesaurus Mundi, 1958.

———. *De praeparatione ad missam*. In *Oeuvres complètes*, edited by Palémon Glorieux, 9:35-50. Paris: Desclée, 1973.

———. *De vita spirituali animae*. In *Oeuvres complètes*, edited by Palémon Glorieux, 3:113-202. Paris: Desclée, 1962.

———. *Oeuvres complètes*. Edited by Palémon Glorieux. 10 vols. Paris: Desclée, 1960-73.

Goez, Werner. "Luthers 'Ein Sermon von der Bereitung zum Sterben' und die spätmittelalterliche ars moriendi." *Lutherjahrbuch* 48 (1981): 97-113.

Grane, Leif. *Contra Gabrielem: Luthers Auseinandersetzung mit Gabriel Biel in der Disputatio contra Scholasticam Theologiam 1517*. Translated by Elfriede Pump. Acta Theologica Danica 4. Copenhagen: Gyldendal, 1962.

Gregory the Great. *Homiliae in evangelia*. In CCSL 141.

Grimm, Jacob, and Wilhelm Grimm. *Deutsches Wörterbuch*. Vol. 3. Leipzig: S. Hirzel, 1862.

Grosse, Sven. "Existentielle Theologie in der vorreformatorischen Epoche am Beispiel Johannes Gersons: Historische Überlegungen zum ökumenischen Disput." *Kerygma und Dogma* 41 (1995): 80-111.

———. *Heilsungewißheit und Scrupulositas im späten Mittelalter: Studien zu Johannes Gerson und Gattungen der Frömmigkeitstheologie seiner Zeit*. Tübingen: J. C. B. Mohr, 1994.

Günter, Wolfgang. "Johann von Staupitz (ca. 1468-1524)." In *Katholische Theologen der Reformationszeit*, edited by Erwin Iserloh, 5:11-31. Katholisches Leben und Kirchenformen im Zeitalter der Glaubenspaltung 48. Münster: Aschendorff, 1988.

Haas, Alois M. "Didaktik des Sterbens: Zur Botschaft der spätmittelalterlichen

Bibliography

Sterbebüchlein." In *Gewißheit angesichts des Sterbens*, edited by Joachim Heubach, 13-31. Erlangen: Martin-Luther-Verlag, 1998.

Haas, Alois M., and Kurt Ruh. "Seuse, Heinrich OP." In *Die deutsche Literatur des Mittelalters: Verfasserlexikon*, vol. 8, cols. 1109-29. Berlin: De Gruyter, 1992.

Hägglund, Bengt. "Luther und die Mystik." In *Kirche, Mystik, Heiligung und das Natürliche bei Luther*, edited by Ivar Asheim, 84-94. Göttingen: Vandenhoeck & Ruprecht, 1967.

Hahn, Gerhard, ed. *Martin Luther: Die deutschen geistlichen Lieder*. Tübingen: Niemeyer, 1967.

Hamm, Berndt. "Den Himmel kaufen: Heilskommerzielle Perspektiven des 14. bis 16. Jahrhunderts." *Jahrbuch für biblische Theologie* 21 (2006): 239-75.

―――. "Einheit und Vielfalt der Reformation — oder: Was die Reformation zur Reformation machte." In *Reformationstheorien: Ein kirchenhistorischer Disput über Einheit und Vielfalt der Reformation*, edited by Berndt Hamm, Bernd Moeller, Dorothea Wendebourg, 57-127. Göttingen: Vandenhoeck & Ruprecht, 1995.

―――. "Die Emergenz der Reformation." In *Die Reformation: Potentiale der Freiheit*, edited by Berndt Hamm and Michael Welker, 1-27. Tübingen: Mohr Siebeck, 2008.

―――. *Frömmigkeitstheologie am Anfang des 16. Jahrhunderts: Studien zu Johannes von Paltz und seinem Umkreis*. Beiträge zur historischen Theologie 65. Tübingen: Mohr, 1982.

―――. "'Gott berühren': Mystische Erfahrung im ausgehenden Mittelalter: Zugleich eine Klärung des Mystikbegriffs." In *Gottes Nähe unmittelbar erfahren: Mystik im Mittelalter und bei Luther*, edited by Berndt Hamm and Volker Leppin, 111-39. Tübingen: Mohr Siebeck, 2007.

―――. "Gottes gnädiges Gericht: Spätmittelalterliche Bildinschriften als Zeugnisse intensivierter Barmherzigkeitsvorstellungen." In *Traditionen, Zäsuren, Umbrüche: Inschriften des späten Mittelalters und der frühen Neuzeit im historischen Kontext — Beiträge zur 11. Internationalen Fachtagung für Epigraphik vom 9. bis 12. Mai 2007 in Greifswald*, edited by Christine Magin, 17-35, 432ff. Wiesbaden: Reichert, 2008.

―――. "Johann von Staupitz (ca. 1468-1524) — spätmittelalterlicher Reformer und 'Vater' der Reformation." *Archiv für Reformationsgeschichte* 92 (2001): 6-42.

―――. *Lazarus Spengler (1479-1534): Der Nürnberger Ratsschreiber im Spannungsfeld von Humanismus und Reformation, Politik und Glaube*. Tübingen: Mohr Siebeck, 2004.

―――. "Die Nähe des Heiligen im ausgehenden Mittelalter: Ars moriendi, Totenmemoria, Gregorsmesse." In *Sakralität zwischen Antike und Neuzeit*, edited by Berndt Hamm, Klaus Herbers, and Heidrun Stein-Kecks, 185-221. Stuttgart: Steiner, 2007.

―――. "Die 'nahe Gnade' — innovative Züge der spätmittelalterlichen Theologie und Frömmigkeit." In *"Herbst des Mittelalters"? Fragen zur Bewertung des 14. und 15. Jahrhunderts*, edited by Jan A. Aertsen and Martin Pickavé, 541-57. Berlin: De Gruyter, 2004.

---. "Normative Zentrierung im 15. und 16. Jahrhundert: Beobachtungen zu Religiosität, Theologie und Ikonologie." *Zeitchrift für historische Forschung* 26 (1999): 163-202.

---. *Promissio, Pactum, Ordinatio: Freiheit und Selbstbindung Gottes in der scholastischen Gnadenlehre.* Beiträge zur historischen Theologie 54. Tübingen: Mohr, 1977.

---. "Die Reformation als Medienereignis." *Jahrbuch für biblische Theologie* 11 (1996): 137-66.

---. "Reformation als normative Zentrierung von Religion und Gesellschaft." *Jahrbuch für biblische Theologie* 7 (1992): 241-79.

---. "Staupitz, Johann(es) von." In *Theologische Realenzyklopädie,* 32:119-27. Berlin: De Gruyter, 2001.

---. "Die Stellung der Reformation im zweiten christlichen Jahrtausend." *Jahrbuch für biblische Theologie* 15 (2000): 181-220.

---. "Theologie und Frömmigkeit im ausgehenden Mittelalter." In *Handbuch der Geschichte der evangelischen Kirche in Bayern,* edited by Gerhard Müller, Horst Weigelt, and Wolfgang Zorn, 1:159-211. St. Ottilien: EOS, 2002.

---. "Toleranz und Häresie: Martin Bucers prinzipielle Neubestimmung christlicher Gemeinschaft." In *Martin Bucer zwischen Luther und Zwingli,* edited by Matthieu Arnold and Berndt Hamm, 85-106. Tübingen: Mohr Siebeck, 2003.

---. "Von der spätmittelalterlichen *reformatio* zur Reformation: Der Prozess normativer Zentrierung von Religion und Gesellschaft in Deutschland." *Archiv für Reformationsgeschichte* 84 (1993): 7-82.

---. "Was ist Frömmigkeitstheologie? Überlegungen zum 14. bis 16. Jahrhundert." In *Praxis Pietatis: Beiträge zu Theologie und Frömmigkeit in der Frühen Neuzeit, Festschrift für Wolfgang Sommer,* edited by Hans-Jörg Nieden and Marcel Nieden, 9-45. Stuttgart: Kohlhammer, 1999.

---. "Was ist reformatorische Rechtfertigungslehre?" *Zeitschrift für Theologie und Kirche* 83 (1986): 1-38.

---. "Wie innovativ war die Reformation?" *Zeitschrift für historische Forschung* 27 (2000): 481-97.

---. "Wollen und Nicht-Können in der spätmittelalterlichen Bußseelsorge." In *Spätmittelalterliche Frömmigkeit,* edited by Berndt Hamm and Thomas Lentes, 111-46. Tübingen: Mohr Siebeck, 2001.

---. *Zwinglis Reformation der Freiheit.* Neukirchen-Vluyn: Neukirchener Verlag, 1988.

Hamm, Berndt, and Thomas Lentes, eds. *Spätmittelalterliche Frömmigkeit zwischen Ideal und Praxis.* Tübingen: Mohr Siebeck, 2001.

Hammann, Konrad. "'Die Allerseligste Vorbereitung zum seligen Sterben': Kontinuität und Wandel lutherischer Frömmigkeit und Sterbekultur vom 16. bis zum 18. Jahrhundert im Spiegel der Göttinger Leichenpredigten." *Jahrbuch der Gesellschaft für niedersächsische Kirchengeschichte* 101 (2003): 117-64.

Harmening, Dieter. "Katechismusliteratur: Grundlagen religiöser Laienbildung im Spätmittelalter." In *Wissensorganisierende und wissensvermittelnde Literatur im*

Mittelalter: Perspektiven ihrer Erforschung, edited by Norbert Richard Wolf, 91-102. Wiesbaden: L. Reichert, 1987.

Harnack, Adolf von. *Lehrbuch der Dogmengeschichte III*. 4th ed. Tübingen: J. C. B. Mohr, 1910.

Hascher-Burger, Ulrike. *Gesungene Innigkeit: Studien zu einer Musikhandschrift der Devotio moderna*. Leiden and Boston: Brill, 2002.

Haskins, Charles Homer. *The Renaissance of the Twelfth Century*. Cambridge: Harvard University Press, 1927.

Heck, Christian. *L'échelle céleste: Une histoire de la quête du ciel*. 2nd ed. Paris, 1999.

Hendrix, Scott H. *Luther and the Papacy: Stages in a Reformation Conflict*. Philadelphia: Fortress, 1981.

Heynck, Valens. "Zur Lehre von der unvollkommenen Reue in der Skotistenschule des ausgehenden 15. Jahrhunderts." *Franziskanische Studien* 24 (1937): 18-58.

Hödl, Ludwig. "'Busse (liturgisch-theologisch),' D. Westkirche, II, Scholastische Bußtheologie." In *Lexikon des Mittelalters*, vol. 2, cols. 1123-41. Munich: Artemis-Verlag, 1983.

―――. *Die Geschichte der scholastischen Literatur und der Theologie der Schlüsselgewalt*. Part I, *Die scholastische Literatur und die Theologie der Schlüsselgewalt von ihren Anfängen an bis zur Summa Aurea des Wilhelm von Auxerre*. Beiträge zur Geschichte der Philosophie und Theologie des Mittelalters, vol. 38 H.4. Münster: Aschendorff, 1960.

Hoffmann, Veronika, ed. *Die Gabe: Ein "Urwort" der Theologie?* Frankfurt am Main: M. Lembeck, 2009.

Hohenberger, Thomas. *Lutherische Rechtfertigungslehre in den reformatorischen Flugschriften der Jahre 1521-22*. Tübingen: J. C. B. Mohr, 1996.

Holl, Karl. "Der Neubau der Sittlichkeit (1919)." In *Gesammelte Aufsätze zur Kirchengeschichte I: Luther*, 155-287. 7th ed. Tübingen: J. C. B. Mohr, 1948.

―――. "Die Rechtfertigungslehre im Licht der Geschichte des Protestantismus (1922)." In *Gesammelte Aufsätze zur Kirchengeschichte III: Der Westen*, 525-57. Tübingen: J. C. B. Mohr, 1928.

―――. "Was verstand Luther unter Religion? (erstmals 1917)." In *Gesammelte Aufsätze zur Kirchengeschichte I: Luther*, 1-110. 7th ed. Tübingen: J. C. B. Mohr, 1948.

Holm, Bo Kristian. *Gabe und Geben bei Luther: Das Verhältnis zwischen Reziprozität und reformatorischer Rechtfertigungslehre*. Berlin and New York: De Gruyter, 2006.

Holm, Bo Kristian, and Peter Widmann, eds. *Word — Gift — Being: Justification — Economy — Ontology*. Tübingen: Mohr Siebeck, 2009.

Hugo of St. Victor. *De Laude caritatis*. In PL 176:970-75.

Iserloh, Erwin. "Luther und die Mystik." In *Kirche, Mystik, Heiligung und das Natürliche bei Luther*, edited by Ivar Asheim. Göttingen: Vandenhoeck & Ruprecht, 1967.

―――. "Die protestantische Reformation." In *Handbuch der Kirchengeschichte*, vol. 4, *Reformation, Katholische Reform und Gegenreformation*, edited by Josef Glazik and Hubert Jedin, 3-436. Freiburg im Breisgau: Herder, 1967.

Iwand, Hans Joachim. "Die Freiheit des Christen und die Unfreiheit des Willens." In *Um den rechten Glauben: Gesammelte Aufsätze*, edited by Karl Gerhard Steck, 247-68. Munich: C. Kaiser, 1959.

Jacobi, Thorsten. *"Christen heißen Freie": Luthers Freiheitsaussagen in den Jahren 1515-1519.* Tübingen: Mohr Siebeck, 1997.

Jacob the Carthusian. *Tractatus de arte bene moriendi.* Microfiche at Wolfenbüttel, Herzog August Bibliothek 112.5 Theol.

Jakobs, Hermann. *Kirchenreform und Hochmittelalter: 1046-1215.* 2nd ed. Oldenbourg Grundriß der Geschichte 7. Munich: R. Oldenbourg, 1988.

Jezler, Peter, ed. *Himmel, Hölle, Fegefeuer: Das Jenseits im Mittelalter.* Exhibition catalogue. Zurich: Verlag Neue Zürcher Zeitung, 1994.

Joest, Wilfried. *Gesetz und Freiheit: Das Problem des Tertius usus legis bei Luther und die neutestamentliche Parainese.* 4th ed. Göttingen: Vandenhoeck & Ruprecht, 1968.

———. "Martin Luther." In *Reformationszeit I,* edited by Martin Greschat, 129-85. Stuttgart: W. Kohlhammer, 1981.

———. *Ontologie der Person bei Luther.* Göttingen: Vandenhoeck & Ruprecht, 1967.

Jüngel, Eberhard. *Zur Freiheit eines Christenmenschen: Eine Erinnerung an Luthers Schrift.* Munich: Kaiser, 1978.

Junghans, Helmar. "Bibelhumanistische Anstöße in Luthers Entwicklung zum Reformator." *Revue d'histoire et de philosophie religieuses* 85 (2005): 17-42.

Juntunen, Sammel. *Der Begriff des Nichts bei Luther in den Jahren von 1510 bis 1523.* Helsinki: Luther-Agricola-Gesellschaft, 1996.

Kaufmann, Thomas. *Martin Luther.* Munich: Beck, 2006.

Kaysersberg, Johannes Geiler von. *Sämtliche Werke.* Part I, section I, vol. 1. Edited by Gerhard Bauer. Berlin and New York: De Gruyter, 1989.

Kienzle, Beverly Mayne, ed. *The Sermon.* Turnhout: Brepols, 2000.

Klein, Luise. "Die Bereitung zum Sterben: Studien zu den frühen reformatorischen Trost- und Sterbebüchern." Diss. theol., Göttingen, 1958.

Köbele, Susanne. "Heiligkeit durchbrechen: Grenzfälle von Heiligkeit in der mittelalterlichen Mystik." In *Sakralität zwischen Antike und Neuzeit,* edited by Berndt Hamm et al., 147-69. Stuttgart: Steiner, 2007.

Kolb, Herbert. *Der Begriff der Minne und das Entstehen der höfischen Lyrik.* Tübingen: M. Niemeyer, 1958.

Köpf, Ulrich. "Monastische Theologie im 15. Jahrhundert." *Rottenburger Jahrbuch für Kirchengeschichte* 11 (1992): 117-35.

———. "Monastische Traditionen bei Martin Luther." In *Luther — Zwischen den Zeiten,* edited by Christoph Markschies and Michael Trowitzsch, 17-35. Tübingen: Mohr Siebeck, 1999.

———. "Monastische und scholastische Theologie." In *Bernhard von Clairvaux und der Beginn der Moderne,* edited by Dieter R. Bauer and Gotthard Fuchs, 96-135. Innsbruck: Tyrolia, 1996.

———. "Mönchtum." In *Luther Handbuch,* edited by Albrecht Beutel, 50-57. Tübingen: Mohr Siebeck, 2005.

———. "Die Passion Christi in der lateinischen religiösen und theologischen Literatur des Spätmittelalters." In *Die Passion Christi in Literatur und Kunst des späten Mittelalters*, edited by Walter Haug and Burghart Wachinger, 21-41. Tübingen: M. Niemeyer, 1993.

———. "Passionsfrömmigkeit." In *Theologische Realenzyklopädie*, 27:722-64. Berlin: De Gruyter, 1997.

———. *Religiöse Erfahrung in der Theologie Bernhards von Clairvaux*. Beiträge zur historischen Theologie 61. Tübingen: Mohr, 1980.

Kroeger, Matthias. *Rechtfertigung und Gesetz: Studien zur Entwicklung der Rechtfertigungslehre beim jungen Luther*. Forschungen zur Kirchen- und Dogmengeschichte 20. Göttingen: Vandenhoeck & Ruprecht, 1968.

Laager, Jacques, ed. *Ars moriendi: Die Kunst, gut zu leben und gut zu sterben. Texte von Cicero bis Luther*. Zurich: Manesse, 1996.

Landgraf, Artur Michael. *Dogmengeschichte der Frühscholastik*. Vol. I/I. Regensburg: Pustet, 1952.

Lecler, Joseph. "Die Gewissensfreiheit." In *Zur Geschichte der Toleranz und Religionsfreiheit*, edited by Heinrich Lutz, 331-71. Darmstadt: Wissenschaftliche Buchgesellschaft, 1977.

Leclercq, Jean. *Wissenschaft und Gottverlangen: Zur Mönchstheologie des Mittelalters*. Translated by Johannes Stöber and Nicole Stöber. Düsseldorf: Patmos, 1963.

Le Goff, Jacques. *Die Geburt des Fegefeuers*. Translated by Ariane Forkel. Stuttgart: Klett Cotta, 1984.

Lehmann, Karl, and Wolfhart Pannenberg, eds. *Lehrverurteilungen — kirchentrennend?* Vol. 1, *Rechtfertigung, Sakramente und Amt im Zeitalter der Reformation und heute*. Freiburg im Breisgau: Herder, 1986.

Lentes, Thomas. "Inneres Auge, äusserer Blick und heilige Schau: Ein Diskussionsbeitrag zur visuellen Praxis in Frömmigkeit und Moraldidaxe des späten MIttelalters." In *Frömmigkeit im Mittelalter: Politisch-soziale Kontexte, visuelle Praxis, körperliche Ausdrucksformen*, edited by Klaus Schreiner and Marc Müntz, 179-220. Munich: Fink, 2002.

———. "Nur der geöffnete Körper schafft Heil: Das Bild als Verdoppelung des Körpers." In *Ausstellungskatalog: Glaube Hoffnung Liebe Tod*, edited by Christoph Geissmar-Brandi and Eleonora Louis, 152-55. 2nd ed. Vienna: Graphische Sammlung Albertina, 1996.

———. "So weit das Auge reicht: Sehrituale im Spätmittelalter." In *Das "Goldene Wunder" in der Dortmunder Petrikirche: Bildgebrauch und Bildproduktion im Mittelalter*, edited by Barbara Welzel, Thomas Lentes, and Heike Schlie, 241-58. Bielefeld: Verlag für Regionalgeschichte, 2003.

Leppin, Volker. "Externe Personenkonstitution bei Johannes Tauler." In *Selbstbewusstsein und Person im Mittelalter*, edited by Günther Mensching, 55-64. Würzburg: Königshausen & Neumann, 2005.

———. "Luther-Literatur seit 1983, Teil II." *Theologische Rundschau* 65 (2000): 431-54.

———. "Luther-Literatur seit 1983, Teil III." *Theologische Rundschau* 68 (2003): 313-40.

———. *Martin Luther*. Darmstadt: Wissenschaftliche Buchgesellschaft, 2006.

———. "'Omnem vitam fidelium penitentiam esse voluit' — Zur Aufnahme mystischer Traditionen in Luthers erster Ablassthese." *Archiv für Reformationsgeschichte* 93 (2002): 7-25.

———. "Tauler, Johannes (ca. 1300-1361)." In *Theologische Realenzyklöpadie*, 32:745-48. Berlin: De Gruyter, 2001.

———. "Transformationen spätmittelalterlicher Mystik bei Luther." In *Gottes Nähe unmittelbar erfahren: Mystik im Mittelalter und bei Luther*, edited by Berndt Hamm and Volker Leppin, 165-87. Tübingen: Mohr Siebeck, 2007.

———. "Von der Polarität zur Vereindeutigung: Zu den Wandlungen in Kirche und Frömmigkeit zwischen spätem Mittelalter und Reformation." In *Frömmigkeit — Theologie — Frömmigkeitstheologie: Contributions to European Church History, Festschrift für Berndt Hamm*, edited by Gudrun Litz, Heidrun Munzert, and Roland Liebenberg, 299-315. Leiden and Boston: Brill, 2005.

———. "Von Sturmgewittern, Turmstuben und der Nuss der Theologie: Martin Luther (1483-1546) zwischen Legende und Wirklichkeit." In *Wittenberger Lebensläufe im Umbruch der Reformation*, edited by Evangelischen Predigerseminar, 11-27. Wittenberg: Drei-Kastanien-Verlag, 2005.

———, ed. *Reformation*. Neukirchen-Vluyn: Neukirchener, 2005.

Lexutt, Athina. "Luthers Verhältnis zur Mystik. Ein kirchengeschichtlicher Lösungsversuch zur Frage: Mystik und Protestantismus — Himmlisches Paar oder Duo infernale?" *Der evangelische Erzieher* 49 (1997): 19-40.

Liddell, Henry George, and Robert Scott. *A Greek-English Lexicon*. 9th ed. Oxford: Clarendon, 1961.

Lienhard, Marc. *Martin Luthers christologisches Zeugnis: Entwicklungen und Grundzüge seiner Christologie*. Göttingen: Vandenhoeck & Ruprecht, 1979.

Link, Wilhelm. *Das Ringen Luthers um die Freiheit der Theologie von der Philosophie*. Munich: Kaiser, 1940.

Litz, Gudrun. *Die reformatorische Bilderfrage in den schwäbischen Reichsstädten*. Tübingen: Mohr Siebeck, 2007.

Loewenich, Walther von. *Luthers theologia crucis*. 5th ed. Witten: Luther-Verlag, 1967.

Lohse, Bernhard. *Luthers Theologie in ihrer historischen Entwicklung und in ihrem systematischen Zusammenhang*. Göttingen: Vandenhoeck & Ruprecht, 1995.

———. "Luther und Bernhard von Clairvaux." In *Bernhard von Clairvaux: Rezeption und Wirkung im Mittelalter und in der Neuzeit*, edited by Kaspar Elm, 271-301. Wiesbaden: Harrassowitz, 1994.

———. *Ratio und fides: Eine Untersuchung über die ratio in der Theologie Luthers*. Göttingen: Vandenhoeck & Ruprecht, 1958.

———, ed. *Der Durchbruch der reformatorischen Erkenntnis bei Luther*. Darmstadt: Wissenschaftliche Buchgesellschaft, 1968.

———, ed. *Der Durchbruch der reformatorischen Erkenntnis bei Luther: Neuere Untersuchungen*. Stuttgart: Franz Steiner Verlag, 1988.

Lüers, Grete. "Die Auffassung der Liebe bei mittelalterlichen Mystikern." *Eine heilige Kirche* 22 (1940): 110-18.

Luther, Martin. *Archiv zur Weimarer Ausgabe der Werke Martin Luthers: Texte und Untersuchungen*. Vols. 1ff. Cologne: Böhlau, 1981ff.

———. *Ausgewählte Schriften*. Edited by Karin Bornkamm and Gerhard Ebeling. 6 vols. Frankfurt am Main: Insel, 1982.
———. *Lateinisch-Deutsche Studienausgabe*. Edited by Wilfried Härle, Johannes Schilling, and Günther Wartenberg. Vols. 1-3. Leipzig: Evangelische Verlagsanstalt, 2006-9.
———. *Luthers Werke in Auswahl*. 8 vols. Edited by Otto Clemen. Vols. 1-4, 6th ed. Berlin: De Gruyter, 1966-68; vols. 5-8, 3rd ed. Berlin: De Gruyter, 1962-66.
———. *Martin Luther Studienausgabe*. Edited by Hans-Ulrich Delius. Vols. 1ff. Berlin: Evangelische Verlangsanstalt, 1979ff.
———. *Martin Luthers Werke: Kritische Gesamtausgabe*. Vols. 1ff. Weimar: H. Böhlau, 1883ff.
———. *Martin Luthers Werke: Kritische Gesamtausgabe, Briefwechsel*. 15 vols. Weimar: Böhlau, 1930-1978.
———. *Martin Luthers Werke: Kritische Gesamtausgabe, Tischreden*. 6 vols. Weimar: Böhlau, 1912-21.
———. *Martin Luther und die Reformation in Deutschland, Ausstellungskatalog*. Frankfurt am Main: Insel Verlag, 1983.
———. *Oeuvres I*. Edited by Marc Lienhard and Matthieu Arnold. Paris: Gallimard, 1999.
Manns, Peter. "Fides absoluta — Fides incarnata: Zur Rechtfertigungslehre Luthers im Großen Galater-Kommentar." In *Reformata Reformanda, Festgabe für Hubert Jedin*, vol. 1, edited by Erwin Iserloh and Konrad Repgen, 288-312. Münster: Aschendorff, 1965.
Mau, Rudolf. "Liebe als gelebte Freiheit der Christen: Luthers Auslegung von G5, 13-24 im Kommentar von 1519." *Lutherjahrbuch* 59 (1992): 11-37.
Maurer, Wilhelm. *Von der Freiheit eines Christenmenschen: Zwei Untersuchungen zu Luthers Reformationsschriften 1520/21*. Göttingen: Vandenhoeck & Ruprecht, 1949.
McGinn, Bernard. *Die Mystik im Abendland*. Vols. 1 and 3. Freiburg im Breisgau: Herder, 1994 and 1999 (English title: *The Presence of God: A History of Western Christian Mysticism* [New York: Crossroad, 1992]).
Meinhold, Peter. *Die Genesisvorlesung Luthers und ihre Herausgeber*. Stuttgart: W. Kohlhammer, 1936.
Melanchthon, Philipp. *Vorrede zu Volume 2 der Gesamtausgabe von Luthers Werken*. Wittenberg, 1546. In *CR* 6, cols. 155-70.
Mennecke-Haustein, Ute. *Luthers Trostbriefe*. Gütersloh: G. Mohn, 1989.
Mertens, Dieter. *Iacobus Carthusiensis: Untersuchungen zur Rezeption der Werke des Kartäusers Jakob vom Paradies (1381-1465)*. Göttingen: Vandenhoeck & Ruprecht, 1976.
Metz, Detlef. "Gabriel Biel und die Mystik." In *Gabriel Biel und die Brüder vom gemeinsamen Leben: Beiträge aus Anlaß des 500. Todestages des Tübinger Theologen*, edited by Ulrich Köpf and Sönke Lorenz, 55-91. Stuttgart: Franz Steiner Verlag, 1998.
Metzger, Günther. *Gelebter Glaube: Die Formierung reformatorischen Denkens in*

Luthers erster Psalmenvorlesung, dargestellt am Begriff des Affekts. Göttingen: Vandenhoeck & Ruprecht, 1964.

Meuthen, Erich. "Gab es ein spates Mittelalter?" In *Spätzeit: Studien zu den Problemen eines historischen Epochenbegriffs*, edited by Johannes Kunisch, 91-135. Berlin: Duncker und Humblot, 1990.

Migne, Jacques-Paul, ed. Patrologiae Cursus Completus: Series Latina. 217 vols. Paris, 1844ff. (5 supplemental vols. Paris, 1958-70).

Modalsli, Ole. "Luther über die Letzten Dinge." In *Leben und Werk Martin Luthers von 1526 bis 1546*, vol. 1, edited by Helmar Junghans, 331-45. East Berlin: Evangel. Verl.-Anst., 1983 (with notes in volume 2, pp. 834-49).

Moeller, Bernd. "Die Anfechtung bei Johann Tauler." Diss. theol., Mainz, 1956.

———. "Das Berühmtwerden Luthers." *Zeitschrift für historische Forschung* 15 (1988): 65-92.

———. *Luther-Rezeption: Kirchenhistorische Aufsätze zur Reformationsgeschichte*. Edited by Johannes Schilling. Göttingen: Vandenhoeck & Ruprecht, 2001.

———. "Sterbekunst in der Reformation: Der 'köstliche, gute, notwendige Sermon vom Sterben' des Augustiner-Eremiten Stefan Kastenbauer." In *Vita Religiosa im Mittelalter, Festschrift für Kaspar Elm*, edited by Franz J. Felten and Nikolas Jaspert, 739-65. Berlin: Duncker und Humblot, 1999.

———. "Tauler und Luther." In *La Mystique Rhénane*, edited by Jeanne Ancelet-Hustache, 157-68. Paris: Presses universitaires de France, 1963.

Moeller, Bernd, and Karl Stackmann. *Luder — Luther — Eleutherius: Erwägungen zu Luthers Namen*. Göttingen: Vandenhoeck & Ruprecht, 1981.

———. *Städtische Predigt in der Frühzeit der Reformation: Eine Untersuchung deutscher Flugschriften der Jahre 1522 bis 1529*. Göttingen: Vandenhoeck & Ruprecht, 1996.

Morris, Colin. *The Discovery of the Individual, 1050-1200*. Church History Outlines 5. London: SPCK for the Church Historical Society, 1972.

Mühling, Andreas. "Welchen Tod sterben wir? — Heinrich Bullingers 'Bericht der Kranken' (1535)." *Zwingliana* 29 (2002): 55-68.

Müller, Gerhard. *Die Mystik oder das Wort: Zur Geschichte eines Spannungsverhältnisses*. Stuttgart: F. Müller, 2000.

Müller, Günther. "Gradualismus." *Deutsche Vierteljahrsschrift für Literaturwissenschaft und Geistesgeschichte* 2 (1924): 681-720.

Munari, Franco. *Ovid im Mittelalter*. Zurich: Artemis, 1960.

Newman, Francis X., ed. *The Meaning of Courtly Love*. Albany: State University of New York Press, 1968.

Nicol, Martin. *Meditation bei Luther*. Göttingen: Vandenhoeck & Ruprecht, 1984.

Oberman, Heiko A. *Contra vanam curiositatem: Ein Kapitel der Theologie zwischen Seelenwinkel und Weltall*. Zurich: Theologischer Verlag, 1974.

———. "Facientibus quod in se est deus non denegat gratiam: Robert Holcot, O.P., and the Beginnings of Luther's Theology." *Harvard Theological Review* 55 (1962): 317-42.

———. *Der Herbst der mittelalterlichen Theologie*. Translated by Martin Rumscheidt and Henning Kampen. Zurich: EVZ-Verlag, 1965 (English title: *The Harvest of Medieval Theology* [Cambridge: Harvard University Press, 1963]).

———. *Luther: Mensch zwischen Gott und Teufel*. Berlin: Severin und Siedler, 1982.

———. *Die Reformation: Von Wittenberg nach Genf*. Göttingen: Vandenhoeck & Ruprecht, 1986.

———. "Simul gemitus et raptus: Luther und die Mystik." In *Die Reformation: Von Wittenberg nach Genf*, 45-89. Göttingen: Vandenhoeck & Ruprecht, 1986.

———. *Werden und Wertung der Reformation: Vom Wegestreit zum Glaubenskampf*. Tübingen: Mohr, 1977.

———. "Wir sein pettler: *Hoc est verum*: Bund und Gnade in der Theologie des Mittelalters und der Reformation." *Zeitschrift für Kirchengeschichte* 78 (1967): 232-52.

———, ed. *Die Kirche im Zeitalter der Reformation*. Neukirchen-Vluyn: Neukirchener Verlag, 1981.

Ohly, Friedrich. *Hohelied-Studien: Grundzüge einer Geschichte der Hoheliedauslegung des Abendlandes bis um 1200*. Wiesbaden: F. Steiner, 1958.

Ohst, Martin. "Die Lutherdeutungen Karl Holls und seiner Schüler Emanuel Hirsch und Erich Vogelsang vor dem Hintergrund der Lutherdeutung Albrecht Ritschls." In *Lutherforschung im 20. Jahrhundert: Rückblick — Bilanz — Ausblick*, edited by Rainer Vinke, 19-50. Mainz: P. von Zabern, 2004.

———. *Pflichtbeichte: Untersuchungen zum Bußwesen im Hohen und Späten Mittelalter*. Beiträge zur historischen Theologie 89. Tübingen: Mohr, 1995.

Otto, Henrik. *Vor- und frühreformatorische Tauler-Rezeption: Annotationen in Drucken des späten 15. und frühen 16. Jahrhunderts*. Gütersloh: Gütersloher Verlagshaus, 2003.

Palmer, Nigel F. "Ars moriendi und Totentanz: Zur Verbildlichung des Todes im Spätmittelalter, mit einer Bibliographie zur 'Ars moriendi.'" In *Tod im Mittelalter*, edited by Arno Borst et al., 313-34. Constance: Universitätsverlag Konstanz, 1993.

———. "Marquard von Lindau OFM." In *Die deutsche Literatur des Mittelalters: Verfasserlexikon*, vol. 6, cols. 81-126. Berlin, 1985.

Paltz, Johannes von. *Coelifodina*. Edited by Christoph Burger and Friedhelm Stasch. Berlin: De Gruyter, 1983.

———. "Collatio funeralis in exsequiis doctoris Theodorici Wissensee." Edited by Walter Simon. In *Opuscula*, edited by Christoph Burger, 414-23. Berlin: De Gruyter, 1989.

———. *Opuscula*. Edited by Christoph Burger et al. Berlin: De Gruyter, 1989.

———. *Supplementum Coelifodinae*. Edited by Berndt Hamm. Berlin: De Gruyter, 1983.

———. *Werke*. 3 vols. Berlin: De Gruyter, 1983-89.

Parshall, Peter, and Rainer Schoch, eds. *Die Anfänge der europäischen Druckgraphik: Holzschnitte des 15. Jahrhunderts und ihr Gebrauch*. In *Ausstellungskatalog des Germanischen Nationalmuseums Nürnberg*. Nuremberg: Verlag des Germanischen nationalmuseums, 2005 (English title: *Origins of European Printmaking:*

Fifteenth-Century Woodcuts and Their Public [New Haven: Yale University Press, 2005]).

Pesch, Otto Hermann. "Freiheitsbegriff und Freiheitslehre bei Thomas von Aquin und Luther." *Catholica* 17 (1963): 197-244.

———. "Neuere Beiträge zur Frage nach Luthers 'Reformatorischer Wende.'" *Catholica* 37 (1983): 259-87.

———. *Theologie der Rechtfertigung bei Martin Luther und Thomas von Aquin: Versuch eines systematisch-theologischen Dialogs.* Mainz: Matthias-Grünewald-Verlag, 1967.

———. "Theologie des Todes bei Martin Luther." In *Im Angesicht des Todes: Ein interdisziplinäres Kompendium,* edited by Hansjakob Becker, Bernhard Einig, and Peter-Otto Ullrich, 709-89. 2 vols. St. Ottilien: EOS Verlag, 1987.

———. "Zur Frage nach Luthers reformatorischer Wende: Ergebnisse und Probleme der Diskussion um Ernst Bizer, 'Fides ex auditu.'" In *Der Durchbruch der reformatorischen Erkenntnis bei Luther,* edited by Bernhard Lohse, 445-505. Darmstadt: Wissenschaftliche Buchgesellschaft, 1968.

Peter Lombard. *Sententiae in IV libris distinctae.* Edited by Collegium S. Bonaventurae. Vol. 1. 3rd ed. Spicilegium Bonaventurianum 4. Rome: Grottaferrata, 1971.

Peura, Simo. *Mehr als ein Mensch? Die Vergöttlichung als Thema der Theologie Martin Luthers von 1513 bis 1519.* Mainz: P. von Zabern, 1994.

Peura, Simo, and Antti Raunio, eds. *Luther und Theosis: Vergöttlichung als Thema der abendländischen Theologie.* Erlangen: Martin-Luther-Verlag, 1990.

Pinomaa, Lennart. *Der existentielle Charakter der Theologie Luthers: Das Hervorbrechen der Theologie der Anfechtung und ihre Bedeutung für das Lutherverständnis.* Helsinki: Finnische Literaturgesellschaft, 1940.

Pleuser, Christine. *Die Benennungen und der Begriff des Leides bei J. Tauler.* Berlin: E. Schmidt, 1967.

Pollmann, Leo. *Die Liebe in der hochmittelalterlichen Literatur Frankreichs. Versuch einer historischen Phänomenologie.* Frankfurt am Main: Klostermann, 1966.

Prenter, Regin. *Spiritus Creator.* Munich: C. Kaiser, 1954.

Preus, James Samuel. *From Shadow to Promise: Old Testament Interpretation from Augustine to the Young Luther.* Cambridge: Harvard University Press, Belknap Press, 1969.

Reinis, Austra. "Evangelische Anleitung zur Seelsorge am Sterbenden 1519-1528." *Luther* 73 (2002): 31-45.

———. *Reforming the Art of Dying: The "Ars Moriendi" in the German Reformation (1519-1528).* Burlington, Vt.: Ashgate, 2007.

Resch, Claudia. *Trost im Angesicht des Todes: Frühe reformatorische Anleitungen zur Seelsorge an Kranken und Sterbenden.* Tübingen: Francke, 2006.

Riedlinger, Helmut. *Die Makellosigkeit der Kirche in den lateinischen Hoheliedkommentaren des Mittelalters.* Beiträge zur Geschichte der Philosophie und Theologie des Mittelalters 38/3. Münster: Aschendorff, 1958.

Rieger, Reinhold. *Von der Freiheit eines Christenmenschen: De libertate Christiana.* Tübingen, 2007.

Bibliography

Rieske-Braun, Uwe. *Duellum mirabile: Studien zum Kampfmotiv in Martin Luthers Theologie.* Göttingen: Vandenhoeck & Ruprecht, 1999.

Rittgers, Ronald K. *The Reformation of the Keys: Confession, Conscience, and Authority in Sixteenth-Century Germany.* Cambridge: Harvard University Press, 2004.

Rogge, Joachim. "Innerlutherische Streitigkeiten um Gesetz und Evangelium, Rechtfertigung und Heiligung." In *Leben und Werk Martin Luthers von 1526 bis 1546: Festgabe zu seinem 500. Geburtstag,* vol. 1, edited by Helmar Junghans, 187-204. Berlin: Evang. Verl.-Anst., 1983 (with notes in vol. 2, pp. 785-87).

Rolf, Sybille. *Zum Herzen sprechen: Eine Studie zum imputativen Aspekt in Martin Luthers Rechtfertigungslehre und zu seinen Konsequenzen für die Predigt des Evangeliums.* Leipzig: Evangelische Verlagsanstalt, 2008.

Romano, Ruggiero, and Alberto Tenenti. *Die Grundlegung der modernen Welt: Spätmittelalter, Renaissance, Reformation.* Frankfurt am Main: Fischer-Bücherei, 1967.

Rorem, Paul. "Martin Luther's Christocentric Critique of Pseudo-Dionysian Spirituality." *Lutheran Quarterly* 11 (1997): 291-307.

Roth, Gunhild. "Die Gregoriusmesse und das Gebet 'Adoro te in cruce pendentem' im Einblattdruck: Legendenstoff, bildliche Verarbeitung und Texttradition am Beispiel des Monogrammisten d. Mit Textabdrucken." In *Einblattdrucke des 15. und frühen 16. Jahrhunderts: Probleme, Perspektiven, Fallstudien,* edited by Volker Honemann et al., 277-324. Tübingen: Niemeyer, 2000.

Rougemont, Denis de. *Die Liebe und das Abendland.* Translated by Friedrich Scholz. Cologne: Kiepenheuer u. Witsch, 1966.

Rudolf, Rainer. *Ars moriendi: Von der Kunst des heilsamen Lebens und Sterbens.* Cologne and Graz: Böhlau, 1957.

―――. "'Ars moriendi,' A: Frömmigkeitsgeschichte." In *Lexikon des Mittelalters,* vol. 1, cols. 1039f. Munich: Artemis-Verlag, 1999.

―――. *Thomas Peuntners "Kunst des heilsamen Sterbens" nach den Handschriften der Österr. Nationalbibliothek.* Berlin: E. Schmidt, 1956.

Ruh, Kurt. *Geschichte der abendländischen Mystik.* Vol. 1, *Die Grundlegung durch die Kirchenväter und die Mönchstheologie des 12. Jahrhunderts.* Munich: Beck, 1990.

Ruokanen, Miikka. "Luther und Ekstase." *Kerygma und Dogma* 32 (1986): 132-47.

―――, ed. *Luther in Finnland — Der Einfluß der Theologie Martin Luthers in Finnland und finnische Beiträge zur Lutherforschung.* Helsinki: Luther-Agricola-Gesellschaft, 1984.

Saak, Eric L. *High Way to Heaven: The Augustinian Platform between Reform and Reformation, 1292-1524.* Leiden: Brill, 2002.

Savonarola, Girolamo. "Prediche sopra Ruth e Michea." In *Opera di Girolamo Savonarola,* vol. 2, edited by Vincenzo Romano. Rome, 1962.

Schäfer, Rolf. "Zur Datierung von Luthers reformatorischer Erkenntnis." *Zeitschrift für Theologie und Kirche* 66 (1969): 151-70.

Scheel, Otto, ed. *Dokumente zu Luthers Entwicklung (bis 1519).* 2nd ed. Tübingen: J. C. B. Mohr, 1929.

Schindele, Gerhard. *Tristan: Metamorphose und Tradition*. Stuttgart: Kohlhammer, 1971.

Schlotheuber, Eva. "Norm und Innerlichkeit: Zur problematischen Suche nach den Anfängen der Individualität." *Zeitschrift für historische Forschung* 31 (2004): 329-57.

Schmidt, Ulrich. *Das ehemalige Franziskanerkloster in Nürnberg*. Nuremberg: Nurnberger Volksseitung, 1913.

Schneider, Karin. "Speculum artis bene moriendi." In *Die deutsche Literatur des Mittelalters: Verfasserlexikon*, vol. 9, cols. 40-49. Berlin: De Gruyter, 1993.

Schreiner, Klaus. *Maria: Jungfrau, Mutter, Herrscherin*. Munich: C. Hanser, 1994.

———. "Der Tod Marias als Inbegriff christlichen Sterbens: Sterbekunst im Spiegel mittelalterlicher Legendenbildung." In *Tod im Mittelalter*, edited by Arno Borst et al., 261-312. Constance: Universitätsverlag Konstanz, 1993.

Schwarz, Reinhard. "Das Bild des Todes im Bild des Lebens überwinden: Eine Interpretation von Luthers Sermon von der Bereitung zum Sterben." In *Gewißheit angesichts des Sterbens*, edited by Joachim Heubach, 32-64. Erlangen: Martin-Luther-Verlag, 1998.

———. *Fides, spes und caritas beim jungen Luther, unter besonderer Berücksichtigung der mittelalterlichen Tradition*. Berlin: De Gruyter, 1962.

———. *Luther*. Göttingen: Vandenhoeck & Ruprecht, 1986.

———. "Luthers unveräußerte Erbschaft an der monastischen Theologie." In *Kloster Amelungsborn 1135-1985*, edited by Gerhard Ruhbach and Kurt Schmidt-Clausen, 209-31. Hanover: Kloster Amelungsborn, 1985.

———. "Martin Luther (1483-1546)." In *Große Mystiker: Leben und Wirken*, edited by Gerhard Ruhbach and Joseph Sudbrack, 185-202. Munich: C. H. Beck, 1984.

———. "Mystischer Glaube — die Brautmystik Martin Luthers." In *Von Eckhart bis Luther: Über mystischen Glauben*, edited by Wolfgang Böhme, 20-32. Karlsruhe: W. Böhme, 1981.

———. "Die Umformung des religiösen Prinzips der Gottesliebe in der frühen Reformation: Ein Beitrag zum Verständnis von Luthers Schrift 'Von der Freiheit eines Christenmenschen.'" In *Die Reformation in Deutschland als Umbruch*, edited by Bernd Moeller and Stephen E. Buckwalter, 128-48. Gütersloh: Gütersloher Verlagshaus, 1998.

Seebass, Gottfried. *Die Himmelsleiter des hl. Bonaventura von Lucas Cranach d.Ä. Zur Reformation eines Holzschnitts*. Heidelberg: C. Winter, 1985.

Seeberg, Reinhold. *Lehrbuch der Dogmengeschichte*. Vol. 3, *Die Dogmengeschichte des Mittelalters*. 6th ed. Darmstadt: Wissenschaftliche Buchgesellschaft, 1959.

Seegets, Petra. *Passionstheologie und Passionsfrömmigkeit im ausgehenden Mittelalter: Der Nürnberger Franziskaner Stephan Fridolin (gest. 1498) zwischen Kloster und Stadt*. Tübingen: Mohr Siebeck, 1998.

Seuse, Heinrich. *Deutsche mystische Schriften*. Edited by Georg Hofmann. Zurich: Benziger, 1999.

———. *Deutsche Schriften*. Edited by Karl Bihlmeyer. Stuttgart: Kohlhammer, 1907; Frankfurt am Main: Minerva, 1961.

Bibliography

———. *Horologium Sapientiae*. Edited by Pius Künzle. Fribourg: Universitätsverlag, 1977.

Slenczka, Notger. "'Allein durch den Glauben': Antwort auf die Fragen eines mittelalterlichen Mönchs oder Angebot zum Umgang mit einem Problem jades Menschen?" In *Luther und das monastische Erbe*, edited by Christoph Bultmann, Volker Leppin, and Andreas Lindner, 291-315. Tübingen: Mohr Siebeck, 2007.

———. "Christus." In *Luther Handbuch*, edited by Albrecht Beutel, 381-92. Tübingen: Mohr Siebeck, 2005.

———. "Communicatio idiomatum." In *Religion in Geschichte und Gegenwart*[4] 2, cols. 433-34. Tübingen: Mohr Siebeck, 1999.

Staubach, Nikolaus, ed. *Kirchenreform von unten: Gerhard Zerbolt von Zutphen und die Brüder vom gemeinsamen Leben*. Frankfurt am Main: P. Lang, 2004.

Staupitz, Johann von. *Gutachten und Satzungen*. Edited by Wolfgang Günter and Lothar Graf zu Dohna. Berlin: De Gruyter, 2001.

———. *Johann von Staupitzens sämmtliche Werke*. Vol. 1, *Deutsche Schriften*. Edited by Joachim Karl Friedrich Knaake. Potsdam: Krausnick, 1867.

———. *Libellus De exsecutione aeternae praedestinationis*. In *Sämtliche Schriften: Abhandlung, Predigten, Zeugnisse*, edited by Lothar Graf zu Dohna et al. Berlin: De Gruyter, 1979.

———. *Tübinger Predigten*. Edited by Richard Wetzel. Berlin: De Gruyter, 1987.

———. "Von der Nachfolgung des willigen Sterbens Christi." In *Johann von Staupitzens sämmtliche Werke*, vol. 1, *Deutsche Schriften*, edited by Joachim Karl Friedrich Knaake, 50-88. Potsdam: Krausnick, 1867.

Steiger, Anselm. *Fünf Zentralthemen der Theologie Luthers und seiner Erben: Communicatio — Imago — Figura — Maria — Exempla, mit Edition zweier christologischer Frühschriften Johann Gerhards*. Leiden: Brill, 2002.

Steinbauer, Karl. *Einander das Zeugnis gönnen*. Vols. 1-4. Erlangen: Selbstverlag, 1983-87.

Steinke, Barbara. "'Den Bräutigam nehmt euch und habt ihn und verlasst ihn nicht, denn er verlässt euch nicht': Zur Moral der mystik im Nürnberger Katharinenkloster während des 15. Jahrhunderts." In *Gottes Nähe unmittelbar erfahren: Mystik im Mittelalter und bei Luther*, edited by Berndt Hamm and Volker Leppin, 139-164. Tübingen: Mohr Siebeck, 2007.

———. *Paradiesgarten oder Gefängnis? Das Nürnberger Katharinenkloster zwischen Klosterreform und Reformation*. Tübingen: Mohr Siebeck, 2006.

Steinlein, Hermann. "Luthers Anlage zur Bildhaftigkeit." *Lutherjahrbuch* 22 (1940): 9-45.

Stock, Ursula. *Die Bedeutung der Sakramente in Luthers Sermonen von 1519*. Leiden: Brill, 1982.

Stoellger, Philipp. *Passivität aus Passion: Zur Problemgeschichte einer "categoria non grata."* Tübingen: Mohr Siebeck, 2010.

Stuiber, Alfred. "Geburtstag." In *Reallexikon für Antike und Christentum*, vol. 9, cols. 217-43. Stuttgart: Anton Hiersemann, 1976.

Swanson, Robert N., ed. *Promissory Notes on the Treasury of Merits: Indulgences in Late Medieval Europe*. Boston: Brill, 2006.

Tauler, John. *Die Predigten Taulers*. Edited by Ferdinand Vetter. Berlin: Weidmann, 1910.

Tenenti, Alberto. *La vie et la mort à travers l'art du XVe siècle*. Paris: A. Colin, 1952.

Thiede, Werner. "Luthers individuelle Eschatologie." *Lutherjahrbuch* 49 (1982): 7-49.

Thomas à Kempis. *De imitatione Christi: Nachfolge Christi und vier andere Schriften*. Edited by Friedrich Eichler. Munich: Kösel, 1966.

Thomas Aquinas. *Summa theologiae*. Editio Leonina, vols. IV-XII. Rome: Apud Sedem Commissionis Leoninae, 1888-1903.

Topsfield, Leslie T. *Troubadours and Love*. Cambridge: Cambridge University Press, 1975.

Vogel, Cyril. "'Buße (liturgisch-theologisch),' D: Westkirche I: Bußdisziplin und Bußriten." In *Lexikon des Mittelalters*, vol. 2, cols. 1132-35. Munich: Artemis Verlag, 1999.

Vogelsang, Erich. *Die Anfänge von Luthers Christologie nach der ersten Psalmenvorlesung, insbesondere in ihren exegetischen und systematischen Zusammenhängen mit Augustin und der Scholastik dargestellt*. Berlin: De Gruyter, 1929.

———. *Der angefochtene Christus bei Luther*. Berlin: De Gruyter, 1932.

Vorgrimler, Herbert. *Buße und Krankensalbung*. Handbuch der Dogmengeschichte, vol. 4, sec. 3. Freiburg im Breisgau: Herder, 1978.

Weinbrenner, Ralph. *Klosterreform im 15. Jahrhundert zwischen Ideal und Praxis: Der Augustinereremit Andreas Proles (1429-1503) und die priviligierte Observanz*. Tübingen: Mohr, 1996.

Werbeck, Wilfrid. "Voraussetzungen und Wesen der scrupulositas im Spätmittelalter." *Zeitschrift für Theologie und Kirche* 68 (1971): 327-50.

Wetzel, Richard. "Staupitz und Luther." In *Martin Luther: Probleme seiner Zeit*, edited by Volker Press and Dieter Stievermann, 75-87. Spätmittelalter und Frühe Neuzeit 16. Stuttgart: Klett-Cotta, 1986.

———. "Staupitz und Luther: Annäherung an eine Vorläufer-Figur." *Blätter für pfälzische Kirchengeschichte und Religiöse Volkskunde* 58 (1991): 369-95.

Wicks, Jared. *Luther's Reform: Studies on Conversion and the Church*. Mainz: Verlag P. von Zabern, 1992.

———. *Man Yearning for Grace: Luther's Early Spiritual Teaching*. Wiesbaden: F. Steiner, 1969.

———. "Martin Luther's Treatise on Indulgences." *Theological Studies* 28 (1967): 481-518.

Williams-Krapp, Werner. "'Dise Ding sint dennoch nit ware zeichen der Heiligkeit': Zur Bewertung mystischer Erfahrungen im 15. Jahrhundert." In *Frömmigkeitstile im Mittelalter*, edited by Wolfgang Haubrichs, 61-71. Göttingen: Vandenhoeck & Ruprecht, 1990.

———. "The Erosion of a Monopoly: German Religious Literature in the Fifteenth Century." In *The Vernacular Spirit: Essays on Medieval Religious Literature*, edited by Renate Blumenfeld-Kosinski, Duncan Robertson, and Nancy Bradley Warren, 239-59. New York: Palgrave, 2002.

———. "Frauenmystik und Ordensreform im 15. Jahrhundert." In *Literarische Interessenbildung im Mittelalter: DFG-Symposion 1991*, edited by Joachim Heinzle, 301-13. Stuttgart: Metzler, 1993.

Winterhager, Wilhelm Ernst. "Ablaßkritik als Indikator historischen Wandels vor 1517: Ein Beitrag zu Voraussetzungen und Einordnung der Reformation." *Archiv für Reformationsgeschichte* 90 (1999): 6-71.

———. "Martin Luther und das Amt des Provinzialvikars in der Reformkongregation der deutschen Augustiner-Eremiten." In *Vita Religiosa im Mittelalter, Festschrift für Kaspar Elm*, edited by Franz J. Felten and Nikolas Jaspert, 707-38. Berlin: Duncker & Humblot, 1999.

Wolff, Jens. *Metapher und Kreuz: Studien zu Luthers Christusbild*. Tübingen: Mohr Siebeck, 2005.

Wriedt, Markus. *Gnade und Erwählung: Eine Untersuchung zu Johann von Staupitz und Martin Luther*. Mainz: Verlag P. von Zabern, 1991.

Zecherle, Andreas. "Die 'Theologia deutsch': Ein spätmittelalterlicher mystischer Traktat." In *Gottes Nähe unmittelbar erfahren: Mystik im Mittelalter und bei Luther*, edited by Berndt Hamm and Volker Leppin, 1-95. Tübingen: Mohr Siebeck, 2007.

Zumkeller, Adolar. *Erbsünde, Gnade, Rechtfertigung und Verdienst nach der Lehre der Erfurter Augustinertheologen des Spätmittelalters*. Cassiciacum 35. Würzburg: Augustinus-Verlag, 1984.

———. *Johannes von Staupitz und seine christliche Heilslehre*. Würzburg: Augustinus-Verlag, 1994.

———. "Das Ungenügen der menschlichen Werke bei den deutschen Predigern des Spätmittelalters." *Zeitschrift für katholische Theologie* 81 (1959): 265-305.

Zur Mühlen, Karl-Heinz. "Affekt II." In *Theologische Realenzyklöpadie*, 1:599-612. Berlin: De Gruyter, 1977.

———. "Luther II." In *Theologische Realenzyklöpadie*, 21:530-67. Berlin: De Gruyter, 1991.

———. "Mystische Erfahrung und Wort Gottes bei Luther." In *Mystik: Religion der Zukunft — Zukunft der Religion*, ed. Johannes Schilling, 45-66. Leipzig, 2003.

———. *Nos extra nos: Luthers theologie zwischen Mystik und Scholastik*. Beiträge zur historischen Theologie 46. Tübingen: J. C. B. Mohr, 1972.

———. "Zur Rezeption der Augustinischen Sakramentsformel 'Accedit verbum ad elementum, et fit sacramentum' in der Theologie Luthers." *Zeitschrift für Theologie und Kirche* 70 (1973): 50-76.

Name Index

Abelard, Peter, 5-7, 17, 67n.26
Agnes von Mansfeld, 115
Agricola, Johann, 103n.74
Albrecht von Brandenburg, 85, 95n.47
Angela de Foligno, 196
Anne, Saint, 52, 58n.128
Anselm of Canterbury, Saint, 6, 122, 129, 232
Aquinas, Saint Thomas, 13n.41, 60n.7, 80n.60, 156
Arndt, John, 225
Augustine, 1-3, 17, 28n.5, 48, 61n.8, 77n.47, 82n.66, 120n.47, 144n.146, 156, 169n.42, 192, 236, 238, 251

Barth, Karl, 191
Bernard of Clairvaux, 4-6, 11, 42, 50, 192, 194, 196, 199, 223
Bernhard von Waging, 119
Biel, Gabriel, 10, 16n.52, 39, 56, 60-62, 70n.32, 106n.81, 194n.13, 197n.19, 235-36
Boniface VIII, 175n.10
Braun, Johannes, 32, 46, 53
Brunner, Emil, 191n.3
Bucer, Martin, 169n.42, 171
Bullinger, Heinrich, 150

Cajetan, Thomas, 155
Calvin, John, 169n.42, 171, 246, 249
Catullus, 1
Charles V, 176n.13
Clovis, 2
Comestor, Petrus, 67n.25
Cyril of Alexandria, 212n.79

Dionysius von Rijkel (the Carthusian), 119
Dorsten, Johannes von, 120n.47
Duns Scotus, John, 13

Eck, Johannes, 155, 236
Eckhart, Meister, 196, 232
Erasmus von Rotterdam, 176n.13

"Frankfurter" (author of *Theologia Deutsch*), 100, 194, 225
Frederick the Wise, 114-15
Fridolin, Stephan, 68n.27, 136, 236n.7

Geiler von Kaysenberg, Johannes, 113, 119, 124n.61
Gerson, Jean, 33, 42, 61n.8, 63-66, 70n.32, 112, 113, 115-16, 119n.44, 121n.50, 194, 230
Gogarten, Friedrich, 191n.3

279

Name Index

Gregory I (the Great), 43n.65, 65n.21
Gregory of Rimini, 48, 169n.42
Güttel, Kaspar, 152n.86

Harnack, Adolf von, 191
Heloise, 6
Hercules, 156
Holbein, Hans the Elder, 9n.31, 123
Huberinus, Caspar, 110

Isolde, 4

Jacob von Paradies (the Carthusian), 119

Karlstadt, Andreas Bodenstein von, 145n.149, 169n.42, 225
Kunigunde of Bavaria, 5n.18
Kydrer, Wolfgang, 119n.40

Lang, Johannes, 225
Leo X, 49n.87, 168n.40, 172-89
Linck, Wenceslas, 174
Lombard, Peter, 10, 46-47, 59, 69-70, 73n.37
Luther, Hans, 38n.42
Luther, Katharina (von Bora), 193n.12

Mechthild von Magdeburg, 196
Melanchthon, Philipp, 171
Miltitz, Karl von, 174, 176
Mörlin, Joachim, 99n.56
Mühlpfort, Hermann, 173, 176n.14
Müntzer, Thomas, 225
Muris, Michael, 176n.13

Ockham, William of, 10, 14, 16, 50, 60n.7, 156
Origen, 212n.79
Osiander, Andreas, 257
Ovid, 3, 11n.37

Paltz, Johannes von, 14n.43, 56, 102n.68, 113, 115, 120n.47, 125-26, 136, 140n.129
Paul, Saint, 82-83, 89, 184, 233, 246
Pelagius, 236
Peuntner, Thomas, 113
Pseudo-Dionysius the Areopagite, 196-97, 219

Rhegius, Urbanus, 110
Richard of Saint Victor, 11n.37
Ritschl, Albrecht, 191
Rupert von Deutz, 4n.15
Ruysbroeck, Jan, 196

Savonarola, Girolamo, 119
Schart, Markus, 114, 117
Scheurl, Christoph, 89n.14, 237n.9
Schwarz, Ulrich, 123n.56
Spalatin, Georg, 28n.7, 173n.6, 174n.7, 175, 176, 186
Spengler, Lazarus, 18n.56, 153n.187
Spenlein, Georg, 100n.61
Staupitz, Johannes von, 5, 15-21, 30, 35n.27, 42, 44-45, 48-52, 56, 61n.8, 63, 68n.27, 69, 82n.66, 96, 102, 106n.81, 114-15, 135n.105, 136, 140n.127, 152n.186, 156-58, 169n.42, 174, 192-93, 205-11, 214-15, 217, 221-25, 229, 236-37
Suso, Henry (Heinrich Seuse), 111-12, 117, 131, 196

Tauler, Johannes, 96, 100-101, 194, 196, 224-29, 250
Thomas à Kempis, 35n.29, 193
Tristan, 4

Weller, Hieronymus, 44
William of Auvergne, 13n.42

Zwingli, Ulrich, 25n.79, 145n.149, 154, 169n.42, 171, 246

280

Topic Index

Absolution, 7-8, 13, 107-8, 143-44, 146
Activity: of cooperation, 245-46, 249, 257; of faith, 242-43, 246, 248, 257
Affect *(affectus)*, 17, 24, 25, 28, 56, 62n.10, 64, 66, 68, 78-79, 80, 232, 248
All *(omnia, universa)*, is provided, 204, 206, 208, 211
Alone *(solus):* late medieval, 235; Reformation, 234
Anfechtung (tentatio), 27-28, 32-34, 41-42, 43-48, 50, 55-58, 101-2, 214-15, 219-21, 222, 224-25, 226-29, 250; experience of nothingness, 226-27; in the hour of death, 117-18, 122, 129-30, 133-35, 152-53
Angst (fear), 215, 250; of death/judgment, 37, 40-41, 117; of punishment, 15
Ars moriendi, 110-53; absence of, in the Reformation, 126-27, 151; for health and dying, 124; late medieval literature, 111-14; of monastic orders, 119; perfection program, 133-34; preparatory program, 133-34; as a way of life, 115, 118, 152
Augustine: anti-Pelagian, 48, 169, 237; observant Order of Augustinians, 174; renaissance of, 3, 17; teachings of Gregory of Rimini, 48; theology, 15, 30, 40, 44, 51, 56, 236-37; thought of, 18, 156
Autonomy, 97, 156

Babylonian Captivity of the Church (Luther), 155, 167, 169, 178
Baptism, 254; and Christian freedom, 178
Biblical interpretation: Luther's Bible lectures, 39-40, 45, 82-83; of the Psalms, 45, 80, 89; of Song of Solomon, 4; tropological, 80. *See also* Paul, interpretation/exegesis of
Birth: day of death as birthday, 130; death as, 130; of God in the soul, 226-27, 229

Care for the poor, 93-94
Catechetical theology and literature, 111, 114-15
Child of God, 212, 213-14
Christ: alone, Lord of the church, 181; alone, Lord over people, 186; body of Christ, 199, 203, 254; as *centrum omnium,* 80n.57; Christ images as images of faith, 137-39, 149; communion with, 199, 203, 230-32, 244n.30, 249; congregation of, 199; doctrine of the two na-

281

tures, 201-3, 207, 220, 253; *humanitas* (humanity), 200n.31, 244; humiliation, 201n.33, 205-7; incarnation of, 203, 206, 253; indwelling, 203-4, 244-45; *pro me/nobis*, 51, 140, 145, 151, 216; *solus Christus*, 153, 234; substitute, 140. See also Passion of Christ

Church: critique of, 166-67, 176-77, 181; critique of ecclesiastical tyranny, 183; *ecclesia sine anima*, 206; reform of, 124; treasure of the, 90

Coercion *(coactio)*, 156

Comfort, 99, 147; letter of, 114n.18; theology of, 151

Commendatio animae (commending the soul), 121

Common priesthood: of all baptized, 214; of all believing, 214

Communicatio idiomatum, 202-3, 207, 253

Communio sanctorum (communion of saints), 37, 122, 125, 135, 148-50, 152; community of the faithful, 230; intercession of, 148; sins borne by, 148

Confession, 8, 12, 28n.7, 35; sacrament of, 19, 91n.24, 107, 142; of sins, 74-75, 160

Confidence (trust), 22-24, 66, 68, 76n.45, 99, 105n.79, 121, 136, 146, 151, 161, 165, 176, 185n.44, 242, 244, 248; not in human powers, 186

Conscience, 20, 36, 42, 165-66, 250, 251-52; "scrupulosity" of, 42, 224n.129

Contemptus mundi literature, 117

Contritionism, 16n.52, 56, 106n.81

Cooperation between God and people, 123, 125, 151, 166, 245, 257

Cross, 218-19, 223; following, 104-5; life of, 93, 98, 102; piety of, 92

Death: accepting, 119, 121, 123n.59, 124, 128; as birth, 130-31; blessed, 110-53; dance of, 117; death of, 128; devotion, 122; endurance of, 119, 121; as formation of the inner person, 121-24; as healing medicine, 128; *imitatio passionis Christi*, 123; joyous, 130-31; as liberation from fear, 128-29; liturgy for, 122, 131; Mary's, 129; perfection of virtues, 121, 123; as punishment, 128; Reformation writings on, 152; rituals, 122, 152; sacraments, 122, 152; as sleep, 128; trust in God, 213; willing, 119, 121, 123n.59, 124, 128

Deathbed (hour of death): angel at the, 122, 132, 148; battle, 129, 151; as chance for perfect repentance, 119; fear at, 130-31, 134; focus on the hour of death, 112, 117, 118-20, 122-23, 127; liberation from fear of, 127, 153; nearness of, 37, 117

Deification: of believers, 204; of the inner humanity, 226-27

Despair, 32, 41; and consolation, 32, 56, 99, 131, 227; self-despair, 56, 65, 95, 99, 105n.79, 108

Devotio moderna, 35

Dialectic, 5-6

Eschatology: distant, 122; imminent, 37, 122

Experience, spiritual, 5, 7, 32, 196, 219; *experientia*, 219; of God's nearness, 196; theology of, 192

Exsurge domine, 174-75, 178, 186, 188

External Word *(verbum externum)*, 107-9, 144n.148, 170, 214, 251

Extra nos, 136-37, 147, 218, 230, 243, 249; Christ, 139, 142, 144, 249; journey outward, 100-101, 215, 221, 250

Extreme unction, 142

Faith, 47, 54, 60-84, 90, 98-99, 101-3, 105-9, 138, 140-52, 165-66, 199-200, 203-4, 212-22, 238-39, 243, 249-50, 251-52; "autarky" of, 185; certainty of, 62, 64-65, 67, 139, 145-46, 150, 216; as gift of God, 152, 211-12, 237, 242; increase of, 186; justifying, 78, 89, 102; knowledge of *(intellectus)*, 62, 64, 69, 73, 80; as lord over "things," 185-86; and love, 179, 181, 214, 216-18, 247-48; reception of, 62, 69, 217, 248; *sola fide*,

59-60, 153, 234, 236; without seeing, 69; in the word of forgiveness, 20n.60, 22-25
Feeling: of faith, 139, 248; religion of, 66, 73
Fraternitas generalis, 91n.24
Freedom: as bondage, 166, 167; Christian, 154-71, 205, 239, 252; of the church, 157-58, 169; of conscience, 165, 166, 240, 252; Eleutherius/Luther, 167, 177n.17; from human powers and statutes, 167, 176, 186; from the law, 165, 167, 240, 252; from mediators to salvation, 256; from the pope, 176-77, 181, 252; from self, 170; from spiritual authority, 184; liberation movement, 154-55; as lord of all, 165, 180, 183-85, 188; Luther's awareness of, 175-78; the right of, 168, 184; as service, 165-66, 171, 181-83, 186, 187; through the word of God, 169; of the will *(liberum arbitrium)*, 155-58, 236
Freedom of a Christian (Luther), 155, 163, 165, 172-89; as a mystical tract, 189

God: anger of, 37-38, 40-42, 48, 52, 228; "condescension" of, 53-54, 206-7; distant, 101, 225-26, 227, 231; lovingkindness of, 46; nearness of, 51-53, 101, 147, 196, 204, 209, 214, 222, 226, 227, 231; present, 147, 196, 222, 229; and sinful humanity, 229-30; sinners acquitted by, 159, 165, 171, 238, 243; unworthiness before, 36, 42, 135, 143, 152, 239; voluntary pledge of, 146-47, 251; worthiness before, 36, 123, 142, 152, 238
Good works, 9, 12, 78n.51, 93, 106, 166, 188, 203, 205, 235-37, 242, 256
Gospel, 90, 107, 169, 213-14, 240, 244n.29; as active and promised word, 212; external dimension, 229, 250; promise of, 107-8, 144-47, 150, 169, 211, 214, 230, 251
Grace, 90-91, 160, 176; alone, 136, 209, 234-36; Christ as image of, 139; dominance of, 237; freedom via, 155-56; justifying, 10, 13, 15, 89-90, 156, 159-60; near, 37, 48, 52, 230-31; preparation for, 10, 234, 236-37
Guilt *(culpa)*, 7

Happy exchange, 100, 162-63, 188, 201-3, 204, 208, 210, 212, 221n.117, 224, 240-41, 246, 253; as struggle, 201n.36
Heaven: open, 52-53; purchasing of, 125-26
Hell, 219, 226, 227-28
Hereafter: freedom from the institutionalization of, 127, 245, 256; institutionalization of, 125-26
Historical periods: break or continuity between the Middle Ages and the Reformation, 83, 150-51, 169n.42, 177-78, 237; late medieval period as early modernity, 83
Holiness: as call to blessedness, 182n.35; of God/Christ *extra nos* (protection), 121-24, 135, 147, 150; imminence of God's/Christ's, 37, 40-42, 147, 240
Holy Communion. *See* Lord's Supper
Holy Scriptures: as basis for legitimacy, 169, 256; freedom for, 169; freedom from, 169, 184; pope and Scripture, 180
Holy Spirit, 152, 157, 165, 203-5, 206, 209, 211, 216, 221, 222, 226, 235, 237, 242, 244, 247, 248-52, 253-54; *filioque*, 203n.43; gifts of, 210; God's word unmediated by, 214; pneumatology, 203n.43
Hope *(spes)*, 41-42, 47, 63-70, 74-79, 97-98; *in spe, non in re*, 77n.47; *iustus in spe*, 164
Humanism, biblical, 39, 45
Humility, 36, 42, 43, 47, 65-68, 75-79, 98, 107, 159, 161, 247

Images: of *ars moriendi*, 122, 129, 133, 148; of comfort, 132-33, 137-39; at the deathbed, 122, 144; of faith, 137-39, 144-46, 251; icon theology, 131-32; religious use of, 117; soul's images, 132-38, 144-45; threatening/terrifying, 132, 134-35, 136-40

Imagination, 131, 138

Imitation of Christ *(imitatio)*, 39, 95, 140, 204n.44; *imitatio passionis*, 123

Immediacy: of Christian to God, 196, 205, 207, 256; to the word of God, 213-14

Imputation *(reputatio, imputatio)*: of the righteousness of Christ, 99, 162-64, 171, 242-45; *sola reputatione*, 242

Individualization, 3, 6

Indulgences, 85-87, 90-91, 103-4, 106; for the dead, 91; financial considerations of, 94; jubilee indulgence, 86, 91; Luther's Ninety-five Theses, 21, 85-109, 167, 177n.17; Peter's, 91; plenary, 91

Inner eye/sight, 132, 139

Internalization, 3, 6, 14, 25, 34, 120, 123-26, 133-35, 137-39, 215, 249-52

Iustitia activa/passiva, 33, 43, 48, 98

Judgment: absence of individual judgment, 127; God's, 160; individual *(iudicium particulare)*, 9, 37, 122n.55; nearness of, 37-38, 40-41, 48, 52, 122; relationship between God and people, 72, 74, 158-59, 161-62, 165, 167; of self before God, 46, 48, 77, 159; word of, 73-78, 98

Justification, 8, 24, 79, 88-89, 98-102, 105, 107-8, 109, 160, 164, 203-5, 207, 209, 211, 215, 233-57; cloak image, 215, 244-45; as creative event, 166; eschatological finality, 126, 164, 238; Reformation profile of, 255-57

Ladder, mystical, 53-54, 197-98, 201, 218, 220, 231

Laity: as audience for theology, 111, 113-16, 119; concept of, 114-15; *simplices* (ordinary people) as religious audience, 116

Law: as accusation, 210-11, 250; as God's beneficial guidance, 171; and gospel, 28-29, 57-58, 151, 182

Lord's Supper, 142, 145-46, 148, 203, 221n.117, 223, 253-54; real presence, 223

Love, 1-25, 60-64, 67-69, 71-72, 77-82, 92-95, 156; brotherly, 179, 181-83, 188; for God/Christ, 1-25, 39, 92, 98, 139, 158, 203, 210, 242, 248; of God/Christ (for humanity), 23; for neighbors, 12, 23, 93-94, 158, 165-67, 182-83, 188, 203-4, 242, 254; spontaneity of, 156-58, 165-66, 237; substitutionary, 254

Mary, 210n.72

Media vita in morte sumus, 117, 124, 127

Memento mori, 117

Mercantile religiosity, 13, 125-26

Mercy of God/Christ, 18, 20, 22, 36, 46-54, 55, 68-69, 88-89, 103-4, 118, 121, 124, 136, 151, 160, 201, 206-9, 211, 235-36, 244-45; gratuitous, 257n.58; *sola liberalitas*, 235; *sola misericordia*, 236

Merits, 120, 133, 235, 255; deeds of *(merita de condigno)*, 43

Mortification of the flesh, 93

Mystical terminology, 131-32, 138, 193

Mystical theology *(theologia mystica)*, 7, 11, 53-55, 96-97, 190-232

Mystical union *(unio mystica)*, 4, 11, 196, 199-201, 203-8, 209, 212, 220, 229; into one body, 199, 208, 209, 224; into one cake, 199, 224n.128; into one person, 199, 208; into one spirit, 200; like iron and fire, 212, 253

Mysticism, 11, 53-55, 81n.61, 100, 190-232; of *Anfechtung*, 221, 224-29, 231; of ascent, 204-5, 220; basic mysticism for all (Christians), 209; bride and marriage, 199-200, 205-9, 215, 219, 231; Christian, 191, 193, 207-8, 210, 221-22; concept and definition of, 195-97, 229-32; democratization, 198; of descent, 205-7, 220, 224; elitist, 197, 210n.72; exegetical, 194, 217-18; faith instead of love, 195, 213-14; of love,

214; of the passion, 50, 193n.10, 198, 221-24; pietism's reception of, 225; popularization of, 198; speculative, 197; of the word, 221, 224

Natural powers (human ability), 14-15, 39
Nature, human, 163-64, 174; natural thought, 63-64, 167-68
Nominalism: Erfurt's *via moderna*, 30, 159

Observance, 31, 34, 39-40
Ockhamism (William of Ockham), 10, 14-16, 39, 60n.60, 156
Odium sui (self-hate), 92, 97, 105
Opus alienum/proprium dei, 32, 220
Ordo salutis of Lutheranism, 247

Paradise: already entered, 53, 164, 222, 240; death as gateway to, 119; foretaste, 210
Passion of Christ, 6, 11-12, 17-20, 50-51; Man of Sorrows as judge, 40, 132-33; as protection, 121-24; trust in death of Christ alone, 121
Passivity, 227; and justification (of faith), 55, 69-70, 101, 166, 205, 216-17, 242, 246, 248, 257
Pastor aeternus gregem, 175n.10
Pastoral care: at the deathbed, 152; to the neighbor, 182; to the pope, 182, 187; theology of, 111, 114-15, 192; Vienna school of, 113
Path to blessedness, 201; and death, dying, 130, 133
Paul, interpretation/exegesis of: Rom. 1:17, 88-89, 160-61; Rom. 8:30-32, 206; 1 Cor. 15:54, 202; Eph. 5:30-32, 199, 206; Phil. 2:5-8, 188
Pauline theology, 156; Luther and, 82
Person: crisis of the inner person, 228-29; inner and outer, 92-95, 104-5
Personal: faith, 62, 71-73, 77-78, 98, 239-40, 241-42; relationship, 159, 161
Piety: late medieval crisis in, 34, 42; of meditation, 146; theology of, 48, 64, 102, 111, 193
Pope, papacy, 28, 85-86, 172-89; as Antichrist, 28n.7, 175-76, 180-81, 186; freedom from, 176, 181; lord of the Holy Scriptures, 180; office of, 174n.7, 179; person, 173-74, 178-79; power of the keys, 186; tyranny, 181, 186
Prayer, 43, 65, 75-77, 79-80, 126; at death, 121; piety of, 66
Predestination, 156, 206, 209, 215n.91, 236; *Anfechtung* concerning, 135n.105, 140-41; necessity *(necessitas)* resulting from, 156, 237; *sola praedestinatio*, 236
Promise of God *(promissio)*: of gospel, 22, 74-76, 211, 216; made true by God (God's faithfulness), 47, 76, 98, 146; of the sacraments, 143, 144-45
Purgatory, 8, 12, 87, 91, 257; absence of, 127, 153; on earth, 95, 119

Quality, religious, 43, 45, 62-63, 71, 77-79, 98-99, 136, 142, 157-59, 161, 213, 215, 230, 238-40, 241-43, 255n.55

Raptus, exstasis (as mystical concepts of faith), 54, 81n.61, 168, 217-20, 221-22, 227, 244n.31
Rationality *(ratio)*, 6
Reformation: breakthrough, 26-30, 44, 169n.42; emergence of, 109; Reformation turn, 26-31, 57, 107, 158, 169n.42, 194; as terminus and category, 31, 169n.42, 255n.55
Repentance *(contritio)*, 1-25, 28, 49-50, 85-109, 247-49, 257; and Christ, 17-20; fear-, love-based, 247; gallows, 15, 19; imperfect *(attritio, attritionismus)*, 13, 56, 126n.81, 143; internalization of, 92, 96-97, 101-2; lifelong, 92-95, 98, 104-5; radical theology of, 97-98; *sola contritio*, 20; true, 6-11, 13, 15-24, 67n.26, 92, 95, 100-101, 102-8, 123, 143
Resignatio ad infernum, 39
Righteousness: external/alien *(externa/aliena)*, 54, 99, 101, 107-8, 161-63, 169,

285

216, 229, 243, 250-52, 253-54; God's judging righteousness, 52-53, 79, 161, 164; God's, as mercy, 163, 244-45; God's, as salvific, 25, 28, 48, 52-53, 79, 88, 98, 102, 161-63, 164, 187, 201-2, 208, 211, 213, 240, 243-45; hen and chicks metaphor, 215, 243-44; love of God's *(amor iustitiae)*, 48-49, 92, 96, 98, 104
Rigor: ethical rigorism, 39; God's claim on a rigorous way of life, 106; rigid observance of commandments, 104; strict image of God, 38

Sacramentalism, 14
Salvation: achievement, 157-58, 160, 164-65, 167, 171; assurance of hope, 51, 66-68, 76-77, 208, 222; certainty of, 36, 47, 126; conditional, 157, 160n.9, 164-65, 166-67, 204-5, 245-46; and faith, 76-77, 140-43, 151, 152-53, 221-23, 229, 230-31, 239, 249, 250-51, 256-57; gift and giving back, 100n.61, 246, 257; means of, 251n.48, 254; necessary and unnecessary features for, 209-10; priestly mediation of, 214, 252; uncertainty and, 64-66, 69, 118; unconditional, 164-66, 171, 238-39, 246, 256-57
Sanctification: as art of dying, 118-19; of life, 106, 108, 203, 205, 244, 249
Satan/Devil, 220, 243, 257n.58; in the papacy, 175, 180, 182, 184, 187
Satisfaction, "doing enough" *(satisfactio)*, 2, 6-9, 12, 91, 93, 96, 123
Secularization, 124
Security/certainty, religious: demand for, 36; and faith, 62, 64, 145; false, 94-95; hereafter, 37; offers of, 36, 91
Sermon: genre, 111, 172n.4; Luther's, 110-11, 172
Sighing *(gemitus)*, 54
Simul iustus et peccator, 163, 202n.38
Sin: awareness of sin, 35, 41, 44, 158; ever sinful, 158-59, 240-41; forgiveness of *(remissio peccatorum)*, 13, 18, 22, 28, 39n.56, 39n.58, 87n.7, 107-8; God's punishment for, 86; original, 25, 215, 240, 241; temporal punishment for, 9, 12, 87, 91
Soul, innermost, 226, 229
Spiritual: embrace, 4, 219, 226, 230; gradualism, 12n.38; kiss, 4-5; perfection, 35, 36, 39-41, 42, 133; poverty, 75n.43, 181-82; steps of faith, 63; steps of love, 210n.72; steps on the mystical path, 226
Storm near Stotternheim (1505), 37-38, 52, 58n.128
Sub contrario (under the form of opposites), 47, 77n.47, 224
Subjects, religious, 14, 156, 166, 245
Sweetness of God/Christ, 46, 50, 53, 226

Theology: communication as foundation of, 203, 252-55; doctrine and life, 179; "elementarization" of, 111, 114; the kernel of the nut, 32; monastic, 30, 192; popularization of, 115; scholastic, 5-8, 177; *theologia negativa*, 219; theological reform, 192; theology of the cross *(theologia crucis)*, 47, 57, 74n.39, 218-20; vernacular, 111-16
Thief on the cross, 119-20, 140n.29
Tower experience, 29
Tribulations, 95
Trinity, 253
Truth/truthfulness: of faith, 43, 61-64, 68-78, 79, 179-80, 183; of God, 90, 146; of God's word, 45, 181-82; of judgment, 159

Unam sanctam, 175, 180n.26

Via purgativa, 12
Virtue(s), 10, 24, 63, 121, 126; and the *ars moriendi*, 133, 150; and sacraments, 143

Will, 62n.10, 64
Word of God, 25, 47; and faith, 69, 71, 73-74, 77, 211-13, 218; of the gospel, 25, 144-46, 168; mysticism of, 221, 224; and the verbal character of the sacrament, 144

www.ingramcontent.com/pod-product-compliance
Lightning Source LLC
Chambersburg PA
CBHW071150070526
44584CB00019B/2737